Labour Law Reforms in India

Labour market flexibility is one of the most closely debated public policy issues in India. This book provides a theoretical framework to understand the subject, and empirically examines to what extent India's 'jobless growth' may be attributed to labour laws. There is a pervasive view that the country's low manufacturing base and inability to generate jobs is primarily due to rigid labour laws. Therefore, job creation is sought to be boosted by reforming labour laws. However, the book argues that if labour laws are made flexible, then there are adverse consequences for workers: dismantled job security weakens workers' bargaining power, incapacitates trade union movement, skews class distribution of output, dilutes workers' rights, and renders them vulnerable. The book:

- identifies and critically examines the theory underlying the labour market flexibility (LMF) argument
- employs innovative empirical methods to test the LMF argument
- offers an overview of the organised labour market in India
- comprehensively discusses the proposed/instituted labour law reforms in the country
- contextualises the LMF argument in a macroeconomic setting
- discusses the political economy of labour law reforms in India.

This book will interest scholars and researchers in economics, development studies, and public policy as well as economists, policymakers, and teachers of human resource management.

Anamitra Roychowdhury teaches economics at Jawaharlal Nehru University, New Delhi, India. Previously, he taught at St. Stephen's College, University of Delhi. He completed his doctoral studies at Jawaharlal Nehru University and his areas of interest include development economics, labour economics, Indian economy and macroeconomics. He has published a number of research articles in many renowned international and national journals including *International Labour Review, Agrarian South: Journal of Political Economy, Economic and Political Weekly* and *Social Scientist*. His commentaries on contemporary economic issues have appeared in *Global Labour Column, Mainstream* and *Macroscan*.

Critical Political Economy of South Asia

Series editors: *C. P. Chandrasekhar and Jayati Ghosh*, both at the Centre for Economic Studies and Planning, Jawaharlal Nehru University, New Delhi, India

At a time when countries of the South Asian region are in a state of flux, reflected in far-reaching economic, political and social changes, this series aims to showcase critical analyses of some of the central questions relating to the direction and implications of those changes. Volumes in the series focus on economic issues and integrate these with incisive insights into historical, political and social contexts. Drawing on work by established scholars as well as younger researchers, they examine different aspects of political economy that are essential for understanding the present and have an important bearing on the future. The series will provide fresh analytical perspectives and empirical assessments that will be useful for students, researchers, policy makers and concerned citizens.

The first books in the series cover themes such as the economic impact of new regimes of intellectual property rights, the trajectory of financial development in India, changing patterns of consumption expenditure and trends in poverty, health and human development in India, and land relations. Future volumes will deal with varying facets of economic processes and their consequences for the countries of South Asia.

Books in this Series

Women, Health and Public Services in India
Why are States Different?
Dipa Sinha

Labour Law Reforms in India
All in the Name of Jobs
Anamitra Roychowdhury

For more information about this series, please visit: www.routledge.com/Critical-Political-Economy-of-South-Asia/book-series/CRPE

'This excellent study skillfully combines information about labour laws with theoretical analysis. It deserves to be read by all, researchers, politicians and practitioners in the field who are not swayed by oversimplified rhetoric of labour market reform.'

Amit Bhaduri, Professor Emeritus, Jawaharlal Nehru University, New Delhi, India

'Dr Anamitra Roychowdhury's book *Labour Law Reforms in India: All in the Name of Jobs* is a careful analysis of one of the major economic questions in recent times. After critically evaluating the voluminous literature, the author builds formal analytical models to explain the empirical findings. The book is a valuable addition to the academic and policy discourse.'

R. Nagaraj, Professor of Economics, Indira Gandhi Institute of Development Research, Mumbai, India

'This book alerts us that increasingly employers will offer contract rather than permanent work. It examines the theory behind labour market flexibility and offers us a macroeconomic perspective that contradicts the one which focuses solely on the labour market without considering the repercussions at the aggregate economy wide level. It is important reading for those concerned about the future of livelihoods and how developing nations should respond to that.'

Errol D' Souza, Professor of Economics and Director, Indian Institute of Management, Ahmedabad, India

'That the inevitable result of flexibility in the labour market – either by legislation or by stealth – has been widening gaps in income and wellbeing is now accepted by many economists with greater equanimity than before. This book will have further sobering effect on the supporters of the so-called labour market flexibility as it critically looks at the theoretical arguments that provide justification for flexibility. With a balanced combination of theoretical arguments and empirical evidence, the book eminently accomplishes what it sets out to do – to show convincingly that the measures advocated to make the labour market more flexible are unlikely to produce the results they are supposed to produce.'

Achin Chakraborty, Director, Institute of Development Studies, Kolkata, India

Labour Law Reforms in India

All in the Name of Jobs

Anamitra Roychowdhury

LONDON AND NEW YORK

First published 2018
by Routledge
2 Park Square, Milton Park, Abingdon, Oxon, OX14 4RN

and by Routledge
711 Third Avenue, New York, NY 10017

Routledge is an imprint of the Taylor & Francis Group, an informa business

© 2018 Anamitra Roychowdhury

The right of Anamitra Roychowdhury to be identified as author of this work has been asserted by him in accordance with sections 77 and 78 of the Copyright, Designs and Patents Act 1988.

All rights reserved. No part of this book may be reprinted or reproduced or utilized in any form or by any electronic, mechanical, or other means, now known or hereafter invented, including photocopying and recording, or in any information storage or retrieval system, without permission in writing from the publishers.

Trademark notice: Product or corporate names may be trademarks or registered trademarks, and are used only for identification and explanation without intent to infringe.

British Library Cataloguing-in-Publication Data
A catalogue record for this book is available from the British Library

Library of Congress Cataloging-in-Publication Data
A catalog record for this book has been requested.

ISBN: 978-1-138-71363-5 (hbk)
ISBN: 978-1-351-05887-2 (ebk)

Typeset in Sabon
by Apex CoVantage, LLC

To those who reposed faith in me:

My parents, Sipra and Tapan K. Roychowdhury, for teaching me to look beyond the everyday;

Nivedita and Aniket, for making every day joyful.

Contents

List of figures   xi
List of tables   xiv
Foreword   xv
Acknowledgements   xix
List of abbreviations   xxi

Introduction   1

1. Present status of labour laws in India and their proposed amendments   12

2. A critical examination of the labour market flexibility debate in India   42

3. Explanation of jobless growth in Indian manufacturing and trends in labour conditions   117

4. Identifying the theoretical structure underlying labour market flexibility and its critical examination   145

5. Some market clearing models on labour market flexibility   190

6. Effectiveness of labour market flexibility in face of effective demand constraint   238

7	Labour market flexibility in an open economy context	264
8	Concluding remarks: labour market flexibility and the proposal for *laissez-faire* capitalism	293
	Bibliography	303

Figures

2.1	Proportion of organised sector employment in total workforce (UPSS)	65
2.2	Share of organised manufacturing sector (ASI) in total organised sector employment	67
2.3	Index number of employment: organised manufacturing	72
2.4	Proportion of contract workers to total workers in organised manufacturing sector	78
2.5	Share of contract workers' wage rate to all workers' wage rate	87
2.6	Share of wages in GVA	88
2.1A	Distribution of total organised employment by sectors	102
2.2A	Share of organised manufacturing employment by sectors	103
2.3A	Share of workers not covered by labour laws: Contract (All) + Regular workers (0–100) employment category	104
3.1	Number of days worked in a year (all manufacturing)	119
3.2	Share of functional (submitting returns) TUs in total registered TUs: all industries	124
3.3	Number of strikes and lockouts in India: all industries	125
3.4	Number of mandays lost due to disputes (work stoppages): all industries	127
3.5	Relative share of mandays lost between strikes and lockouts: all industries	128
3.6	Share of unionised workers in total workers: manufacturing sector	129
3.7	Number of disputes (strikes and lockouts) in the manufacturing sector	131

3.8	Number of workers involved in disputes and its share to total workers: manufacturing sector	132
3.9	Share of mandays lost to total mandays worked: manufacturing sector	133
3.10	Labour absenteeism rate in organised manufacturing	134
3.11	Index number of real wage (RW) and product wage (PW)	136
3.12	Share of fatal injuries in total industrial injuries in factories	138
3.13	Proportion of retrenchment-and layoff-related disputes to all disputes	139
3.1A	Index number of labour productivity (LP), product wage (PW) and real wage (RW)	141
4.1	Diagrammatic representation of I-O theory	157
4.2	Scrutinizing the existence of unemployment in a two-tier wage system	163
5.1	Freedom to develop voluntary contracts based on initial conditions	212
5.2	Examining the case to develop voluntary contracts based on initial conditions	216
5.3	Examining the case to develop voluntary contracts with commodity market intervention	217
5.4	Examining the case to develop voluntary contracts with firm-specific knowledge	220
5.5	Superiority of F-regime over N-regime when industry size is endogenously determined	225
5.6	Examining the superiority of F-regime over N-regime when industry size is endogenously determined	226
5.7	Relationship between severance pay and equilibrium wage	227
5.8	Relationship between severance pay and equilibrium wage with demand management	228
6.1	Aggregate labour market	243
7.1	Current account deficit and trade balance as percentage of GDP	271
7.2	Share of manufacturing exports in total merchandise exports: India	272
7.3	Mean total hourly compensation cost of manufacturing employees, selected countries and regions, 2005	273

7.4	Comparative unit labour cost of selected countries, 1990–2005 (USA = 1)	275
7.5	Real Effective Exchange Rate (REER) 36-currency index: India	277
7.6	Monthly growth rate of index of industrial production: manufacturing sector	278
7.7	Net capital inflows to India	284
7.8	Short-term debt to forex reserves	285
8.1	Unions and shared prosperity	295

Tables

1.1A	List of central labour laws	32
1.2A	Current provisions of IDA, 1947	33
1.3A	Amendments to the IDA, 1947	34
1.4A	Differences in provisions relating to layoff, retrenchment and closure in IDA 1947 and SNCL Report	35
2.1	Growth rate of employment in different segments of the organised sector	68
2.2	Coefficient of variation by size of employment	73
2.3	Coefficient of variation (employment): by employment size	75
2.4	Growth rates of output, employment and number of factories: by size of employment	76
2.5	Growth rate of employment: by employment size	77
2.6	Growth rate of output and employment in organised and unorganised manufacturing	84
2.7	Correlation coefficient between point growth rate of output and employment: by size of employment	94
2.8	Growth rate of employment, capital intensity (K/L) and real wage rate (RW) between 1980–81 and 1985–86	95
2.9	Growth rate in registered manufacturing, 1979–80 to 1988–89	98
2.1A	Coefficient of variation: decadal	105
3.1	Growth rate of output, employment, labour productivity, capital intensity and capital productivity between 1980–81 and 1985–86	120
3.2	Growth rate of labour productivity (O/L), capital intensity (K/L) and capital productivity (O/K)	122

Foreword

For some time now there has been a demand in some quarters that the labour market in India should be made 'flexible', in the sense that employers should be given the absolute and unfettered freedom to hire and fire workers at will. This demand has not come only from employers' representatives or neo-liberal 'think-tanks'; it has been voiced by several academic economists of repute. And an array of empirical and theoretical arguments has been advanced in its support.

While the empirical demonstration that India's industrial growth has been hamstrung by the absence of labour market flexibility has been rather weak and unconvincing, a point that even votaries of labour market flexibility concede, and has also drawn powerful critiques, the theoretical arguments in favour of such flexibility have not been much debated. The outstanding merit of the present book by Dr Anamitra Roychowdhury is that he gives not only an overview of this entire discussion and a powerful rebuttal of the attempts that have been made to demonstrate empirically the need for labour market flexibility but also a detailed critique of the theoretical arguments adduced in its favour, including even by such well-known economists as Assar Lindbeck and Robert Solow.

In general, the theoretical argument for labour market flexibility assumes that the economic system is not demand-constrained. This is hardly surprising. Labour market flexibility entails an enfeebling of trade unions and hence a level of real wages lower than would have prevailed in its absence. But in a demand-constrained system, a rise in the real wages of organized workers, by *ceteris paribus* increasing aggregate demand (since the workers' propensity to consume is higher than that of those living off the surplus they produce), *increases* output and employment in the economy and hence serves to benefit the unorganized workers as well.

There is, therefore, no conflict of interest between the organized and the unorganized workers, no question of high real wages of organized workers resulting in a lower social output and no basis for claiming that trade unions hold back the growth rate of the economy. Since all these are propositions asserted by the votaries of labour market flexibility, a demand-constrained system obviously undermines this general theoretical position.

There is, however, one strand of argument in favour of labour market flexibility that has been advanced even in the context of a demand-constrained system. This states that investment would be larger in an economy where employers are free to hire and fire workers at their will than in one where they are not. This argument goes as follows. Whenever any investment project is planned, the investor hopes to earn an expected rate of return from it. But in the event of expectations going wrong (e.g. the sales being more or less than expected, the rate of return would turn out to be more or less). The expected rate of return in short is the 'best guess' rate of return, the mean of a probability distribution whose standard deviation can be taken as a measure of risk. The investor would wish to get compensated for this risk by earning a risk premium. Investment, therefore, would be pushed up to the point at which the expected rate of return on the marginal project (what Keynes had called the 'marginal efficiency of capital') would equal the sum of the interest rate and the marginal risk premium (which depends not only on the risk associated with the marginal project itself but also on the ratio of borrowed to own funds of the entrepreneur, or the gearing ratio, on the entire portfolio).

Now we can visualize two alternative situations, in one of which workers can be hired and fired at will, while in the other there are a certain number of workers who cannot be easily fired. Compared to the first situation, the 'best guess' rate of expected return would be lower in the second situation and the desired risk premium higher. This is because in the event of sales being higher than expected, more workers can be hired in both situations to produce more, while in the event of sales being lower, the damaging effect on profits would be greater if workers cannot be retrenched (i.e. if their wages constitute an 'overhead') than if they can. It follows that since the best guess rate of return would be lower and the risk premium higher on any project in the absence of labour market flexibility, the magnitude of investment planned by any entrepreneur (and hence, it is inferred, the magnitude of total investment) would be lower in such a case.

This argument for labour market flexibility even in a demand-constrained system, however, has two obvious lacunae. First, it is of course an *ex ante* argument (its point of reference is an individual investor planning his investment on the assumption that other things remain the same). But even as an *ex ante* argument it does not hold in a world dominated by oligopolies and monopolies, in whose case, as John Hicks had pointed out long ago, the marginal efficiency of capital schedule is vertical (i.e. investment is determined by the expected growth of the market). Investment in this case, not being an interior equilibrium (where the marginal efficiency of capital equals the sum of the interest rate and the marginal risk premium, as suggested above) is unaffected by changes in the interest rate or in the risk premium or in the expected rate of return itself (as long as it is above a certain level).

Secondly, labour market flexibility affects the share of wages and hence also the size of the Keynesian multiplier, so that we cannot carry on the discussion only on a *ceteris paribus* basis. In fact, with an accelerator-type investment function, we can arrive at a certain obvious conclusion. During the slump in a business cycle, the 'floor' level of activity will be higher in a world without labour market flexibility than in one that has such flexibility; the 'ceiling' of the cycle, however, is unlikely to be affected one way or the other by whether the economy has such flexibility. Hence the *average* level of output and employment in any cycle is likely to be higher in a world which has no labour market flexibility than in a world which has. (Cycles in an open economy, of course, are not going to be of the simple multiplier-accelerator sort, but the theoretical arguments advanced for labour market flexibility, and examined by Roychowdhury, are all in the context of a closed economy anyway.)

It follows, therefore, that the theoretical case for labour market flexibility is not sustainable in a demand-constrained system, and since capitalism is quintessentially a demand-constrained system, the argument for such flexibility lacks any theoretical substance.

Roychowdhury discusses, of course, the infirmity of the theoretical argument for labour market flexibility in the context of a demand-constrained system, but he is not content with that alone. He actually critiques the theoretical arguments that have been advanced for labour market flexibility *on their own grounds* (i.e. by pointing to the *internal inconsistencies* in such theoretical arguments). In fact, this part of the book is a real intellectual treat for all academic economists.

This book is an extremely valuable one precisely because it caters to such a large variety of readers: those who are interested in knowing simply what labour market flexibility is and the debate around it; those who wish to have a detailed picture of the Indian labour situation and those who wish to savour internal logical critiques of theories of labour market flexibility, including those advanced by some internationally respected figures of the economics profession. And above all it is an extremely timely contribution, since the demand for such flexibility is becoming more and more strident.

Prabhat Patnaik, Professor Emeritus
Jawaharlal Nehru University, New Delhi, India

Acknowledgements

This book developed out of my doctoral thesis written at the Centre for Economic Studies and Planning (CESP), Jawaharlal Nehru University (JNU), New Delhi, India. When I started my doctoral studies in 2005, two things got me interested in the subject of labour reforms: (a) at the macro level, the national labour commission had submitted its report a few years earlier, and a major debate on labour flexibility ensued; (b) at the micro level, the 2005 version of the Indian Society of Labour Economics conference was hosted by JNU, and labour reforms were discussed with great enthusiasm. I made up my mind, and fortunately my thesis adviser Professor Prabhat Patnaik – believing in complete academic freedom – gave me a green light.

When I started working on this book there was, indeed there is, very little in terms of theory explaining – at least in case of India – how exactly labour laws hold back employment creation. Instead, the literature almost entirely developed in the empirical terrain, confining me initially to enquire along similar lines. It was my inability to answer Professor Patnaik's penetrating questions that forced me to engage with theory. Over the years his main influence has been – other than shaping my ideas – to provide the courage for asking basic questions in my quest for analytical precision. I sincerely thank him for the care with which he nurtured my intellectual growth.

I am also grateful to Professor Jayati Ghosh for constant support and encouragement. At various stages of the book, I have greatly benefited from her insightful suggestions. I want to thank Professor C. P. Chandrasekhar for providing me this opportunity – as one of the series editors – and granting enough time to complete this book. I thank Surajit Das, Debabrata Pal and Zico Dasgupta for reading previous drafts of the manuscript and helping me improve the arguments presented in the following pages. Long discussions with my wife, Nivedita Sarkar, on most ideas developed here saved me, on several occasions, from committing minor and major errors. Needless to say, none of them is responsible for the errors that may remain.

Writing a book more often than not is a lonely affair, and friends, seldom realizing, contribute in many indispensable ways through the journey. Taposik Banerjee and Sayantan Bera supported me enthusiastically throughout the project. Among others, Sakti Goldar, Shouvik Chakraborty, Tirthankar Mandal and Indranil Mukhopadhay need special mention. Thanks are due to Jyotirmoy Bhattacharya, Rohit, Indranil Chowdhury, Debabrata Roy, Amarjoyti Mahanta, Kaushik Bhadra and Anil K. Mani, who were all helpful in various ways. Library staffs of JNU, EXIM Bank, NIPFP, RTL, IEG and St. Stephen's College were resourceful and generous throughout the period, and my various demands were enthusiastically accommodated by colleagues at St Stephen's College and then at JNU. Shreya Sharma ably proofread the manuscript in full.

Finally, I must express my gratitude to my parents, who steadfastly stood by my side and never lost faith in me. It is their unfailing encouragement that gave me the confidence to finish this book. At the end, I am short of words to express my indebtedness to Nivedita. It is only because she tight-roped, balancing her own doctoral research while single-handedly taking charge of every worldly need of our family, that I could work for long stretches. But for her constant support, this work would have never seen the light of day. I also drew enormous motivation from my smiling little son, Aniket.

A heartfelt thanks to Shoma Choudhury of Routledge, without whose patient reminders to write the last lines, this book would have never gone to press.

Abbreviations

AD	Aggregate Demand
AP	Andhra Pradesh
APC	Aggregate Propensity to Consume
ASI	Annual Survey of Industries
BoP	Balance of Payments
CAD	Current Account Deficit
CLA	Contract Labour Act
CPI	Consumer Price Index
CPI (IW)	Consumer Price Index (Industrial Workers)
CV	Coefficient of Variation
DB	Doing Business
DGET	Directorate General of Employment and Training
DIPP	Department of Industrial Policy and Promotion
EPF	Employees' Provident Fund
EPL	Employment Protection Legislation
ESI	Employees' State Insurance
FDI	Foreign Direct Investment
FII	Foreign Institutional Investment
GDP	Gross Domestic Product
GoI	Government of India
GT	General Theory
GVA	Gross Value Added
IDA	Industrial Disputes Act
I-O	Insider-Outsider
JSR	Job Security Regulation
LMF	Labour Market Flexibility
LP	Labour Productivity
LTC	Labour Turnover Cost
MEC	Marginal Efficiency of Capital

MNC	Multinational Corporation
MPL	Marginal Productivity of Labour
NRF	National Renewal Fund
NSS	National Sample Survey
OECD	Organization for Economic Co-operation and Development
OGL	Open General License
PFC	Principle of Free Contract
POL	Petroleum, Oil and Lubricant
PPP	Purchasing Power Parities
PSU	Public Sector Unit
PW	Product Wage
R&D	Research and Development
RBE	Real Balance Effect
REER	Real Effective Exchange Rate
RW	Real Wage
SEZ	Special Economic Zone
SNCL	Second National Commission on Labour
ToR	Terms of Reference
TU	Trade Union
ULC	Unit Labour Cost
UNCTAD	United Nations Conference on Trade and Development
UNICEF	United Nations Children's Fund
UPSS	Usual Principal plus Subsidiary Status
VRS	Voluntary Retirement Scheme
WPI	Wholesale Price Index

Introduction

The background

One of the chief defining features of second generation economic reforms in India has been the country's strong commitment to undertake labour market reforms. Only a cursory look at the government documents testifies to this fact. In the terms of reference (ToR) of the Second National Commission on Labour (SNCL) 2002 appointed by the Government of India (GoI), it is clearly stated that one of the two *key* tasks[1] the Commission set itself to resolve was 'to suggest rationalisation of existing laws relating to labour in the organised sector' (SNCL 2002: 6).[2] To the Commission, rationalisation[3] meant: 'In our understanding, rationalisation in this context, *means only making laws more consistent with the context*, more consistent with each other, less cumbersome, simpler and more transparent' (emphasis added) (ibid.: 10). The *context* is clearly identified 'as the emerging economic environment: the *globalization of the economy and liberalisation of trade and industry*; the rapid changes in technology and their consequences and ramifications; . . . and the responses that are necessary *to acquire and retain economic efficiency and international competitiveness*' (emphasis added) (ibid.: 6).

Now a major source of retaining efficiency and international competitiveness is recognised to be achieved by taking recourse to 'cost-cutting' – especially saving on labour costs. This is apparent from the following observation – '*Because of global competition most of the companies want to reduce costs and be competitive. The first casualty is the number of workers employed, and since 1992 many Indian companies have resorted to downsizing by introducing Voluntary Retirement Schemes (VRS)*' (emphasis added) (ibid.: 245). However, resorting to VRS often proves to be costly and time consuming. Thus, the Commission sought to rationalise the labour laws, such that 'rationalisation of labour' (interpreted as 'retrenchment of workers', as pointed out by the critiques) could be smoothly (and costlessly) carried out. This is amply clear from the following statement:

> The Commission is conscious of the fact that in the fast changing economic scenario and changes in technology and management, which are entailed in meeting current challenges, *there cannot be a fixed number of posts in any organization for all time to come. Organizations must have the flexibility to adjust the number of their workforce based on economic efficiency.*
> (emphasis added) (ibid.: 364)

The Commission through its recommendation proposed to facilitate such flexibility by rationalising the labour laws. However, the Commission cautiously noted that such 'rationalisation of labour' – which in its view, is inevitable to withstand global competition, would lead to unemployment. So the Commission emphasized the 'need to provide some form of public assistance to meet the distressing consequences of unemployment [which] has become more urgent after globalisation' (ibid.: ch.8: 8). This is because the 'Commission observed a continuous downsizing of workers in the organized sector and the miseries that it is causing to the retrenched working population' (ibid.: 1304). Therefore, the view of the Commission seems to be – *allowing for retrenchment, of course with some safety measures for the workers thus rendered unemployed.*

Such an outlook comes out most clearly from this detailed observation:

> [T]hose who demand the right to hire and fire also want to bring about a fundamental change in the nature or perception of employment. They want all employment to be on the basis of contracts for stipulated periods. Without going into the need or merits of the contract system, it must be admitted that this introduces a basic or fundamental change in the current system in vogue in most kinds of employments. . . . We have been accustomed to distinguish jobs as permanent and ad hoc or nonpermanent. While we understand that nonpermanent jobs or temporary assignments can be on contract for specified

periods, with the possibility of extensions, we are accustomed to look upon employment against permanent jobs as permanent service. Any attempt, therefore, to change the basis of tenure in all jobs (permanent as well as nonpermanent) to contractual, and for stipulated periods, no doubt involves a basic change in attitudes and notions. . . . *If transforming the basis of all employment is a social necessity because it has become an economic necessity for industrial or commercial enterprises, then, it is equally necessary to create social acceptability for the change, and the social institutions that can take care of the consequences.*

(emphasis added) (ibid.: 303–304)

As regards creating social acceptability of contract jobs for institutionalizing free hire and fire, the Commission recommended:

(T)o pay adequate compensation, offer outsourced jobs to retrenched workers or their cooperatives, if any enterprise decides to close down give workers or Trade Unions a chance to take up the management of the enterprise before the decision to close is given effect to: underwrite facilities for medical treatment, education of children, etc. and provide for a third party or judicial review of the decision, *without affecting the right of the management to decide what economic efficiency demands.*

(emphasis added) (ibid.: 350)

The necessity for such an arrangement, in the Commission's view, in the present context is on the following grounds:

In the new circumstances of global competition, it may not be possible for some enterprises to continue and meet the economic consequences of competition. In such cases, one cannot compel non-viable undertakings to continue to bear the financial burden that has to be borne to keep the concern going. There is no justice or benefit in compelling a loss-making undertaking to bear burdens that it cannot carry, to sink further. They should, therefore, have the option to close down. It would be good if there can be a prior scrutiny of the grounds on which the closure is sought, and the reasons for the loss of viability. It is precisely for this reason that the provision for prior permission was incorporated in the Law. But experience has shown that governments do not want to give quick decisions, even though they know that delay in taking decisions only adds to the burdens that such enterprises are forced to carry. Applications to permit closure are kept pending for months and years. . . . *In these circumstances the Commission came to the conclusion that the best, and more honest and equitable course will be to allow closure, provide for adequate compensation to workers* . . . [and] *prior permission is not* [deemed] *necessary in respect of lay off and retrenchment in an establishment of any employment size. Workers will, however, be entitled to two months' notice or notice pay in lieu of notice, in case of retrenchment.*

(emphasis added) (ibid.: 350)

The Commission, therefore, forcefully articulated its position as follows: allow for free retrenchment, layoff of workers and closure of units along with suitable compensation for the workers thrown out of employment. This, however, is a sea change in perspective if we compare it with the view government held immediately after independence.

Changing sensibilities of government towards labour

Since the stated objective of the government is to boost efficiency and international competitiveness through rationalisation of labour laws – it may be interesting to note the exact process through which this is sought to be achieved. As already pointed out, rationalisation of labour laws is only a means to bring in *rationalisation of labour*. Now enhancing competitiveness by introducing rationalisation of labour is a long-standing argument in the literature. Rationalisation, it is typically argued, is one of the principal means of increasing output and reducing production costs (Singh 1967). According to the International Economic Conference of 1927 (Geneva), rationalisation, *interalia*, aimed at – 'securing maximum efficiency of labour with minimum effort'; therefore, ' "rationalisation" may be said to mean any measure (or measures) aimed at maximizing output with minimum *effort* and *cost*' (emphasis in original) (Singh 1967: 44). Thus, the process of rationalisation predicts enhancing international competitiveness through a reduction in costs, especially labour costs (Bhaduri 2005: 41) and '[a]ll forms of rationalisation from employers are prompted by the desire to reduce cost in wages' (Prasad 1963: 275).

However, while rationalisation emphasizes minimizing *both* effort and cost, 'the term in India is often understood to mean reorganization of labour and working conditions so as to reduce labour costs [alone]' (Singh 1967: 45). A typical means of reducing labour cost is simple labour retrenchment.[4] Such singular focus of rationalisation on reducing labour costs in India – resulting in retrenchment of labour – is typically associated with widespread labour protests. The prolonged workers' strikes waged against introduction of rationalisation in the early 1930s in the Ahmedabad textile industry is an interesting case in point. Special interest in this case arises from the resolution adopted for settlement of the stand-off between employers and employees. The strike was called off only after the intervention of Mahatma Gandhi in 1935 and adoption of a resolution reached through mutual negotiation between employers and employees; among other things, the resolution specified that 'on introduction of rationalisation, *no worker shall be retrenched except by voluntary retirement on payment of gratuity*' (emphasis added) (ibid.: 45).

Professor V. B. Singh documents the continuation of such labour unrest even after independence:[5]

> [T]he employers in India continued to introduce rationalization, specially in the post Second World War period, in the restricted sense of the term, namely, reorganization of production methods with a view to reduce labour costs. The workers' opposition to this sort of rationalization culminated in an eighty-day strike in Kanpur in 1955.
>
> (ibid.: 46)

This dispute caught so much public imagination that the then Prime Minister, Jawaharlal Nehru on 31 May 1955 chose to speak on the subject – clearly defining the aims and scope of rationalisation – as follows:

> We want higher techniques, greater efficiency, a more rationalized system of working, but we certainly do not want people to be thrown out of work. Therefore, the broad policy, the government have adopted, is that where any rationalization takes place the people must be guaranteed work, that is, no one

> should be thrown out. If that is so, then we consider it. Also broadly speaking our approach is this: All new plants that we put in must be of the latest technique, the newest type, and generally speaking, we should employ our resources on additional production units which necessarily give additional employment rather than in improving an old unit which might create unemployment. We do the latter only when we can provide employment for those who might become unemployed.
>
> (quoted in Singh 1967: 47)

These views were also echoed in the Second Five-Year Plan document:

> In the context of growing unemployment, rationalization has an adverse psychological effect on workers. Even so, to freeze the existing techniques of production is not in the larger interests of a developing economy. Rationalization should, therefore, be attempted when it does not lead to unemployment, is introduced in consultation with workers, and is effected after improving working conditions and guaranteeing a substantial share of gains to workers.
>
> (quoted in Prasad 1963: 270)

Thus, protection of *existing* employment was an overwhelming and even primary objective of the government in the period immediately after independence, and rationalisation was encouraged only when it was *not* in conflict with this employment objective.[6] It follows that the current position of the government in the context of labour rationalisation, namely, allowing for retrenchment with suitable social security measures for the unemployed, appears to be in sharp contrast to the view that the government held during the early planning era. This is probably because government previously realized that the best way of offering social security to workers was through jobs.

However, this is not to suggest that retrenchment and layoffs were unknown in the early planning period. But the newly decolonized country felt the necessity to maintain the balance of power between labour and capital through passing of legislations that progressively strengthened the bargaining position of labour compared to what it had been before independence. One such piece of legislation was the Industrial Disputes Act (IDA) of 1947 – which, *interalia*, dealt with retrenchment and layoffs. With the 1954 amendment to IDA, it was stipulated that any industrial establishment employing more than 50 workers (except for casual workers) has to meet the following norms for carrying out layoffs and retrenchment: (a) Provide layoff compensation equal to 50 percent of basic wages and dearness allowance up to a period of 45 days of a year (in case employee is ready to accept reasonable alternative employment and is not already employed elsewhere), and (b) No worker who has been in continuous employment for more than a year under an employer is to be retrenched unless s/he has been given one month's notice and also a gratuity of 15 days' average pay for every completed year of service (Punekar 1963: 244–245).

The necessity for such a stipulation arose mainly out of the pre-independence experience. Buchanan (1934: 417) noted that for the period between April 1921 and March 1926, 'disputes in Bombay Presidency due to "dismissal or reinstatement of individuals" were 22.3% of the total [disputes], and were second only to those due to "pay and allowances"'. Thus, it was realized that peaceful discharge of industrial activity required some form of restraint on free hire and fire. More importantly, such necessity arose out of the understanding that unfettered hire and fire was damaging for the development of trade unionism itself. A labour leader, N. M. Lokhanday, president of Bombay Mill-hands' Association in 1884, noted that 'so jealous are the employers of labour here [Bombay] of any combination among workers for their mutual benefit' that they penalized workers for forming any kind of association and identified the fear of losing employment to be the main obstacle in the way of building a trade union movement (quoted in Buchanan 1934: 419). This aspect comes out most clearly from the set of resolutions adopted by the Bombay Mill-owners Association around 1882 to deal with their workers; for instance, Rule number 13 specified as follows: 'Persons striking work, or intimidating or conspiring with other persons employed in the factory to strike work, may be summarily dismissed, and shall be liable to forfeit all wages then accrued to them, and also to be prosecuted' (ibid.: 419). It is clear that without safeguarding employment itself, none of the workers' demands can be enforced or even tabled. As Buchanan (1934: 430) notes, 'the real secret of the employers' opposition [to trade unionism] appears to be that they hate to surrender the position in which they can "hire and fire" without notice and at their untrammelled will'. After decolonization, legislation was passed precisely to protect workers from facing such caprices of employers.

After the 1954 amendment, a major amendment governing layoff, retrenchment and closure of industrial units was passed at the time of Emergency in 1976. The 1976 amendment to IDA stipulated the requirement for obtaining *prior* permission from government – at the threshold level of at least 300 (permanent) workers – for carrying out retrenchment, layoff and closure of industrial units. A similar amendment was passed in 1982 which reduced the threshold level of (permanent) workmen from 300 to 100. Under the current stipulation of IDA (after amendments), *prior* permission is necessary, for industrial establishments employing 100 or more workers, to bring about layoff, retrenchment and closure of units (IDA 1947; Khan 2005: 88).[7]

This current provision of IDA – requiring *prior* government permission for implementing retrenchment, layoff and closures – occupies the centre stage of the labour market flexibility (LMF) debate. As noted earlier, this is seen as an obstacle to efficiency gains and competitiveness, hindering growth and development of the economy. More importantly, it is identified as the principal factor behind meagre employment growth in the organised sector. This is apparent from the following observation:

> Indian Labour Laws are highly protective of labour, and labour markets are relatively inflexible. These laws only apply to the organised sector. Consequently, these laws have restricted labour mobility, have led to capital-intensive methods in the organised sector and adversely affected the sector's long-run demand for labour.
> (Economic Survey 2005–06: 209)

The changed perspective of the government towards labour directly follows from the above understanding. Such a change is best captured by the Second Labour Commission's observation:

> The attitude of the Government, especially of the Central Government, towards workers and employers seems to have undergone a change. *Now, permissions for closure or retrenchment are more easily granted. . . . The labour adjudication machinery is more willing to entertain the concerns of industry.*
> (emphasis added) (SNCL 2002: 249)

It may be interesting to note the *nature* of economic thinking that is responsible for such a stark change in government's attitude. Now the objective behind rationalisation of labour laws is to bring in free hire and fire – such that labour rationalisation (i.e. retrenchment) could be easily and costlessly carried out. However, such a crucial policy prescription, affecting lives of millions of workers, must be based on sound theoretical and empirical foundations. *One of the main objectives of the book is to study in detail the logical consistency of the theoretical framework and the empirical underpinnings underlying labour market flexibility.* A detailed description of the objective of the book is provided below.

Plan of the book

Chapter 1 forms the background of the book, where we present in detail the current status of legal provisions available to labour. Next, we discuss the main proposals put forward in the LMF debate for rationalising labour laws in India. This is followed by a discussion of some recently amended labour laws in India. In Chapter 2 we take up the ongoing debate on LMF in India, which has mostly taken place in the empirical terrain. Here we closely scrutinize the validity of the empirical studies on both sides of the debate. Chapter 3 outlines the factors contributing to the phenomenon of 'jobless growth' observed in Indian manufacturing for a considerable stretch of time. It also assesses labour conditions in the industrial sector; in particular, whether rise in labour militancy – creating labour market rigidities – results in work stoppages. Anybody acquainted with the literature on the LMF debate in India clearly realizes the lack of proper theoretical understanding on the subject. It is precisely because of this that most of the debate in the Indian context has remained confined to the empirical terrain. One of the main objectives of the book is to fill this present lacuna and clearly identify the theoretical framework that recommends LMF. This forms the subject matter of Chapter 4, where we not only identify the theoretical framework underlying LMF but also check its internal consistency. In Chapter 5 we take up another genre of theoretical models for discussion that prescribes LMF. Once more the robustness of results thrown up by these studies is checked. However, both strands of theoretical arguments, it would be apparent in the course of discussion, not for once recognise the problem of effective demand deficiency in the economy. But this is a perennial feature of any capitalist economy, where wealth is held at least partly in the form of money. Therefore, in Chapter 6 we explicitly take note of the autonomous role played by effective demand and investigate how the results suggested by the theories discussed in Chapters 4 and 5 are liable to change. The discussion until Chapter 6 is carried out in a closed economy context. However, there could be an argument in favour of LMF in an open economy context. In Chapter 7 we bring in the open economy context into the discussion and analyse whether LMF would help India to penetrate the export market. The book ends with some concluding remarks and policy suggestions.

Notes

1 The other major task facing the Commission was 'to suggest an Umbrella Legislation for ensuring a minimum level of protection to the workers in the unorganised sector' (SNCL 2002: 6). The other avowed objective was to take account of various factors that contributed to the creation of the *context* which necessitated the appointment of the Commission. Labour Commissions were set up in India on two earlier occasions. First, the Royal Commission on Labour was appointed in 1928 and is widely known as the Whitley Commission. Second, the First National Commission on Labour was formed after independence under the chairmanship of Justice Gajendragadkar and is popularly known as the Gajendragadkar Commission, which submitted a report in 1967.
2 The organised sector comprises only those establishments employing at least ten or more total workers (Indian Labour Year Book 2007: 2).
3 The Commission had to clearly state the meaning of rationalisation since there was some critique that 'the word "rationalization" means the retrenchment of workers or cutting down the labour force engaged in an industry or plant, and, therefore, indicates an attempt to sanctify "retrenchment"' (SNCL 2002: 10–11).
4 Now such retrenchment may or may not be associated with technological progress. If it is not accompanied by technological progress, then it simply increases the burden of work on each employee. On the other hand, technological progress (of labour-saving variety with non-commensurate wage increases as compared to labour productivity increases to save on labour costs) also necessitates retrenchment, whenever growth of labour productivity surpasses output growth. In such a situation, the effect on effort per employee (either in the form of intensity of work or prolonged working hours) depends upon a number of other factors such as bargaining power of employees, unemployment rate in the economy and so on.
5 Labour unrest related to rationalisation in pre- and post-independent India are also reported in some detail in Prasad (1963: 263–275).
6 The broad framework to meet these apparently conflicting objectives is described below: 'Rationalization should be introduced gradually

and its pace should be so set that labour rendered surplus by it is absorbed . . . and no one is retrenched or thrown out of employment' (Prasad 1963: 277) and this is practically feasible since:

> There is always some reduction in the number of workers by death, resignation and abandonment. Such of the vacancies as occur for these causes should not be filled till the intended rationalization is completed and labour likely to be rendered surplus by rationalization should be set off against such vacancies.
>
> (ibid.: 276)

7 A detailed analysis of the different sections and aspects pertaining to the current provisions of IDA is carried out in Chapter 1.

Chapter 1

Present status of labour laws in India and their proposed amendments

As already mentioned in the Introduction, approaches for achieving efficiency and international competitiveness through rationalisation of existing labour laws have been elaborately documented in various government reports. Before discussing the suggested contours of labour market reforms (proposed changes and already amended labour laws), it may be worthwhile to look at the present status of legal provisions available to labour.

1.1 Present status of labour laws in India

In the Indian Constitution, the subject of Labour appears in List III of the Seventh Schedule, known as the Concurrent List. Therefore, Union and State legislatures simultaneously enjoy the constitutionally provided right to design laws relating to labour. There are 45 Central[1] laws and 170 State statutes directly governing the labour market in India (Debroy 2005; World Bank 2010). Such laws were originally formulated to safeguard the interests of the labour constituency vis-à-vis that of capital. Most of these legislations are the product of the Nehruvian era, when the country pursued the goal of a Socialistic pattern of society – probably to respect the implicit social contract that developed during the course of struggle for independence. However, most – but not all – labour laws apply to the organised sector.[2]

The several laws governing the Indian labour market can be broadly categorized under three distinct heads: (a) laws relating to industrial relations, (b) laws relating to wages and (c) laws relating to social security (Hazra 2005). *This study exclusively concentrates on the implications of the proposed changes in laws governing industrial relations.* Industrial relation pertains to the relations between an employer and his/her employee or between two employees. Hence, there are bound to be 'potential areas of conflict between them [various participants] and consequently laws relating to industrial relations are perhaps the most important of the labour laws' (Hazra 2005: 138).

Essentially, three main statutes govern industrial relations in India: (a) The Trade Unions Act 1926 specifies the right of workers to organise themselves, (b) The Industrial Disputes Act (IDA) 1947, created for settling industrial disputes and securing industrial peace and (c) The Contract Labour (Regulation and Abolition) Act (CLA) 1970, which strictly stipulates the activities and norms for using contract labour in industrial units. *In what follows we shall restrict ourselves to a discussion of certain provisions of IDA 1947 and CLA 1970.*[3] This is because much of the rationalisation of labour laws sought after (and discussed due to their sensitivity and profound implications on labour) in various government documents and subsequently debated in the literature pertains to changing the current provisions of IDA and CLA.

Let us first discuss certain present provisions in the IDA.[4] We shall further confine ourselves to only those sections of the Act which have raised intense debate in recent times with respect to proposals for amendment. These are Chapter II-A (Sections 9-A and 9-B), Chapter V-A (Sections 25-C, 25-F and 25-FFF) and Chapter V-B (Sections 25-M, 25-N and 25-O). In what follows we shall discuss them seriatim.[5]

Chapter II-A deals with the Notice of Change and comprises Sections 9-A and 9-B. Section 9-A stipulates that an employer must serve three weeks of advance notice in writing, informing the worker[6] of any change in his/her working conditions. These changes include: (1) changes in shift work, (2) changes in grade classification, (3) changes in rules of discipline, (4) a technological change that may affect the demand for labour and (5) changes in employment, occupation, process or department. The worker, of course, has the right to object to these changes and can go to the court, which can result in an industrial dispute with all its implications in terms of time and cost. In particular the law suggests:

> No employer, who proposes to effect any change in the conditions of service applicable to any workman in respect of any matter specified in the Fourth Schedule, shall effect such change, – (a) without giving to the workman likely to be

affected by such change a notice in the prescribed manner of the nature of the change proposed to be effected; or (b) within twenty-one days of giving such notice...

(IDA 1947)[7]

The aforementioned stipulations of Section 9-A also apply as employers propose to change working conditions under the following contingencies: Items 10 and 11 of the Fourth Schedule. Item 10 of the Fourth Schedule reads: 'Rationalisation, standardization or improvement of plant or technique which is likely to lead to retrenchment of workmen', and Item 11 of the Fourth Schedule reads: 'Any increase or reduction (other than casual) in the number of persons employed in any occupation or process or department or shift (not occasioned by circumstances over which the employer has no control)' (SNCL 2002: 347). The foregoing provisions of Section 9-A, it is widely argued, prevent an establishment from undertaking effective industrial restructuring and technological upgradation, and responding quickly to the rapidly changing international market environment, which are essential to remain competitive and economically viable in a globalised world (SNCL 2002; Debroy 2005; Hazra 2005; Khan 2005).

However, government has the option to *exempt* employers from the provisions of Section 9-A, and this is stipulated under Section 9-B, which suggests:

> Where the appropriate Government is of opinion that the application of the provisions of Section 9-A to any class of industrial establishments or to any class of workmen employed in any industrial establishment affect the employers in relation thereto so prejudicially that such application may cause serious repercussion on the industry concerned and that public interest so requires, the appropriate Government may, by notification in the Official Gazette, direct that the provisions of the said Section shall not apply or shall apply, subject to such conditions as may be specified in the notification, to that class of industrial establishments or to that class of workmen employed in any industrial establishment.
>
> (IDA 1947)

Although government reserves the right to exempt an establishment from serving the notice of change in advance, citing Section 9-B, it has been particularly criticized on grounds of creating uncertainty among employers (Hazra 2005; Khan 2005).

Chapter V-A applies only to establishments employing 50 or more workers (but is inapplicable to establishments with 100 or more workers).[8] Chapter V-A requires giving a workman[9] (1) in case of layoff, 50 percent of his/her normal basic wage plus dearness allowance for a period of 45 days (under Section 25-C),[10] (2) in case of retrenchment[11] (under Section 25-F), written notice 30 days in advance or wages in lieu of the notice[12] – additionally 15 days' average pay for every completed year of service needs to be paid, (3) in case of closure or sale of an establishment, the employer must fulfil the same conditions as for retrenchment unless its successor takes on these obligations (under Sections 25-FF and 25-FFF). However, the advance notice period in prescribed manner for closures is sixty days.

As for Chapter V-B, it is applicable to:

> an industrial establishment (not being an establishment of a seasonal character or in which work is performed only intermittently) in which not less than one hundred workmen are employed on an average per working day for the preceding twelve months.[13]

After the 1982 amendment of Chapter V-B, which reduced the threshold level of workmen from 300 to 100 for obtaining prior permission before layoff, retrenchment and closures, this is the current stipulation in IDA.[14] In case of layoff, Section 25-M of Chapter V-B is applicable and stipulates:

> No workman (other than a *badli* workman or a casual workman) whose name is borne on the muster-rolls of an industrial establishment to which this Chapter applies shall be laid off by his employer except [with the prior permission of the appropriate Government or such authority as may be specified by that Government by notification in the Official Gazette (hereafter in this section referred to as the specified authority), obtained on an application made in this behalf, unless such lay-off is due to shortage of power or to natural calamity, and in the case of a mine, such lay-off is also due to fire, flood, excess of inflammable gas or explosion].
>
> (IDA 1947)

Cases of retrenchment are governed by Section 25-N, which requires three months' notice in writing to the workman or wages in lieu of the notice. Retrenchment additionally requires prior permission from the appropriate government, failing which retrenchment is deemed illegal. Therefore, unlike Chapter V-A, only serving prior notice is *not* sufficient in case of establishments governed by Chapter V-B, where *prior* permission has to be sought from government authorities. If permission is granted, the workman must be paid 'compensation which shall be equivalent to 15 days' average pay for every completed year of continuous service' (IDA 1947). Under Section 25-O, identical provisions – similar to retrenchment – apply for closure of an enterprise, requiring prior governmental permission.

Therefore, the crucial difference between Chapters V-A and V-B is that whereas establishments covered by the former are only required to serve an *advance notice* to the workers and appropriate government, in a prescribed manner to carry out the proceedings of layoffs, retrenchments and closures, in the *latter* case the law specifies a further stringent condition, namely, in addition to serving advance notice, *prior* permission has to be sought from government to execute layoffs, retrenchments and closures.[15] These, in short, are certain current provisions (of only those sections which have raised intense debate in recent times) of the IDA 1947. Next, we turn to the current provisions of the Contract Labour (Regulation and Abolition) Act 1970.

Now the above regulations guiding adjustment of workers in an establishment apply only to the category of permanent workers. But those hired as contract/temporary workers *do not* enjoy such protection; their retrenchment and layoffs are out of the purview of Chapters V-A and V-B. Therefore, it is widely argued that contract labour provides flexibility to the firm since it can hire and fire contract workers at will (without legal hassles) and quickly adjust the workforce according to changing market conditions (Debroy 2005; Guha 2009; World Bank 2010).

This technique of using the device of contract labour to bypass labour laws was largely anticipated by the legislators. Therefore, CLA 1970 was formulated to restrict the use of contract labour, clearly specifying the areas in which such workers *cannot* be used. Specifically, Chapter 3 (Section 10) prevents the use of contract labour for most core functions (main activity) of a firm and stipulates that such labour should be abolished from carrying out these activities.[16] Section 10 further stipulates:

> Notwithstanding anything contained in the Act, the appropriate Government may, after consultation with the Central or a State Board, prohibit by notification in the National Gazette, employment of contract labour in any process, operation or other work in any establishment.
>
> (CLA 1970)

Later, in a landmark judgement, the Supreme Court ruled that contract workers (after abolition of contract labour from core activities) must be absorbed within the firm itself.[17] In 1976 the Central Government issued a notification that in establishments run by the Central Government, contract labour should not be used for sweeping, cleaning, dusting and watching of buildings. The law also prevents firms from hiring workers on temporary contracts for more than 120 days (anyone so employed can demand permanent employment status) and currently applies to establishments employing at least 20 workers. Presently, firms bypass such legal obligations by compulsorily instituting a one-day break in service after 120 days.[18]

Among various laws[19] which guide the balance of power between the constituencies of capital and labour, the bone of contention has been Chapter V-B of IDA 1947. Major amendments proposed to the IDA are discussed in Appendix 1 (Table: 1.3A). Having discussed the present legislative provisions in place, we are now in a position to discuss the major proposals in vogue for their rationalisation.

1.2 Approaches to rationalisation of labour laws in India

It is widely asserted in official circles that the current legal provisions perversely affect economic growth and employment generation in the organised sector. This sentiment is clearly captured in the recommendations of the Task Force on Employment Opportunities, constituted by the Planning Commission in 2001, chaired by Montek Singh Ahluwalia:

> India's labour laws have evolved in a manner which has greatly reduced the flexibility available to the employers to adjust the

labour force in the light of changing economic circumstances. In a globalised world, persisting with labour laws that are much more rigid than those prevailing in other countries only makes us uncompetitive not only in export markets but also in domestic markets. Some changes in the laws are therefore necessary if we want to see rapid [economic] growth.

(Task Force on Employment, Planning Commission 2001: 171)[20]

It is with this general perception in official circles that the proposals for rationalisation of labour laws in India are put forward.[21] We now turn to the detailed recommendations for rationalisation of the specific laws discussed in Section 1.1.

With regard to Notice of Change (i.e. Section 9-A), it is recommended:

[A] source of rigidity in our labour market arises from the provisions regarding service rules in the Industrial Disputes Act. . . . The requirement of a 21-day notice can present problems when units have to deploy labour quickly to meet the requirement e.g. time bound export orders. More generally, the requirement of consent of workers means that employers cannot easily shift workers between different plants and locations, or even shift them to do new jobs within the same plant. It is necessary to amend the Act to introduce much greater flexibility in this area.

(Task Force on Employment, Planning Commission 2001: 156–157)

This clause, it is argued, obstructs firms from quickly responding to technological changes and exigencies caused by genuine economic reasons, which are considered to be central to withstand global competition. Therefore, commentators have argued on the relevant (Notice of Change) portion of Section 9-A that '[w]orkmen are protected in so many different ways that a logical outcome would be to scrap Section 9-A altogether' (Khan 2005: 100).[22] Furthermore, it is also argued that since government does not follow any well-defined procedure and invokes Section 9-B in a discretionary manner, this creates considerable confusion among employers, and therefore Section 9-B should be scrapped as well (Khan 2005). Adopting the above recommendations would certainly render Sections 9-A and 9-B redundant. This view has gained some support in the policy establishment, as SNCL (2002: 348) recommended:

> (T)he Commission is of the view that notice of change, issued by an employer as per provisions of Section 9A, *should not operate as a stay* [on employers' action] under Section 33 though such a decision of the management will be justiciable under Section 33 A. Section 33 may be amended accordingly.
>
> (emphasis added)

Now items 10 and 11 of the Fourth Schedule in effect deal with retrenchment and determination of size of employment under foreseeable situations. It is held that employers should be allowed to make them operational unilaterally:

> [I]tems 10 and 11, in a manner, deal with the very employment of persons and in the present situation, the size of employment is a matter which can be best decided by the employer himself or herself keeping in view various attendant circumstances.
>
> (ibid.: 347)

Further, this should not be a long, drawn-out process as it is suggested that 'there need be no statutory obligation for the employer to give prior notice, in regard to item 11 of the Fourth Schedule for the purpose of increase in the workforce, as is the position now under Section 9A' (ibid.: 348). In fact, it is held that '[t]he entire Chapter, Chapter II-A should be deleted . . . we should have "rationalisation without tears". Retrenchment, on account of automation, and modernization, is acceptable provided the employees accept retraining and re-deployment' (Hazra 2005: 148).[23] However, for workers (solely dependent on labour power for subsistence) retrenchment from current occupation may be acceptable – *only if guaranteed alternative employment opportunities (with remunerations equivalent to current income) are available*. Next, we turn to the proposed amendments in the Contract labour laws.

It is argued that the CLA in its present format is designed to prohibit rather than allow the use of contract labour and thereby introduces considerable uncertainty in the working of this increasingly important contractual arrangement. It is noted:

> The present legal provisions introduce a disincentive to expansion of contractual services because enterprises can freely outsource those services which do not have to be performed on the premises (e.g. laundry) but for those services which are of a regular nature and have to be performed on the premises (e.g. waiters serving in

workers canteens, cleaning, gardening, watch and ward services, loading and unloading etc.) employers outsourcing these services run the risk that the labour used in such services may be treated as contract labour, and may have to be absorbed permanently on the payroll. This obviously discourages employers from using such [regular] services to the extent that they otherwise might have done, with the net effect of reducing total employment.

(Task Force on Employment,
Planning Commission 2001: 158)[24]

Therefore, the flexibility enjoyed by organizations at present, in the matter of using contract labour is greatly diminished – which is argued to be of manifold importance especially in a globalised world that necessitates discharge of short-term contracts mainly in export consignments. So SNCL recommended that the use of contract labour should not be restricted to only noncore activities of an establishment but also extended to *core* activities, provided the demand is of transitory nature, stating: 'Organizations must have the flexibility to adjust the number of their workforce based on economic efficiency . . . [therefore] *for sporadic seasonal demand, the employer may engage temporary labour for core production/service activity*' (emphasis added) (SNCL 2002: 364).[25] A further measure, it is argued, would be to clearly 'identify certain specialized and supporting occupations that "naturally" tend to use contractual work for a variety of industries' (World Bank 2010: 137) and allow the use of contractual labour in them.[26] In short, it is envisaged that the CLA should be made flexible and accommodating by tightening Section 10 so that ambiguity about absorption of contract workers following abolition of contract labour is removed. However, it is conceded that this move should be accompanied by introducing social security schemes for contract workers.

At the centre of debate, however, is Chapter V-B (although there are concrete reform proposals for Chapter V-A as well, but they are only of secondary importance to the debate). A major debate started in the early 1990s with the proposals of two committee reports commissioned by the Government of India which suggested means, as part of the larger reform measures, for revamping the industrial sector. These reports were The Report of the Inter-Ministerial Working Group on Industrial Restructuring, which was submitted in March 1992, and The Goswami Committee Report on Industrial Sickness and Corporate Restructuring, which was submitted in July 1993. Both committees forcefully recommended complete deletion of Chapter V-B. This view was considered too aggressive; therefore, a softer proposal by the Prime Minister's Council on Trade and Industry, under convenorship of Kumar Mangalam Birla in the year 2000, was agreed upon. On its recommendation, the then Union Finance Minister, Yaswant Sinha, in his Budget Speech of 2001–02 announced that the IDA should be amended to see that only establishments with 1,000 or more workers are covered by Chapter V-B.[27] However, there was repeated resonance of the original proposal. The employment task force suggested:

> We . . . recommend a more radical step of deleting Chapter V-B from the Industrial Disputes Act completely and restoring the position prior to 1976. This was recommended in 1992 by the Inter-Ministerial Working Group on Industrial Restructuring and subsequently also by the Committee on Industrial Sickness 1993.
> (Task Force on Employment, Planning Commission 2001: 156)

These policy prescriptions address a major problem pointed out by employers, namely, obstacles faced in adjusting workforce due to fluctuating product demand and technology upgrading. These are, it is emphasized, absolutely essential for withstanding global competition (see Chapters 1 and 6: SNCL 2002). Note that in the current statute there are already provisions for both these contingencies. A close reading of Chapter V-B suggests that it *does not* apply for *casual/contract* workers[28] or establishments of a *seasonal* character or in which work is performed *intermittently*. Hence, firms already enjoy some leeway to adjust (temporary) workforce in a moderately fluctuating economy, in which technological obsolescence is not very rapid. However, it is argued that such moderate flexibility is not enough to face global competition – even the permanent workforce has to be suitably adjusted. In other words, such an argument must admit that uncertainty faced by firms due to integration with the world economy has increased manifold. However, this observation may also suggest a decoupling from the world economy (up to a certain degree), rather than pushing the working class towards vulnerability through socialization of risk.[29]

It is further argued that 'Chapter V-B and Clause 25-O [governing closure of units] effectively make labour a fixed factor. . . . [it] creates incentives for employers to choose more capital-intensive techniques and increase wages instead of employment' (World Bank 2010:

118. Also see Lucas 1988; Ghose 1994). Specifically, the argument is: 'Chapter V-B ends up biasing against labour, the cheaper input promotes its substitution by capital, leading to inefficiency as the employers partake an artificial labour by capital substitution' (Hazra 2005: 156). Moreover, with Clause 25-O in place: 'In the long-run, firms would realize that plants they contemplate setting up in the near future will be difficult to close down at some later date should the economic environment turn adverse' (Khan 2005: 90).[30] Therefore, it is argued that there has been a decrease in demand for labour in existing firms on one hand and lower investments in terms of forsaking setting up of new firms – consequently, government policies aimed at protecting jobs end up destroying them in the first place.

However, this is a logically fallacious argument since firms go for capital-intensive technology, it is argued, since workers become a fixed factor of production due to Chapter V-B. Therefore, wage costs are like fixed costs, and to safeguard against such contingencies, firms go for capital substitution. First, note that traditionally capital is treated as the fixed factor of production – therefore, rental costs are normally considered to be fixed (at least in the short run). Thus, without additional reasoning, it is patently unclear why restrictions on 'hire and fire' would *necessarily* lead to adoption of capital-intensive technology. Second, the *degree* of capital intensity in production depends upon the nature of market imperfection firms are confronted with (Kaldor 1939: 45). Specifically, in an oligopolistic set-up, assuming labour as the only input used in the production process, suppose any rise in wage costs can be fully passed on to the final price of outputs. Then, an across-the-board rise in wages (translating to an all-round increase in prices) would only have scale effect, leaving the relative ordering of the marginal efficiency of capital schedules (MEC) for different techniques unchanged. Hence, the choice of technique, in this case, would be exactly the same as before (i.e. wage increase). Even when wage costs cannot be fully passed on to the final output prices, since oligopolistic firms have fixed market share, an all-round increase in wages – due to job security regulations (JSR) – is likely to leave the choice of technique for firms unaffected. This is due to the following reason: since firms have fixed market share under oligopoly, the gross revenue of any firm would continue to remain the same as before the wage rise. Now an across-the-board rise in wages by the same percentage would leave the relative ordering of the net revenue obtained from different techniques unchanged. Therefore, relative ordering of the MEC schedules under such circumstances would remain unaffected, leaving the choice of technique the same. Hence, in an oligopolistic setting, capital intensity of production may remain unaltered following introduction of JSR. Third, the notion of availability of *multiple* techniques (of varying capital intensities), at the *same* point in time, to produce a 'given good' is something of a chimera. As Patnaik (2011a) cogently puts it:

> If a modern steel plant is to be built then there is a *particular* technology for doing so and there is *not* much scope for *varying* the employment-intensity within that technology; on the other hand it is true that backyard steel can be produced with a far higher employment-intensity than in a modern steel plant, but then for the purposes for which steel is typically required in the economy the outputs of the two *cannot* be deemed to be the 'same'. *So, this entire assumption of employment-intensities being different for the production of the "same good" is a bit of a red herring.* A "good", strictly defined, has *only one particular technique of producing it at any particular time*. In an economy, given its pattern of income distribution, certain types of goods are demanded, and they are typically produced with certain *fixed* techniques (or even when there is a multiplicity of techniques for producing a "good", the employment-intensities do not vary much among them); *labour market flexibility as such makes little difference to the choice of technique.*
>
> (emphasis added)

Currently, the debate revolves around SNCL proposals, to which we now turn. SNCL (2002: 352) took the view: 'Chapter VA should apply ... to all establishments with 20 or more workers', governing layoff, retrenchment and closure, 'as it [commission] is inclined to recommend a separate set of legal provisions covering all aspects of layoff, retrenchment and closure for all kinds of establishments with less than 20 workers'.

For Chapter V-B it recommended:

> [Firms] should ... have the option to close down ... the Commission came to the conclusion that the best ... course will be to allow closure, provide for adequate compensation to workers, and in the event of an appeal, leave it to the Labour

Relations Commission to find ways of redressal: – through arbitration or adjudication.

(ibid.: 351)

However, this was subject to the condition that prior government permission would still be necessary for closures, layoffs and retrenchments in establishments employing 300 or more workers – 'It would however, recommend that in the case of establishments employing 300 or more workers where layoff exceeds a period of one month, such establishments should be required to obtain post facto approval of the appropriate Government' (ibid.: 352). This recommendation is true for retrenchments and closures as well; with its (requiring government permission for 300 or more workers) reach extending to *all* establishments instead of the present provisions covering only plantations, mines and factories. SNCL also recommended that applications seeking permission for closures, retrenchments and layoffs should be responded to within 60 days of filing them, failing which permissions will be deemed to have been granted. Essential difference in scope and content between the current provisions of IDA and the SNCL proposals are reported in Appendix 1 (Table 1.4A). SNCL's recommendations played a crucial role, as we shall see below, in shaping the recent proposals for changing the labour laws.

1.3 Recent changes in labour laws

We discuss below major proposals for change/amendments in labour laws in recent times very briefly.[31] A comprehensive coverage of labour law changes is not attempted here; instead, focus is on such laws which are likely to have far-reaching impact on labour. These changes are taking place both at the level of Union and State governments (mainly Rajasthan and Madhya Pradesh). We shall discuss legal changes at the Union level first and then in Rajasthan.[32]

Labour law changes by Union government

Labour Code on Industrial Relations Bill, 2015: It proposes to amalgamate the following three regulations (with crucial change in provisions): (a) Industrial Disputes Act, 1947, (b) Trade Union Act, 1926 and (c) Industrial Employment (Standing Order) Act, 1946.

Industrial Disputes Act, 1947: The new code proposes to restrict the applicability of Chapter VB to establishments employing 300 or more workers (current threshold 100). However, amendment to IDA is the most controversial of all labour law reforms and trade unions (TUs) are expected to resist it the most. Therefore, it is tactically left to the states to raise workers' threshold by amending their respective IDAs with clear signal of providing tacit support. This would in effect decentralize the Indian labour market, with 29 states each vying to offer the most lucrative labour regime to attract industries.

Trade Union Act, 1926: With the 2001 amendment, trade unions (TUs) for getting registered, require at least 10 percent or 100 workers (whichever is less) engaged in an establishment or industry as its members. The earlier norm for registration was only seven members (which now applies only for units where 10 percent of the workforce is fewer than seven). Traditionally, non-worker members of TUs or outsiders (not engaged or employed in the establishment or industry with which the TU is concerned) play a crucial role in the formation of TUs and strengthening its activity as office-bearers. Earlier, a maximum of up to five persons could be non-working office-bearers of TUs in the organised sector, and in the unorganised sector at most 50 percent of office-bearers could be outsiders. However, the proposed code does not allow any office-bearer from outside in TUs engaged with the organised sector and allows only two non-worker office-bearers in the unorganised sector. These moves are likely to weaken TUs in particular by starving them of the expertise/specialized knowledge (notably legal) that outsiders bring from different fields.

Industrial Employment (Standing Order) Act, 1946: It proposes application of Standing Orders only to industrial units with 100 or more workers. A standing order clearly delineates policies and provisions on various aspects of working conditions with the objective of protecting labour by defining workers' rights and fixing the responsibilities/duties of employers. In many states (Uttar Pradesh, West Bengal, Maharashtra and Assam, among others) it is applicable to industrial units with 50 or more workers – thus, with the new code, workers in these states might stand to lose.

Factories (Amendment) Bill, 2016: It proposes to amend the Factories Act, 1948. Before this, another bill, Factories (Amendment) Bill, 2014, was introduced in the Lok Sabha on 7 August 2014. It proposed amendments to reduce the eligibility of paid leave from 240 to 90 days; also establishments liable to provide restrooms or shelters have been reduced from 150 to 75 workers. These are positive developments. However, the bill proposes that only factories employing 20 or more workers (using power) or 40 or more workers (without using power) shall be governed by the Factories Act [up from the present cut-off of 10 workers (using power) and 20 workers (without using power)]. Further, in response to the demand for revising the list of hazardous industries and hazardous substances in the first schedules of the Factories Act, the first schedule has been altogether deleted. However, deleting first schedule may complicate matters further, rather than resolving them, resulting in lengthy deliberations between management and workers to the detriment of the latter. Moreover, the bill allows women workers to work in night shifts (7 p.m.–6 a.m.), of course with proper safety measures. This would certainly help firms in cutting down wage cost through substitution of men by women workers, since women workers' wages are typically half of their male counterparts, even in the organised manufacturing sector. The bill also proposes to increase the spread of working hours from the existing 10.5 hours to 12, causing harassment to workers. Another major change has been to raise the limit of overtime work across the board. The overtime limit for shift workers has been raised from 50 to 100 hours per quarter (a three-month period). The same has been raised for adult workers from 75 to 115 hours per quarter (and up to 125 hours per quarter for public utilities). This move would definitely extend working hours (thereby thwarting fresh job creation) and further help in depressing labour costs, as 'overtime wages' do not include complimentary allowances (otherwise to be paid to new workers) such as house rent allowance, transport and small family allowance. But the proposals got stuck in the parliamentary standing committee on labour and were sent back to government for review (unanimously rejecting some of them). Another problem was introducing the bill in parliament without tripartite consultations – violating Convention 144 of the International Labour Organisation. Following this, Factories (Amendment) Bill, 2016, was introduced in Lok Sabha on 10 August 2016. It retains exactly the proposals on overtime work and disturbingly introduces proposals to stretch working hours of certain workers and curb their periods of rest (additionally specifying that these rules will *not* be limited to a five-year period, unlike now). Further, the bill has enabling conditions allowing each state to decide on the threshold of workers in a unit that would continue to be governed by Factories Act. However, TUs have opposed this move.

The Small Factories (Regulation of Employment and Conditions of Services) Bill, 2014: It proposes to exempt factories employing less than 40 workers (defined as 'small factory') from 14[33] labour laws, if these units complied with the stipulations laid down in the bill. Women are allowed to work in night shifts, of course, with proper safety measures in small factories, and the spread over of work has been increased from 10.5 to 12 hours. However, with the poor state of inspection, implementing the stipulations in the bill remains highly questionable. Further, these units can buy health insurance and provident fund products from the market instead of subscribing to the mandatory social sector schemes of Employees' State Insurance (ESI) and Employees Provident Fund (EPF). Moving to a market-based health insurance may deny the workers 'sickness benefit' (i.e. periodical payments to any insured person in case of his/her sickness). Similarly, moving away from EPF advocating: 'Every employer shall ensure that all worker in the small factory are covered by a Provident Fund scheme, approved by the Insurance Regulatory and Development Authority set up under the Insurance Regulatory and Development Authority Act, 1999' would deny workers 'defined benefit' and subject them to the risk of the 'defined contribution' scheme (where benefits vary according to the market performance).

Child Labour (Prohibition and Regulation) Amendment Act, 2016: On 29 July 2016, the President consented to the provision of allowing employment of a child below 14 years of age, 'where the child helps his family or family enterprises, which is other than any hazardous occupations or processes set forth in the Schedule, after his school hours or during vacations'. Along with encouraging child labour in home-based work, the new Act substantially reduced the list of professions considered hazardous. However, United Nations Children's Fund (UNICEF) India's Chief of Education, Euphrates Gobina, noted: 'Under the new Child Labour Act, some forms of child labour may become invisible and the most vulnerable and marginalised children may end up with irregular school attendance, lower levels of learning and could be forced to drop out of school' (www.unicef.org/media/media_92021.html; last accessed 19 July 2017). Therefore, to provide a protective legal framework, UNICEF strongly recommended removal of the provision 'children helping in family enterprises' from the Act.

The Apprentices (Amendment) Act, 2014: It amended Apprentices Act, 1961. With the amendment, definition of workers is changed to *include* workers employed through a contractor (contractual workers). Earlier workers with only regular contracts (regular workers) were considered for determining the number of workers in an enterprise. This restricted the number of apprentices an enterprise could appoint, given the fixed worker-to-apprentice ratio prescribed by government. Thus, broadening the definition of workers would help firms in hiring more apprentices (earning stipend which is only a fraction of the wage received by workers). Further, until now, daily (and weekly) hours of work an apprentice has to put in was decided according to the norms prescribed by the Central Apprenticeship Council. With amendment, employers are given the power to *unilaterally* decide on the daily (and weekly) working hours of an apprentice. Thus, working hours of apprentices would now depend on the vagaries of employers. Similarly, employers are given *full freedom to formulate their own policies* regarding recruitment of apprentices, which is bound to increase employers' discretionary power. Moreover, failing to comply with the provisions of the Act would now attract only monetary penalties and unlike before, offending employers cannot be put behind bars.

The Labour Laws (Exemption from Furnishing Returns and Maintaining Registers by Certain Establishments) Amendment Act, 2014: It amended the Labour Laws (Exemption from Furnishing Returns and Maintaining Registers by Certain Establishments) Act, 1988. The Bill containing the proposed amendments was rejected twice (2005 and 2011) on grounds of being excessively employer-friendly by the Parliamentary Standing Committee on Labour. Yet the 2011 Amendment Bill (with minor modifications) was passed in the Rajya Sabha in 2014 and got President's approval the same year. The original legislation exempted 'very small establishments' (employing up to nine workers) and 'small establishments' (employing 10 to 19 workers) from maintaining registers and filing returns *individually/separately* for nine[34] labour laws (about meeting the prescribed norms/standards), if these establishments provided a *consolidated* account for the same. *The basic reason for such exemption is to facilitate business by curtailing the transaction/compliance costs.*

The recent amendment changed the definition of 'small establishments' and allowed consolidated submission of returns for seven[35] *additional* labour legislations. The threshold for determining 'small establishments' has been increased from 19 to 40 workers. This is clearly a business-friendly move, since a larger set of firms would now come under the Act; additionally, they would now be exempted from separately furnishing information for 16 (instead of 9) labour laws subsumed under the Act. Note that certain newly added laws are very sensitive, such as the Child Labour Act and the Migrant Workers' Act, which require strict implementation. However, there is evidence of labour inspection sharply deteriorating in India in the recent past (Sood *et al.* 2014); therefore, implementation of these laws remains questionable (a concern shown by the Standing Committee; see Roychowdhury 2015) which may potentially lead to pervasive violation of these laws.

Labour law changes in Rajasthan

Industrial Disputes (Rajasthan Amendment) Act, 2014: Rajasthan amended its IDA, raising the applicability of Chapter VB to 300 or more (instead of 100 or more) workers. Madhya Pradesh also amended its IDA along these lines.[36] Both states stipulated three years for raising any case of retrenchment or layoff for conciliation, failing which it will not be considered as an industrial dispute. Rajasthan also increased the membership requirement for recognition of a trade union from 15 to 30 percent.

Contract Labour (Regulation and Abolition Rajasthan Amendment) Act, 2014: Rajasthan amended its CLA, which applies to establishments employing 50 or more workers, instead of the current 20. This move may potentially abolish all permanent jobs in establishments with fewer than 50 but more than 20 workers.[37] This employer-friendly move would implicitly encourage contract workers' use more liberally in establishments employing more than 50 workers.

Factories (Rajasthan Amendment) Act, 2014: It amended the Factories Act, 1948. Previously, it covered factories employing 10 or more workers (using power) or 20 or more workers (without using power). The recent amendment increased this threshold to 20 workers (using power) and 40 workers (without using power). An attempt to amend the Factories Act by Union government along similar lines has been rejected by the Standing Committee on Labour (Third Report, December 2014: 56; http://164.100.47.193/lsscommittee/Labour/16_Labour_3.pdf; accessed 19 July 2017) noting:

> if the amendment is carried out more than 70 percent of the factory establishments in the Country will be out of the coverage

of the Factories Act [with the increase in threshold] and workers will be at the mercy of employers on every aspect of their service conditions, rights and protective provisions laid down under the Act.

Yet Rajasthan went ahead. Another amendment is in the area of 'cognizance of offence'.

Previously, labour inspectors could directly report an offence to the court; now, inspectors require permission in writing from State government before reporting any offence to the court. Certainly, this is going to delay the proceedings and curb the power of labour inspectors.

Conclusion

This chapter formed the background of the study. It drew attention to various government documents which considered Indian labour laws rigid and self-defeating; therefore, recommending labour market reforms. It was necessary, therefore, to document the present provisions of labour laws in India in order to understand clearly the concrete proposals for their rationalisation. However, only those Chapters (and Sections therein) of the laws which have raised intense debate were discussed. Relevant portions of IDA and CLA were discussed in some detail. Next, we discussed concrete government proposals for reforming the current legal provisions. Among various proposals, it was pointed out that Chapter V-B of IDA occupied the centre stage of debate. Employers saw Chapter V-B as a formidable obstacle in adjusting the workforce, even in face of fluctuating product demand and technology upgrading – which, it is argued, is of exceptional importance in withstanding global competition. As a result, firms were believed to artificially opt for capital-intensive techniques. Currently, SNCL proposals are seriously debated, and they provide a road map for future reforms. The Labour Code on Industrial Relations proposed to restore the original threshold of 300 workers – introduced with the 1976 amendment – for Chapter V-B. Recent amendments/proposals of change in labour laws were also discussed briefly.

However, intense debate on reforming labour laws in India, particularly Chapter V-B, has been largely carried out in the empirical terrain without any conclusive outcome.[38] Nonetheless, it did not stop SNCL and the Ministry of Labour from proposing an increase in the threshold of workers for application of Chapter V-B. Next, we turn to review the empirical studies relating to the Indian (registered) manufacturing sector and assess the major conclusions drawn, which argue for complete labour market flexibility. The argument adopted to arrive at those conclusions will later help us in identifying the underlying theory. It will also be shown that the government's recent stand is directly derived from the conclusions arrived at by these studies.

Appendix

Table 1.1A List of central labour laws

Sr. no.	Name of the law
1	Apprentices Act, 1961
2	Bidi and Cigar Workers (Conditions of Employment) Act, 1966
3	Bidi Workers Welfare Cess Act, 1976
4	Bidi Workers Welfare Fund Act, 1976
5	Bonded Labour System (Abolition) Act, 1976
6	Child Labour (Prohibition and Regulation) Act, 1986
7	Children (Pledging of Labour) Act, 1933
8	Cine-Workers and Cinema Theater Workers (Regulation of Employment) Act, 1981
9	Cine-Workers Welfare Cess Act, 1981
10	Cine-Workers Welfare Fund Act, 1981
11	Coal Mines Provident Fund and Miscellaneous Provisions Act, 1948
12	Contract Labour (Regulation and Abolition) Act, 1970
13	Dock Workers (Regulation of Employment) Act, 1948
14	Dock Workers (Safety, Health and Welfare) Act, 1986
15	Employees' Provident Fund and Miscellaneous Provisions Act, 1952
16	Employees' State Insurance Act, 1948
17	Employers' Liability Act, 1938
18	Employment Exchanges (Compulsory Notification of Vacancies) Act, 1959
19	Equal Remuneration Act, 1976
20	Factories Act, 1948
21	Fatal Accidents Act, 1855
22	Industrial Disputes Act, 1947
23	Industrial Employment (Standing Orders) Act, 1946
24	Inter-State Migrant Workmen (Regulation of Employment and Conditions of Services) Act, 1979

Sr. no.	Name of the law
25	Iron Ore Mines, Manganese Ore Mines and Chrome Ore Mines Labour Welfare Cess Act, 1976
26	Iron Ore Mines, Manganese Ore Mines and Chrome Ore Mines Labour Welfare Fund Act, 1976
27	Labour Laws (Exemption from Furnishing Returns and Maintaining Registers by Certain Establishments) Act, 1988
28	Limestone and Dolomite Mines Labour Welfare Fund Act, 1972
29	Maternity Benefit Act, 1961
30	Mica Mines Labour Welfare Fund Act, 1946
31	Mines Act, 1952
32	Minimum Wage Act, 1948
33	Motor Transport Workers Act, 1961
34	Payment of Bonus Act, 1965
35	Payment of Gratuity Act, 1972
36	Payment of Wages Act, 1936
37	Personal Injuries (Compensation Insurance) Act, 1963
38	Plantations Labour Act, 1951
39	Public Liability Insurance Act, 1991
40	Sales Promotion Employees (Conditions of Service) Act, 1976
41	Trade Unions Act, 1926
42	Weekly Holidays Act, 1942
43	Working Journalists and Other Newspaper Employees (Conditions of Service) and Miscellaneous Provisions Act, 1955
44	Working Journalists (Fixation of Rates of Wages) Act, 1958
45	Workmen's Compensation Act, 1923

Source: Debroy (2005)

Table 1.2A Current provisions of IDA, 1947

Establishments by employment range	Restrictions on layoff	Restrictions on retrenchment	Restrictions on closure	Change in work conditions*
0–49 workers	No restriction	No restriction	No restriction	Notice of 21 days before introducing the change
50–99 workers	Compensation to workers	Compensation and prior notice to workers	Compensation and prior notice to workers	Notice of 21 days before introducing the change

(Continued)

Table 1.2A (Continued)

Establishments by employment range	Restrictions on layoff	Restrictions on retrenchment	Restrictions on closure	Change in work conditions*
100+ workers	Prior permission of government necessary	Prior permission of government necessary	Prior permission of government necessary	Notice of 21 days before introducing the change

Note: * However, Taskforce on Employment Opportunities (2001: 156) specifies that 21 days' prior notice is *only* applicable for establishments with 100 or more workers. All the provisions apply to only permanent workers.

Source: Author's compilation from IDA 1947

Table 1.3A Amendments to the IDA, 1947

Central amendments	Major change/clause introduced
1953	Layoff compensation
1956	Layoff compensation rules detailed
1965	Section 29: Penalty on employers for breach of Section 25 (layoff compensation) introduced.
1971	Revision of layoff rules for mines that close because of exhaustion of resources.
1976	Chapter VB is introduced. Sixty days' notice required for closure of industrial undertakings employing more than 300 workers.
1982	A number of changes based on the National Commission on Labour (1969) recommendations. The most important change is the revision of VB in view of the Excel Wear case in which the Supreme Court rejected the government's right to refuse closure. The government is now empowered to refuse or grant closure to units employing 100 or more workers.
2002	Amendments to Sections 2(a) and 2(s) defining 'appropriate government' and 'workmen'. Higher salaried employees brought under the Act; the state governments are the appropriate governments to issue orders refusing or granting permission for retrenchment, closure, or layoffs.

Central amendments	Major change/clause introduced
Major state clauses and amendments	
Industrial Disputes (West Bengal Amendment) Act, 1971	First introduced requirement of prior notice for closure of undertakings with 50 or more workers. Generalized in the 1972 Central amendment.
Layoffs, retrenchment and closure	• Government is authorized to force an undertaking to maintain 'continuity and normalcy' of work (West Bengal). • Maharashtra and Andhra Pradesh stipulate compensation payments before closure. • Permission required for retrenchment and closure of undertakings with 50 or more workers (West Bengal), 100 or more workers (Karnataka), 300 or more workers (Rajasthan and Madhya Pradesh). • Notice required for 90 days before closure (West Bengal, later Maharashtra). • Closure is valid when it occurs due to non-renewal of licenses (Maharashtra). • Full compensation to workers for retrenchment on any ground other than discontinuance of power supply (Maharashtra).

Source: India's Employment Challenge: Creating Jobs, Helping Workers, The World Bank, OUP, 2010 and Author's compilation.

Table 1.4A Differences in provisions relating to layoff, retrenchment and closure in IDA 1947 and SNCL Report

Particulars	IDA, 1947	SNCL Report
Scope	Factories, Mines and Plantations	All Industries
Notice period or pay in lieu of it	30 days	60 days
Government permission required for		
(a) Layoff	Yes (100+) workers	Yes (300+) workers
(b) Retrenchment	Yes (100+) workers	Yes (300+) workers
(c) Closure	Yes (100+) workers	Yes (300+) workers

Source: SNCL Report 2002

Notes

1. Table1.1A in the Appendix provides the list.
2. Establishments in the organised sector employ at least 10 or more workers.
3. However, discussions on other labour laws that have undergone recent changes are taken up in Section 1.3, albeit very briefly.
4. Section 2(j) of IDA 1947 defines an industry (to identify the scope of its application) as:

    industry means any systematic activity carried on by co-operation between an employer and his workmen (whether such workmen are employed by such employer or through any agency, including a contractor) for production, supply or distribution of goods and services with a view to satisfy human wants or wishes (not being wants or wishes which are merely spiritual or religious in nature), whether or not, – (a) any capital has been invested for the purpose of carrying on such activity; or (b) such activity is carried on with a motive to make any gain or profit. . .

5. Appendix 1 (Table: 1.2A) documents these legal provisions, according to their domain of application in establishments categorized by employment ranges.
6. Section 2(s) of IDA 1947 defines a worker as follows; Workman,

    means any person (including an apprentice) employed in any industry to do any manual, unskilled, skilled, technical, operational, clerical or supervisory work for hire or reward, whether the terms of employment be express or implied, and for the purposes of any proceeding under this Act in relation to an industrial dispute, includes any such person who has been dismissed, discharged or retrenched in connection with, or as a consequence of, that dispute, or whose dismissal, discharge or retrenchment has led to that dispute, but does not include any such person – (a) who is subject to the Air Force Act, 1950, or the Army Act, 1950, or the Navy Act, 1957; or (b) who is employed in the police service or as an officer or other employee of a prison; or (c) who is employed mainly in a managerial or administrative capacity; or (d) who, being employed in a supervisory capacity, draws wages exceeding one thousand six hundred rupees per month or exercises, either by the nature of his duties attached to the office or by reason of the powers vested in him, functions mainly of a managerial nature.

7. Inter-state variations exist in the time period specified – for example, Andhra Pradesh and West Bengal stipulate 42 days instead of 21 days.
8. IDA specifies that Chapter V-A

    [shall *not* apply to industrial establishments to which Chapter V-B applies, or] – (a) to industrial establishments in which less than fifty workmen on an average per working day have been employed in the preceding calendar month; or (b) to industrial establishments which are of a seasonal character or in which work is performed only intermittently.

(emphasis added)

The 1964 amendment to the IDA introduced this provision.

9   It requires emphasis that subclause (iv) of Section 2 (s) [which defines a workman] of IDA (with the 2010 amendment) *excludes* any person in a supervisory capacity drawing wages exceeding Rs. 10,000 per month from the definition of workman; hence it is outside the purview of law governing *only* workmen/women.

10 Adding a rider that the workman must 'present himself for work at the establishment at the appointed time during normal working hours at least once a day' (IDA 1947). If layoff continues beyond seven days at a stretch, West Bengal stipulates the workman to be present only once a week.

11 Retrenchment means permanent removal from the establishment and therefore is more damaging, whereas layoff means temporarily put on bench.

12 Importantly, serving advance notice to the workman concerned is a mandatory requirement, failing which retrenchment is not possible. Section 25-F further stipulates that 'notice in the prescribed manner is served on the appropriate Government [or such authority as may be specified by the appropriate Government by notification in the Official Gazette]' (IDA 1947).

13 Note both Chapters V-B and V-A are applicable only to establishments which have some record of stability in activity (preceding 12 months) and are *not* traditionally engaged in serving markets facing idiosyncratic demand (more on this later).

14 According to the original requirement of ID Act 1947 – to retrench a factory worker, under contingent situations, with more than 240 days of service, no prior permission was necessary if the following conditions were satisfied: 'last come first go' rule was followed in drawing up a list of workmen to be retrenched, one month's notice in writing stating the reasons of retrenchment and 15 days compensation for each year of completed service at 50 percent of basic wages plus dearness allowance were payable (see Report of the Task Force on Employment Opportunities, Planning Commission 2001 and Introduction). The requirement for obtaining prior permission at the threshold level of at least 300 workers was first-time introduced with the 1976 amendment to IDA, and Chapter V-B was introduced as the guiding principle for governing layoffs, retrenchments and closures. However, there are considerable inter-state variations in determining the threshold level of workmen. For instance, in West Bengal the provision is stricter and applies to industrial establishments employing only 50 workers instead of 100. In Karnataka, Chapter V-B applies even to industrial establishments where work is of *seasonal* nature. Rajasthan and Madhya Pradesh, on the other hand, very recently increased the threshold of workers back to 300 (from 100), relaxing the application of Chapter V-B.

15 Otherwise, it is illegal to carry out these activities under Chapter V-B.
16 This prohibition of contract workers in 'core' areas followed from two Supreme Court judgements (Standard Vacuum Refinery Company of India Limited vs. Its Workman, 1960 III SCR 466 and Vegoils Private Limited vs. The Workmen, 1972 I SCR 673). It prohibited temporary labour in tasks that are (a) perennial, (b) necessary for the work of the factory, (c) sufficient to employ a considerable number of wholetime workmen and (d) being done in most concerns by regular workers (Debroy 2005; World Bank 2010).
17 Judgement of Air India vs. United Labour Union (1996 9 SCC 70) case.
18 This is a widely held practice in all spheres of the economy. For example, in Delhi University, ad hoc (contract) teachers are offered work for at most 120 days, after which there is a compulsory break in service. In recent times, around 40 percent of the faculty members in the University are appointed on a contract basis (The Indian Express 28 November 2016).
19 For a comprehensive discussion on existing labour laws in India, see the chapter on Review of Laws (SNCL 2002: ch.6); Debroy and Kaushik (2005); Ahsan et al. (2008).
20 Relatively rigid labour law in a particular country, it is alleged, makes it uncompetitive in the export market – for the country in question cannot adopt cost-cutting measures through wage restraint and wage cuts – which is believed to be the key instrument through which countries penetrate the international market. However, the United Nations Conference on Trade and Development [(UNCTAD) 2011: IV] notes that if many countries take recourse to such a strategy, then this would lead to a 'race to the bottom' in terms of wages, ultimately proving counterproductive: 'The simultaneous pursuit of export-led growth strategies by many countries implies a race to the bottom with regard to wages, and has a deflationary bias' (more on this in Chapter 7).
21 Interestingly, the judiciary was much ahead of the legislators in appreciating the need for rationalising labour laws in favour of employers. The Supreme Court quite consciously initiated a change of course in its interpretation of the IDA, stating that its earlier verdicts were excessively pro-worker, and a more 'balanced' approach was necessary. This is a crucial development, since India follows a common-law system. Thus, apart from deciding on the constitutional validity of a law, the higher judiciary can bring about substantial changes in the *way* it is enforced, with no change in the statute itself. The following Supreme Court judgement in Excel Wear vs. Union of India AIR 1979 SC 25 is a case in point:

> Gradually, the net [of laws] was cast too wide and the freedom of the employer tightened to such an extent by the introduction of the provisions that it has come to a breaking point from the point of view of the employers. . . . It is not quite correct to say that because compensation is not a substitute for the remedy of prevention of unemployment, the latter remedy must be the only one. If it were so, then in no case closure can be or should be allowed. . . . But, so long

as the private ownership of an industry is recognised and governed on overwhelmingly large proportion of our economic structure, is it possible to say that principles of socialism and social justice can be pushed to such an extreme so as to ignore completely, or to a very large extent, the interest of another section of the public, viz. the private owners of the undertakings?

(Quoted in Task Force on Employment, Planning Commission 2001: 155)

More recent Supreme Court verdicts invoke similar sentiment: see, *State of U.P. vs. Jai Bir Singh*, (2005) 5 *Supreme Court Cases* 1; *Allahabad Jal Sansthan vs. Daya Shankar Rai*, (2005) 5 *Supreme Court Cases* 124; *U.P. State Brassware Corporation vs. Udai Narain Pandey*, (2006) 1 *Supreme Court Cases* 479; and *Hombe Gowda Educational Trust vs. State of Karnataka*, (2006) 1 *Supreme Court Cases* 430, among others.

22 Other proposals include reducing the period of advance Notice of Change from 21 days to 7 days as per the recommendation of the Report of the Inter-Ministerial Working Group on Industrial Restructuring 1992 (popularly known as the J. L. Bajaj Committee).

23 It may be interesting here to note H. Mahadevan's observation, Dy. General Secretary, All India Trade Union Congress, New Delhi, on the proposals for re-training and re-deployment: 'It is pertinent to point out that the Indian employers' apex fora have refused to accept to contribute to the proposed "Skill Development Fund", which indicates that they are not prepared for investment in education and training' (Mahadevan 2005: 262). Now if employers are not interested in re-training, it could be extremely difficult for the employees to acquire the same even with the best of intentions.

24 Without clearly specifying an alternative route of carrying out these regular (on premises) activities currently accomplished through outsourcing, the claim on reduced total employment remains idle speculation.

25 Andhra Pradesh readily accepted this recommendation and immediately amended its contract labour legislation to allow engagement of contract labour not only in peripheral areas but also in core activities, under certain circumstances [see *The Contract Labour (Regulation and Abolition), Andhra Pradesh Amendment Act 2003*, FICCI-AIOE (2005: 277)].

26 The World Bank's tentative list includes cleaning, security, maintenance, housekeeping, laundry, loading, information technology, support services, ports, airports, hospitals and export-oriented units in SEZs.

27 Under current provisions, the stipulation on the number of workers is 100. Hence, the finance minister envisaged a tenfold increase in the number of workers, for whom the law would apply. The most recent demand has been to raise the limit to at least 500 workers (World Bank 2010). This would render Chapter V-B de facto irrelevant. For instance, under the current provisioning, the proportion of workers protected by Chapter VB is 72 percent (actually lesser, for contract workers are *not* protected) according to 2008–09 data (other years show a similar

outcome). However, if the cut-off is raised to 500, then merely 40 percent would receive employment protection and with the threshold raised to 1,000, it drastically falls to 27 percent.

28 This is recognised in the literature; Fallon and Lucas (1991: 399) note:

> The legislation [IDA] does make an exception for retrenchment resulting from power shortages or natural disaster. Moreover *badli*, or casual workers, are not covered by either the compensation formula or the permission requirements, which apply to permanent workers (those paid for 240 days or more in a year).

29 It is argued that labour regulations apply for only a small section of the workforce, a fraction of the organised sector that forms the labour aristocracy. This is used as an argument to repeal the labour laws:

> These [labour] regulations. . . , encourage informality, and deepen dualism (division or extreme disparities, especially between formal and informal sectors). They also foster inequality between a very small segment of workers in the organised sector and the vast majority, about 90 percent of workers, in the informal sector.
> (World Bank 2010: 105)

However, in our view this is an inverted logic for repealing labour laws; instead, the goal should be to extend protection to a larger section of the workforce.

30 Bhattacharjea (2006) makes an interesting observation regarding Section 25-O, questioning the *extent* to which it could *actually* be considered as a constraint. Bhattacharjea (2006: 8–9) notes:

> 25(O) was struck down as unconstitutional by the Supreme Court as early as 1978 [Excel Wear vs. Union of India (1978) 4 Supreme Court Cases 224.]. . . . The 1982 amendment . . . incorporated several procedural changes in 25(O) so as to satisfy the Supreme Court. It was brought into effect in 1984. . . . After conflicting verdicts by various High Courts, *it upheld the amended 25(O) only in 2002* [Workmen vs. Meenakshi Mills (1992) 3 SCC 336, Papnasam Labour Union vs. Madura Coats Ltd (1995) 1 SCC 501, and Orissa Textile and Steel Ltd vs. State of Orissa (2002) 2 SCC 578]. Thus, 25(O) would have remained *inoperative* all over the country between 1978 when it was struck down by the Supreme Court and 1984 when the curative amendment took effect. Along with the other two sections [25(M) and 25(N)], it would have remained unenforceable in certain states unless the relevant High Court's judgements were stayed while the appeals were pending in the Supreme Court.
> (emphasis added)

31 Discussion below liberally draws upon Roychowdhury (2015).
32 Legal changes in Madhya Pradesh are not separately discussed, since these are largely the same as Rajasthan.
33 These are: 1. The Factories Act, 1947; 2. The Industrial Disputes Act, 1947; 3. The Industrial Employment (Standing orders) Act 1946; 4. The

Minimum Wages Act, 1948; 5. The Payment of Wages Act, 1936; 6. The Payment of Bonus Act, 1965; 7. The Employees State Insurance Act, 1948; 8. The Employees Provident Funds and Miscellaneous Provisions Act, 1952; 9. The Maternity Benefit Act 1961; 10.The Employees Compensation Act, 1923; 11. The Inter-state Migrant Workmen (Regulation of Employment and Conditions of Service) Act, 1979; 12. (State) Shops and Establishments Act; 13. The Equal Remuneration Act, 1976; 14. The Child Labour (Prohibition and Regulation) Act, 1986.
34 These are: 1. The Payment of Wages Act, 1936; 2. The Weekly Holidays Act, 1942; 3. The Minimum Wages Act, 1948; 4. The Factories Act, 1948 (63 of 1948); 5. The Plantations Labour Act, 1951 (69 of 1951); 6. The Working Journalists and other Newspaper Employees (Conditions of Service) and Miscellaneous Provisions Act, 1955; 7. The Contract Labour (Regulation and Abolition) Act, 1970; 8. The Sales Promotion Employees (Conditions of Service) Act, 1976; 9. The Equal Remuneration Act, 1976.
35 Seven additional laws are: 1. The Motor Transport Workers Act, 1961; 2. The Payment of Bonus Act, 1965; 3. The Beedi and Cigar Workers (Conditions of Employment) Act, 1966; 4. The Inter-State Migrant Workmen (Regulation of Employment and Conditions of Service) Act, 1979; 5. The Dock Workers (Safety, Health and Welfare) Act, 1986; 6. The Child Labour (Prohibition and Regulation) Act, 1986; and 7. The Building and Other Construction Workers (Regulation of Employment and Conditions of Service) Act, 1996.
36 Maharashtra is reported to be moving along similar direction (*The Times of India* 17 October 2015).
37 According to 2010–11 data, around one-third of 2.15 lakh regular workers in the manufacturing sector of Rajasthan were located in establishments employing less than 50 workers.
38 For a comprehensive review of the arguments on both sides, see Shyam Sundar (2005); Bhattacharjea (2006); Sharma (2006).

Chapter 2

A critical examination of the labour market flexibility debate in India

From the discussion in Chapter 1, it is clear that the government is keen on pursuing labour market reforms in order to remove the alleged inflexibilities that characterize the Indian labour market.[1] Therefore, it may be interesting to note how far the Indian labour market may actually be called inflexible with regard to the widely accepted definition of an inflexible labour market, following Solow (1997: 190). A labour market is inflexible:

> if the level of unemployment-insurance benefits is too high or their duration is too long or if there are many restrictions on the freedom of employers to fire and to hire, or if the permissible hours of work are too highly regulated, or if excessive generous compensation for overtime work is mandated, or if trade unions have too much power to protect incumbent workers against competition and to control the flow of work at the site of production, or perhaps if statutory health and safety regulations are too stringent.

It is clear from above that Indian labour markets may be demarcated as inflexible in only a very limited sense. For example, provisions of unemployment-insurance or safety norms are meagre or non-existent by international standards. Therefore, the provision of job security regulations (JSR) has been singularly identified as the root of the problem.

More specifically, Chapter VB of IDA has occupied the centre stage of debate on proposals for amendment. Such a view gained currency mainly in light of the employment experience of the 1980s,[2] in the organised/registered manufacturing sector of the economy.[3] Employment trends in the 1980s in organised manufacturing were indeed puzzling when read in conjunction with the experience of the previous one-and-a-half decades (1965–1979). During that period, whereas value added in organised manufacturing grew at a modest rate of 5 percent per annum, employment also registered a decent growth rate of 3.5 percent per annum (Goldar 2000: 1191). Thus, employment growth in organised manufacturing outpaced population growth, since the latter was growing at 2.2 percent per annum during the same period (Visaria 2008–09). This is in sharp contrast to the experience of the subsequent period. While the growth rate in value added accelerated to 8.66 percent per annum during the period 1980–81 to 1990–91, employment growth plummeted to a mere 0.53 percent per annum (Kannan and Reveendran 2009: 80).[4] This is widely regarded as the phenomenon of 'jobless growth' in the literature (Papola 1994; Ghose 1994; Goldar 2000; Nagaraj 2000, 2004; Sundaram and Tendulkar 2002). To offer an explanation of 'jobless growth' during the 1980s, some observers have *uniquely* identified the supposedly rigid labour laws (especially the provisions of Chapter VB of IDA), as being the *central* cause, and recommended increasing their flexibility (Fallon and Lucas 1993; Besley and Burgess 2004). There is another strand of argument which points to the sharp hike in real (and product) wages as being the *dominant* cause for employment stagnation during the 1980s (Lucas 1988; World Bank 1989; Ahluwalia 1992; Ghose 1994).[5] Findings of these studies, however, did not go uncontested, and both strands were thoroughly criticized. However, the whole debate has been carried out almost entirely in the empirical terrain, and the two strands of argument are *not* completely independent of one another.[6]

In what follows, we shall provide a survey of the literature, in Section 2.1, which confines itself to the discussion (and criticism) of the first strand only. In Section 2.2, we provide some fresh results to scrutinize the validity of the first strand – accomplished by some simple statistical analysis on distribution of employment (often referred as 'threshold effect' in the literature). Section 2.3 is devoted to the literature review of the second strand along with its critical examination.

2.1 Impact of labour laws on employment generation: a review of the empirical literature

This section is devoted to the literature review of the first strand, which singularly identifies the operation of rigid labour laws [amendments to IDA in 1976 and 1982] to be the *main* reason behind the employment downturn during the 1980s in the organised manufacturing sector. In the Indian context, this literature developed primarily in the empirical terrain. In what follows, we will discuss this literature critically – with an eye on the quality of results thrown up by these studies and the soundness of methodology employed to establish causality.

The paper by Fallon and Lucas (1991; and the 1993 revised version) was the earliest contribution in this genre. They employed a dummy variable (i.e. 'before and after') technique to examine the impact of the 1976 amendment on organised manufacturing employment at the national and industry level. The authors clearly state their purpose of study as: 'One of our key concerns therefore is to examine the effects that the job security provisions in the 1976 amendment to the Industrial Disputes Act have had on industrial employment' (Fallon and Lucas 1991: 397). In particular, the authors estimated the dynamic labour demand functions of Indian manufacturing industries in the organised sector between the period 1959–60 and 1981–82.[7]

Now dynamic labour demand functions typically attempt to capture the impact of hiring, training and firing costs of workers on labour demand by incorporating adjustment lags in the relationship between past levels of employment and present labour demand. In this technique, employment is typically regressed on its own lagged value and the current and lagged values of demand-related variables such as the output level, shifts worked per employee and wages, among others (normally involving multi-period lags). In what follows, we take a simple version of the dynamic labour demand equation:[8] for a single labour demand variable (N) involving only one period lag, for industry 'i' in period 't' – as follows:

$$N_{it} = \beta_0 + \beta_1 X_{it} + \beta_2 X_{i,t-1} + \beta_3 N_{i,t-1} + \beta_4 J + \beta_5 J N_{i,t-1} + v_{it}$$

where X represents the vector of demand-related variables and J is the job security dummy variable that switches from 0 to 1 in the year change occurs (in this case, 1976, when the new amendment to IDA came in place). β_1 and β_2 capture the effect of how current and previous values of demand-related variables affect current labour demand.[9] β_3 measures the degree of inertia in the labour adjustment process. If the cost to a firm in adjusting its labour force rises with the rapidity of transition made, then employment changes will tend to occur slowly; consequently, today's employment decisions will be strongly influenced by the inherited employment level from yesterday. Now, if even *before* JSR were imposed there were considerable costs associated with rapid adjustment of the size of the workforce, then evidently it would result in some sluggishness in changing employment levels as well. And this would be reflected by a statistically positive β_3 coefficient in the regression equation. The authors' estimation results indeed showed that:

> [i]n more than half of Indian industries ... the estimated coefficient associated with the lagged value of the dependent variable proves significantly positive. In other words, *even before* the new permission clauses were imposed, employers in many industries were reluctant to adjust rapidly firm employment levels under varying market conditions. Presumably this was because such speedy adjustments were costly [even earlier].
>
> (emphasis added) (Fallon and Lucas 1991: 406)

The next interesting question that arises is the following: whether JSR impose even *higher* adjustment costs (over and above already existing adjustment costs) for rapidly changing the workforce – in which case we might expect to see a *rise* in the inherited employment effect. This is because new regulations by *raising* the cost to a firm – of changing its workforce – would make employment adjustments even *more* sluggish following the new enactment. In the regression equation this would be captured by the coefficient β_5 – on the interaction between the lagged dependent variable and the dummy variable (set equal to 1 after enactment of JSR). If adjustment costs rise with new enactment – then this coefficient should prove positive (showing an increase in the inherited employment effect). The authors' findings, however, do not substantiate this hypothesis. Fallon and Lucas (1991: 406) note:

> It seems that rapid adjustments in employment levels were costly even before the new permission clauses were enacted. The coefficient on the interaction between job security dummy and lagged employment is found to be statistically indistinguishable from zero in most sectors.

Thus, foregoing finding suggests that employment adjustments were sluggish even *before* the 1976 amendment and that there was *no* evidence of an increase in the *degree* of employment inertia after the enactment.

However, Fallon and Lucas (1993: 263) noted:

> But this certainly does not imply that the new regulations had little or no effect on labor demand. Rather, the focus of our attention with respect to job security provisions falls upon any quantum shift in desired level of employment, following the imposition of the permission clause, instead of alterations in how rapidly employers adjusted their work force.

In particular, the authors hypothesized that the new amendment might have increased the effective cost of employing a *given* level of workers rather than adjustment costs. This is because Fallon and Lucas (1991: 401–402) noted:

> Even if a firm wishes to maintain a *constant* overall level of employees, labor adjustment [hiring and firing] costs affect the firm's employment decisions. There will be turnover in the specific composition of individuals comprising the steady number of employees because of quits and retirements, dismissals for disciplinary purposes, and the process of on-the-job screening. Again, the effect of raising the cost of such adjustments in workforce composition is to raise the cost of employing a *given* level of employees.
>
> (emphasis added)

Such cost escalations, the authors hypothesized, would normally result in a *decline* in the firm's desired level of employment – reflected by a *negative* coefficient β_4, on the job security dummy variable. In fact, the quantum of shift in employers' desired level of employment is represented by the magnitude of the job security dummy coefficient. Note that the authors once again drew attention to rising labour adjustment costs following job security amendment to explain the drop in labour demand. Indeed Fallon and Lucas (1993: 263) found some evidence to this end, noting:

> Among Indian industries this estimated coefficient proves negative in 29 out of 35 industries. In 25 out of these 29 cases this negative effect is statistically significant on at least a 75 percent confidence level test and in 14 cases a 90 percent confidence level test is passed.

Based on these results, the authors concluded that 'there is indeed quite *strong evidence* consistent with the job security regulations having diminished employment across a wide range of industries, compared to what it might otherwise have been' (emphasis added) (ibid.: 263). More specifically, averaging over the coefficients on the job security dummy across industries the authors noted: 'In India, the weighted average drop in long-run demand for employees, at given output levels, is estimated to be 17.5 percent. . . ' (ibid.: 269).[10] Most estimates were robust to the inclusion of a time trend.

We now examine how strong Fallon and Lucas' evidence is. Bhalotra (1998: 7) noted that the 17.5 percent overall drop in employment, attributed to the 1976 amendment by Fallon and Lucas, was based on the questionable procedure of averaging across all industry-specific coefficients on the dummy variable, many of which were statistically insignificant at conventional significance levels. Bhalotra pointed out that Fallon and Lucas had found coefficients on the job security dummy to be statistically significantly negative in 25 out of 35 industries – but only at a 25 percent level of significance. At the more conventional 10 percent and 5 percent levels of significance, only 14 and 11 industries respectively, displayed statistically significant negative dummy coefficients. Under these circumstances when more than half of the industries considered *did not* show any sign of employment decline (at more conventional level of significance) following amendment – clearly it puts to question the robustness of Fallon and Lucas' result.

In fact, there is a fundamental problem in employing the dummy variable technique to capture the effect of an amendment to employment protection law on employment creation. By adopting such a technique, the authors could *only* conclusively establish the phenomenon of jobless growth; however, it *does not explain* the underlying reasons *conclusively*. This is because the observable fact might be *primarily* driven by some *other* underlying structural factors in operation not accounted for in the model. Such objections have, in fact, been raised against the methodology adopted by Fallon and Lucas. Bhattacharjea (2006) clearly points out the difficulty of using a dummy variable technique in this particular case. Bhattacharjea (2006: 7–8) notes:

> [B]ut one very obvious political development makes it difficult to treat the 1976 amendment as causing a structural break. . . .

> The amendment was passed during the 1975–77 State of Emergency, during which democratic rights were effectively suspended. *It is likely that taking advantage of this situation, employers retrenched labour en masse.*
>
> (emphasis added)

Thus, it is possible that the sudden employment downturn in 1976 was actually due to the State of Emergency rather than the new JSR coming into place; both occurring simultaneously was a coincidence. However, using dummy variables, there is no way we can *separate out* the effect of these two events on employment. Hence, the authors' technique does not permit them to draw any conclusive inference.

Moreover, Anant *et al.* (2006: 254) noted:

> (A) puzzling feature of Fallon and Lucas' result is that the 1976 amendment affects labor demand but *not the speed of adjustment of employment*. Presumably, if new labor regulations had significant bite, firms would take *longer* than before to adjust employment levels in response to unanticipated shocks to labor demand.
>
> (emphasis added)

Thus, Fallon and Lucas' result seems to suggest that the 1976 job security amendment had a one-shot effect in reducing employment *immediately* but no *sustained* effect in slowing down employment adjustments in the long run. However, this result is unexplained by the authors and forces one to search for other possible explanations of the sudden employment drop in 1976. This is plainly because, if JSR was the *main* reason for employment downturn, then it should have been operative (manifested by sluggish employment adjustments) in the subsequent periods as well, of which Fallon and Lucas find no evidence.

Bhalotra (1998), recognising the *nature* of her study and the short time period covered [1979–87], submitted that the impact of 1982/84 amendment could not be investigated. However, she did comment critically on the subject noting that 'there are several reasons to be sceptical of the claim that it [1982/84 amendment] is the primary explanation of the downturn in manufacturing employment in the 1980s' (Bhalotra 1998: 7). These reasons are listed below: First, according to her own estimates, on an average the length of time required for employment to adjust following an exogenous shock was on the order of five to six years. Therefore, she concluded that the *immediate* fall in manufacturing employment after the 1982/84 amendment, normally cited in the literature, could be purely accidental. Second, she cited various micro-level studies reporting widespread evasion of labour laws. Third, she cited evidence on manufacturing wages being lower in regions which reported higher unemployment rates. She pointed out this could not be the case if labour regulations truly protected workers. Fourth, she noted that employment increased in enterprises employing 100 to 1,000 workers and fell only in the greater than 1,000 employment range. However, 1982/84 amendment determined the cut-off (for the application of Chapter V-B, IDA – that stipulates firms to secure *prior* government permission for carrying out layoff and retrenchment) at 100 workers. Therefore, if employment growth was mainly hurt by labour regulations – how could employment grow in the enterprises employing 100 to 1,000 workers? Finally, Bhalotra pointed out that

> the view has no firm theoretical backing. That is, since job protection lowers hiring *and* firing rates [i.e. frequencies], its direct impact on employment is, *a priori*, just as likely to be positive as negative and, indeed, investigations of job protection in the OECD are inconclusive about its impact on labour demand.
> (emphasis in original) (ibid.: 8)

Based on her own estimates of a simpler dynamic labour demand function (similar to the one employed by World Bank [1989] although for a different time span), Bhalotra found a *decline* in employment inertia (i.e. the propensity or tendency of employment to remain *static* once it reaches a particular level) during the period 1979–87. She explains this apparent *increase* in labour market flexibility (LMF) in terms of a growing trend towards subcontracting output to small firms which are outside the ambit of the law, alongside the relatively easy recourse to firing *even* in those enterprises governed by JSR. Thus, Bhalotra (1998: 22) concludes: 'To the extent that the decline in employment inertia [i.e. increased LMF] reflects lower adjustment costs, *it reinforces scepticism of the view that the extension of job security in 1982 was responsible for the employment decline*' (emphasis added).

Another study, by Aggarwal (2002), covering the time period 1960–98, reported the inertia of employment, estimating the dynamic labour demand function to be increasing (hence reducing LMF) during the sub-period 1976–85. But the author found evidence on the measure of inertia becoming insignificant for the sub-period 1985–98, when employment responded swiftly to growth in value added. Thus, the study indicates that while the 1976 amendment might have reduced labour flexibility, the 1982/84 amendment paradoxically increased it. So with respect to the effect of job security amendments on LMF, the evidence obtained by the author deters one from inferring conclusively, either way.

In another study, Dutta Roy (2002) tried to analyse the impact of JSR on LMF in an innovative manner, namely, the *ease* with which employers use accession[11] rates and separation[12] rates as instruments to bring about *changes* in employment. Her sample period extends from 1963 to 1992, involving 18 two-digit industry-level data on turnover (both, accession and separation) for only directly employed regular workers in the Census sector of the manufacturing segment. Inspired by the literature of job search models, the author tried to explain/determine accession and separation rates through (among other variables) planned/desired employment changes. In particular the author's empirical model specification tried to uncover the response of accession rates[13] and separation rates[14] to desired changes in employment. This is done to capture the impact of JSR through the coefficients on planned employment growth (contemporaneous) and the gap in actual and planned employment growth (lagged).[15] To meet this objective, in the regression equations she took the following route:

> To relate turnover decisions to those of employment, we include two variables, the planned growth in employment in the current period and the difference between actual and planned employment growth in the previous period in both the accession and separation equations.
>
> (Dutta Roy 2002: 148)

However, the major challenge remains – to derive the main explanatory variable, namely, desired/planned employment growth. The author points out that earlier literature for developed countries estimated this variable by dynamic factor demand functions (given factor prices and other determinants of employment demand).

However, for the purpose of the present study, the author was only interested in *directly* employed regular workers in the *Census* sector.[16] But she was unable to separate the regular workers from contract workers *and* Census sector data from the Sample sector. This prevented her from estimating planned employment growth by employing dynamic factor demand functions. Instead, she modelled planned employment growth as determined by output growth and growth in labour cost. She realizes this to be a shortcoming of her study and comments: 'In light of this simple characterization of labour demand the results of our exercise, while intuitive, should only be taken as indicative' (ibid.: 149). Now we turn to her results.

Dutta Roy (2002: 156) finds that 'the pre-1976 era was characterized by significant responsiveness of worker turnover to employment decisions, with both accession and separation rates responding positively to planned growth in employment in the current period'. Thus, evidence suggests that there was significant flexibility in the pre-1976 era. Between 1976 and 1983 accession and separation rates became negatively associated with planned employment growth. Therefore, employment growth took place by separation rates being lower than accession rates. Note that the coefficients might change in sign post-1976, but they still remained responsive, implying that planned employment growth could be undertaken by suitable adjustment of turnover instruments and hence reflecting flexibility. Finally, the post 1984 period was marked by a significant decline in flexibility, with planned employment growth and a gap between actual and planned employment growth no longer significant in either the accessions or separations equation. Thus, Dutta Roy (2002: 158) argues:

> Put together, in terms of the responsiveness of turnover to employment decisions, our results indicate a positive response of both accession and separation in the pre-JSR period, a negative response post-IDA 1976 and non-responsiveness in the post-IDA 1982 period. These results indicate significant impact of job security regulations on the use of turnover decisions to effect desired changes in employment.

In particular, she drew attention to the fact that the post-1982 period was indicative of a significant decline in LMF. However, we also need to remember the caveat that the author regards this result to be only tentative.

In a different study, Dutta Roy (2004) estimated the dynamic interrelated factor demand functions for the time period 1960–95, spanning over 16 two-digit industry groups – in order to understand (a) whether there are rigidities in employment adjustment following an exogenous shock and (b) if rigidities at all exist, then what are the causes/sources of these rigidities? With regard to the first objective, Dutta Roy found evidence on industries displaying significant rigidities in the adjustment of labour (of course exhibiting inter-industry variations). The author estimated the speed of labour adjustment to come back to an equilibrium state after an initial shock and reported that on an average it takes about five to six years for the impact to die out completely. With regard to the second objective, the author specifically tested the following hypothesis:

> From an Indian policy perspective, it would seem particularly important at this point to examine whether the rigidities are due, in any way, to the job security regulations embodied in the 1976 and 1982 Amendments to the Industrial Disputes Act. If most of the observed rigidities, for instance, are attributable to the inherent characteristics of the industries under consideration, then relaxation of the provisions of the Industrial Disputes (Amendments) Act may not reflect in enhanced flexibility of employment adjustment.
>
> (Dutta Roy 2004: 244–245)

From her results, she found that most industries exhibited substantial rigidity in their employment adjustment *even before* 1976 (with the only exception of the cement industry). Paradoxically, in four industries, flexibility was reported to have *increased* post-amendment, and was explained in terms of the growing use of contract/casual workers coupled with greater flexibility in hours worked. The author's main conclusion was the following:

> To sum up, our findings indicate that the imposition of job security regulations can, by no means, be identified as the sole, or even the primary, cause for the observed rigidities in employment adjustment in the Indian manufacturing sector. Major proportion of the industries studied revealed rigidities even in the pre-JSR period, indicating that these may be attributable to industry-specific characteristics.
>
> (ibid.: 247)

In fact, she submits: 'In summary, our findings reveal that the impact of job security legislation was, contrary to popular perception, minimal' (ibid.: 248).

In another study, Guha (2009) tried to empirically examine the validity of the claim made by Lucas and others – namely, increased LMF gives a boost to output and employment growth. The author drew attention to the fact that the category of workers employed through contractors (i.e. with casual or non-permanent status) in establishments falling within the ambit of Chapter VB of IDA are nonetheless *not protected* by labour regulations. This provision clearly gives leeway to employers to introduce LMF in a sector otherwise governed by law. Therefore, Guha (2009: 45) notes:

> (A) substantial degree of labour market flexibility has already been achieved in the Indian labour market. To capture the extent of these labour market flexibilities we have indexed them as the ratio between workers employed through contractors and the total number of factory workers.

Noting that contractualization of workforce (i.e. LMF) has increased manifold in the reform era, the author tried to scrutinize the impact of this increased LMF on output and employment growth.[17] His study period was 1994–95 to 2003–04 and spanned 44 three-digit sectors. In particular, the author estimated the following two regression equations. For examining the impact of LMF on output growth, the author estimated the following equation:

$$\frac{(Y_t - Y_{t-1})}{Y_{t-1}} = \alpha + \beta_1 \frac{(Y_{t-1} - Y_{t-2})}{Y_{t-2}} + \beta_2 \frac{(K_{t-1} - K_{t-2})}{K_{t-2}} + \beta_3 \frac{(K_{t-2} - K_{t-3})}{K_{t-3}}$$
$$+ \beta_4 \frac{\frac{(K_t - K_{t-1})}{K_{t-1}}}{\frac{(L_t - L_{t-1})}{L_{t-1}}} + \beta_5 \frac{1}{\frac{W_{t-1}}{Y_{t-1}}} \left(\frac{W_t}{Y_t} - \frac{W_{t-1}}{Y_{t-1}} \right) + \beta_6 \frac{1}{\frac{INP_{t-1}}{Y_{t-1}}}$$
$$\left(\frac{INP_t}{Y_t} - \frac{INP_{t-1}}{Y_{t-1}} \right) + \beta_7 \frac{1}{\frac{CL_{t-1}}{L_{t-1}}} \left(\frac{CL_t}{L_t} - \frac{CL_{t-1}}{L_{t-1}} \right) + u_t$$

where Y_t is the output of a particular sector at the tth period. Similarly, K_t, L_t, and W_t are respectively the capital stock, number of workers and total wage bill of a particular sector at the tth period. INP_t denotes the total input cost (raw materials, energy etc.) of a particular sector in period t and CL_t denotes the total labourers employed through contractors (therefore, outside JSR) of a particular sector in period t.

The expression in the left-hand side of the equation is output growth of a particular sector in period t. The second term from the left in the right-hand side of the equation is output growth of a particular sector with one period lag. The third and fourth terms from the left in the right-hand side of the equation are, respectively, capital stock growths of a particular sector with one period lag and two period lag. The fifth, sixth, seventh and eighth terms are, respectively, technological change, growth in wage cost per unit of output, growth in total input cost per unit of output and growth in LMF for a particular sector. Now the author contends that if β_7 is positive and statistically significant, only then LMF boosts output growth. However, from the regression result, the author found β_7 to be statistically insignificant, implying LMF had no statistically significant influence on output growth.

In order to trace the impact of LMF on employment growth, the author estimated the following equation:

$$\frac{(L_t - L_{t-1})}{L_{t-1}} = \alpha + \beta_1 \frac{(Y_t - Y_{t-1})}{Y_{t-1}} + \beta_2 \frac{\frac{(K_t - K_{t-1})}{K_{t-1}}}{\frac{(L_t - L_{t-1})}{L_{t-1}}}$$

$$+ \beta_3 \frac{1}{\frac{W_{t-1}}{L_{t-1}}} \left(\frac{W_t}{L_t} - \frac{W_{t-1}}{L_{t-1}} \right)$$

$$+ \beta_4 \frac{1}{\frac{CL_{t-1}}{L_{t-1}}} \left(\frac{CL_t}{L_t} - \frac{CL_{t-1}}{L_{t-1}} \right) + u_t$$

where each term has exactly the same meaning as above. Here, the expression on the left-hand side of the equation represents employment growth rate of a particular sector in period t. The first expression on the right-hand side of the equation represents output growth rate of a particular sector in t^{th} period. The second and third expressions on the right-hand side of the equation denote technological change and growth in wage rate of a particular sector in t^{th} period.

Finally, the fourth expression on the right-hand side of the equation denotes growth in LMF of a particular sector in period t. As before, only if β_4 is positive and statistically significant can one argue that LMF has given a boost to employment growth. However, from the regression result, the author found β_4 to be statistically insignificant and concluded that growth in LMF has no statistically significant influence on employment growth.

Therefore, on the basis of his empirical inquiry Guha (2009: 51) concluded:

> From the regression analysis that we have undertaken, we conclude that increasing labour market flexibility – defined as an increase in the proportion of non-permanent/casual workers in total workers – has no positive impact on output and employment growth. The neoliberal proposition that an increase in labour flexibility would lead to higher output growth and greater labour absorption does not seem to be valid as far as Indian manufacturing industries are concerned. Therefore, the reasons for an amendment to the Contract Labour Act, 1970 and IDA, 1947, which are being proposed in order to facilitate greater labour market flexibilities, appear quite dubious.

Next, we shall discuss a widely quoted study by Besley and Burgess (2004). Besley and Burgess draw attention to the fact that 'labour matters' occur in the Concurrent List of the Indian Constitution. Thus, subnational governments can amend IDA. The authors note that there were 133 state-level amendments to the Act since it was passed. So they concluded: 'Thus although all states have the same starting point, they diverged from one another over time' (Besley and Burgess 2004: 6). Their objective is to assess the impact of such (differential) state-level amendments on states' (diverging) manufacturing outcomes: 'This paper studies the role of labor market regulation in explaining [variations in] manufacturing performance in Indian states between 1958 and 1992' (ibid.: 2).

It may be interesting to delineate the *method of construction* of the labour regulatory index/measure used as the main explanatory variable. It is best to quote the authors:

> We code legislation based on our reading of all state-level amendments to the Industrial Disputes Act of 1947.... There were 113 such amendments since the Act was passed.... Each

amendment is coded as being either neutral, pro-worker or pro-employer. While this method of classification required a number of judgement calls, we found surprisingly few cases of uncertainty. For the purpose of quantitative analysis, we coded each pro-worker amendment as a one, each neutral amendment as a zero, and each pro-employer amendment as a minus one.[18]

(ibid.: 6)

Finally, to develop the index, the authors adopted the following method: 'Having obtained the direction of amendments in any given year, we cumulated the scores over time to give a quantitative picture of how the regulatory environment evolved over time. This is our basic regulatory measure used below' (ibid.: 7). Going by their regulatory index, the authors classified 16 major states as control states (where no changes have occurred in any direction benefiting either workers or employers), pro-employer states and pro-worker states.[19]

Next, the authors developed an econometric model, taking all states together, to study the impact of this regulatory index on manufacturing performance – more specifically to analyse whether regulation can account for the cross-state pattern of manufacturing performance over time. Within a panel data framework, they used this index, along with several control variables,[20] to explain (with a one year lag) state-level variables pertaining to the organised manufacturing sector like output per capita, employment,[21] intensity of labour use, fixed capital, number of factories and labour productivity. Their results show 'pro-worker labor regulation resulted in lower output, employment, investment, and productivity in the formal manufacturing sector. Output in the informal sector increased. We also find that pro-worker labor regulation is also associated with increases in urban poverty' (ibid.: 3). Their innovative technique of treating endogeneity issues allows them to infer that poor manufacturing performance was a *consequence* and *not a cause* of pro-worker labour regulation.

Further, using industry dummies, the authors find similar negative effects – for a different time period (1980–97) – on industrial performance at the three-digit industry level within each state. This exercise allows them to conclude that their results at the aggregate level are *not* driven by inter-state variations in industrial specialization or technological progress. They also provide evidence on pro-worker legislation having no effect either on earnings per worker in the organised sector or on aggregate or rural poverty in the state, but that increased urban poverty. They attribute this to its adverse effect on organised sector employment. Hence, Besley and Burgess (2004: 21) conclude:

> It is apparent that much of the reasoning behind labor regulation was wrong-headed and led to outcomes that were antithetical to their original objectives. . . . Our finding that regulating in a pro-worker direction . . . suggest that attempts to redress the balance of power between capital and labor can end up hurting the poor.

However, there are several problems with their analysis, as shown painstakingly by Bhattacharjea (2006), to which we now turn. Bhattacharjea mainly pointed out two sets of flaws in Besley's and Burgess's analysis: (a) econometric specification and, more importantly, (b) construction of the regulatory index itself. We take up these issues seriatim.

Bhattacharjea (2006) noted that Besley's and Burgess's use of the *same* set of control variables (an exercise to check the robustness of their basic result) in their regression analysis seeking to explain outcomes as diverse as output, employment, wages, entry and poverty is disquieting. Therefore, expectedly the coefficients on most of the control variables were statistically insignificant. Moreover, it was pointed out that Besley's and Burgess's claim of their results being robust to imposing different lag structures on the regulatory index were *not* tested by incorporating these control variables. Bhattacharjea further pointed out that the inclusion of state-specific time trends in the regression equation consistently made the coefficients on their regulatory index insignificant.[22] The author noted: 'State-level IDA amendments, as we saw above, were very infrequent, so it is disturbing that their effect is so comprehensively knocked out by the inclusion of time trends' (Bhattacharjea 2006: 18).[23]

Further, Besley and Burgess, by putting excessive emphasis on legal statutes missed out on important counts like implementation of the law and larger macroeconomic issues during their sample period (1958–92). For example, Anant et al. (2006) note that reading off directly from state amendments to measure rigidities could be exceedingly misleading, since the effect of laws could only be fully realized into labour market outcomes only through proper implementation. Implementation, in turn, depends upon a range of intermediate factors like enforcement environment, culture of governance and compliance, among others. Limited consideration of these aspects can very easily deflect or nullify the presumed effect of the statutes and hence impair accurate construction of the regulatory index.[24] With regard to the larger macroeconomic issues, Bhattacharjea (2006) notes that Besley and Burgess have completely ignored the allocation of industrial licenses by the central government, a central feature in determining industrial performance of any state (by determining industrial location) during their sample period. This is indeed an important feature, since allocation of licenses considerably influenced the regional distribution of industrial activity *independent* of state-level regulations, and was in turn influenced by political considerations. These are important considerations neglected by Besley and Burgess and should have been modelled in terms of control variables for a robustness check of their basic results. Bhattacharjea (2006: 18), in fact, lists a few of them, and these are difficult to contest:

> There are thus far too many potentially relevant omitted variables for comfort in the BB [Besley and Burgess] regressions, which could seriously bias the estimated coefficients on the index if they are correlated with it. For example, the state of pro-worker IDA amendments in West Bengal in the 1980s coincided with crippling power cuts and adversarial relationship with the central government which controlled industrial licenses. Pro-employer amendments in Tamil Nadu in the same decade coincided with the rapid expansion of technical education which fed the growth of industry. And the collapse of the textile mills, which caused a major fall in registered manufacturing employment in Gujarat, Maharashtra and West Bengal in 1980s, was not entirely attributed to labour market conditions.

These considerations are far too important to be omitted and seriously question the econometric specification and results of the Besley and Burgess study. Next we discuss the *method* of construction of the regulatory index used as the main explanatory variable.

Bhattacharjea (2006) closely examined the appendices[25] of the Besley and Burgess (2004) paper and concluded that the methodology employed to construct the regulatory index is incorrect on two counts: (a) assigning scores to individual amendments and (b) the method used to combine these scores.

Bhattacharjea (2006) pointed out that Besley's and Burgess's scoring system allows a state to be categorized as pro-worker or pro-employer on the basis of *just one or two amendments* at any time over the long period of 50 years of IDA history (1947–97). As a result, we reach strange conclusions such as Gujarat being designated as a pro-worker state[26] while Kerala is classified as a pro-employer state.[27] A similar problem arises with classifying Andhra Pradesh as a pro-employer state. Andhra Pradesh obtains pro-employer status because of three amendments: (a) 1949, which is unquestionable, (b) 1968, described in Appendix 2 as 'limits strikes and lockouts in designated public utilities' and (c) 1982, which 'facilitates settlement of industrial disputes in labour courts'. Bhattacharjea (2006), going by the detailed text, notes that the 1968 amendment merely included hospitals and dispensaries in the list of public utilities, which is completely irrelevant for assessing manufacturing outcomes. The interpretation of the 1982 amendment is also incorrect. This amendment merely conferred on labour tribunals and labour courts the powers of a civil court to enforce their awards and need not be necessarily pro-employer. Similarly, their interpretation of the Madhya Pradesh amendments of 1982 (empowering labour courts) and 1983 (extending closure rules to undertakings engaged in construction activities are irrelevant for the manufacturing sector) is fraught with analogous errors.

There are still other problems with Besley's and Burgess's coding system, as exposed by Bhattacharjea (2006) in the case of supposedly pro-worker amendments made by Maharashtra [1981], Orissa [1983] and Rajasthan [1984] to Section 25-K of the IDA-Chapter VB. In their shorter appendix, the authors summarize these changes as 'Extends rules for layoff, retrenchment and closure to smaller firms'. However, their detailed appendix gives a more vivid account for Maharashtra and Rajasthan:

> The rules for layoff, retrenchment and closure may according to the discretion of the state government be applied to industrial establishments of a *seasonal character* and which employ *more than 100 but less than 300 workers*. Under the central act these rules only apply to permanent establishments which employ more than 300 workers.
>
> (emphasis added)

Therefore, the pro-worker coding of these amendments must be on two counts: (a) to establishments of seasonal character and (b) to establishments employing between 100 and 300 workers. However, Bhattacharjea (2006) notes that the coding is erroneous on both counts. So far as (a), Maharashtra and Rajasthan amendments *specifically excluded* establishments 'of a seasonal character' (Radhakrishnaiah 2003: 190). This error is not repeated for Orissa, which earns a pro-worker coding merely because of reducing the threshold to 100 workers. But Bhattacharjea (2006) points out that the reduction in threshold (primarily on the basis of which these three states were awarded 'pro-worker' status) was already undertaken by the central government in the 1982 amendment to Section 25-K and put into effect in August 1984. This clearly shows that Besley and Burgess cannot justify their classification of the three states as pro-worker on the basis of (b).[28] Although, in spite of this the three states mentioned above would retain their pro-worker status in the respective years (for there was at least one other IDA section simultaneously amended in pro-worker direction), it would leave the overall pro-worker characterization of Orissa resting on just one minor (1983) amendment in 50 years[29] (giving power of appeal to workers to overturn a decision on the closure of the firm).[30]

Next, it was pointed out that assigning a score of just +1 or −1 to a year in which a state passed *more than one* amendment is itself problematic on several grounds. This is because all amendments are coded as either +1 or −1 (of course, looking at their *general direction* of change in a year), regardless of their relative importance or the extent to which they were actually implemented. The limitation of this exercise at once becomes clear when we look at the amendments made in Rajasthan in 1960. These are summarized and coded in Besley's and Burgess's (2004) paper as follows:

> Exact criteria for being union member defined [-1]; Defines employers in firms sub-contracted to industry as employers for industrial disputes purposes [1]; Defines who is allowed to be involved in bargaining process on behalf of unions [-1]; Gives definition of what a union is in an industrial dispute [-1]; Definition of worker for industrial disputes purposes extends to those subcontracted with an industry [1].

Now Bhattacharjea (2006) comments that the second and fifth amendments are essentially the same. Moreover, interpretation of the third amendment is erroneous as it only required the state government to appoint a Registrar of Unions and local Assistant Registrars, with no suggestion that these officials were supposed to represent unions. These varied changes were then clubbed together and classified as pro-employer, with a summary score of –1 for the year 1960. However, the same score is assigned to Kerala and Andhra Pradesh for minor amendments in 1979 and 1968, respectively. Legitimately, Bhattacharjea questions the method of treating *all* these episodes of reform at par (in terms of coding).[31]

Problems of the coding procedure come to the fore in case of Uttar Pradesh as well. The problem relates to *only* looking at state amendments to the Central IDA.[32] Uttar Pradesh amended its *own* IDA in 1983 to insert Section 6-V, *changing* the threshold for permission of layoffs, retrenchment and closure at 300 – which was set at 100 by the 1982 central amendment of IDA. Since the Uttar Pradesh amendment came at a *later* date than the central amendment of IDA, the Supreme Court upheld the UP amendment, citing Article 254 of the Constitution. Thus, going by the above instance, UP should have received a pro-employer status, but Besley and Burgess designate it as a control state, with no amendments to central IDA, in their sample period.[33]

In terms of combining the scores for each state, a different problem arises.[34] Bhattacharjea (2006) notes that Orissa passed two pro-worker amendments in the *same* year (1983) and therefore Orissa's score was raised by +1. However, Maharashtra passed the *same* two amendments but in *different* years (1981 and 1983), so its score increased by +2 under the cumulation rule. Therefore, Bhattacharjea (2006: 14) asks the following question: 'Why should a state that *spreads the same reforms* over a number of years be considered *more* pro-worker than one that enacts them in the *same* year?'

The discussion above shows that the Besley and Burgess (2004) study is riddled with too many errors, at various levels, to be considered seriously. Next, we review studies that use with some modification the Besley-Burgess index. The study by Hasan *et al.* (2003) modifies the Besley-Burgess classification of states in three respects. The three categories of states are collapsed into only two categories. Pro-employer states are designated as states with flexible labour markets, and pro-worker and neutral states are designated as states with inflexible labour markets. They also changed the strange classification of Gujarat, Maharashtra and Kerala in the Besley-Burgess study. As pointed out earlier, the first two were designated as pro-worker states and Kerala was designated as a pro-employer state. Hasan *et al.* (2003) simply reversed these classifications, citing a World Bank report. Lastly, Madhya Pradesh was designated as pro-employer in the earlier study and is categorized as having inflexible labour markets, since pro-employer amendments in 1982 were offset by a pro-worker amendment in 1983.

Using this new classification and allowing for lagged adjustment of employment, Hasan *et al.* (2003) calculated the own-price elasticities of demand for labour in Indian manufacturing. Comparing the own-price elasticities of demand for labour in the post-reform period (1992–97) with the pre-reform era (1980–91), they concluded that trade liberalisation has *increased* the own-price elasticities. These elasticities were higher and more sensitive to trade reforms in states with more flexible labour markets, indicating that employment responds more actively to liberalisation in states with flexible labour markets. However, the authors also found evidence on the volatility of wage and employment increasing *due to* volatility of productivity and output in the post-reform era, which is a theoretical consequence of high labour-demand elasticities. From these results, Bhattacharjea (2006: 22) concludes: 'This destroys the result that labour demand becomes more elastic in response to liberalisation in states with flexible labour markets, showing how sensitive it is to the classificatory scheme'.

In another study, Ahsan and Pagés (2009) recoded the 113 state-level amendments listed by Besley-Burgess along two *different* categories: (a) those amendments that affected the ability of parties to initiate or sustain industrial disputes, and (b) employment protection legislative (EPL) amendments that increased job security and reduced labour flexibility. The authors constructed a Besley-Burgess type index for each of these two *different* types of amendment separately. For (a) they constructed the disputes index, giving scores of +1 to amendments that increased the costs of settling disputes and −1 to those that reduced it. For (b) they constructed the EPL index, with more protective legislation restricting labour flexibility coded as +1 and −1 given to those that increased flexibility. Additionally, following the same methodology, they also constructed an index considering *exclusively* amendments to Chapter VB alone, namely, Chapter VB index.[35] From their regression analysis, it turned out that the adverse effects of the disputes index on various industrial outcome/performance indicators for organised manufacturing were much *stronger* than in the EPL index.[36] Thus, Ahsan and Pagés concluded that EPL affects industrial activity and employment creation *less adversely* than the ability of firms to resolve industrial disputes.

However, Bhattacharjea (2009) pointed out – as Ahsan and Pagés (2009) use the Besley-Burgess summary of amendments as well as their aggregation and cumulation techniques – that his criticisms discussed above also apply in this case.[37] This is particularly crucial for state amendments affecting the coverage of Chapter VB. This is because there were *only* five such amendments in all, among which three were miscoded (having only transient effect in light of the 1984 central amendment). In the Besley-Burgess case, this miscoding *by itself* did not alter their index since in all three states (i.e. Maharashtra, Rajasthan and Orissa) there was at least one supporting pro-worker amendment in those years. However, this is not the same for Ahsan and Pagés (2009). As they singled out amendments to Chapter V-B for a *separate* index, under the cumulation rule these amendments *permanently* increased the state's score, although some of them had *only a transient effect*. Further, Bhattacharjea (2006) points out that the coding of amendments affecting procedural matters, union recognition and so on had to heavily depend upon the *subjective* judgement of individual researchers. Robustness of the estimates was also open to question.

Additionally, in a celebrated paper Bhattacharjea (2009) launched a devastating critique of the Besley and Burgess (2004) and Ahsan and Pagés (2009) papers. Bhattacharjea (2009) drew attention to the fact that both Besley-Burgess and Ahsan-Pagés tried to capture the impact of the central amendments of 1976 and 1982 (coming into effect only in August 1984) by year fixed effects. But the effect of these amendments was definitely *not* confined to the year of enactment. Therefore, to have constructed the index correctly, the central amendments should have been captured by dummy variables that switch from zero to one, the year after these amendments took effect.

Bhattacharjea (2009) pointed out that there were still other problems. The problem with the dummy variable technique is that it implicitly assumed that the central amendment took effect *simultaneously* in *all* states. But he provided concrete examples that this was *not* the case. Bhattacharjea cited the Supreme Court *Excel Wear* judgement of 1978 in which section 25-O (pertaining to closure of a firm) of IDA (amended only in 1976) was constitutionally invalidated.[38] Later he showed, through a detailed analysis of the cases, that the high courts of Madhya Pradesh, Maharashtra, Orissa, Uttar Pradesh, Karnataka, West Bengal and Rajasthan passed curative judgements [also in some cases to restore the provisions of Sections 25-N and 25-M] to uphold Section 25-O, *but at different points in time* (Bhattacharjea 2009: 57). Evidently these events, which go to the heart of construction of the Besley-Burgess type index, were not at all accounted for by the authors; neither was the dummy variable technique adequate for getting around the problem. There were still other problems associated with the construction of the index, namely, the convention of judgements to be operative *retrospectively* from the date legislation was enacted. This, it was argued, might prove to be enormously costly for the firms,[39] and judgements in more *recent* times (i.e. *after* the sample period considered by Besley-Burgess or Ahsan-Pagés) might completely reverse the characterization of a state (from pro-worker nature to pro-employer status or vice-versa) *retrospectively*. Since the indices are likely to change, these circumstances obviously would alter the results of the Besley-Burgess and Ahsan-Pagés studies.

In light of the aforementioned inadequacies in the empirical literature advocating LMF, Bhattacharjea (2009: 62) infers: 'As in my 2006 paper, I can only conclude that the evidence [in favour of carrying out LMF] is inconclusive and my own views on the impact of EPL [employment protection legislation] remain agnostic'. Our inference is along similar lines. In the next section, we provide some fresh evidence on employment adjustments (along with output and number of firms) in spite of JSR in place.

2.2 Evidence on employment adjustments in the presence of labour laws

In light of the discussion of the previous section, it is clear that the empirical evidence in favour of instituting LMF in India is far from satisfactory. In this section, we provide some fresh evidence on labour adjustments, *precisely in those factory segments in which JSR applies*, implying labour regulations *do not* come in the way of employment adjustment. But before undertaking such an exercise – to clear a long-standing confusion in the literature – a brief digression is in order.

This pertains to the commonplace explanation of our very small size of *overall* organised sector employment compared to the vast economy-wide workforce. Figure 2.1 shows that the share of the

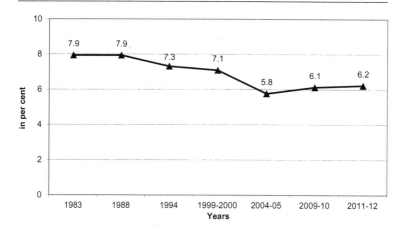

Figure 2.1 Proportion of organised sector employment in total workforce (UPSS)

Source: Data on total workforce according to Usual Principal plus Subsidiary Status (UPSS) from NSS, various rounds and Organised sector employment data from DGET, various years.

organised workforce – for almost three decades – never crossed 8 percent; moreover, it has steadily fallen between 1988 and 2004–05. This falling trend, however, got arrested after 2004–05, showing some improvement in 2009–10 (6.12 percent) and further gaining marginally in 2011–12 (6.22 percent). Even then, in 2011–12, the proportion of the organised workforce could not recover from the loss suffered in previous periods.

Thus, the share of organised workforce is not only minuscule but is in fact falling over the years. This is a cause of concern, since organised sector workers enjoy certain social security benefits (making organised sector jobs better in quality) which their informal sector counterparts are denied.[40]

It is common in the literature to ascribe such failure of the organised sector *as a whole*, in generating formal jobs, *primarily* to the rigid labour laws. It is alleged that labour laws create, 'a dualistic set-up in which the organised or formal sector necessarily remains limited in terms of aggregate employment and most workers, who remain in the unorganised sector, are therefore denied the benefits of any protection at all' (Ghosh 2004: 2). For instance, Zagha (1999: 163) points out, 'India's labour laws . . . encourage firms to remain small and in the informal sector'. Similarly, Sharma (2006: 2079) notes:

> Employment protection laws are also believed to be inefficient and inequitable ... dividing workers into protected and unprotected categories. *Social security, of a limited kind, is enjoyed by only 8 to 9 percent of workforce.* Over-protection of a small section of workers is not only ostensibly inimical to the growth of employment, but also goes against social justice as more and more workers are faced with deplorable working conditions.
>
> (emphasis added)

Notice that *no* distinction is drawn *within* the organised sector regarding the application of job security law.[41] It is further alleged that the organised sector workers aided by protective labour laws have become a selfish 'labour aristocracy' and enjoy privileges at the cost of employment growth that would benefit millions of unemployed or underemployed in the informal sector (Douglas 2000). Such perception permeates the official circles as well:

> Indian Labour Laws are highly protective of labour, and labour markets are relatively inflexible. *These laws only apply to the organised sector.* Consequently, these laws have restricted labour mobility, have led to capital-intensive methods in the organised sector and *adversely affected the sector's long-run demand for labour.*
>
> (emphasis added) (Economic Survey 2005–06: 209)

Immediately, the question arises: how good is it to singularly identify JSRs for explaining the failure of the organised sector, *as a whole*, to generate quality jobs?

A close reading of the domain of application of Chapter VB (IDA 1947) reveals that it applies to *only* manufacturing units, mines and plantations (with more than 100 workers, *not* run seasonally)[42] and *not* to firms providing services or related to agricultural activity.[43] However, firms employing 10 or more workers qualify for the 'organised' sector *irrespective* of the nature of activity (Indian Labour Year Book 2007: 2). Figure 2.2 shows that the share of the organised manufacturing sector (where JSR applies) workers in the *total* organised workforce has been consistently below 35 percent (except 2011–12) for the whole study period. However, JSR applies

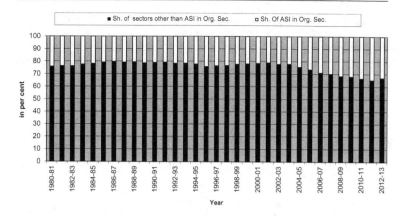

Figure 2.2 Share of organised manufacturing sector (ASI) in total organised sector employment

Source: Data on Organised Manufacturing Sector from Annual Survey of Industries (ASI), various years and Total Organised sector employment data from DGET, various years.

only to a subset of the *total* organised sector, namely, the organised manufacturing sector (constituting at most 35 percent of the total organised workforce) and does not extend to the organised sector *as a whole*.

Therefore, it is patently wrong to identify the labour laws as an explanation for the slowdown in employment growth in the *overall* organised sector. Let us now look at the employment trends in different segments of the *total* organised sector and compare them with the organised *manufacturing* sector. Refer to Table 2.1.

The first row shows employment growth in the long period (1980–2008)[44] in organised manufacturing (1.31 percent) is more than double that of the *total* organised sector (0.59 percent). If, for the same period, we disaggregate *total* organised sector employment data by private and public sector, then employment growth in the private sector (0.88 percent) turns out to be almost double that of the public sector (0.45 percent). Thus, collapse of the public sector in generating formal employment was an important factor for the slowdown of employment growth in the *overall* organised sector.

This is so, since the relative strength of the public sector in total organised sector employment is throughout above 60 percent for the whole period under study (see Figure 2.1A in Appendix). It has

Table 2.1 Growth rate of employment in different segments of the organised sector (%)

Period	Organised manufacturing (ASI)[45]	ALL organised sector	Private organised sector	Public organised sector	Org. sectors other than ASI
1980–2008	1.31	0.59	0.88	0.45	0.34
1980–90	−0.05	1.60	0.15	2.24	2.08
1991–97	3.17	0.87	2.02	0.39	0.21
1998–2008	3.48	−0.58	0.73	−1.22	−1.95
1980–91	0.10	1.57	0.25	2.15	2.00
1992–2000	0.56	0.53	1.62	0.07	0.53
2001–08	5.8	−0.31	1.7	−1.35	−2.45

Source: Author's calculation. Data on Organised Manufacturing Sector from ASI and All Organised Sector employment data from DGET.

to be also kept in mind that employment in the public sector is driven more by autonomous policy decisions rather than the pure profit motive. Now the fall in public sector employment growth could be at least partially attributed to large-scale privatization of public sector units (PSUs) for 'enhancing efficiency' (that typically sheds workers to reduce labour costs in search of accounting profits). Thus, a fall in public sector employment could be simply due to a *change in the classification of units following privatization*, where employment expansion in *erstwhile* PSUs would now show up as employment dynamism in the private organised sector. On the whole, it may be argued that the quest for achieving accounting profits in the private sector, coupled with a conscious policy decision to rationalise the public sector workforce (translating into the shedding of existing workers or freezing new appointments), turns out to be a decisive reason for the incapacity of the *overall* organised sector to generate quality employment.[46] In any case, private organised sector (0.88 percent) employment growth, in the long period, is also *less* than the organised manufacturing sector (1.31 percent). Now, in both the private organised and the organised manufacturing sector, employment is determined by the profit motive, since there is a large overlap between these sectors.[47] Therefore, in the private organised sector, *other than manufacturing*, employment growth must have been *lower* than in the manufacturing sector, implying that the employment slowdown cannot be explained by labour laws. Finally, it can be seen that employment growth in the *overall* organised sector (0.34 percent) (*other than* the manufacturing sector *not* governed by law) is well *below* the manufacturing sector. These trends clearly suggest that labour laws could not have been the reason for the slowdown in *overall* organised sector jobs, since the sector where labour laws apply experienced an employment growth rate *higher* than *every* other sector where they do not apply, in the long period.

Let us now turn to the sub-period analysis. First, we concentrate on the sub-period 1980–90, where employment growth in the *total* organised sector (1.6 percent) is *greater* than the manufacturing sector (–0.05 percent). But interestingly, this cannot be attributed to the operation of labour laws in the manufacturing sector – since the employment growth almost entirely took place in the public sector (2.24 percent) of the organised segment – which, in the pre-liberalisation era continued with its responsibility to generate quality jobs.[48] Moreover, the difference between employment growth in the private organised sector (0.15 percent) and the organised manufacturing sector (–0.05 percent) was only marginal. However, labour laws do not apply to the whole of the private organised sector but only to the manufacturing segment, thus the slowdown in employment must have been due to some reason *other than* labour regulations.

Finally, if we consider the next two sub-periods – 1991–97 and 1998–2008 – then it can be even more forcefully argued that labour laws were *not* the reason for employment downturn. In both sub-periods, employment growth in organised manufacturing is *greater* than *all* other sectors. Therefore, the sector where labour laws apply experienced a growth rate that is substantially *higher* than *every* sector where they do not operate. It is especially interesting to note that in the public sector and organised sector *other than* manufacturing, employment growth slowed down with the advent of economic reforms in 1991 (see sub-period 1991–97) and *subsequently turned negative* (see sub-period 1998–2008). However, precisely during these two sub-periods, the organised manufacturing sector, where labour laws apply, showed robust positive growth. Hence, labour laws could not be the reason for employment slowdown in the *overall* organised sector. These results broadly hold for an alternative periodisation (1992–2000 and 2001–2008) of the long period – except for manufacturing and private organised sector in the sub-period 1992–2000 – primarily because there was an absolute decline of 1.3 million workers after 1995 in the organised manufacturing sector (Nagaraj 2004: 3387).

Let us now restrict our attention to the organised manufacturing sector solely, where JSR apply. In this sector, '[I]t is argued that the legal provisions of job security and institutional factors like the pressure of trade unions make *adjustment* of the workforce of enterprises difficult, and discourage organised sector enterprises from expanding employment' (emphasis added) (Sharma 2006: 2080). In what follows, we shall assess the validity of this claim empirically.

The underlying reason and the policy implication that follows from such an argument are simple:

> In face of adverse shocks employers have to reduce the workers' strength; but they are not able to do so owing to the existence of stringent job security provisions. On the other hand, when the going is good and the economic circumstances are favourable, the firms may want to hire new workers. But they would hire only when they would be able to dispense with workers as and when they need to. Thus, separation benefits accruing to workers become potential hiring costs for the employers. This affects the ability and the willingness of firms to create jobs.
>
> (Sundar 2005: 2274)

Therefore, it is argued, 'a shift towards a more universal contract-based system of labour relations, with no assumptions of permanence of employment, is often deemed to be necessary to ensure economic progress based on private sector . . .' (Ghosh 2004: 29). Interestingly, '[J]ob security regulations apply . . . also to restructuring firms that need to permanently discontinue an activity or to close a plant [and] . . . discontinuing an activity, or closing a plant in India is as closely regulated as retrenchment of labour' (Zagha 1999: 165).[49] These stipulations, it is alleged, had major detrimental consequences for employment creation since,

> the laws have made it more costly for firms to adjust to changes in market conditions and technology. There are numerous references in the literature to hoarding of labour which is believed to have become particularly serious since the mid-1980s, and to how restrictions on retrenchment have been an obstacle to urgently needed industrial restructuring, particularly since 1991.
>
> (Zagha 1999: 170)[50]

From the above discussion it is clear that there exists a pervasive view in the literature ascribing the supposedly limited *adjustment* in workforce and industrial restructuring to the labour laws, even when such adjustments are deemed necessary for continuing in business – hence impeding employment creation in the first place.[51] Let us check the claim.

Before delving into a detailed analysis of the employment trends, it is essential to identify the time period on which one needs to focus in order to scrutinize the supposedly negative impact of labour laws on employment adjustment (hence creation). Let us consider the index number of absolute employment figures in the organised manufacturing sector in the recent past (Figure 2.3).

It is clear even from a cursory look at the index number of employment that organised manufacturing sector employment started to rise secularly (except 2012–13) from 2003–04 onwards (Goldar 2011 documents this) in spite of the labour laws in place.[52] However, prior to this period, for more than two decades (between 1979 and 2002) the employment trend shows a clear mark of stagnation (with a very slight upturn in the mid-1990s); so much so that the value of employment index, which stood at 100 in 1979, merely increased to 114 in 2003–04. Thus, if labour regulations have negatively affected employment at all, they must have done so during *this* period. Hence, the period we need to focus on here must be 1979 to 2002. Next, we turn to test the hypothesis just formulated.[53]

In order to do so, we calculate a simple indicator for capturing employment *adjustment* (through its variation), namely, coefficient of variation (CV).[54] Even at the risk of repeating, it is worth recapitulating the pro-LMF claim here: employment adjustments are typically difficult to undertake due to rigid labour laws.[55] However, it must be clear from our earlier discussions that Chapter VB of IDA *does not apply uniformly* to *all* firms in the organised manufacturing segment – but only to a subset of it. It was categorically pointed out that government permission for retrenchment, layoff and closure is required *only* for those establishments which routinely employ 100 or more workers. Thus, if labour laws were a true deterrent for employment adjustment, then we would expect the CV of those segments of the organised manufacturing sector where labour law applies (i.e. establishments with more than 100 workers) to be *consistently lower* than the segments where they do not apply (i.e. establishments with less than 100 workers). This is often referred to in the literature as the 'threshold effect' (Bhalotra 1998: 8;

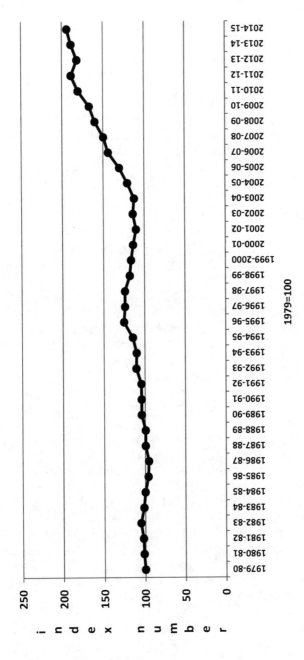

Figure 2.3 Index number of employment: organised manufacturing
Source: ASI, various years

Anant *et al.* 2006: 257). Commenting on the 1976 amendment to IDA, Fallon and Lucas (1993: 264) noted: 'The 1976 Amendment imposed a permission requirement for retrenchment and closure only for factories having 300 or more employees. *Naturally there may be a tendency to keep employment below the 300 cut-off...*' (emphasis added). In fact, they found evidence of this: '[T]he estimated decline in employment as a result of the 1976 amendment is greater in industries in which the fraction of employees in private sector enterprises employing more than 300 workers is greater' (Fallon and Lucas 1991: 411). Against this backdrop, we examine the empirical evidence on employment adjustment in order to assess the pro-LMF claim of finding 'threshold effects' (Table 2.2).

Table 2.2 Coefficient of variation by size of employment

Panel: A coefficient of variation (output)

Size of empt.	1979–02	1979–90	1991–97	1998–02
0–99	52	31	25	4
100–199	62	35	40	7
200–499	56	35	32	12
500–999	49	36	25	12
1,000 &>	32	22	12	10
Total	44	26	22	6

Panel: B coefficient of variation (workers)

Size of empt.	1979–02	1979–90	1991–97	1998–02
0–99	13	9	8	2
100–199	20	8	16	2
200–499	19	13	19	4
500–999	17	10	17	3
1,000 &>	17	16	8	7
Total	8	3	8	3

Panel: C coefficient of variation (factories)

Size of empt.	1979–02	1979–90	1991–97	1998–02
0–99	12	6	6	2
100–199	22	8	18	1
200–499	24	6	21	3
500–999	22	7	19	5
1,000 &>	17	14	11	9
Total	13	5	7	1

Source: Author's calculation. Data from ASI, various years.

We calculated in addition to employment CV (Panel: B) (for employment figures we considered workers *both* directly employed and also employed through contractors),[56] CVs of (real) output (Panel: A) and number of factories (Panel: C), for it is also argued that JSR impede output growth and smooth closure of factories (Besley and Burgess 2004; Zagha 1999). In the first column, firms are arranged according to their *size of employment*. Thus, labour laws for undertaking retrenchment, layoff and closure would apply to establishments of all employment sizes, *other than* the 0–99 category. Note that the second column looks at the variations in the long period (1979–2002). It is clear from Panel: A that the CV of the 0–99 category (52) is distinctly *below* that of the 100–199 (62) and 200–499 (56) category. However, output CVs of 500–999 and above 1,000 categories are *less* than the 0–99 category. Such qualifications disappear in Panel: B and C, where it is seen – for employment and number of factories – the CVs of 0–99 category are consistently *lower* than *all* other categories. Thus, available empirical evidence does not corroborate the pro-LMF claim.

Next, we carry out a sub-period analysis (Table 2.2). Sub-periods are chosen keeping in mind the fluctuations of the business cycle.[57] It is easy to see that for each of these sub-periods (i.e. 1979–90, 1991–97 and 1998–02) the CV of output (Panel: A) in the 0–99 category is consistently *lower* than (or, at best equal to) other categories, except for the above 1,000 category. Interestingly for *all* the sub-periods, the CV of employment (Panel: B) in the 0–99 category is throughout *lower* than the other categories. Even for factories (Panel: C), the CV of establishments in the 0–99 category is all through *lower* than the other categories.[58] Further, if we extend this analysis for the subsequent years (i.e. 2003–07) for employment – employment CV (Table 2.3) in the lowest employment range is persistently *lower* than the higher employment categories.[59]

Therefore, it is patently wrong to suggest that JSR hinders either output or employment adjustment. We also find no evidence of obstacles faced in the course of factory closures due to the law. Hence, the conventional claim appears unsubstantiated in the face of the available empirical evidence.

Further, it is claimed that JSR deters employment generation *even if* economic circumstances warrant such a move. Zagha (1999: 163) noted:

> Indicative of the burden on firms implied by these stipulations [of JSR], employment [growth] in firms with more than 100

Table 2.3 Coefficient of variation (employment): by employment size 2003–07

Size of empt.	CV (workers)
0–100	8
101–200	13
201–500	13
501–1,000	15
1,000 &>	16
Total	12

Source: Author's calculation. Data from ASI, various years.

employees has been virtually stagnant in the ten years following 1984, where as it has increased to 3.6 percent per year in firms with less than 100 employees.

Let us scrutinize this argument in light of the experience of the 1990s (Table 2.4). Panel: A reports the growth rate in value added, Panel: B reports the growth rate in employment and Panel: C reports the growth rate in number of factories. Note that the growth rate in value added markedly increased from the first sub-period (1979–90) to the second sub-period (1991–97). This is true for the overall factory sector as well as for all employment categories. Now if JSRs were truly a deterrent for employment expansion (based on the assumption that firms hire only when they are able to dispense with workers), then one would expect employment *not* to respond to output growth. However, evidence is at odds with such a hypothesis, since employment *did* respond to output growth. For the factory sector as a whole, as well as in all the categories, employment growth in the sub-period 1991–97 was higher than in the sub-period 1979–90. Moreover, employment growth in the 0–99 category accelerated by only 1 percent between 1979 and 1990 (2.4 percent) and 1991 and 1997 (3.4 percent) in response to acceleration in output growth, whereas for the higher employment categories, acceleration in employment growth was *faster*.[60]

Such trends continue to hold in case of the number of factories also. In Panel: C for the overall factory sector and employment size-classes, coming of new firms was faster, with acceleration in output growth in the second sub-period compared to the first sub-period. Thus entry of firms was *not* thwarted by restrictions on closure

Table 2.4 Growth rates of output, employment and number of factories: by size of employment (%)

Panel: A value added

Size of employment	1979–90	1991–97	1998–02
0–99	8.6	11.5	−0.4
100–199	9.5	18.6	2.9
200–499	9.4	14.9	2.8
500–999	9.9	11.5	7.5
1,000 &>	4.9	5.1	−1.7
Total	7.1	10.3	1.4

Panel: B number of workers

Size of employment	1979–90	1991–97	1998–02
0–99	2.4	3.4	−0.4
100–199	1.9	6.9	0.4
200–499	2.2	8.2	−0.3
500–999	2.3	7.2	−1
1,000 &>	−3.3	−2.7	−3.6
Total	0.2	3.4	−1.2

Panel: C Number of factories

Size of employment	1979–90	1991–97	1998–02
0–99	1.1	2.6	−0.8
100–199	1.8	7.4	0.2
200–499	1.3	8.9	−0.2
500–999	1.7	8.1	1.3
1,000 &>	−3.3	3.2	−3.6
Total	1.1	3.2	−0.9

Source: Author's calculation. Data from ASI, various years.

of units. Hence, there is little to suggest that JSR hampers either employment growth or expansion of factory units when the underlying economic condition justifies such a move. Further, it is interesting to note that between sub-periods one and two, for all three variables, growth in the categories where labour laws apply was mostly *higher* than for the 0–99 category, where they do not apply (except 1,000 and above employment category).[61]

It is easy to show that already Indian labour markets are effectively quite flexible. This is because: either government permission is easy to obtain, or the restrictions in the statute books seldom translate into rights due to the lack of attending institutional support in a developing country like ours. Thus, employers easily resort to layoff, retrenchment and closure without facing litigation (and hence saving on transaction costs) in spite of the laws in place, due to laxity in implementation of the law. Experience of the third sub-period lends support to this hypothesis.

Note that output growth (Panel: A) plummeted in the third sub-period (1998–2002) in the overall factory sector and in all employment categories. Associated with it were significant adjustments in *both* employment (Panel: B) and the number of factories (Panel: C). Interestingly, expansion of *both* variables turned *negative* in the overall factory sector. This trend was true for the majority of employment categories in the case of both the variables. Thus, evidence suggests that firms *could* adjust *both* employment and production units unhindered, according to the fluctuations of the business cycle. Clearly the conventional hypothesis finds no support from the employment experience of the factory sector in the 1990s. Even if we extend our analysis to the more recent period (2003 to 2007), when output growth recovered significantly,[62] it is clear from Table 2.5 that employment growth responded; further, employment growth in the 0–99 employment range was *less* than all other employment categories where labour law applies.

In light of the preceding results, the question may be asked: how could entrepreneurs adjust employment according to the swings of the business cycle if government permission is a mandatory prerequisite for undertaking such activities? For this, refer to Figure 2.4,

Table 2.5 Growth rate of employment: by employment size

2003–07	
Size of empt.	gr.rt. (workers)
0–100	5.2
101–200	7.9
201–500	8.7
501–1,000	9.9
1,000 &>	9.9
Total	8.0

Source: Author's calculation. Data from ASI, various years

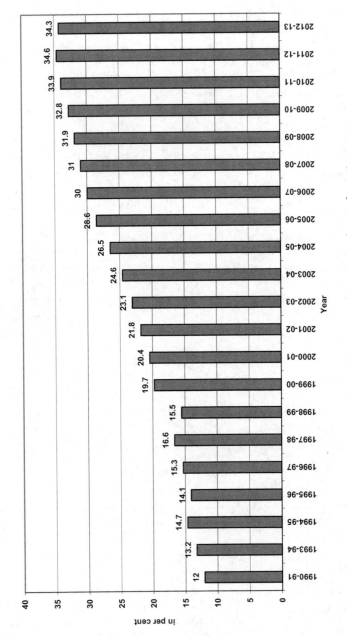

Figure 2.4 Proportion of contract workers to total workers in organised manufacturing sector
Source: Statistics on Employment and Labour Cost, ASI, Volume I, Labour Bureau, various issues

which shows that the share of contract workers in total workers has been continuously increasing in the last two decades.[63]

Chapter VB stipulates that employers have to obtain government permission for labour adjustments only in the case of regular workers but not for contractual workers.[64] Thus, the secular rise in the share of contract workers provides an inbuilt flexibility to the system which employers can manoeuvre whenever the necessity arises.[65] This is a principal means of introducing 'reform by stealth' (Nagaraj 2004: 3388; Guha 2009: 47). The contractual contingent essentially serves as an active army of labour subject to hire and fire, for a sector otherwise governed by labour laws. Thus, government needs to strictly regulate and limit the use of contract labour in the organised manufacturing sector – otherwise, overtime Chapter VB and VA would simply become redundant – as a progressively larger proportion of workers would fall out of their ambit. The pitfall of this phenomenon would be a sharp drop in the wage rate (and wage share) and the consequent *negative* repercussion on effective demand that may arise out of this (more on this below). However, the share of contract workers in total workers depicted in Figure 2.4 is an *underestimate* of the proportion of workers *not* covered by Chapter VB – *this is because even regular workers employed in establishments employing fewer than 100 workers are out of the ambit of law*. Thus, if we add the number of regular workers in the 0–100 category to the contract workers, then in 2012–13 the proportion of workers for whom *no prior* permission from the government was necessary for carrying out retrenchment, layoff and closure of units stood at 58.7 percent (this trend has been increasing since 2003–04; see Figure 2.3A in the Appendix).

Although employing contract workers is the most important tool for bypassing JSR, employers resort to other innovative ways of circumventing it. Moreover, flexibility has indeed been introduced by certain central and state-level amendments in IDA and Contract Labour Act (CLA), 1970. We discuss below the amendments and commonly used methods to evade IDA and CLA, seriatim.

Interestingly, in addition to contract workers, retrenchment rules are not applicable to even certain *directly* employed (i.e. through principal employer) workers. This is due to a 1984 amendment in Section 2(oo) of IDA, which changed the definition of retrenchment. In the new definition, termination of service due to non-renewal of contract or under a stipulation contained in the contract is no longer viewed as retrenchment (Bhattacharjea 2006). This amendment greatly increased employers' flexibility in adjusting even the directly employed workforce by deploying them for fixed periods. In practice, firms increasingly employed 'fixed-term workers' since their retrenchment did not require adherence to the usual norms (Sood *et al.* 2014). Further, state-level amendments also reduced the scope of IDA. In very recent amendments, Rajasthan and Madhya Pradesh raised the threshold of workers from 100 to 300 (Uttar Pradesh did it way back in 1983), for application of Chapter VB (see Chapter 1). Moreover, states like Andhra Pradesh, Gujarat, Tamil Nadu, Karnataka and Goa passed amendments to exempt special economic zones (SEZs) from the purview of IDA (ibid.). Another legal method actively pursued by employers is the Voluntary Retirement Scheme launched in May 1999, since it requires no permission from the state for removing workers (Nagaraj 2004).

Additionally, IDA is flouted in myriad ways. A prominent way is not to properly recognise a worker and his/her length of service. As Bhattacharjea (2006) noted, employers often dispute if a working person actually fits the definition of worker in IDA and whether she or he was in continuous service for 240 days required to benefit from IDA's retrenchment clauses. When inspection rates in factories have come down from 63.05 percent in 1986 to merely 17.88 percent in 2008, and even regular workers with no written job contract are 72.73 percent of organized manufacturing workers in 2011–12, disputing workers' status can be a very effective way of evading Chapter VB (Sood *et al.* 2014: tables 2.3 and 2.7). The 240 days continuous service clause required of getting retrenchment benefits is often flouted by declaring lockouts. Moreover, the judiciary has shifted the burden from the employer to the non-regular worker for proving that s/he continuously worked for 240 days in a firm to seek regularization of work and avert any arbitrary termination (ibid.).[66]

Prior government permission is also not needed for termination of workers in the case of transfer of entitlement of an enterprise. This loophole in the law was rampantly utilized in Maharashtra (Shyam Sundar 2008). Even illegal means are adopted to circumvent the law, as D'Souza (2010: 130) notes: '[G]overnment authorities are often manipulated to delay consent sought for retrenchments because after two months it is considered automatically to have been approved'. Also, the meagre penalty of Rs 5,000 is hardly a deterrent, and there is no instance of anyone going to jail for the violation of the law (ibid.). Another potent way of introducing labour reforms bypassing formal amendment is to use the administrative route (Dougherty 2009). It appears, then, that JSR remained largely confined to the statute book rather than translated into workers' rights.

Similarly, the phenomenal rise in contract labour noted earlier is fuelled by a combination of formal state-level amendments and informal circumvention of CLA, allowing unfettered utilization of contract labour by firms without any fear of absorbing them in future. CLA restricts utilization of contract workers to noncore activities and applies to establishments employing 20 or more workers on any day in the preceding year.

However, Andhra Pradesh (AP) amended its CLA in 2003 and took out a large number of tasks from the list of core activities and designated them as noncore – thus paving the way for unrestricted use of contract workers in these newly added noncore areas. Rajasthan in a recent amendment relaxed the application of CLA by raising the threshold of workers from 20 to 50. Therefore, firms with 20–49 workers can now use contract labour unfettered. Further, the director of a company can also assume the role of labour contractor, thereby circumventing JSR by changing the composition of workers, which in this case would simply mean hiring workers in the capacity of labour contractor and not as the principal employer (i.e. director).

However, legislative procedures were not the only means to encourage contractualization; as Sood *et al.* (2014) notes in 2009–10, the proportion of contract workers in organized manufacturing in Bihar (55.8 percent), Haryana (42.1 percent) and Orissa (41.4 percent) was higher than in AP (41 percent), although CLA was amended only by AP. Hence they concluded, 'CLA in perennial and core activities of the firm seems to have been done away with for all practical purposes and serves as a law only on paper' (ibid.: 64). Evading regulations is often preferred to the legislative route emboldened by weak enforcement (specially for contract and migrant workers) and as Shayam Sundar (2008) observed, the paltry sum of Rs 100 or 200 charged as a fine for violation remains inconsequential. The Supreme Court judgement of 2001,[67] by relieving the principal employer from the statutory obligation of absorbing contract workers following abolition of the contract labour system, significantly boosted the use of contract workers. Hence, CLA in practice is hardly a deterrent for employing contract labour.

Therefore, JSR and CLA have been greatly diluted by formal amendments and with rampant use of contract workers. This has resulted in low-quality job creation on vulnerable terms, making labour laws largely ineffective and the labour market *de facto* flexible. As Sood *et al.* (2014: 61) note,

> The increasing contractualisation of the workforce has resulted in severe degradation in the quality of employment being generated and has in effect made the labour market far more flexible for the employer. Workers (even those employed as regular wage workers) in the organized manufacturing sector are experiencing increasingly vulnerable terms of employment which has affected their bargaining power in the labour market.

Widespread evasion and weak enforcement further reduced the reach of labour laws. D'Souza (2010) points out that employers and labour inspectors often colluded to evade laws, which anyway are seldom enforced. Additionally, State governments jeopardized workers' interest by recommending compulsory arbitration for public utilities in the case of labour disputes; knowing workers have shallow pockets, 'all that firms were then required to do was to ensure the proceedings dragged on for months, which in many cases they did' (ibid.: 130). As labour laws lost effectiveness, our empirical finding of labour laws not putting a drag on employment or output growth is hardly surprising.

This analysis also casts doubt on the hypothesis that the small size of the Indian factory sector compared to China is primarily due to labour laws – in order to reap incentive by withholding employment below 100 workers. However, when the labour market is found to be *de facto* flexible, such apprehension seems misplaced. Bardhan (2014) cites the case of highly labour-intensive garment industry,

> [A]bout 92 percent of garment firms in India have fewer than eight employees (the bunching of firms is around the eight-employee size, not the below-100-employee size, as one would have expected). Labour law cannot discourage an eight-employee firm from expanding to an 80-employee firm since Chapter VB of the IDA does not kick in until the firm reaches the size of 100 employees. So the binding constraints on the expansion of that eight-employee firm may have to do with

inadequate credit and marketing opportunity, erratic power supply, wretched roads, bureaucratic regulations etc.

Thus, it is incorrect to suggest that the small size of Indian manufacturing is *primarily* due to JSR. Incidentally, the preceding discussion also suggests that holding legislation like the Factories Act, 1948, and IDA, 1947, and so on singularly responsible for the long-term decline in the average factory size of Indian manufacturing is patently wrong. In addition to the array of constraints pointed out by Bardhan, another constraint considered to have played an important role is the small size of the home market.[68] Thus, explaining the small size of Indian manufacturing solely in terms of a few pieces of legislation is fraught with difficulties.

Next, we compare the employment experience of the manufacturing sector in the unorganised segment (defined as fewer than 10 workers), where labour laws do not apply, with its organised counterpart.[69] There is a view in the literature that labour market rigidities encourage migration of activities and employment out of the formal sector into informal fringes – precisely to bypass labour regulations (Lucas 1988: 189–190). It is stated that

> a stagnation of employment levels in the organised sector accompanied by faster expansion of employment in the unorganised sector is often seen as a *consequence* of high labour cost and, more particularly, stringent job security regulations in the organised sector' (emphasis added).
>
> (Papola 1994: 10)

Therefore, it is suggested that to circumvent the law, 'enterprises . . . contracted out increasing volumes of work to smaller [informal] enterprises where provisions of government permission did not apply' (Goldar 2000: 1191) or, '[formal sector] employers . . . make greater use of casual [contract] labour' (Zagha 1999: 170). Let us check the validity of this argument in the light of the empirical evidence at hand (Table 2.6).[70]

It is crucial to remember at this juncture that in trying to offer an explanation for the sluggishness of employment growth – primarily during the 1980s in the organised manufacturing sector in India – various analysts drew attention to the supposedly stringent JSR. Therefore, if the hypothesis (and its *modus operandi*) just mentioned were correct, then it is reasonable to

Table 2.6 Growth rate of output and employment in organised and unorganised manufacturing (%)

	Growth rt. in value added		Growth rt. in employment	
Period	Organised	Unorganised	Organised	Unorganised
1984–85 to 1989–90	7.2	0.99	0.65	–0.95
1989–90 to 1994–95	8.25	–0.99	2.13	–1.73
1994–95 to 1999–2000	6.94	6.92	0.7	2.16
1999–00 to 2004–05	7.24	4.91	0.65	5.70
2004–05 to 2009–10	11.53	10.36	7.14	–2.90
2009–10 to 2011–12	6.63	5.06	6.76	8.70

Note: Cut-off points are based on the availability of unorganised manufacturing sector data.
Source: Rani and Unni (2004: 4569) up to 1999–00; Author's calculation thereafter

expect that – accompanied with a stagnation of employment growth in the organised segment during the 1980s – there would be a surge of activity (and employment) in the informal segment during the same period. *In fact, stringent JSR in the organised segment would manifest itself through employment dynamism in the unorganised segment.* However, Table 2.6 shows that the available evidence is at odds with such a thesis. Output growth in the unorganised manufacturing segment (0.99 percent) was much below the organised segment (7.2 percent) during the 1980s, and employment growth turned negative (–0.95 percent) precisely in the period when employment growth in the organised segment (0.65 percent) was also low. Therefore, when the organised segment of manufacturing failed to generate employment, its unorganised counterpart also trailed. This goes against the basic tenet of the migration thesis. This, in turn, also casts doubt on the principal explanatory factor used for explaining the slowdown of employment growth during the 1980s in the organised manufacturing sector, namely, stringent JSR. In effect, the above evidence suggests that *independent* forces were at work to withhold employment expansion in each of these sectors.[71]

Experience of the subsequent period (1989–90 to 1994–95) gives a further blow to the migration thesis. Output (8.25 percent) and employment (2.13 percent) growth in the organised manufacturing segment surged quite substantially during this period, whereas both these variables turned negative for the unorganised segment. This is opposite of the prediction of migration thesis. Also note that labour laws did not change in-between, but now, with acceleration of output in the organised segment, employment growth also responded. This further invalidates the explanation provided for employment stagnation of the previous period in this segment.

However, between 1994–95 and 1999–2000, the organised manufacturing sector experienced substantial deceleration in output and employment growth despite the labour regulations in place (already noted in Table 2.4). The employment plunge is explained by a sharp absolute decline of 1.3 million workers after 1995 in the organised manufacturing sector, largely driven by a conscious government policy of rationalising the workforce through institution of the National Renewal Fund (Nagaraj 2004: 3387–3388). Interestingly, after a decade of retrogression, both output and employment in the unorganised segment surged between 1994–95 and 1999–2000. No doubt part of this dynamism was due to subcontracting and hence constitutes a relocation of activity from the formal sector. However, the underlying reason was *not* simply bypassing JSR but a diverse set of factors like cost-cutting in the face of intense international competition after liberalisation, increased product differentiation, volatility in the export market and so on (for details see Ramaswamy 2003: 162).

Relative employment stagnation in the organized segment coupled with employment dynamism in the unorganized sector (at even greater pace) continued during 1999–00 to 2004–05 and was associated with modest output growth in both segments. However, with unprecedented acceleration of output growth (11.53 percent) between 2004–05 and 2009–10 in the organized segment, employment growth revived (7.14 percent). Paradoxically, output acceleration in the unorganized segment (10.36 percent) during this period was accompanied by job destruction (–2.9 percent). Therefore, the employment experience during 2004–05 and 2009–10 in *both* manufacturing segments invalidates the 'relocation hypothesis'.

Between 2009–10 and 2011–12, employment growth was positive and accompanied by moderate output growth in both segments (although this trend may be ignored because of its very short period). Further, it is self-evident from the results that the limited relocation of activity from formal to informal sectors must have been primarily for reasons *other than* bypassing labour laws – otherwise such tendencies should have been *persistently visible across all* quinquennium rounds.[72]

One also remains doubtful of the claim that formal sector employers use contractual labour *primarily* to bypass the law. However, such a strategy can be adopted purely for maximizing profits through cost-cutting. To see this, refer to Figure 2.5, which shows the share of contract workers' wage rates to *all* workers' wage rates (which also includes contract workers).[73] Available evidence shows that contractual workers consistently receive lower wages than regular workers, although the gap has been reduced overtime. Now, so long as a wedge exists between regular and contract workers' wages, rational profit-maximizing employers will have full incentive to hire workers on a contractual basis rather than on regular basis (although this would affect the *quality* of work adversely, see Chapter 5), *irrespective of the labour regime in place*.

Indeed, there is some evidence that the twin effects of rising share of contract workers in total workers (Figure 2.4) coupled with marked *wage differentials* between two sets of workers (Figure 2.5) has translated itself into depressing the wage share in total output (Figure 2.6). The share of wages (or unit labour cost) started to fall sharply from 1987–88 [when it was 26 percent of gross value (GVA)], precisely the period during which the share of contract workers was on the rise. The share of wages reached its nadir (9.2 percent) in 2007–08 and recovered only slightly to reach 12.1 percent in 2014–15. However, substitution of regular by contractual workers, of course, was not the sole reason for the decline in wage share. This analysis clearly shows that coupled with JSR, we need to strictly monitor and limit the use of contract labour in the factory sector, otherwise JSR would be drained out of its content, taking recourse to the contract labour route. Interestingly, it also shows that once LMF is introduced, *all workers now reduced to the category of contract labourers* would face a sharp reduction in wage rate by at least 19 percent, resulting in a further compression of wage share in output and depressing effective demand and employment (see Chapter 6).

However, this is not to suggest that wage differentials alone explain the preference of employers to use contract workers – another major driving factor is to weaken workers' bargaining

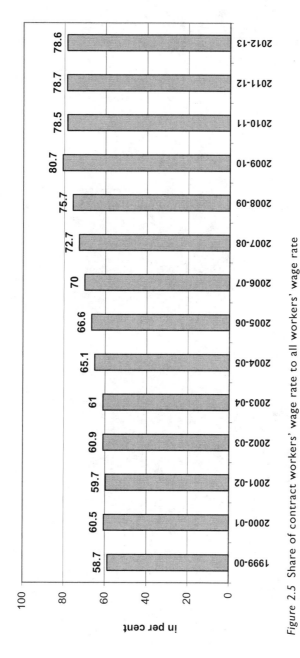

Figure 2.5 Share of contract workers' wage rate to all workers' wage rate

Source: Report on Absenteeism, Labour Turnover, Employment and Labour Cost, ASI Volume 2, Labour Bureau, various issues.

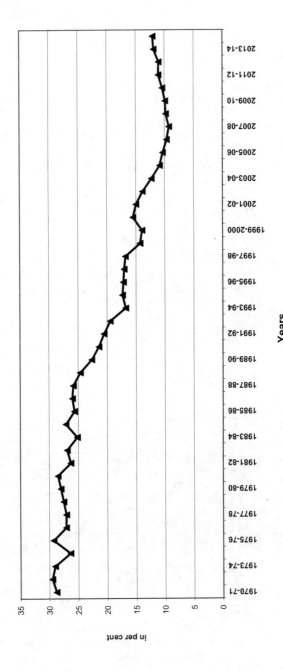

Figure 2.6 Share of wages in GVA
Source: ASI, various issues

power – since contract workers are typically vested with limited bargaining strength. From the discussion above it is clear that, even in those segments of the factory sector where labour law applies, employers have been successful in undertaking labour adjustments whenever deemed necessary. Rapid contractualization of the manufacturing workforce was the principal means to achieve such flexibility. In the next section, we explore the validity of the second strand of the argument, which seeks to explain the employment slowdown during the 1980s in terms of a sharp rise in real wages (and product wages).

2.3 Rise in real wages as an explanation for employment downturn

The analytical framework underlying this strand of argument is the neoclassical view of labour market functioning. According to this view, the aggregate labour market must *always* clear, if real wage adjusts freely. Thus, the existence of unemployment in this framework must ultimately arise from incomplete real wage adjustments normally attributed to labour unions running a closed shop (prohibiting wage cuts) or minimum wage legislation. For example, World Bank (1989: 110) – one of the principal proponents of this genre – concludes: '[T]he faster growth of real wages in the 1980s indeed did play an important role in slowing down employment creation'. Further, Lucas (1988: 189), one of the earliest contributors in this vein, notes:

> [E]vidence certainly suggests that the rising industrial wage has been a significant factor in the observed move toward more capital intensive techniques. But why have wages in the manufacturing sector been rising? . . . it is clear that the comparative power of unions in pressing for wage settlements has grown substantially. . .

However, this explanation of unemployment due to real wage rigidity never recognises either the role of technological progress or effective demand constraint that characterizes any modern money-using economy where wealth can be held in money form. Consequently, the possibility of unemployment arising out of technological progress or effective demand deficiency, independently, simply cannot be accommodated within such a framework. A detailed critique of this approach would, however, be premature at this stage and must wait until Chapter 6 is reached. In what follows, we pursue a different approach altogether, namely, to check the robustness of the empirical studies conducted by the commentators, who attribute stagnation of employment during the 1980s to rising real (and product) wages.

Lucas' (1988) study tried to show that there are some long-term tendencies for capital intensity to increase in the Indian manufacturing sector and that it started at least two decades before the 1980s. Lucas (1988: 188) notes: 'Between 1959–60 and 1979–80. . . the bulk of the increase in capital intensity is thus a reflection of choice of production technique within the thirty-nine manufacturing activities. . . '. In order to explain this rising trend in capital intensity, Lucas relies on the following:

> Towards understanding these factors [that contributed to rising capital-intensity], it is worth noting that the real product wage . . . has increased steadily. . . . the real product wage rate in manufacturing increased by some 86 percent between 1960–61 and 1979–80. Relative to the national accounts deflator for capital formation the manufacturing wage rate rose by some 47 percent over the same period, and *it seems that this rise has indeed significantly encouraged reliance on more capital-intensive techniques in most manufacturing industries.*
> (emphasis added) (ibid.: 189)[74]

However, it is important for us to check how Lucas reaches such conclusions. They are based on the regression analysis stated as follows:

$$\ln(l/k) = \alpha + \beta \ln(w/p_k) + \lambda \ln(l/k)_{-1}$$

where l represents man-hours, k is fixed capital, w is hourly wage rate and p_k is the price index for capital formation. Here, 'ln' represents natural logarithm and –1 represents a one period lag. Now the author runs this regression for 39 two-digit industries separately – from the sign and statistical significance of the β coefficients [i.e. the coefficient on $\ln(w/p_k)$] – and draws his conclusions. Let us now turn to the author's results and their interpretation.

Surprisingly, the author simply does not report the results of those industries for which β coefficient turns out to be *positive*;

however, he provides no justification for doing so. The author simply says: 'Regressions for eight industries in which the point estimates for the coefficient on $\ln(w/p_k)$ prove positive are omitted...' (ibid.: 195 footnote 14).[75] But these industries throw up results which are just the *opposite* of the hypothesis the author contemplates; therefore, simply ignoring these results is clearly a shortcoming of the study. For rest of the industries, however, results are reported and interpreted. For the interpretation of the results, it is best to quote Lucas (1988: 189) in full:

> For twenty-seven of the thirty industries for which regressions are reported, increases in the wage rate relative to price of capital are estimated to have significantly encouraged more capital-intensive techniques on at least a *75 percent confidence level test* and in seventeen cases the significance level is 5 percent or better.
>
> (emphasis added)

Now it is amply clear that a 75 percent confidence level test means that the regression coefficients are *not* statistically different from zero in 25 percent of the cases. But the standard practice in any statistical exercise *never* conventionally puts any credence on results beyond the 10 percent significance level. Now if we reconsider the author's results and use the conventional 10 percent significance level (rather than 25 percent level), then a further nine industries show *insignificant β coefficient* on $\ln(w/p_k)$.[76] Thus, out of 39 industries considered by the author, 18 industries do not support his hypothesis; under this circumstance it is difficult to conclude that a rise in capital intensity was brought about *primarily* by the rise in relative price of labour to capital. Surely we need to search for other reasons.

Next, we turn to a well-cited study by the World Bank (1989). It sought to explain the slowdown in employment generation in the first half of the 1980s (1979–80 to 1984–85) when compared with the period 1973–74 to 1979–80, in spite of the growth rate in value added accelerating in the later period. The rapid rise in real wages during the 1980s was found to be *primarily* responsible for the slowdown in employment creation. The study noted: 'Real wage growth was much higher in the 1980s than in the 1970s, and employers not surprisingly responded by economizing on the use of labour and investing in more capital-intensive techniques' (World

Bank 1989: 108). In passing, the study also mentioned the possible dampening effect of acrimonious, dysfunctional labour laws and employment overhang inherited from the past on employment growth. But the study insisted on rapid real wage growth as the *main* explanatory factor for the employment slowdown during the first half of the 1980s. It argued:

> The rising real cost of labor to firms appears to have been a major proximate cause of the observed fall in labour-output ratios. Whereas real wages in terms of cost to employer (nominal emoluments per worker deflated by the wholesale price index for manufacturing) fell by 1% p.a. in 1973/74–1979/80, they rose by an astonishing 7.2% p.a. in 1979/80–1984/5... there was also substantial acceleration in real wage growth measured in terms of workers' consumption basket (from 1.7% p.a. in 1974/5–1979/80 to 3.4% p.a. in 1979/80–1984/5). Employers not surprisingly responded to sharply rising labor costs by economizing (i.e. by virtually stopping new hiring and retrenching existing workers to the extent possible) on the use of labor.
>
> (ibid.: 109)

To establish causality, the study estimated employment elasticities from the employment functions of the manufacturing sector as a whole and its broad sub-sectors (at two-digit level).[77] These estimates were for the pooled cross section and time series data for the period 1974/75–1984/85. From the regression results, the study concluded:

> The estimates are fairly robust and point to a significant trade-off between the higher real cost of labor and employment. . . . The estimated long run elasticities, clustered around (–) 0.8, imply that the annual increase in the real cost of labor of 7.2% in the 1980s reduced the annual growth employment by 5.7%.
>
> (ibid.: 110)[78]

Notice that both studies explained the employment downturn and the consequent adoption of capital-intensive techniques in terms of rising real wages. Now economic theory suggests that such a negative causal relationship between real wages and employment is valid *only if movement is along a given production function*.

However, if there is technological progress (to argue otherwise would be surprising since it would amount to assuming that there was no technological progress in Indian manufacturing for two decades) which causes production function to shift upwards, no such causality can be established. This is because if the underlying *nature* of technological progress is of a labour-saving variety (we find evidence on this in Chapter 3), then *higher* labour productivity would *cause* a rise in wages, and slowing down of employment growth is explained in terms of labour productivity rising at a faster rate relative to output growth.[79] Therefore, a rise in real wages and employment downturn are brought about by a third independent factor, namely, rising labour productivity, and the negative causal relationship between real wages and employment is snapped. Hence, it is clear that in interpreting their results, both Lucas (1988) and the World Bank (1989) implicitly assumed that the Indian manufacturing sector during the respective period of their studies *operated along a single production function*.

Let us hypothesize for a moment along the lines of Lucas and the World Bank, that indeed there was no technological progress introduced in the Indian manufacturing sector for two decades, and that the economy operated along a single production function. Only then can the negative causal relationship between real wages and employment be evoked and only then could the reduction in employment growth be explained by rising real wages. The question immediately arises: *what* contributed to the rising real wages in the manufacturing sector? There is a view in literature that the sharp rise in real wages was brought about by the introduction of strict JSR. As Ghose (1994: 143) points out: 'A popular perception in India today is that rising labour costs, [are] attributable to labour market rigidities generated by inappropriate [labour] regulations and the nature of industrial relations. . . .'.

Under the assumption that the manufacturing sector *operated along a single production function*, we would expect 'threshold effects' to be present. Specifically, if we assume remaining on the *same* production function, it is expected that the correlation coefficient between the growth rate of output and employment would be unity in the '0–99' employment category, where labour laws *do not* apply. This is so because workers in this category would *fail* to claim higher wages, owing to low bargaining power in the *absence* of JSR. Consequently, firms would *not* hesitate to hire labour, whereas we would expect the correlation between the growth rate of output and employment to breakdown in employment ranges (100 and above) where labour laws apply. In order to test this hypothesis, we calculated the correlation coefficients of year-to-year growth rates between output and employment (Table 2.7). Interestingly, the correlation coefficients for employment categories where labour law applies turned out to be positive and statistically significant.[80] *Paradoxically, where labour laws do not apply we cannot find statistically significant coefficients with the correct sign.* Hence, even if we assume that the manufacturing sector operated along a single production function, the conventional claim of negative relationship between real wages and employment expected to prominently manifest itself in the employment range of 100 and above workers remains uncorroborated.

Now we shall examine a study by Ahluwalia (1992), which categorized the manufacturing industries by use-based classification. The study covers a time period of 1959–60 to 1985–86 and divides it into four sub-periods. However, for our purpose we shall only concentrate on the last sub-period, namely, 1980–81 to 1985–86. The author draws attention to the fact that the first half of the 1980s was characterized by a peculiar phenomenon: growth rate in value added accelerating, but employment expansion plummeting. Ahluwalia (1992: 79–80) notes:

> As for employment growth, the first half of the eighties was marked by an across-the-board slowdown. In particular, consumer non-durables recorded a decline in employment at the rate of 3 percent per annum during the period. The intermediate

Table 2.7 Correlation coefficient between point growth rate of output and employment: by size of employment

Factories by size of employment	1980–90	1991–97	1998–02
0–99	0.536***	−0.646	0.039
100–199	0.511	0.878*	0.891**
200–499	0.765*	0.709***	0.886**
500–999	0.823*	0.781**	0.878***
1,000 &>	0.666**	0.289	0.842***
Total	0.086	0.73***	0.803

Notes: Reported results are for 2-tailed test: *significant at 1% level; **significant at 5% level; ***significant at 10% level; others insignificant.

Source: Author's calculation. Data from ASI, various years.

good also experienced a slowdown in employment growth . . . to 0.8 percent per annum. . . . Even for the manufacturing sector as a whole, employment declined at the rate of 0.7 percent per annum.

These facts are based on Table 2.8. Now although employment growth rates were positive in *other than* consumer non-durable segments, overall manufacturing growth still turned negative. This phenomenon is explained by the author:

> For a sector [i.e. consumer non-durables] which accounts for 47 percent of the total employment in manufacturing, this negative growth was a major contributor to the stagnation in employment (growth rate of – 0.7 percent per annum) in manufacturing during this period.
>
> (ibid.: 82)

Immediately the question arises: what contributes to this slowdown? The author argues: 'The sharp increase in the capital-labour ratio in the first half of the eighties was associated with a sharp increase in the real wage rate during this period after a prolonged phase of wage stability . . .' (ibid.: 82). Ahluwalia clearly attributes the employment slowdown to rising real wages.[81] This is further made clear from the following:

> While the cause and the effect can be debated at length, the data seem to suggest that the consumer non-durables sector experienced the maximum increase in capital intensity as well as the maximum increase in the real wage rate during this period. Consumer durables were next in line recording real

Table 2.8 Growth rate of employment, capital intensity (K/L) and real wage rate (RW) between 1980–81 and 1985–86 (%)

Used based classification	Empt.	K/L	RW
Manufacturing	–0.7	8.4	6.8
Intermediate goods	0.8	6.8	2.9
Consumer non-durables	–3	10.5	9.1
Consumer durables	2.4	8.4	8.2
Capital goods	1.6	5.7	5.7

Source: Ahluwalia (1992: 74–76)

wage increases of the order of 8 percent per annum. By contrast, faster growth of the capital labour ratios in the intermediate goods and capital goods sector was associated with much more modest increases in the real wage rates during this period
(ibid.: 83–84)

Note that Ahluwalia (1992) also assumes implicitly – along the lines of Lucas and the World Bank – that the organised manufacturing sector during the period of her study operated along a *given* production function. Let us check the robustness of the conclusions reached by the World Bank (1989) and Ahluwalia (1992).

Both studies were contested on grounds of methodology in a celebrated paper by Nagaraj (1994). It is worth remembering that both studies pointed towards rising real wages as the main proximate reason for the employment downturn during first half of the 1980s. Therefore, it is important to probe closely the *method* employed by these two studies to *derive real wage rates*. Both studies simply took the category of 'wages to workers' (available with ASI) and divided it by the number of workers reported in that year (of course, adjusting for inflation to derive real wages). Let us see whether this is a *correct method* for computing the real cost of labour.

Now ASI defines the category of 'wages to workers' as follows:

> Wages are defined to include all remuneration capable of being expressed in monetary terms and also payable/paid more or less regularly in each pay period to workers as compensation for work done during the accounting year. It includes: (a) Direct wages and salary (i.e. basic wages/salaries, payment of overtime, dearness, compensatory, house rent and other allowances); (b) Remuneration for period not worked (i.e. basic wages), salaries and allowances payable for leave period, paid holidays, lay-off payments and compensation for unemployment (if not paid from source other than employers); (c) Bonus and ex-gratia payment paid both at regular and less frequent intervals (i.e., incentive bonuses and good attendance bonuses, production bonuses, profit sharing bonuses, festival or year-end bonuses etc.). It excludes layoff payments and compensation for employment except where such payments are for this purpose, i.e., payments not made by the employer. It excludes employer's contribution to old age benefits and other social security charges, direct expenditure on maternity benefits and

creches and other group benefit in kind and travelling and other expenditure incurred for business purposes and reimbursed by the employer. The wages are expressed in terms of gross value, i.e., before deductions for fines, damages, taxes, provident fund, employee's state insurance contribution etc. Benefits in kind (perquisites) of individual nature are only included.
(ASI Report Volume I, 2008–09: A-631-A-632)

Nagaraj (1994), going by the definition mentioned above, rightly pointed out that the rise in real labour cost, defined as real wage by the World Bank and Ahluwalia, could represent *additional* remuneration for workers' *additional* effort and may not *necessarily* imply an increase in the real wage rate. It is best to quote the author in some detail to fully appreciate his basic critique of the *methodology* employed by the World Bank and Ahluwalia to derive the real wage rate:

Ahluwalia and the World Bank use Annual Survey of Industries (ASI) data on 'wages to workers' to compute the wage rate (or wages). As the ASI definition includes all payments made to workers – excepting layoff payments not made by the employer and the imputed value of benefits in kind – it evidently refers to workers' *total earnings*, which covers not only the wage rate – that is, the basic wage plus dearness allowance, wherever applicable – but also all *additional* remuneration for workers' *additional* effort. Conceptually, earnings per worker is a function of the wage rate for the standard working day, remuneration for additional hours of work (and more shifts) and incentive income from more intensive work that is linked to output. In the decade beginning 1979–80, while the employment growth turned negative, total person days (or mandays) worked in registered manufacturing – and hence mandays per worker – recorded a positive trend growth rate; suggesting that the observed increase in earnings per worker could, at least partly, represent his (or her) compensation for greater effort and may not *necessarily* imply an increase in the wage rate, as has been argued.
(emphasis in original) (Nagaraj 1994: 177–178)

Based on this understanding, Nagaraj tried to eliminate *additional* remuneration for workers' *additional* effort and enumerated *earnings per manday* to more appropriately proxy for the real wage rate. These results are reported in Table 2.9. The author notes:

> We examine the trends in earnings per worker and earnings per manday, although the latter as a proxy for the wage rate ignores additional remuneration due to plausible intensification of the working day. While earnings per worker in registered manufacturing increased at 3.2 percent in the decade beginning 1979–80, earnings per manday increased only 1.6 percent per annum, which is less than the corresponding real per capita GDP growth rate during the same period (2.7 percent).
>
> (ibid.: 178)

Therefore, it cannot be claimed that the real cost of labour increased excessively in organised manufacturing during the period under consideration.

Nagaraj (1994: 178–179) further notes:

> Ahluwalia, . . . observed the inverse movement between employment and wage rate in these [use based classification] industries was associated with an above average increase in capital-labour ratio. The foregoing evidence, however, suggests

Table 2.9 Growth rate in registered manufacturing, 1979–80 to 1988–89 (%)

Used based classification	Empt. of workers	Mandays per worker	Earnings per worker	Earnings per manday
Intermediate goods	0.5* (0.336)	1.0* (0.870)	2.6* (0.843)	1.6* (0.751)
Capital goods	(–) 0.02 (0.0)	0.3 (0.134)	3.0* (0.900)	2.7* (0.965)
Consumer durables	1.6* (0.791)	0.7 (0.181)	2.7* (0.776)	2.0* (0.588)
Consumer non-durables	(–) 1.6* (0.706)	2.3* (0.750)	3.0* (0.829)	0.5* (0.653)
Registered manufacturing	(–) 0.5* (0.301)	1.5* (0.663)	3.2* (0.579)	1.6* (0.800)

Notes: *(1) Indicates statistical significance of the estimated coefficient at 90 percent confidence level or above. (2) Employment growth rate for registered manufacturing is for the nine-year period since 1980–81 as the same for the period since 1979–80 is statistically significant at 80 percent confidence level.
Source: Nagaraj (1994: 178)

that while earnings per worker undoubtedly went up in the 80s, it was mainly on account of an above average increase in the number of days worked per worker. The rise in earnings per mandays in consumer non-durable good industries, as shown above, is considerably lower (0.5 percent per annum) than the average for registered manufacturing (1.6 percent per annum).

The foregoing observation allows the author to conclude:

> If it is conceded that the definition of the wage rate (by Ahluwalia) and wages (by the World Bank) *represent earnings per worker*, then these diverging trends seem to suggest that much of the reported increase in the wage rate or wages noted by them, represents additional remuneration for workers' extra effort . . . and *perhaps not a substantial increase in the wage rate for the standard working day.*
>
> (emphasis added) (ibid.: 179)

Thus, the claim that the real cost of labour has gone up excessively and that *this primarily explains* the employment slowdown during the first half of the 1980s finds no empirical support.[82]

From the foregoing discussion, it is clear that the neoclassical hypothesis of a *negative* trade-off between wages (both product and real) and employment remains unsubstantiated *throughout* in light of the available evidence. However, what caused the observed employment downturn during the 1980s still remains unexplained. This is taken up for discussion in Chapter 3.

Conclusion

This chapter was devoted to scrutinizing empirically the claims normally advanced in favour of undertaking LMF. It was pointed out that there are two broad emerging trends in this respect, namely, stringent JSR and rising real wages, not necessarily as competing explanations for the slowdown in employment growth, especially during the 1980s. In Section 2.1, we critically reviewed the empirical literature which associates employment downturn with strict job security laws in some details. Discussing Fallon and Lucas (1991), we noted that the robustness of their result was open to question. The dummy variable technique adopted by the authors was inadequate for drawing a *conclusive* inference. It was further pointed out that Fallon and Lucas found evidence on plummeting employment in the immediate aftermath of the 1976 amendment but *no sustained* effect on employment adjustment in the long run. Bhalotra (1998), estimating dynamic labour demand functions, found evidence on labour flexibility *increasing* during her sample period [1979–87]. Further, Aggarwal (2002) found mixed results on this subject. Although Dutta Roy (2002) reported a significant decline in labour flexibility after the 1982 amendment, she regards her result to be only tentative. However, in another study, Dutta Roy (2004), estimating dynamic labour demand functions, found no evidence on labour rigidities increasing post-JSR amendment. Guha (2009), constructing his own labour flexibility index, found no evidence of labour flexibility affecting industrial outcomes. Compiling state-level amendments, Besley and Burgess (2004) and Ahsan and Pagés (2009) found evidence on negative effects of JSR on industrial outcomes. However, Bhattacharjea (2006, 2009) thoroughly criticized both studies on the grounds of the methodology employed by these studies in constructing their LMF index as well as the econometric technique adopted by them. Thus, it can be safely concluded that the available empirical evidence in favour of LMF is far from satisfactory.

In Section 2.2, we noted that at most 35 percent of the workers in the organised sector – those working in organised manufacturing – are covered by JSR. Thus, it is patently wrong to argue that the small size of India's organised sector *as a whole* is *due to* job security legislations. It was further shown that the conscious policy decision to rationalise the public sector workforce (by shedding existing workers or freezing new appointments) coupled with privatization of PSUs for enhancing 'efficiency' (typically shedding workers to reduce labour costs to boost accounting profits) stand out to be decisive reasons for the incapacity of the *overall* organised sector to generate quality employment. Next, we provided evidence on employment fluctuations being *higher* precisely in those employment categories where labour laws apply compared to employment segments where they *do not* apply. We also showed employment growth being *greater* in sectors where labour laws apply compared to where they do not apply. Finally, we contested the proposition that employers, in order to escape labour laws, subcontract economic activity to the unorganised sector and hence employment growth takes place in the informal segment. Moreover, a simpler explanation of employers' preference for contract workers over permanent workers was provided in terms of wage differentials – fulfilling basic profit maximization criteria – *irrespective* of the labour regime in place.

In Section 2.3, we examined the second strand that claims rapid real (product) wage growth to be the *primary* proximate reason for employment downturn. Examining Lucas' (1988) study, we showed that his results were not robust. In the course of the discussion it also became clear that, in interpreting their results (of *negative* association between wages and employment), both Lucas (1988) and the World Bank (1989) implicitly assumed that the Indian manufacturing sector *operated along a single production function throughout, and there was no technological progress for nearly two decades*. Even assuming this, contrary to the expectations, a statistically significant *positive* association between output and employment growth could be discerned in employment segments *governed* by labour laws; whereas no such association was visible in employment categories *not governed* by labour laws.

Commenting on the World Bank's (1989) and Ahluwalia's (1992) study, we noted that they were confusing wage rates and earnings per worker. Nagaraj (1994) pointed out this confusion, and in order to assess the real cost of labour, calculated earnings per manday. Nagaraj's estimates firmly established that the growth in real costs of labour claimed by Ahluwalia (1992) were *overestimates*. Thus, scrutinizing the *methodology* adopted by the empirical studies reviewed, it was concluded that there are logical infirmities (on grounds of definitions used and robustness of results) involved in these studies.

Appendix

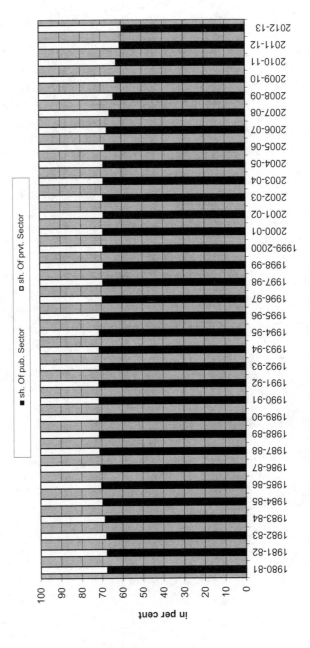

Figure 2.1A Distribution of total organised employment by sectors
Source: Indian Labour Year Book, various issues.

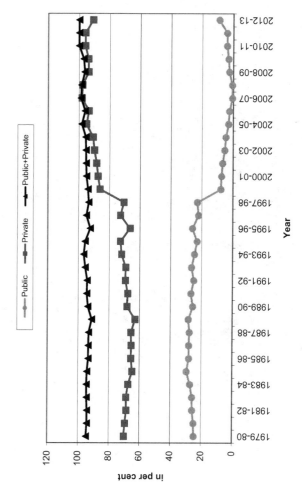

Figure 2.2A Share of organised manufacturing employment by sectors

Note: Shares may not always add up to 100, since rest of the employment is in the Joint Sector not shown in graph.

Source: ASI, various issues.

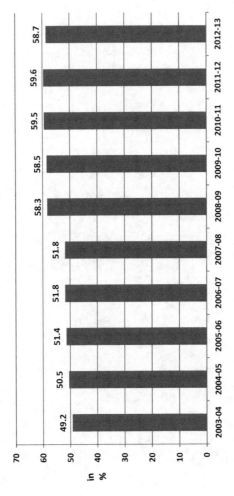

Figure 2.3A Share of workers not covered by labour laws: Contract (All) + Regular workers (0–100) employment category

Source: ASI, various issues.

Table 2.1A Coefficient of variation: decadal

Panel: A Coefficient of variation (output)

Size of employment	1979–91	1992–02
0–99	33	19
100–199	34	24
200–499	36	21
500–999	35	16
1,000 &>	22	8
Total	27	13

Panel: B Coefficient of variation (workers)

Size of employment	1979–91	1992–02
0–99	10	8
100–199	8	13
200–499	13	14
500–999	9	16
1,000 &>	16	11
Total	3	9

Panel: C Coefficient of variation (factories)

Size of employment	1979–91	1992–02
0–99	6	3
100–199	9	13
200–499	7	14
500–999	7	12
1,000 &>	14	18
Total	6	4

Source: Author's calculations. ASI various years.

Notes

1 In concrete terms this involves, among other things, mainly dilution of certain current provisions of IDA 1947 and the Contract Labour Act 1970.
2 In particular, employment growth turned negative during the period 1979–87 – registering a fall in employment to the tune of (-) 0.3 percent per annum (Bhalotra 1998: 5). However, employment growth is reported to be positive, albeit negligibly, with an alternative periodisation – 1980–81 to 1989–90 (Goldar 2000: 1191).
3 The organised manufacturing sector covers only those establishments which are engaged in the manufacturing process and employ (a) 10 or more workers, where activity is carried out with the aid of power,

or (b) 20 or more workers, where activity is carried out without the aid of power, whereas the total organised sector of the economy covers a much larger set of establishments (including those in the agricultural and services sector) employing at least 10 or more total workers. Therefore, the organised manufacturing sector is only a subset of the whole organised sector of the economy (Nagaraj 1994: 180). Interestingly, JSR applies only to certain firms in the organised manufacturing sector (those employing more than 100 workers) and not to the whole of the organised sector of the economy. However, there is some confusion in the literature, about the domain of application of Chapter VB of IDA, 1947, and this has unnecessarily clouded the discussion on the necessity of LMF (more on this later).

4 However, population during the 1980s continued to grow at 2.2 percent per annum (Visaria 2008–09).

5 That these two lines of argument are patently cited by orthodox economists to explain employment downturn in the 1980s has been widely accepted in the literature:

> The labour flexibility argument is based on twin notions of the presence of labour market rigidities in the form of protective legislation and trade union militancy and downward rigidity of real wages or rising product wages (these arguments were used to explain the decline in formal manufacturing employment especially in the 1980s).
>
> (Shyam Sundar 2009: 28)

Also see Papola (1994: 5); Ghose (1994: 143); Nagaraj (1994: 179–180); Sharma (2006: 2080); Shyam Sundar (2005: 2276); Kannan and Reveendran (2009: 80); Goldar (2000: 1191–1192).

6 For example, Ghose (2005: 238) notes: 'The sharp rise in real wages in the 1980s could conceivably be attributable to the introduction of strict job security regulations in 1982'.

7 Other studies in this genre also estimate different versions of the dynamic labour demand functions. For example, among the studies reviewed below, Bhalotra (1998) and Dutta Roy (2004) estimate such functions.

8 Such a version can also be found in Bhattacharjea (2006: 4).

9 Authors argue that the sign of these coefficients cannot always be predicted a priori – for wages it would be typically negative, for output it is likely to be positive. However, for hours of work and number of workers it is ambiguous in sign depending upon whether these operate as substitutes or complements to each other.

10 Employment reduction following the 1976 amendment was found to be stronger in plants employing more than 300 workers (the threshold level at which the amendment applied), those in the private sector and those with lower union membership. In order to strengthen their claim, Fallon and Lucas (1991: 407) also showed the following:

> Thus no evidence is found to suggest that job loss in the census sector as a result of the 1976 amendment produced job gains in parallel

sample sector factories through transfer of across establishments, through sub-contracting, through putting-out of work, or through major adjustments in establishment size. Nor does this evidence suggest that the significant drops in census sector employment were a result of spurious industry developments, which also caused drops in the parallel sample sector factories.

11 Accession is defined as the total number of workers added to employment during a period, whether new or re-employed or transferred from other establishments or units under the same management. Interdepartmental transfers within the same establishments are ignored.

12 Separation is defined as severance from employment at the instance of employers or workers. It includes termination of service due to death or retirement. Retirement as a result of modernisation or rationalisation or any other cause is also treated as separation. This includes transfers out of the establishment.

13 The accession rate is assumed to depend upon the following variables, and the equation is: accession rate = f (relative wage, relative plant size, absenteeism, union power, accession rate lagged one period, planned employment growth, gap in employment growth in previous period).

14 The separation rate is assumed to depend upon the following variables, and the equation is: separation rate = f (relative wage, relative plant size, job hazard rate, union power, separation rate lagged one period, planned employment growth, gap in employment growth in previous period).

15 In particular, Dutta Roy (2002: 149) argues:

> If turnover decisions are sufficiently responsive, hiring and firing decisions can be suitably used to effect desired changes in employment. As a corollary, regulations of firing decisions would reduce labour market flexibility, the impact of which could be gauged via the effect on these coefficients. The expected signs of the coefficients on 'pgemp' [planned growth in employment] and 'empgap$_{-1}$' [gap in actual and planned employment growth] are negative and positive respectively in the separation equation. The expected signs are reversed for the accession equation.

Clearly, reduced flexibility would make turnover unresponsive to the coefficients on planned employment changes.

16 JSR applies neither to the Sample sector (because it is defined below the employment threshold of 100 workers) nor to the workers employed through contractors.

17 This index is defined by the author as the proportion of contract workers to all workers in the manufacturing sector. As the proportion of contract worker increases, this index attains higher values and demonstrates a rise in LMF.

18 Needless to say, pro-worker (pro-employer) amendments were meant for benefiting workers (employers). Neutral amendments had no a priori impact on either group. For coding purposes, the following procedure was adopted:

In years in which there were multiple amendments, we use an indicator of the general direction of change. So, for example, if there were four pro-worker amendments in a given state and year, we would only code this as plus one rather than plus four. Coding in this manner gives us a total of nineteen changes in our period.

(Besley and Burgess 2004: 7)

19 Control states were: Assam, Bihar, Haryana, Jammu and Kashmir, Punjab and Uttar Pradesh. Pro-employer states were: Andhra Pradesh, Karnataka, Kerala, Madhya Pradesh, Rajasthan and Tamil Nadu. Pro-worker states were: Gujarat, Maharashtra, Orissa and West Bengal.
20 This was done to check the robustness of their basic result. These variables were: state's development expenditure on health, education, infrastructure and administration. The state's installed power generation capacity per capita; Bhattacharjea 2006 draws attention to the fact that the installed capacity parameter is misleading when assessing the general status of infrastructure in a state, for, among other things, there can be trade in power between states via regional grids. So power consumption need not be circumscribed by power generation, population, ruling political parties and state or year fixed effects.
21 With regard to employment, the authors took the total number of employees (as against workers) from the ASI, which includes both production workers and those in supervisory or managerial positions. However, IDA explicitly states that Chapter VB applies only to workers and not to persons in a supervisory or managerial capacity.
22 This was true for industrial performance at both state and industry levels, and also for poverty.
23 Besley and Burgess (2004: 21–22) anticipate this criticism and argued:

> The fact that our results are not robust to state specific time trends does raise the question of whether the effects that we are picking up are those due to labor regulations per se or the consequences of a poor climate of labor relations – union power and labor/management hostility – which affect the trend rate of growth within a state.

However, they failed to give a satisfactory answer to this question.
24 It is indeed intriguing to note the peculiar outcomes of the coding procedure followed by Besley and Burgess. Gujarat and Maharashtra emerge as pro-worker states, whereas Kerala is designated as a pro-employer state. However, a World Bank study [quoted in Anant et al. (2006): 256] reports that small and medium enterprises in Kerala receive twice as many factory inspections per year as did Maharashtra and Gujarat. Scepticism with the coding procedure further arises as Bhattacharjea (2006) draws attention to the findings of an India Labour Report (Team Lease Services 2006). This Report, using a different coding technique of state-level amendments to the IDA, along with many direct indicators of enforcement and industrial disputes, ranks Maharashtra, Karnataka, Punjab and Gujarat, in that order, as being most conducive to employment creation. In Besley's and Burgess's study, these states are respectively categorized as pro-worker, pro-employer, neutral and pro-worker (more on this below).

25 There are two appendices describing the procedure of assigning scores to each state-level amendment (coding) adopted by the authors. Appendix 2 of the paper by Besley and Burgess (2004) provides a synopsis of the amendments. Another appendix is available at Burgess's website (www.lse.ac.uk/economics/people/facultyPersonalPages/facultyFiles/Robin-Burgess/LabourRegulationData0803.pdf; accessed on 12 July 2017), which furnishes a more detailed summary of the amendments.

26 Gujarat is designated as a pro-worker state because of only one amendment in 1973, allowing for a penalty of Rs.50 per day on employers for not nominating representatives to firm-level joint management councils. Bhattacharjea (2006) provided examples from micro-level studies in Gujarat about why such specifications can be completely misleading. He cited Streefkerk (2001), a study which shows a rise in casualisation, feminization and contractualization of the workforce and factory inspectors being routinely paid off by employers. Quoting Breman (2004: 160–169), Bhattacharjea adduced evidence on thousands of workers having lost their jobs in the collapse of Ahmedabad's textile factories in the 1980s and 1990s and being unable to secure their statutory benefits.

27 Kerala is designated as pro-employer, notwithstanding other factors, on the basis of just two amendments (in 50 years), both passed in 1979. These are: (a) Prohibition of strikes and lockouts when in public interest, and (b) Imposing a penalty for not complying with an order prohibiting industrial disputes.

28 For Maharashtra there was another amendment coded as +1 (i.e. in a pro-worker direction, namely, 'gives power of appeal to workers to overturn decision to close down firm') [see Appendix 2 of Besley and Burgess (2004)]. However, Bhattacharjea (2009: 57) notes:

The Maharashtra amendment gave both employers and workers the right to appeal, and should be regarded as neutral rather than pro-worker. Even if we regard it as pro-worker, it took effect from 1981, rather than 1983 as erroneously tabulated by BB [Besley and Burgess], thus according to aggregation rule should not have affected Maharashtra's score in 1981 because other pro-worker amendments took effect in the same year.

(emphasis added)

29 However, Bhattacharjea (2009: 57) notes that 'the Orissa amendment did nothing of the sort, and was identical to the central amendment'.

30 The experience of Maharashtra shows why the coding system is extremely misleading. Bhattacharjea (2006) notes that although Maharashtra passed supposedly 'pro-worker' amendments to the IDA in the early 1980s, the textile workers' strike was brutally suppressed in the state. Subsequently, mass retrenchment of employees was undertaken to stop the formation of a union in Reliance Textile Industries. State government, despite repeated High Court orders, refused to refer the matter to a labour court as stipulated under Section 12(5) of IDA.

31 Failure to appreciate the relative importance of different amendments [to Sections 25-K and 25-O] in various states also come to the fore in

case of Maharashtra, Orissa and West Bengal. For details, see Bhattacharjea (2009: 57).

32 Bhattacharjea (2006) points out that Section 31 of the Industrial Disputes (Amendment and Miscellaneous Provisions) Act of 1956 stipulates that IDA would not override any state laws on industrial disputes that were already in force. Moreover, according to Article 254 of the Constitution, if any provision of a state law is 'repugnant to' a central law on a matter falling within the Concurrent List, the state law will be void to the extent of the repugnancy. But the state law will prevail if it has been enacted later and has received the assent of the President of India.

33 For further discussion on the subject, see Bhattacharjea (2009: 57).

34 The state of Andhra Pradesh is an interesting case in point; see Bhattacharjea (2006) for details.

35 The original Besley-Burgess index was strongly correlated with the disputes index, but only weakly to the employment protection legislative (EPL) index and the Chapter VB index.

36 Interestingly, this is so, even though they found evidence for these two types of amendments to be mutually reinforcing each other.

37 For an elaborate discussion on this subject and the implications of non-inclusion of high court judgements in construction of Besley-Burgess index and Ahsan-Pagés index, see Bhattacharjea (2009: 58).

38 This was on the ground that it was restricting one's constitutional right of carrying on business.

39 Bhattacharjea (2009: 58) concretely provides an example of the bitter legal battle between Rajasthan Trade Union Kendra (RTUK) and J K Synthetics.

40 These benefits, however, are not uniformly available to all organised sector workers but vary considerably across firms and industries. These benefits include health insurance for employees, accidental benefits, severance pay, maternity leave, provident funds and other post-retirement benefits, availability of physical amenities like crèches, rest rooms and subsidized canteens, among others.

41 This holds true for other studies also. See, for example, Sundar (2005: 2275); Papola (1994: 11); Ghosh (2004: 2); Chandrasekhar (2005: 774).

42 Chapter VB of IDA 1947 clearly demonstrates:

> The provisions of this Chapter [VB] shall apply to an industrial establishment (not being an establishment of a seasonal character or in which work is performed only intermittently) in which not less than 2*[one hundred] workmen were employed on an average per working day for the preceding twelve months.
>
> (2*: means it applies to whole of India)

43 With regard to Chapter VB, IDA 1947 clearly states its domain of application as: 'For the purposes of this Chapter[VB], – (a) "industrial establishment" means – (a) a factory as defined in clause (m) of section 2 of the Factories Act, 1948... (b) a mine ... or (c) a plantation... [are considered]'. Now Sections 2m(i) and 2m(ii) of the Factories Act 1948 define a factory as:

'factory' means any premises including the precincts thereof- (a) whereon ten or more workers are working, or were working on any day of the preceding twelve months, and in any part of which a *manufacturing* process is being carried on with the aid of power, or is ordinarily so carried on, or (b) whereon twenty or more workers are working, or were working on any day of the preceding twelve months, and in any part of which a *manufacturing* process is being carried on without the aid of power.

(emphasis added) (Factories Act 1948)

Notice that the Factories Act emphasizes the working unit to be engaged in *manufacturing* activity as borne out from the following: '[A]ny premises or part thereof, *shall not be construed to make it a factory if no manufacturing process is being carried on in such premises or part thereof*' (emphasis added) – hence it is clear that firms engaged in the services industries and agriculture are *not* governed by Sections 2m(i) and 2m(ii) of the Factories Act and therefore are also *out* of the ambit of Chapter VB of IDA.

44 The analysis restricted up to 2008–09 since inclusion of later years may vitiate analysis, because global financial crisis adversely affected India's manufacturing sector, in particular (see Economic Survey 2012–13: ch.9).
45 Data on the organised manufacturing sector are taken from ASI, various issues. Due to changes in the coverage of the ASI frame over the years, suitable adjustments were made in data to make it comparable over time following the procedure suggested by Kannan and Reveendran (2009: 82).
46 In fact, to implement its view on rationalisation (i.e. reduction) of the workforce by various means, including voluntary retirement schemes (VRS), the Indian government constituted a dedicated fund to that end, namely, the National Renewal Fund (NRF), as part of its 1991 reform process 'to provide funds [among others] . . . for compensation of employees affected by restructuring or closure of industrial units both in the public and private sector' (Zagha 1999: 167). However, the NRF was mainly used for shedding off workers from the public sector. As of July 1995, it was estimated that the dedicated fund enabled the retrenchment of 78,000 labourers from the public sector and further aimed to reduce 2 million workers (Zagha 1999). For a similar argument, see Nagaraj (2004).
47 Organised manufacturing employment in private ownership enterprises was more than 70 percent on average during the period 1979–97, according to the ASI data. After that, due to a revision in the tabulation scheme of ASI, certain sectors, such as electricity and water supply were deleted from the ASI frame and were covered separately. Hence, data for the subsequent years are not strictly comparable. Interestingly, the share of the public sector in organised manufacturing employment plummeted to only 8 percent in 1999 after the revision of the ASI frame from 23 percent in 1997 (with the private sector now constituting 86 percent in 1999, up from 71 percent in 1997), and its share has been continuously falling since then. For example, in 2007–08, the

public sector's share was only 1 percent of organised manufacturing employment (see Figure 2.2A in Appendix).

48 This had a major impact in pulling the overall growth rate of the organised sector, since, as already discussed, the share of the public sector in the total organised sector employment has been 60 percent or above throughout the period under observation.

49 Papola (1994: 13) points out that even removing legal obstacles on the labour front for closure of units is not a sufficient condition for smooth closures, since additionally, 'provisions in company and insolvency law, and legal procedures associated with them are found to be serious bottlenecks in eventually closing down a unit legally'.

50 Labour hoarding is claimed to be an undesirable consequence of stringent JSR. This is because firms may have to unwillingly carry forward a portion of their redundant workforce, pending government permission. Now, since firms unwillingly retain a part of their unused labour force – labelling it as 'hoarding' is a misnomer. This is because economic agents typically 'hoard' voluntarily for profit motives; they never do it unwillingly. It is argued that with the economic environment turning bright, firms first use up their unused or hoarded (as well as employed) labour force too exhaustively and only then go for fresh recruitments. It is undesirable from the point of view of firms since, they cannot shed their unused labour force (as large parts of their capital stock are left unused due to lack of aggregate demand); it is also undesirable for the workers since existing workers are used up more vigorously and new recruitments are delayed until such intensive margins are reached.

51 Fallon and Lucas (1991: 396) notes:

> In very broad terms one might expect that making jobs more secure would make employers less able to make rapid adjustments to changing market conditions. But, in addition, restricting employers' ability to fire workers may actually reduce the size of the work force employers wish to maintain.

52 Although we shall show later that there is very little to celebrate this phenomenon.

53 We shall discuss, albeit briefly, the employment trends beyond this time period as well.

54 Coefficient of Variation (CV) is a pure number used for measuring relative dispersion (variability). It is calculated as, CV = (Standard Deviation / Mean) × 100. See Das (1997: 242).

55 Even when genuinely warranted for sustaining in business putting a drag on employment creation.

56 Workers employed through contractors are not governed by Chapter VB of IDA.

57 Output growth in the manufacturing sector showed a distinctly upward jump (see Panel: A of Table 2.4 below) with the advent of economic reforms in 1991 in response to the 'pent-up demand' in the economy. Once this demand was met by 1997, such growth petered out thereafter (Ghosh and Chandrasekhar 2002: 60).

58 Except for the 100–199 category in one of the sub-periods (1979–90) for employment and sub-period (1998–02) for number of factories. The

reported trends of CVs for output, employment and factories broadly remain the same, albeit with minor exceptions, for a decadal analysis and are reported in appendix Table 2.1A.

59 We restricted our analysis until 2007–08 because the inclusion of 2008–09 data may vitiate the analysis due to the possible repercussions of the global financial crisis on India.

60 Except for 1,000 and above category where employment growth is negative in all sub-periods. But this phenomenon of employment growth being higher in small and midsized firms (categorized by employment-size class) in organised manufacturing and turning negative in large sized firms is a long-term trend and has little to do with JSR [see Goldar (2000: 1193)]. Nagaraj (2000: 3446) notes:

> [T]he faster growth of employment in smaller sized factories, and loss of employment in larger [employment] size classes . . . has been taking place over the last five decades. For instance, in the factory sector, the average factory size fell from over 140 workers per factory in 1950, to less than 60 in 1976.

However, JSR came into existence only in 1976.

61 Micro-level evidence on labour flexibility also reports such anomalies. Findings from a survey carried out in Bombay during 1987–88 testify the following: 'In fact, it was the medium and large firms – though supposedly constrained by restrictive laws and unions – that increased employment *more* than the small firms' (emphasis added) (Sudha Deshpande *et al.* 1998 quoted in Sundar 2005: 2277). The exception of 1,000 and above category is well appreciated in the literature. Anant *et al.* (2006: 257) report (Figures 5.11 and 5.12 in their page 258):

> What we see [during the period 1973/4 to 1997/8] is that the 100–999 size class has increased (as a percentage of total employment) much more than the below-100 size class. *The presumed deceleration of employment seems valid only in the case of 1000+ size class employment.* It is possible that the employment decline of 1000+ size establishments is due less to the labor laws than to the substantial restructuring of large public sector units and traditional manufacturing units (cotton textiles, jute manufacturing, steel and engineering). Thus, these data do not seem to support the presumed employment effect of the labor laws.
>
> (emphasis added)

Sharma and Sasikumar (1996), studying 233 manufacturing firms in Ghaziabad and Noida industrial belt, found that neither employment growth nor fixed capital investments of firms were constrained by labour laws.

62 See Goldar (2011: Table 2: 21).

63 Except for 1998–99, most probably due to the revision in the ASI frame undertaken that year.

64 See Guha (2009). Bhattacharjea (2006: 9) points out the 1984 amendment to IDA as the source (through contractual labour) which introduced labour flexibility *within* the organised manufacturing segment:

> the 1984 amendment also changed the definition of 'retrenchment' in Section 2(oo) so as to exclude from its purview any termination

of service resulting from the non-renewal of a contract or under a stipulation contained in the contract. This would be conducive to *greater* flexibility, because retrenchment requires notice and payment of compensation for establishments covered by Chapter V-A (those employing at least 50 workers), plus official permission for those covered by Chapter V-B.

(emphasis in original)

65 Micro-level studies lend support to such a hypothesis on the basis of an extensive survey of 1,300 manufacturing firms in nine industries across 10 states of India. Lalit Deshpande *et al.* (2004) observe that contract labour is a principal means of introducing flexibility in the labour market. Sundar (2005: 2277) notes the following from the findings of Deshpande's study:

> The percentage of permanent manual employment decreased during 1991–98 [from 69 percent to 62 percent]; percentage share of casual among non-permanent increased; more than one-third of manual employment belonged to the non-permanent category (i.e. temporary plus casual); if contract labour is added then the share of non-regular (non-permanent plus contract) is 42 percent. Large firms (1,000+ workers) reported using more non-permanent especially casual labour; . . . The macro data offers support to flexibisation tendencies in the labour market.

Further, undertaking retrenchment was not a problem, as Papola (1994: 12) reports that about 36,000 workers lost their jobs due to closure of several mills in Ahmedabad during 1983 and 1984.
66 Supreme Court case, 2010: GM, BSNL & Ors vs. Mahesh Chand.
67 Steel Authority of India Ltd (SAIL) & Others vs. National Union of Waterfront workers & Others.
68 On how aggregate demand constraint precipitated the industrial stagnation of mid-sixties, see Nayyar (1994).
69 Bagchi's (2002: 245) observation in this context is interesting:

> In the neo-liberal theology of adjustment in developing countries, the informal sector has been assigned a special place at the altar. It is supposed to correct the rigidities in the labour market introduced by government regulations, and act as a shock absorber when the economy is rocked by the need to correct serious imbalances.

70 Discussion below partially draws upon Roychowdhury (2014b).
71 For an explanation of employment slowdown in the organised segment, see Chapter 3. However, the experience of the 1980s in the unorganised manufacturing sector is consistent with the earlier finding of rising contractualization of the workforce in the organised segment. The inability of the unorganised manufacturing sector – arguably where all employment is on contractual basis – to grow (both in terms of output and employment) during the 1980s could be due to entirely different reasons. For a discussion see footnote 72.
72 A number of studies provide detailed analyses of the observed output and employment patterns in the unorganised sector for different periods. Between 1984 and 1989, there was a marked departure in

industrial policy from earlier periods under the Rajiv Gandhi government. It is widely recognised that in an attempt to foster domestic competition, the economy was partially liberalised, having 'delicensed several industries; increased the ceiling of investment for big business houses; relaxed rules for importation of foreign technology; replaced quantitative trade restrictions with tariffs, and lowered tariff barriers overall...' (Varshney 2001 quoted in Rani and Unni 2004: 4569). The unorganised manufacturing sector was adversely affected by these policy changes – as it had limited capacity to withstand such competitive pressures (Subrahmanya 2009 discussed in Kapila 2009: 361–367). The two major changes in this period were: (a) first delicensing 32 groups of industries without any investment limit and then in 1988 exempting all industries from obtaining license except for a specified negative list of 26 industries (Kapila 2009: 326) and (b) exposing a set of domestic producers to foreign competition by the import policy of 1980s – by including some capital goods and intermediate goods in the open general license (OGL) category. Thus, in the face of the rising competition from large domestic firms and foreign competition in the capital and intermediate goods sector, the performance of the unorganised manufacturing sector turned dismal during the second half of the 1980s. With the advent of liberalisation in 1991, both these tendencies got accelerated, along with progressive dereservation of manufacturing items previously preserved only for the small-scale sector. As the competitive forces were unleashed more vigorously, it caused 'displacement of existing domestic production either directly by imports or indirectly by new products assembled domestically from imported inputs' (Ghosh and Chandrasekhar 2002: 56). This trend was more prominent in the unorganised manufacturing segment, causing both output and employment growth to turn negative in the first half of the 1990s.

73 Wage rates are defined as wages per manday worked.
74 Lucas elsewhere identifies the source of rising wages in collective bargaining: 'A rather complex minimum wage law prevails in India, but collective bargaining, rather than updating of the legal minimum, has probably been the main force behind the steady rise in real, industrial wages over at least the last three decades' (Fallon and Lucas 1993: 245).
75 Actually, there are nine (not eight) industries for which β are not reported, since they turned out to be positive. These were: Dairy Products, Cotton Mills, Paper, Leather, Rubber Products, Toiletries, Railway Equipment, Motor Vehicles and Cycles (compare Table 9.4: 201–202 with the table in Appendix to the Chapter).
76 The nine industries for which β are not statistically significant even at 10 percent significance level were: Tobacco Products, Synthetic Textiles, Oil Products, Plastics, Other Chemicals, Cement, Non-ferrous Metals, Agricultural Machineries and Miscellaneous Manufacturing (see the t-statistics in Appendix table).
77 The dependent variable of the employment function is employment, and independent variables are real wage, value added and employment, with one period lag. All variables are expressed in terms of their natural logarithm values.

78 However, Bhalotra (1998: 18), from the World Bank, estimating a capital-constraining model for a slightly different time period [1979–87], noted:

> Given trend wage growth of 4.2 percent p.a. [per annum], a long-run elasticity of -0.44 implies a decline in employment of 1.85 percent p.a., ceteris paribus. Using the unrestricted model produces an even more conservative figure of 1.26 percent p.a. In either case, the claim that wages alone can account for a rate of employment decline of 5.7 percent p.a. (World Bank 1989: 110) is seriously undermined.

Estimating the output constrained model similar to the World Bank, with some modifications (like introducing actual hours worked, productivity and cyclical demand as explanatory variables in the regression equation), Bhalotra noted:

> Holding constant output and other factors, trend growth in the wage of 4.2 percent p.a. over the sample period implies a decline in employment of 1.18 percent p.a. This is again substantially smaller than the 5.7 percent p.a. decline claimed by the World Bank report.
>
> (ibid.: 22)

In her study, the employment downturn in the 1980s was explained mainly in terms of growth in productivity and actual hours worked and less in terms of hourly product wage.

79 Labour augmenting technical progress would also explain the observed rise in capital intensity in production.

80 With the exception of the 100–199 category in sub-period 1980–90; and 1,000 and above category for 1991–97.

81 Ahluwalia also accepts the employment overhang argument (acting as a dampener on current employment prospects).

82 Papola (1994), in fact, argues that the observed employment downturn during the 1980s is a mere reflection of industry specific effects in two industries. Papola (1994: 10) notes:

> a stagnation or a slight decline in employment in this sector [organised manufacturing] during this period [first half of the 80s] was, to a large extent, accounted for by a large reduction in employment in only two major industry group, namely Cotton Textiles and Food Products. Accounting for a share of about 20 percent in total employment, cotton textiles experienced a decline of about 3.6 percent per annum in employment, reducing the number of workers by about 3 lakhs between 1980–81 and 1988–89. Similarly, food products group, accounting for the next largest share of 13 percent in organised manufacturing employment, also experienced a similar rate of decline in employment, primarily in the sub-group of sugar where employment in absolute terms declined by about two lakhs during this period. Decline in these two industries was caused mainly by the closure of a large number of mills due to sickness caused by several reasons and rationalisation of many of them to overcome obsolescence. Most other industry groups, including those with high wage levels and capital intensity, experienced growth in employment.

Chapter 3

Explanation of jobless growth in Indian manufacturing and trends in labour conditions

Discussions in Chapter 2 confirmed that the two propositions normally advanced in the literature to explain jobless growth in Indian manufacturing could not stand scrutiny. However, the question remains – what explains the observed phenomenon of jobless growth in registered manufacturing? In Section 3.1, we advance the true reason (in our view) for the employment downturn in the 1980s and afterwards. The observed rise in capital intensity of production in the organised manufacturing sector is also explained. Another crucial objective of this chapter – in view of the alleged rise in labour militancy causing work disruptions – is to examine the trends in labour conditions in the organised sector (with special reference to organized manufacturing) between 1980 and the present. This is done in Section 3.2.

3.1 What caused jobless growth in Indian manufacturing? An empirical investigation

Below we investigate the reason behind the employment downturn in the 1980s and employment stagnation thereafter. Since the variable of interest is 'number of workers' (actually we are interested in its growth rate), let us directly investigate the *method* applied by the Annual Survey of Industries (ASI) to enumerate workers. The figure on 'number of workers' furnished by ASI is a *derived* estimate. ASI follows the following methodology: 'The number of workers or employees is an average number obtained by dividing mandays worked by the number of days the factory had worked during the reference year' (ASI Report 2011; *Annexure-III*: Concepts and Definitions). Now if the numerator (i.e. number of mandays worked) rises only moderately, while the denominator shows a sharp upturn (i.e. number of days factory had worked), then this would simply manifest itself as *smaller size* of the workforce.

The available evidence suggests that something of this nature has happened in the first half of the 1980s (Figure 3.1). While there is no evidence of an exceptional rise in total mandays worked, registering annual growth of 0.88 percent between 1981–82 and 1986–87 – however, during the same period, number of days factory had worked[1] went up very sharply, recording 2.33 percent growth per annum – precisely when employment growth turned negative.[2] Now extending the number of days (in a year) factories worked is analogous to extending the working time (during a day) of existing workers, in the face of rising demand. In the latter case, workers work overtime, whereas Indian manufacturing seem to have extended the number of working days in a year (which might have also been accompanied by the extension of working hours in a day).[3] Thus, the employment downturn in the early 1980s is largely interpreted as a mere statistical outcome of the *way* the number of workers is estimated by ASI.[4] Simply put, in estimating 'number of workers' – as the term occurring in the numerator, namely, number of mandays worked increased at a *slower* rate than the denominator, namely, number of days factory worked – this resulted in persistently throwing up *lower* estimates of employment during the 1980s (compared to the 1970s).

But coupled with the above phenomenon, data suggests that another force may be at work to put a drag on employment during the first half of the 1980s. Employment (L) growth in any period is determined by the difference between two variables, namely, the growth rate of output (O) and the growth rate of labour productivity (O/L). Moreover, the growth rate of labour productivity can be expressed as the sum of the growth rate of capital productivity (O/K) and the growth rate of capital intensity (K/L). Further, if it is the case in any period that capital intensity increases whereas capital productivity remains constant, then this is regarded as labour-augmenting (saving) technological progress (Hahn and Matthews 1964).[5] Let us now try to make sense of Table 3.1, taken from Ahluwalia (1992).

It is easy to see that the negative employment growth of the manufacturing sector as a whole during the period 1980–81 to 1985–86 can be explained by a faster growth in labour productivity over output growth, due to the underlying nature of technical progress being labour-augmenting in nature. Ahluwalia (1992: 79)

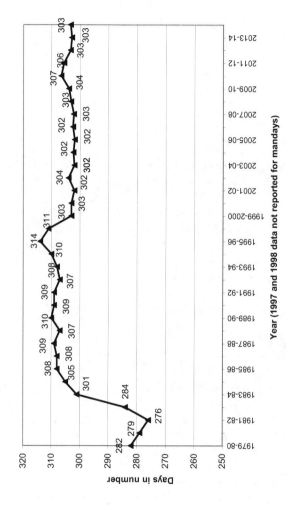

Figure 3.1 Number of days worked in a year (all manufacturing)
Source: ASI, various years

Table 3.1 Growth rate of output, employment, labour productivity, capital intensity and capital productivity between 1980–81 and 1985–86 (%)

Used based classification	Output	Empt.	O/L	K/L	O/K
Manufacturing	7.5	–0.7	8.3	8.4	0
Intermediate goods	6.5	0.8	5.6	6.8	–1.1
Consumer non-durables	7.6	–3	10.9	10.5	0.4
Consumer durables	14.2	2.4	11.5	8.4	2.8
Capital goods	7.8	1.6	6.1	5.7	0.4

Note: O/L represents labour productivity, K/L represents capital-intensity and O/K represents capital-productivity.
Source: Ahluwalia 1992: 74–76

recognises this phenomenon but strangely explains the employment downturn in terms of rising real wages:

> In terms of partial productivity measures the most notable development in the first half of the eighties was that capital productivity was no longer declining. As capital intensity recorded a strong acceleration over the eighties compared with earlier period, there was understandably a strong acceleration in the growth of labour productivity. *But this was not associated with a decline in capital productivity.*
>
> (emphasis added)

Now the phenomenon of rising capital intensity associated with *non-declining* capital productivity (in fact, for the manufacturing sector as a whole Ahluwalia finds the output-capital ratio to be *constant* during her study period; see Table 3.1) *cannot* be explained if movements along a *given* production function are considered (yet we found in Chapter 2 that Lucas, the World Bank and Ahluwalia for theoretical consistency must assume this in interpreting their empirical results).[6] This phenomenon can only be explained by labour-augmenting technological progress (Harrod-neural type) where the production function shifts upward (see Hanh and Matthews 1964: 827). Under conditions of technological progress, when production function shifts, *no causal relationship between wages and employment can be ascertained, a priori.*

This trend of labour-saving technological progress was also prominent in the consumer non-durables and capital goods segment, where the rise in capital intensity was coupled with almost close to zero change in capital productivity, whereas in the intermediate goods segment no such trend was visible. However, in the consumer durables section, labour productivity was boosted due to the dual effect of a rise in *both* capital intensity and capital productivity. Hence, the fall in manufacturing employment in the first half of the 1980s is better explained by an almost across-the-board technological upgrading (barring intermediate goods segment) of a labour-saving variety and *not* by rising real wages.[7]

Finally, it may be argued that the *nature* of technological progress was of the labour-saving variety *due to* the rising real cost of labour. But there is no empirical evidence or theoretical model to support this claim. In fact, it has been pointed out by observers that in developing countries like India, hardly any research and development (R&D) activity and innovation take place; mostly these activities are undertaken in the advanced capitalist world, and developing countries simply *adopt* them over time (Patnaik 2011b: 113). Thus, technological progress in developing countries are mostly *exogenously* determined by the *nature* (mostly labour-saving variety) and pace (introduced with a lag) of technological innovations carried out in the developed world (ibid.: 113). On the other hand, in so far as production in developing countries takes place under the aegis of multinational corporations (MNCs), capital goods are often directly imported from the metropolis. Essential features of the production techniques embodied in these imported capital goods were noted by Joan Robinson (1979: 112) as:

> The high capital to labour ratio in such plants is accounted for by the fact that they embody highly mechanised techniques of production, pioneered in the West in conditions of scarcity of labour, and the low level of utilization is due to the large minimum size of investment required to produce such outputs at all . . . but the cost of capital to the transnational corporation is lower because the research and development were paid for long ago, and sometimes the physical equipment is second hand.

In such a scenario, it is impossible to attribute labour-saving technological progress – that characterized the organised manufacturing sector – *to* the rising real cost of labour. In any case, technological progress is normally treated in the literature as an exogenous factor *autonomously* determined rather than driven by factor prices.[8]

Table 3.2 Growth rate of labour productivity (O/L), capital intensity (K/L) and capital productivity (O/K)

Period	O/L	K/L	O/K
1974–75 to 1981–82	1.31	−0.48	1.79
1983–84 to 1991–92	5.78	4.26	1.46
1992–93 to 2004–05	6.72	7.26	−0.5
1983–84 to 2004–05	6.29	5.97	0.3

Source: Figures for 1974–81 are from Ghose (1994: 149) and others from Kannan and Raveendran (2009: 87–88)

The *nature* of technological upgrading mentioned above in the manufacturing sector has been its characteristic feature of late. From Table 3.2 it is clear that in the long period of partial-to-widespread liberalisation (1983–84 to 2004–05), the nature of technological progress was of a labour-saving variety; giving a boost to labour productivity – which explains the general tendency of 'joblessness' during this period. This phenomenon is, by and large, true for the period of rapid liberalisation as well (1992–93 to 2004–05).

Thus, the employment slowdown during the 1980s can be seen as a result of *two* separate forces, each contributing to increase labour productivity growth (and hence putting a drag on employment expansion *given* the growth rate of output). The sharp rise in labour productivity was due to the *joint* effect of rapid growth in capital intensity *and* capital productivity, indicating an across-the-board upgradation in technology. Note that although output growth rate was reported to rise during the 1980s, labour productivity also rose sharply during this period compared to the 1970s. This basically explains the phenomenon of 'jobless growth' during the 1980s. This explanation holds true for the long period (1983–84 to 2004–05) as well. Thus, it is labour-saving technological progress and *not* the real cost of labour that seems to be the *key* force behind employment deceleration during the 1980s and stagnation in the subsequent period.

3.2 Assessing labour conditions in the organised sector: special reference to the organised manufacturing sector

In this section, we investigate the conditions of labour in the organised sector, with special emphasis on the organised manufacturing sector. It is often alleged in policy circles that there has been a rise in labour militancy in the organised sector – owing to inflexible labour laws – resulting in developing labour market rigidities. These rigidities, causing frequent work stoppages, ultimately dampen employment and output growth.[9] In what follows, we shall adopt a method devised by Lucas (1988) for scrutinizing rigidities in the labour market, as pointed out by Nagaraj (1994: 180), namely: 'Following Lucas in examining *the trends in union power as a proxy for the alleged rigidities*[in labour market] . . . ' (emphasis added).

For examining the trends in union power, we choose certain indicators (some of these used by Lucas) both for the organised sector as a whole and particularly the manufacturing sector. Overall the organised sector is studied to test the following hypothesis empirically: whether labour regulations *contribute* to labour rigidities, *separately*. Specifically, it is tested whether the results of the indicators in case of organised manufacturing (where labour law applies) are very *different* from the overall organised sector (where labour law applies only to a subset) or, are there *similarities* in outcome between these indicators? If these show *similar* trends, then one can conclude that labour regulations *separately* do not cause labour rigidities.

First, we look at the proportion of functional (i.e. those submitting returns) trade unions (TUs) to total registered TUs for all organised industries. Figure 3.2 shows that this share is steadily declining from the mid-1980s to the present. The share of functional TUs rapidly fell from just below 25 percent in the mid-1980s to marginally above 10 percent in 2008–09.[10] Thus, trade unionism at the all (organised) industries level clearly shows a declining trend during the period under observation.

Let us now look at the number of disputes (strikes and lockouts) at the all (organised) industries level. Figure 3.3 shows that the number of strikes – identified with labour militancy and expected to go up with a rise in union power – has been steadily declining during the last three decades. However, the same cannot be claimed in the case of lockouts, widely identified as a disciplining device in the hands of employers[11] – which showed a stable trend until 1998–99, falling only thereafter. It is interesting to note that in the early 1980s, the number of disputes due to strikes were nearly four-times the number of lockouts, whereas from the mid-1990s they tend to converge. From this it may be inferred that the union power in recent years has declined considerably relative to that of

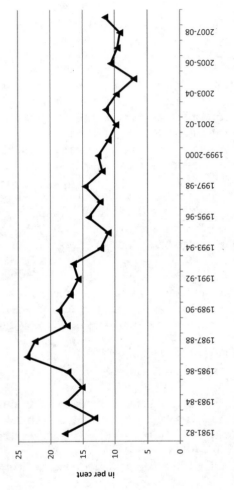

Figure 3.2 Share of functional (submitting returns) TUs in total registered TUs: all industries

Note: Data after 2008–09 not comparable as number of registered TUs fell by 75% due to large number of non-responding States and UTs; (Report on Trade Unions in India 2010: 18; www.labour-bureau.gov.in/Trade_Unions_In_India_2010.pdf).

Source: Indian Labour Year Book, various issues

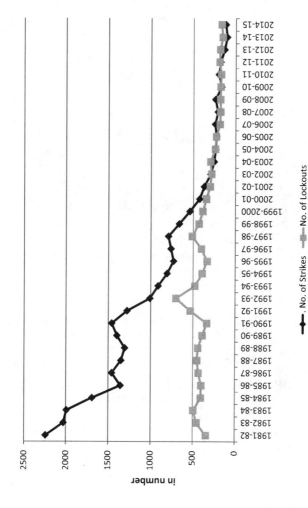

Figure 3.3 Number of strikes and lockouts in India: all industries

Source: Indian Labour Year Book, various issues

the employers. There is some recognition of this fact in the literature: 'For example, the fear of losing jobs has impelled unions to accept relocation, downsizing, productivity linked wages, freezes in allowances and benefits, voluntary suspension of trade union rights for a specific period and commitment to modernization' (Sharma 2006: 2083). This has further led to: 'The weakening of workers' bargaining capacity and rise in the militancy of employers are also manifested in the significant increase in the incidence of lockouts and a decline in the incidence of strikes' (ibid.: 2083).

However, it may be argued that the *effectiveness* of disputes does not depend on the number of disputes but on the number of mandays lost during such disputes.[12] Thus, we provide two more indicators for the organised sector as a whole, namely: (a) number of mandays lost per dispute (for both strikes and lockouts) (Figure 3.4), and (b) relative share of mandays lost due to strikes and lockouts (Figure 3.5). Both indicators reveal that lockouts are by far more effective than strikes. Note in Figure 3.4, the number of mandays lost per lockout far exceeds the number of mandays lost per strike (except for two years) over the last 34 years. Similarly, Figure 3.5 reveals that the share of mandays lost due to strikes exceeded that of the lockouts only for a brief period in the mid-1980s. From then onwards, the share of mandays lost due to lockouts has considerably exceeded the strikes (except for 2007–08 and 2010–11). Thus, it can be safely concluded that the bite of strikes in disrupting economic activity has been far less than lockouts.

Next, we turn to the manufacturing sector itself, where job security regulations (JSR) apply. It is frequently argued in the literature that workers protected by JSR (termed labour aristocracy) often indulge in unwarranted labour union activity (labour militancy), hampering output growth and employment creation, that goes against both the interest of enterprise as well as the larger society. From Figure 3.6 we investigate whether the 1982 amendment to the Industrial Disputes Act (IDA), 1947 boosted labour activism in the manufacturing sector.

For this, we calculate the share of unionized workers to total workers in the manufacturing sector (Figure 3.6). This, however, shows a stable trend over the last 28 years, with some improvement in the last two years under observation. Thus, there is no evidence of JSR translating to greater labour activism – in which case we would have witnessed a rising trend in unionized workers. But this may be argued as an insufficient proof of the proposition at hand,

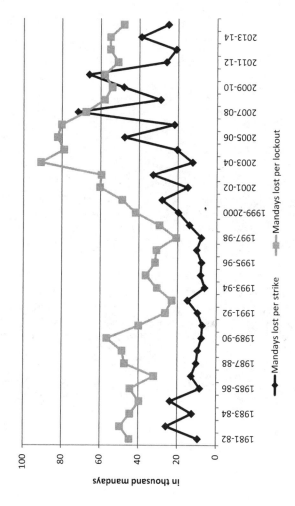

Figure 3.4 Number of mandays lost due to disputes (work stoppages): all industries
Source: Indian Labour Year Book, various issues

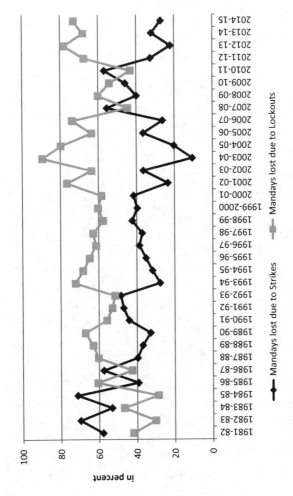

Figure 3.5 Relative share of mandays lost between strikes and lockouts: all industries

Source: Indian Labour Year Book, various issues

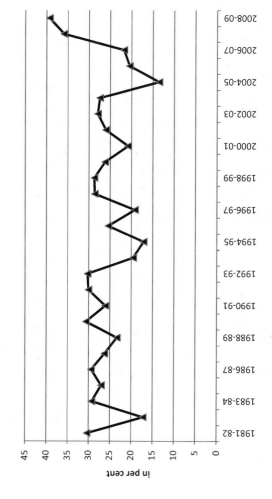

Figure 3.6 Share of unionised workers in total workers: manufacturing sector
Source: Indian Labour Year Book, various issues (see notes in Figure 3.2)

for even if unionisation of manufacturing workers was not on the rise, labour activism of *existing* unionized workers might nonetheless have increased. Therefore, we attempt a more direct proof. We investigate the number of disputes (Strikes + Lockouts) in organised manufacturing over the years (Figure 3.7). It is evident that the number of disputes came down drastically, which is inconsistent with the hypothesis of a rise in labour militancy.

For further evidence, we plot the number of workers (log value) involved in disputes and its share to total number of (organised) manufacturing sector workers. Figure 3.8 shows that both variables are consistently declining over time except for a brief period of four years – between 2002 and 2005 – when both variables registered an upturn. However, for more recent years both variables were far below the values attained at the advent of liberalisation in 1991. Thus, there is little evidence to suggest that labour militancy was on the rise during last three decades.

It may still be argued that the number of disputes or the number of workers involved and their proportion are not sufficient to adjudge the effectiveness of labour disputes since a small but strong union may paralyse economic activity and inflict large losses to enterprises in the manufacturing sector. To rule out such confusion, we calculate the share of mandays lost to the total number of mandays worked in Figure 3.9. This can be seen to fall unambiguously over time – leaving little room to substantiate any rise in labour militancy.

Next, we turn to the labour absenteeism rate[13] in the organised manufacturing sector. These data are compiled by ASI and pertain only to directly employed regular workers during the calendar year. They cover all establishments under Sections 2m(i) and 2m(ii) of the Factories Act, 1948 and bidi and cigar workers.

We find no evidence of labour indiscipline in terms of *increase* in labour absenteeism in the organised manufacturing sector (Figure 3.10). Note that after the 1982 amendment to IDA, there is no indication of an increase in the labour absenteeism rate. Labour absenteeism showed a rising trend only briefly with the advent of economic reforms in 1991; however, after 1993 it declined almost *secularly* – seen from the three-year moving average trend line.[14] Thus, absenteeism data do not corroborate a rise in labour militancy.

The foregoing empirical evidence broadly suggests that there are *similarities* in outcomes discernible between the organised sector as a whole and the organised manufacturing sector with respect to the

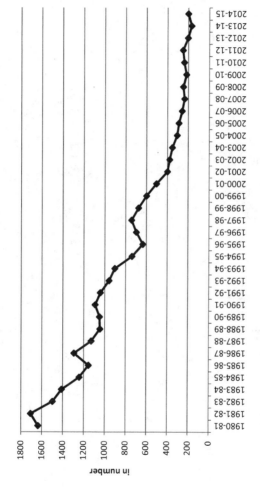

Figure 3.7 Number of disputes (strikes and lockouts) in the manufacturing sector

Source: Indian Labour Year Book and Indian Labour Statistics, various issues

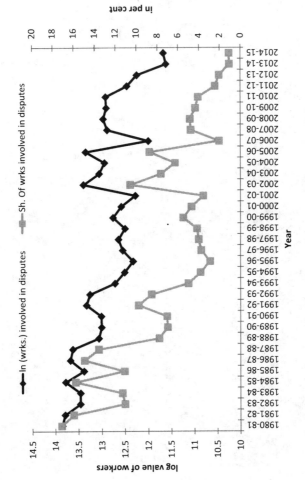

Figure 3.8 Number of workers involved in disputes and its share to total workers: manufacturing sector

Source: Indian Labour Year Book and Indian Labour Statistics, various issues

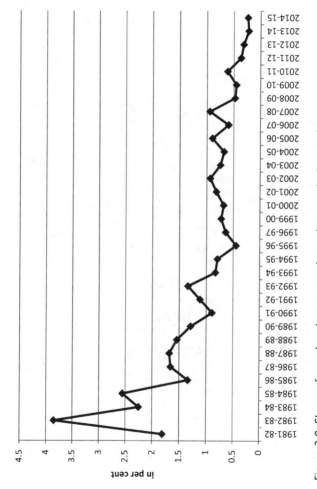

Figure 3.9 Share of mandays lost to total mandays worked: manufacturing sector
Source: Indian Labour Year Book, various issues

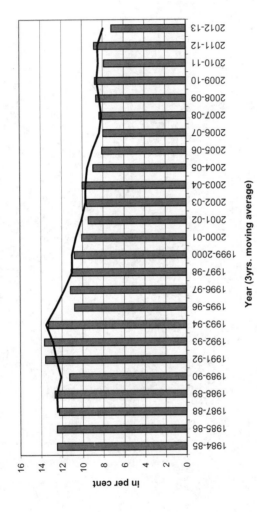

Figure 3.10 Labour absenteeism rate in organised manufacturing

Source: ASI Report on Absenteeism, Labour Turnover, Earnings, Employment and Labour Cost, various issues

indicators considered; hence, these indices confirm the hypothesis that labour regulations *separately do not* cause labour rigidities. In fact, they confirm that labour market rigidities captured by trend in union power – as suggested by Lucas – were on the *decline*.

Now we turn to see what happened to real and product wages.[15] Note that the living standard of workers does not depend on product wages but real wages, since industrial workers *inter alia* consume food which is produced *outside* the manufacturing sector.

Wages are considered as an important indicator of workers' bargaining power for:

> The increase in wage rate that is presumed to have taken place is seen as an evidence of growing rigidities in the labour market – namely, minimum wage legislation, (growing) strength of trade unions and increasingly stringent job security laws – as reflected in the power of organised labour to appropriate a share of output disproportionate to their contribution, at the expense of additional employment generation and with a socially undesirable rise in capital intensity.
>
> (Nagaraj 1994: 179–180)

To examine what happened on the ground, we plot the index number of real and product wages in Figure 3.11.

It can be seen that real wages and product wages were increasing roughly at a comparable pace up to 1995–96. From then onwards they started to diverge. The increase in the gap between product and real wages signifies that although workers were somewhat successful in bargaining for higher money-wages (looking at the price of their own products, although this was no match to the rapid rise in labour productivity; see Appendix Figure 3.1A) in the factory floor, it was not enough to keep up with the rise in the cost of living index.[16] Especially after the downturn hit the manufacturing sector in 1997–98, there was a sharp *absolute* decline in both product and real wages. Moreover, as the pace of product wage growth decelerated thereafter (up to 2008–09), real wages virtually stagnated for the next 15 years (even as product wage growth showed some recovery after 2008–09).[17] Chandrasekhar and Ghosh (2007) document the trends in real wages in the post-reform era:

> Meanwhile, contrary to public perception, the average real wage of workers in the organised manufacturing sector has

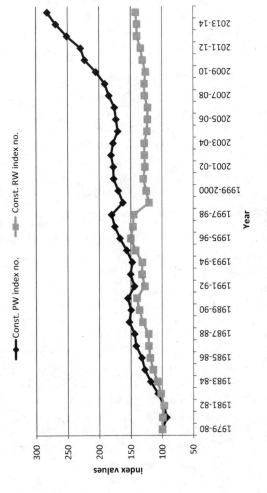

Figure 3.11 Index number of real wage (RW) and product wage (PW)
Source: Annual Survey of Industries, various issues

been more or less constant right through the 1990s. Average real wages increased in the early years of the 1990s, until 1995–96, and then fell quite sharply. The subsequent recovery after 1998 has been muted, and real wages have stagnated since 2000. *As a result, real wages in the triennium ending 2003–04 were around 11 percent lower than real wages in the triennium ending 1995–96.*

(emphasis added)

The foregoing discussion shows that since workers are interested in their real wages, there is little evidence to show that unions could successfully raise real wages and (real) product wages through bargaining.

Next, we look for an indicator which captures the basic working conditions in the industrial units covered under the Factories Act, 1948. These data pertain to the whole of the organised sector. As a proxy for safety in the workplace, we enumerate the share of fatal injuries as a percentage of total industrial injuries (Figure 3.12).[18] This shows a secularly rising trend throughout, especially after economic liberalisation in 1991.[19] Thus, unions were incapable of addressing even workers' basic safety issues in the workplace. This was because firms were now engaged in cost-cutting and as a result reduced safety norms in order to withstand intense international competition. Under these circumstances, it is difficult to believe that their grip over determining industrial outcomes in favour of the workers' group was actually rising. All the above indicators, in fact, show the very *opposite* of what is usually claimed by the orthodox economists. If the trend in union power is taken as a proxy for labour market rigidities – following Lucas – then it can be safely concluded that labour rigidities were on the *decline* in the last three decades. On the other hand, the employers' bargaining position seems to have strengthened during the same period – implying a sharp rise in 'employers' militancy' rather than growing 'workers' militancy'.[20]

Finally, we compute at the all-industry level the share of retrenchment- and layoff-related disputes in all disputes. These figures are furnished by employers.[21] Figure 3.13 shows the share of retrenchment- and layoff-related disputes to all disputes. It is interesting to note that, according to employers' reporting, the share of retrenchment- and layoff-related disputes never crossed four percent of total disputes in the last three decades. Even this share is falling

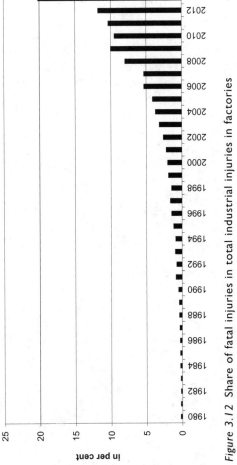

Figure 3.12 Share of fatal injuries in total industrial injuries in factories

Source: Indian Labour Year Book, various issues

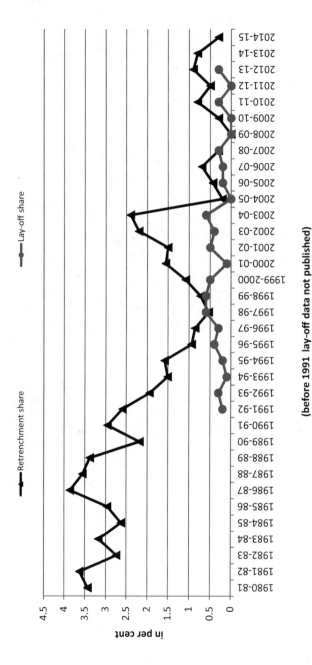

Figure 3.13 Proportion of retrenchment-and layoff-related disputes to all disputes

Source: Indian Labour Year Book, various issues

in the long run. Share of other disputes, from causes like workers' indiscipline and wage-related issues, far exceeds retrenchment- and layoff-related disputes. Thus, employers themselves do not perceive retrenchment and layoffs to be major impediments in the general working of factories. Therefore, highlighting this issue as one of critical importance finds no support in the data.

Conclusion

In this chapter I have tried to explain the observed behaviour of employment during the study period. Discussions in the first section revealed that the employment dynamics are better understood in *pure statistical* terms (how workers' estimates are derived by ASI) and in terms of the underlying *nature* of labour-saving technological progress rather than rising (real) labour cost.

In the second section, I analysed the trends in labour union activity using various indicators. Specifically following Lucas (1988), I examined trends in trade union power, regarded as a proxy of labour market rigidities. Any rise in trade union power is interpreted as a confirmation of rising labour market rigidities. Going by various indicators, we concluded that labour rigidities were *falling* in the last three decades. If anything, 'employers' militancy' was on the rise. Further, comparing the results of the organised manufacturing sector (JSR applies) with the organised sector *as a whole*, we inferred that labour regulations *do not* contribute to labour market rigidities, *separately*.

From the discussions carried out in Chapters 2 and 3 it can be safely concluded that the empirical evidence in favour of implementing LMF stands on rather shaky grounds. In subsequent chapters, we investigate the soundness of the theoretical foundations underlying LMF.

Appendix

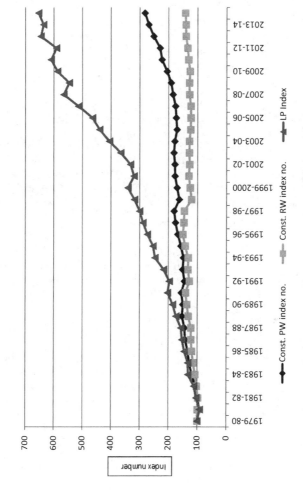

Figure 3.1A Index number of labour productivity (LP), product wage (PW) and real wage (RW)
Source: Annual Survey of Industries, various issues

Notes

1 This figure is obtained by dividing 'total mandays worked' by the 'number of workers' reported in ASI.
2 With alternative periodisation 1980–81 to 1985–86 used by Ahluwalia (1992), the same result holds: while total mandays worked increased in this time span by 1.8 percent per annum, annual growth in the number of days the factory had worked increased by 2.5 percent. Probably due to increased competitive pressures – after partial liberalisation in the 1980s – the factory sector had to operate more intensively. Operations at the intensive margin were possible by using up days which were earlier unutilized. In response to greater output demand, firms simply responded by utilizing the existing workforce more intensively and not by furthering new recruits. In fact, a portion of the existing workforce had to be retrenched.
3 That extension of working days could be successfully implemented (resulting in some retrenchment) shows that the bargaining power of workers was on the decline. Further, the extension of the number of working days became feasible, possibly due to the nature of technological progress (labour-saving type, discussed later) which made it physically possible to work for more days.
4 Note that there was some pressure to make the production process still more intensive until the mid-1990s; but since this method had already reached its limit by then, it was not possible to further intensify the production process. Hence, beyond the mid-1990s employment more or less varied proportionally with the fluctuations of aggregate demand.
5 However, if capital productivity falls then this is explained as pure substitution of labour by capital. If capital productivity increases, then this is explained as technical progress of a capital-saving variety. This is a standard result in economic growth theory:

When capital intensity rises, if capital productivity either remains unchanged or rises, production efficiency can be unambiguously said to have improved. In other words, with a positive rate of growth of capital intensity, if the rate of growth of labour productivity either equals or exceeds the rate of growth of capital intensity, a part of the growth of labour productivity is unambiguously attributable to an improvement in production efficiency. In these cases, the rise in capital intensity is most likely to have been associated with technology upgrading. When a rise in capital intensity is associated with a substantial decline in capital productivity, it is likely that there has been a mere substitution of capital for labour (Hahn and Matthews 1964; quoted in Ghose 1994: 148–149).

6 This is because along a given production function, the output-capital ratio must fall with rising capital intensity in production.
7 In any case, Papola (1994: 9) notes that:

> Increase in labour productivity measured as value added per worker increased in registered manufacturing sector at an annual average rate of 6.7 percent. And productivity growth has been much faster

than the increase in real wages in practically every industry group at 2-digit level. Also, high increases in real wages have generally been closely associated with high increase in productivity across industry groups. Overall correlation coefficient between annual in wages and in productivity during 1970–71 to 1987–88 for all industries works out as high as 0.91; in most industries it was higher than 0.70, significant at 1 percent level. Only industries it was not significant though positive are: Beverages, Tobacco and Tobacco products, Textile Products and Basic Metals, where real wage increases exceeded productivity. In leather and leather products where the coefficient is negative though not significant, productivity has increased much faster than wages.

So the causation may well run in the opposite direction, namely – from higher productivity to higher wages.

8 Ghose (1994) also recognises technical upgrading taking place in the 1980s but somehow tries to explain the increase in capital intensity in terms of relative factor price movements (and not labour augmenting technical progress, although he finds evidence of capital productivity remaining constant).
9 Perhaps by raising the effective labour cost (deterring employment creation) due to repeated halts in work and discouraging investment (deterring output growth) by raising the level of uncertainty in economy.
10 Figures for subsequent years are not included in the study since the number of states furnishing data fell drastically after 2008–09. For example, in 2009–10 the number of registered TUs and those submitting returns were just one quarter of those reported in 2008–09.
11 Sundar (2005: 2277) notes: 'The post-Bombay textile strike period witnessed more lockouts than strikes, the former being an important managerial strategy to weaken union power and is a flexibility device'.
12 Interestingly, Besley and Burgess (2004), conducting a regression analysis, explained mandays lost due to strikes and lockouts by the regulatory index constructed (for the details of index construction see Chapter 2) by them. Their result 'shows that labor regulation is strongly positively correlated with work days lost to strikes and lockouts per worker' (Besley and Burgess 2004: 8). Hence, there is some tradition in the literature to associate mandays lost due to strikes and lockouts with labour regulations; specifically, a fall in mandays lost is explained by falling labour rigidities.
13 The absenteeism rate is defined as the percentage of mandays lost due to absence to the number of mandays scheduled to work. Absence means failure of a worker to report for work when s/he is scheduled to work (i.e. when the employer has work available for him/her and the worker is aware of it). Authorised absence is also treated as absence, while presence for even part of a day or a shift is not considered as absence. Absence on account of strike, lock-out or layoff is not taken into account.
14 Up to 2000–01, data pertain to Census Sector only. From 2001 onwards, Labour Bureau clubbed the Census Sector data with the Sample Sector.

Hence, later years are not strictly comparable. However, a falling trend is discernible even if we restrict our analysis up to 2001. Absenteeism data for the years 1986–87, 1990–91 and 1998–99 were not collected.

15 Real wages are obtained by deflating nominal wages by the consumers' price index [for industrial workers; CPI(IW)] and for product wages, the deflator used is the producers' price index [WPI in India].

16 Ghose (1994: 157) underscores the point that the relative price of food to non-food articles plays an important role in determining the relationship between product and real wages:

When the relative price of food rises, consumer price rises faster than manufacturing price; when the relative price of food falls, manufacturing price rises faster than consumer price. It follows that the product-wage rate will rise faster (slower) than real wage rate whenever the relative price of food rises (falls).

17 Of course, the rise in relative price of food to non-food articles also played its role, after the mid-1990s, in withholding real wage growth. The wage stagnation hypothesis is well documented in the literature; Bhattacharjea (2006: 28) notes:

Several recent studies have shown that during the 1990s, real wages in organised manufacturing were almost stagnant on average, and actually declined in many industries; the growth rate of product wages decelerated; and both wage series lagged far behind labour productivity, whose growth accelerated. Consequently, the wage share of value added declined.

18 Statistics on injuries are obtained from industrial accidents by reason of which persons affected are prevented from attending work for a period of 48 hours or more immediately following the injury. Data on injuries pertain to only those factories submitting returns, as no estimate can be made for defaulting units.

19 A plausible explanation of rising share of fatal injuries could be under-reporting of non-fatal injuries and difficulty in concealing fatal injuries.

20 The decline in trade unionism is amply recognised in the literature; Anant et al. (2006: 251) notes: 'The final phase (1991 to present), coinciding with a vigorous acceleration of economic reforms, has seen a greater decline in public sector employment and a continued decline in the power of centralized unions'.

21 Hence, there is some suspicion among observers that the figures are under-reported (Nagaraj 2004: 3388). But since figures on all categories of disputes are furnished by employers and further we are considering percentage shares; therefore, we hope to normalize for under-reporting everywhere (there is no way we can check for the extent of under-reporting in each case and there is no evidence to claim that retrenchment, layoff figures carry any special bias).

Chapter 4

Identifying the theoretical structure underlying labour market flexibility and its critical examination

The argument

Earlier chapters clearly revealed that the empirical evidence in favour of introducing labour market flexibility (LMF) in India is far from satisfactory. Let us now examine the theoretical argument underlying LMF, *specifically, whether the theoretical foundation underlying the proposal for labour flexibility – that is essentially tantamount to watering down of job security regulations – can stand logical scrutiny.*[1]

Unfortunately, the theory which leads to the policy conclusions (of complete freedom to hire and fire) recommended by the labour commission has not been stated clearly in the literature, at least in the Indian context, and empirical studies have been conducted instead with an impression that the underlying theory is unambiguously true. We propose to examine the theory in some detail. But before such an exercise, a recapitulation of the presumed theoretical links underlying the empirical studies may be useful.

We closely follow here the *explanations* provided by the empirical studies in interpreting their results rather than the *methodology* they adopt to arrive at those results, which in any case has been discussed in Chapter 2. Hence, the robustness of their empirical results is not of immediate concern here; instead, their underlying theoretical framework is the object of inquiry.

Fallon and Lucas (1991) and Fallon and Lucas (1993) are extremely influential papers in this debate.[2] They argue that job security regulations (JSR) act as an impediment to employment growth; in particular, '[by] restricting employers' ability to fire workers [JSR] may actually reduce the size of the workforce employers wish to maintain' (Fallon and Lucas 1991: 396). The authors explain this reduced ability to fire workers in terms of *increased* adjustment costs or labour turnover costs *due to* the 1976 amendment to the IDA 1947.[3] They argue that labour adjustment costs negatively impact firms' employment decisions in the following manner:

> By raising turnover costs, . . . job security regulations may thus act as a tax on employment, effectively raising the cost of labour. Job security regulations would then tend to encourage adoption of more capital intensive production techniques, to shift production away from more labour intensive processes, and hence to reduce the demand for labour.
> (emphasis added) (ibid.: 402)

The question arises: *how* do labour turnover or adjustment costs raise labour cost? The authors argue: since hiring cost has *already* been bestowed on the *currently* employed workers of a firm (during hiring process) and further some firing cost is required to retrench them (for JSR) – this *secures* the position of *currently* employed workers and increases their bargaining power, translating to higher wage claims.[4] A rise in wages post-regulation is explained by:

> This [empirical] finding would be consistent with *the theory that enhanced job security endows insiders with greater bargaining strength, thus enabling them to achieve higher wages.*
> (emphasis added) (ibid.: 404)

Thus, they are using a theoretical framework in which JSR *introduces* labour turnover costs (LTCs), which, in turn, are *functional* in enhancing insiders' bargaining power (explained below) – translating to higher wage claims thereby raising labour costs.[5] Since employment is supposed to be inversely related to wages, this explains sluggish employment growth.

Another important contribution is the study by Besley and Burgess (2004), which looks into, among other things, the impact of labour laws (state-level amendments) on employment. In their study, they point out two main theoretical routes through which labour regulation affects employment creation: (a) relative price effect, and (b) expropriation effect.

With regard to the first route, the following impact is pointed out:

> The relative price effect is relevant if the effect of labour regulation is to raise the (fixed or marginal) cost of employing

labourers. Labour regulations will typically create *adjustment costs in hiring and firing labour* and in making adjustments in the organization of production. We would expect firms in the registered sector to substitute away from labour (reducing employment) towards other labour-saving inputs (including capital if labour and capital are substitutes) (emphasis added)

(ibid.: 8)

Hence, once again we find that an employment downturn is explained in terms of adjustment (or turnover) costs.

In explaining the second route, Besley and Burgess (2004: 9) argue:

The expropriation effect . . . by increasing the *bargaining power* of the workers, . . . [causes firms to] face a problem *if workers can expropriate part of that return* [hence pushing up wages] once the capital is sunk. . . . This effect shows why pro-worker labour regulations is similar to insecure property rights for owners of capital as their sunk investments are subject to workers expropriation.

Thus, workers' rent-seeking activities explain higher wage claims – over and above their supply price.[6] Now the bargaining power of the worker is enhanced following institution of JSR – presumably due to the LTCs associated with hiring and firing.

Therefore, as before, we find that labour regulations impair employment adjustment by amplifying turnover costs (thus acting against the interest of *currently unemployed*),[7] which existing workers *use* to seek higher wages for themselves (these workers are therefore *currently employed*).[8] Therefore, pro-labour regulations, in their theory, operate through introducing labour adjustment costs, which secure the position of the current workers against free dismissal (since the hiring cost has already been conferred on them and the firing cost has to be further borne by the firm for carrying out retrenchment). Knowing this fact, currently employed workers, it is argued, even when they are *not* retrenched – ask for higher wages (to the extent of labour adjustment cost) – since they know that if they have to be replaced then the firm has to bear LTCs. This can be demonstrated in terms of the following notations: Let the reservation wage of currently unemployed workers be denoted by *RW*; also let '*h*' be the marginal hiring cost of labour and '*f*' be the marginal firing cost. It is argued that the currently employed workers manipulate to increase their wages (W_I) above the reservation wage of the currently unemployed by the amount of marginal hiring and firing costs (i.e. $W_I = RW + h + f$). However, the firm would be *indifferent* between retrenching an existing worker and employing a hitherto unemployed worker in his/her place – for the cost of replacing an existing worker by a new worker would be $RW + h + f$; which is exactly the same as retaining an existing worker (more on this below).

Thus, it may be argued that the impact of JSR – through turnover costs – is *instrumental* in raising real wages of existing workers. Hence, LTCs provide existing workers the *bargaining tool* for increasing their wages. Thus, *this* theory explains the source of bargaining power of existing workers in terms of labour adjustment/turnover costs. Such an explanation is provided by the Insider-Outsider (I-O) theory of employment and unemployment – which explains how LTC is *instrumental in raising* the real wages of *existing* workers (above market clearing levels).

That this line of reasoning is banked upon by the empirical studies in the Indian context to explain rising real wages, which in turn is held responsible for generating unemployment, is not difficult to establish. Ghose (2005: 238) notes,

> The sharp rise in real wage in the 1980s could be conceivably be attributed to the introduction of strict job security regulations in 1982. By making labour retrenchment practically impossible, these regulations suddenly increased the bargaining power of the workers already in employment in organised manufacturing and effectively created an "insider-outsider" problem. *It is obviously possible to suppose that the workers used this increased bargaining power to increase real wages.*
>
> (emphasis added)

Similarly, Fallon and Lucas (1991: 402) observe: 'The inability of employers to dismiss striking workers may actually *strengthen the bargaining position of unions and insider workers more generally, which could result in an enhanced overall reward package including both greater job security and higher pay*' (emphasis added). Finally, discussing the various arguments in the literature to explain the employment slowdown in the 1980s, Dutta Roy (2004: 234) noted: 'Ahluwalia (1991) and the World Bank (1989) . . . explain the employment decline as the impact of a high rate of growth of wages, *in turn made possible by job security legislation'*. Footnote to this sentence reads: 'A possible basis for the latter possibility is provided by the Insider-Outsider framework of Lindbeck and Snower (1988)' (Dutta Roy 2004: 234 n: 2). (Also see Besley and Burgess (2004: 9); Sharma (2006: 2078)).

It is this explanation of rigidity[9] of real wages and its prevention from underbidding by the currently unemployed which explains involuntary unemployment. However, this explanation of unemployment – in terms of rent-seeking activity of the currently employed workers (insiders) is somewhat misleading due to the following reason: in light of LTCs, although it is true that firms are indifferent between paying higher wages to insiders (above the supply price of labour) and hiring an outsider (currently unemployed) in his/her place, insiders may not be in a position to exploit this fact – as argued above – precisely because there is unemployment in the economy. Let us elaborate on this point.

Clearly, insiders prefer their employed status rather than joining the ranks of outsiders. Knowing this, suppose that firms – to teach a lesson and contain higher wage claims – replace some of the insiders by outsiders. Firms *indifferent* between insiders and outsiders can easily do this. As a result, erstwhile insiders lose their privileged status and join the ranks of the unemployed, which they clearly dislike. Firms can evidently use this threat of replacement to instil fear among insiders, who desist from asking for higher wages even in the presence of LTCs. But, if insiders *cannot* indulge in rent-seeking activity and fail to raise wages above the supply price of labour, then the illustration of unemployment described above loses its meaning. Aware of this basic lacuna in the I-O framework, we now turn to its detailed examination.

4.1 The insider-outsider theory of employment and unemployment: a critical assessment of Lindbeck and Snowers' argument

The Insider-Outsider (I-O) theory of employment and unemployment, discussed below, is primarily due to the contribution of Professors Assar Lindbeck and Dennis J. Snower. In a series of articles[10] appearing in the late 1980s, the authors drew attention to one critical *source* of labour market power enjoyed by incumbent workers in a firm, namely, labour turnover costs (LTCs). The authors claim that incumbent workers (or insiders) *utilize* LTCs in their own favour without taking into account the interests of outsiders (unemployed)[11] and thereby generate involuntary unemployment. As Lindbeck and Snower (1988: 72) state: 'A central implication of the insider-outsider theory is that labor turnover costs are responsible for unemployment'. Therefore, this theory promises to offer an explanation of involuntary unemployment based on insiders' market power derived from LTCs. It clearly states, 'The insider-outsider theory was originally designed to explain the existence of involuntary unemployment in market economies and, in particular, the failure to underbid wages in the presence of such unemployment' (ibid.: 238).[12]

The authors claim that although I-O theory was originally designed to study the employment stagnation in European labour markets in the 1980s, the scope of the theory is wider. In their words:

> [T]he insider-outsider theory in *not* just about European labor markets, and in particular, it is *not* just designed to explain the persistence of unemployment in Europe during the 1980s. Rather, the theory is meant to apply to any labor markets in which labor turnover costs are significant and workers have some say in wage negotiations.
> (emphasis in original) (ibid.: 10)

The purpose of this chapter is to show that it is precisely this wider application of the theory which is being relied upon to prescribe policies of free hire and fire in developing economies like India.

It is now time to illustrate *how* insiders' activity generates involuntary unemployment. In order to understand this clearly, it is important to look at what constitutes the LTCs in detail. The authors focus on certain kinds of costs associated with worker turnover [i.e. either when workers are entering a firm or leaving it (therefore known as LTCs)]. Further, these costs can be divided into 'production-related' and 'rent-related' turnover costs. The former arises with new recruitments into the firm and are normally called hiring costs. These costs arise, according to the authors, due to advertising, screening, negotiating and training the fresh employees. Firms have an incentive to incur such costs so as to ensure that the right people (with certain guaranteed productivity) are chosen. Since hiring costs are primarily incurred to secure productive services, they are known as 'production-related' turnover costs. The second set of turnover costs arise at the time of separation of an incumbent worker from the firm. These costs are *not* aimed at ensuring productive services and hence are avoidable from the firm's point of view. Nonetheless, they exist due to JSRs that protect incumbent workers from free dismissal. Such regulations stipulate that before dismissal of incumbent employees, firms may have to follow costly firing procedures like engaging in litigation, incurring severance pay, serving advance notice of dismissal or seeking permission from concerned authorities. Costs incurred on such accounts are known as firing costs. The authors contend that firing costs fall into the category of 'rent-related' turnover costs (see ibid.: 7).

Note that the 'rent-related' turnover costs described above are *exogenous* to workers' conscious decision making and are entirely determined by legislation. This, however, need not be the case since some 'rent-related' turnover costs can also be *endogenous*.[13] However, since we are only interested in analysing the underlying theory that recommends free hire and fire by amending the law (IDA 1947), these endogenous routes need not detain us here.

We are now in a position to examine *how* insiders' *use* these LTCs to generate involuntary unemployment. The authors' explanation is based on the labour market and relies on wages:

> In the simple models presented in this book, we have seen that the insider wage is . . . positively related to the magnitude of labor turnover costs. . . . Moreover, a rise in the insider wage may be expected to lead to a rise in the level of unemployment, . . . because labor demand in the primary [i.e. organized] sector may be inversely related to the insider wage. . .
>
> (ibid.: 251)

Therefore, like all neoclassical explanations of involuntary unemployment, I-O theory tries to provide an answer *solely* based on the labour market and quite predictably explains it through rigid[14] real wages set above the market clearing level.[15] The authors draw a parallel with the efficiency wage theory and argue:

> Both theories seek to explain persistent involuntary unemployment on basis of optimizing microeconomic activities. . . . In the efficiency wage theory firms have incentive to *set wages above*

> *their full-employment levels*, whereas in the insider-outsider theory [insider] workers have such an incentive.
>
> (emphasis added) (ibid.: 61)

Obviously the question arises, even if there is an incentive for insiders to drive wages up: what is the *tool* at their disposal by which they actually do so? The authors provide the following answer:

> The rent-related turnover costs [i.e. firing costs] play a crucial role in the insider-outsider explanation of involuntary unemployment. Since the insiders are assumed to use their market power to further their own interests, they drive their wages above the market clearing level ... the reason why the insiders may be able to drive their wage up sufficiently ... is to be found in the rent-related turnover costs.
>
> (ibid.: 63)

Note that it is *only* the firing costs [i.e. rent-related turnover costs] which the authors emphasize as the underlying reason for generating involuntary unemployment and *not* hiring costs [i.e. production-related turnover costs]. However, we shall later show that the economy *can* reach full employment even in presence of firing costs.[16] Thus, it would be argued that the I-O theory *cannot* provide an adequate explanation of involuntary unemployment in the first place – hence, its policy recommendation of instituting free hire and fire is not theoretically well grounded.

Clearly, the question that now arises is: what stops profit-maximizing firms from replacing the insiders by outsiders? This question is important since if replacement occurs, there is no case for unemployment.[17] In addressing this question, the authors argue:

> [T]he insiders are able to raise their wage above the minimal level required to induce workers to become entrants, but *firms nevertheless have no incentive to hire outsiders. For this reason, aggregate labor supply may exceed aggregate labor demand.*
>
> (emphasis added) (ibid.: 64)

Hence, it becomes necessary to discuss why firms have no incentive to replace insiders by outsiders.

Note that even if wage claims of insiders exceed what outsiders are willing to work for (adjusted for productivity differentials), outsiders may still not find work since 'experienced incumbent employees whose positions are protected by various job-preserving measures... *make it costly for firms to fire them [insiders] and hire someone else [outsiders] in their place*' (emphasis added) (ibid.: 1). Now if this replacement (or adjustment) cost is of such magnitude (at the margin) that it makes *no difference* between choice of insiders and outsiders for firms, then replacement is negated. This, indeed, is the case as pointed out by the authors: 'the insider-outsider wage differential may fall short of total turnover costs (i.e., production and rent-related turnover costs), and thus firms do not find it worthwhile to replace insiders [by outsiders]' (ibid.: 63). This can be expressed in symbols as follows: if we denote w^I as the wage of insiders and w^E as reservation wage of outsiders, where 'h' is marginal hiring cost and 'f' is marginal firing cost, then the condition for no replacement can be written as: $(w^I - w^E) \leq h + f$; or, $w^I \leq w^E + h + f$. Clearly, so long as this condition holds, there is no incentive for the firm to replace insiders by outsiders. Similarly, this is also the reason why successful underbidding cannot take place.

Here we arrive at the result that insiders can raise their wage above those of the outsiders but by no more than the associated LTCs. This is known as the 'relative profitability constraint' in the I-O literature. There is another constraint faced by the insiders – 'absolute profitability constraint' – in the I-O literature. The relative profitability constraint specifies that 'insiders must remain profitable to the firm' (ibid.: 5). The absolute profitability constraint implies that 'the insider wage must not exceed the marginal revenue product of the firm's incumbent workforce plus the marginal firing cost. If this condition were not fulfilled, the firm would dismiss the insider' (ibid.: 5–6). Now which constraint would be operative depends upon the *initial size* of insiders in the firm.[18] According to the authors, insiders' wage setting following both conditions can explain involuntary unemployment, and the policy stance recommended by I-O theory (forming the basic cornerstone of LMF argument) proposes to cure unemployment – either when the relative profitability constraint or the absolute profitability constraint is binding, as we shall see later.

It is clear from the preceding discussion that insiders can raise their wage above the outsiders' reservation wage[19] by the magnitude of marginal hiring and firing costs. Yet the authors claim that it is *only* the rent-related turnover costs (or firing costs) which are responsible for generating involuntary unemployment and *not* production-related turnover costs (or hiring costs). It is to the discussion of this set of issues to which we now turn.

In order to demonstrate why production-related turnover costs (or hiring costs) do not contribute to creating unemployment, the authors bring in another category of workers, namely, entrants. Entrants are defined as those 'who have recently acquired jobs with a future prospect of gaining insider status, but whose current positions are not associated with significant turnover costs' (ibid.: 3). In plain terms, when an outsider is hired, s/he becomes an entrant to the firm. Note that since workers are usually recruited through a selection procedure (advertising, screening etc.), some costs are already expended over the entrants (whereas no such costs are incurred on the unemployed/outsiders). These are precisely the hiring costs (or production-related turnover costs). Also note that it was just mentioned that entrants have 'a future prospect of gaining insider status'. This is because normally it takes some time to acquire insiders' status (referred to in the literature as 'initiation period'). Therefore, entrants are *yet to* achieve insider status, so there is *no firing cost associated with the retrenchment of entrants*. Consequently, entrants (unlike insiders) *cannot* drive their wages above the reservation wage of outsiders by *both* hiring *and* firing costs.

Nonetheless, entrants *can* exploit/utilize the hiring costs (expended on them but not on outsiders) to drive their wages *above* the reservation wage of outsiders – but only by the magnitude of hiring costs.[20] This is amply clear from below:

> the entrant wage could be greater than the reservation wage [of outsiders]. . . . Entrants may have some rent to exploit (e.g., because the firm may already have expended advertising, screening, and some training costs on them and may incur even further costs to fire them).
>
> (ibid.: 44)

Thus, with three types of workers – insiders, entrants and outsiders – we have a graded wage structure where insider wage exceeds the entrant wage (by the magnitude of firing cost) which, in turn exceeds the reservation wage of outsiders (by the magnitude of hiring cost).

However, the difference between the reservation wage of outsiders and the entrants' wage does not generate involuntary unemployment for the reasons stated below:

> The outsiders may be willing to work for a wage that falls short of the insider wage by an amount sufficient to compensate the firms for insider-outsider productivity differences and *all production-related turnover costs* [i.e. hiring costs], but outsiders may nevertheless be unable to find jobs. The reason, obviously, is that the rent-related labor turnover costs [i.e. firing costs], may be sufficiently high to discourage firms from hiring the outsiders.
> (emphasis added) (ibid.: 7)

This condition can be expressed in symbols as follows: w^I, w^E, h and f have similar meanings as above. Here, a^I denotes the productivity of the insiders and a^E denotes the productivity of the outsiders. The authors state that although $(a^E - w^E - h) \geq (a^I - w^I)$ may hold and outsiders are also willing to work,[21] as $(a^E - w^E - h - f) < (a^I - w^I)$ happens, it is therefore firing costs that discourage the firm from hiring outsiders. The implication of this, according to the authors, is:

> Under these circumstances, the economy may get stuck in an equilibrium with involuntary unemployment. Here, the relative bargaining power of the firms and workers gives rise to a wage structure in which the insider wage exceeds the entrant wage, which, in turn, may exceed the reservation wage. *Consequently, workers [outsiders] prefer being employed to being unemployed.* Yet there may nevertheless be unemployed workers whom no firm has incentive to hire.
> (emphasis added) (ibid.: 44–45)

Note that in the above line of reasoning involuntary unemployment is explained by the firm's inability to replace insiders by outsiders, *due to the presence of rent-related (firing) LTCs, since by assumption, production-related turnover (hiring) costs do not pose a problem at all*. However, this argument is not correct; later we show that *rent-related turnover costs cannot explain the existence of involuntary unemployment*.

According to the authors, the argument that involuntary unemployment is due to rent-related turnover costs and not due to production-related turnover costs can also be presented from another[22] perspective:

> Underbidding may be unsuccessful on account of rent-related labor turnover costs [i.e. firing cost]. In particular, the outsiders may be willing to work for less than the insider wage minus production related turnover costs [i.e. hiring cost] (which account for the insider-outsider productivity differences), but the outsiders may nevertheless remain jobless because they are *not* willing to work for less than the insider wages minus the production – *and* rent-related turnover costs.
> (emphasis in original) (ibid.: 59)

However, we will show later that such an assumption cannot hold, for it violates the standard concept of reservation wages firmly established in the literature (see below). Next we will look at the diagrammatic representation of the I-O theory, which explains involuntary unemployment in terms of rent-related turnover costs and recommends policy prescriptions[23] of how such unemployment could be cured. It would be apparent from the following diagram that the basic contours of LMF directly follow from the policy recommendations of I-O theory.

The basic argument of I-O theory can be demonstrated through Figure 4.1. In the diagram, W^E represents the reservation wage (RW) of outsiders, and AB represents the marginal product curve of workers (MPL).[24] Now E represents full employment equilibrium outcome – where the MPL curve cuts the RW of outsiders. Let 'h' be the exogenously given marginal hiring cost (production-related turnover cost), represented by MN in the diagram, and let 'f' be the exogenously given marginal firing cost (rent-related turnover cost), represented by NS in the diagram. From the preceding discussion it is clear that if there were only hiring costs, then insiders would be able to increase their wage by no more than K (on the MPL curve). Additionally, if there is firing cost – as a consequence of JSR – then insiders can manipulate to raise their wages up to J (on the MPL curve). Also, suppose the initial group of insiders is L_I in the above diagram such that all insiders are employed when insiders' wage is OS (i.e. insiders' wage is increased up to J on the MPL curve above the RW of outsiders; in terms of notation, $W_I = RW + h + f$).[25]

Now without hiring and firing costs, the firm's profit-maximizing behaviour would result in a full employment outcome at E.

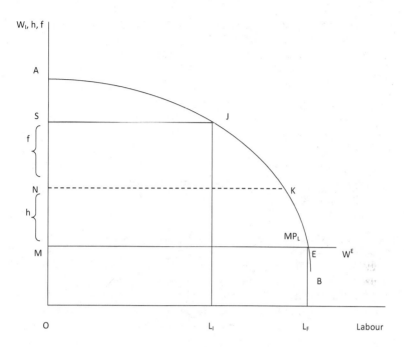

Figure 4.1 Diagrammatic representation of I-O theory

However, with hiring and firing costs L_I, the pool of insiders would claim wages equivalent to OS (= JL_I). Now even if insiders ask for insider wages above reservation wages up to W_I (= RW + h + f), the firm would nonetheless have no incentive to replace insiders and employ outsiders in their place, for the effective cost of employing an outsider in place of an insider at the margin would be RW + h + f, which is exactly the *same* as insiders' wage (JL_I). Thus, outsiders cannot successfully underbid insiders' wage below OS (= JL_I); hence, employment gets stuck at L_I (initial insiders pool) below full employment level (L_F). Hence, $L_I L_F$ represents involuntary unemployment, and this is explained by insiders' activity described above.

However, it is simply assumed that outsiders are willing to work for less than the insider wage if all LTCs were production-related (i.e. hiring costs). But, outsiders are not willing to work for less than the insider wage if LTCs include both hiring and firing costs. Thus, in the policy prescription the authors argue (discussed in detail below) that if firing costs are removed, then the economy would automatically move towards full employment (L_F) – for it is assumed by the authors that hiring costs do not generate unemployment. Thus, the authors recommend scrapping of JSR. In terms of the figure, this means that if firing cost is scrapped, then the economy moves to K (from J) and eventually to E (for it is assumed by the authors that outsiders do not mind working for a wage less than the insiders' wage minus hiring costs). However, we shall demonstrate below that both assertions are erroneous; specifically, (a) full employment is achieved even in the presence of firing costs (if, we assume, for argument's sake, that firms do not have to bear hiring costs), and (b) hiring costs alone are enough to generate unemployment. For now, we look at the policy implication of I-O theory in detail.

Policy implications of insider-outsider theory

The authors prescribe detailed policy suggestions based on I-O theory and explicitly rely on government to implement them. They try to address the following question: 'In face of substantial unemployment and high labor turnover costs, what can governments do to stimulate employment and reduce unemployment?' (ibid.: 260). In particular, they suggest 'government policies that are designed to *change the structure of institutions, laws and contractual agreements* with a view to creating greater equality of opportunity in the labor market' (emphasis added) (ibid.: 260). Such interventions are termed as 'structural labour market policies'. The authors bifurcate structural labour market policies into two categories, namely: (a) policies to diminish insider power designated as 'power-reducing policies', and (b) policies to 'enfranchise' outsiders in the wage negotiation process, called 'enfranchising policies'.

Power-reducing policies broadly take the form of 'limit[ing] the preferential treatment insiders receive in the labor market . . . by reducing firms' costs of firing insiders. . . ' (ibid.: 260), whereas enfranchising policies are aimed at inducing firms to hire more outsiders, operating through reducing firms' cost of hiring outsiders.[26] In what follows, we engage in a detailed examination of both policies.

Power-reducing policies: reducing insiders' power

In advocating 'power-reducing policies', the authors advance the following reason:

> When insiders use their power [conferred to them by legislatively determined exogenous hiring and firing costs] to discourage firms from hiring outsiders, then there is a case of egalitarian fairness to be made in favor of *policies that reduce the legal protection and rent-creating opportunities associated with insiders' jobs. A macroeconomic case can be made as well, since a reduction in the insiders' bargaining power may lead to a fall in unemployment and to a rise in production.*
>
> (emphasis added) (ibid.: 261)[27]

Now let us see what constitutes – in the authors' opinion – the removal of legal protection and rent-creating opportunities for the insiders:

> On the one hand, they may involve dismantling some existing job-security legislation, such as laws to reduce severance pay or to simplify firing procedures. On the other hand, they may cover legislation to reduce union power, such as legal restrictions on strikes and picketing.
>
> (ibid.: 260–261)

As it has been claimed that rent-related turnover costs or firing costs are responsible for generating unemployment, naturally the policy recommendation that follows clearly delineates removal of such impediments to firing, which unnecessarily – in their view – makes the labour adjustment process lengthy (and costly) for firms. This move, it is argued, pushes the economy towards full employment.

Nonetheless, the authors are sceptical about the practical application of such a policy. The reason is as follows:

> note that power-reducing policies are usually not Pareto-improving. Rather, they tend to raise the outsiders' chances of employment at the cost of reducing the insiders' real wages and job security. Thus, when a government attempts to implement these policies, it is likely run into all the various social and political difficulties that characteristically arise when there are conflicts of interest over income distribution and vested interested groups are stripped from power.
>
> (ibid.: 261–262)

The vested interest group referred to above is the group of 'insiders'. Therefore, I-O theory advocates a pushing through steadfastly of unpalatable reforms in the face of stiff opposition likely to surface from organised sector workers (where labour laws apply) under the aegis of trade unions. This is the content of power-reducing policies; which aims to produce a frictionless labour market closely resembling the Classical labour market. Next, we turn to the 'enfranchising policies'.

Enfranchising policies: enhancing outsiders' power

It is worthwhile restating what constitutes these enfranchising policies designed to 'fight unemployment'. The authors argue: 'Enfranchising policies are *designed to reduce firms' cost of hiring outsiders* and thereby give more workers insider status . . .' (emphasis added) (ibid.: 260). Note that enfranchising policies envisage to 'stimulate employment' by cutting down on firms' hiring costs. Further, the authors identified rent-related turnover costs *alone* to be responsible for generating involuntary unemployment and *not* production-related turnover costs.[28] However, we will show that hiring costs *alone* are capable of generating involuntary unemployment – *if the standard definition of reservation wages is not violated.*

Nonetheless, 'enfranchising policies' have genuine distributional effects. Consider the specific policy prescription by the authors – that of adopting an apprenticeship system which lengthens the 'initiation period' (i.e. time span that elapses *before* a newly hired worker gains insider status and can renegotiate a wage). Basically, an apprenticeship system elongates the time period covered under entrants' wage contracts (in common parlance, this is often referred to as probation period in a job), which in turn reduces firms' hiring cost and allows 'firms a longer span of time in which to take advantage of the differential between insiders' and entrants' wage claims' (ibid.: 264). It is easy to see that the extension of the initiation period clearly *raises* profits at the margin, at the cost of wages. In this context, it is difficult to miss the close resemblance between the policy prescription of 'enfranchising policies' and recent amendments to the Apprentices Act, 1961, by the Government of India (GoI) discussed in Chapter 1.

Similarly, it is argued, specific policies of the enfranchising variety like vocational training programmes – subsidized or run by government – might help to 'enfranchise' outsiders. This raises the productivity of outsiders through training (making them more attractive), the cost of which firms do not bear – thus firms save on training costs.[29] The effectiveness of these vocational training programmes, it is argued, depends on the relative importance of general skills vis-à-vis firm-specific skills in affecting overall worker productivity. If the former dominates the latter, then these programmes are more effective. Clearly, once again, effects are distributional.

Finally, the authors recommend an enfranchising policy which can truly enhance employment, namely, 'reducing barriers to the entry of new firms' (ibid.: 265). The reason they argue is the following: 'New firms generally have no insiders, though with the passage of time their employees may eventually become insiders. Consequently, new firms may be in an especially good position to create employment opportunities'; however, the problem lies elsewhere since, 'incumbent firms may have an incentive to erect entry barriers against new firms' (ibid.: 265). Therefore, to facilitate entry they recommend 'government measures to reduce the industrial, occupational, and geographical coverage of union wage agreements [which] may also encourage the entry of new firms, since these agreements determine the degree to which new firms are legally bound to pay insider wages' (ibid.: 265). Note that the authors explicitly visualize entry barriers to the market – therefore this closely resembles oligopolistic market structure. However, this view is inconsistent with the formal description of the model – where price faced by the representative firm in the output market is assumed to be *exogenously* given. Nonetheless, once again we find that the proposed wage restraint can only have distributional implications over claims on gross value added. Now we turn to examine the internal consistency of I-O framework.

Checking the consistency of the arguments: a critique of the Lindbeck and Snower argument

In this section, we show that the conclusions drawn from the model are *not* internally consistent. At the outset, note that the entire theoretical literature which identifies JSR as the main obstacle to reach full employment assumes that *job security legislation extends to all sectors of the economy*. In other words, coverage of JSR in the economy is *universal*. For if this is not the case, then – according to their theory – there should not be obstacles to reach full employment. Instead there would be two segments in the economy – a high-wage sector governed by JSR alongside a low-wage sector *not* governed by JSR. Competition among workers in the non-JSR sector would result in full employment. In other words, there exists no theory which predicts that the same results will hold, when JSR applies to only a *sub-sector* of the economy. Thus, to apply a theory which assumes *universal* JSR – for recommending LMF – to an economy characterized by a large unorganised sector (notably India) is clearly untenable.

Further, it can be shown that even in the *presence* of rent-related LTCs, the representative firm can reach full employment level E. This is the case if we consider a two-tier wage system in the I-O framework. Let us, for argument's sake, assume zero hiring cost. It requires the following: let the insiders continue to receive a higher wage consistent with marginal rent-related LTCs (i.e. firing cost) and let the representative firm maintain its incumbent workforce. Until now, as full employment is not reached, entrants are employed as new recruits at a lower wage, since entrants are *yet to attain insider status* (so no firing costs are associated with entrants and we have assumed for the time being zero hiring costs).[30]

In terms of the Figure 4.2, consider that the initial incumbent workforce for the firm is L_I – where insiders receive W_I (= OB) wage [remember, we assumed – for argument's sake – zero hiring costs]. Now suppose the representative firm does not consider replacement of its insiders by outsiders but instead continues to retain its existing pool of incumbents (L_I) at insiders' wage rate W_I (= OB). The question arises – is there any opportunity for the firm to *add* to its existing set of insiders?

Remember, it takes some time for newly hired workers to attain insider status. And it is only *after* attaining insider status that workers are protected from free dismissal by firing cost. Therefore, new workers can be recruited at the reservation wage (RW) of outsiders[31] [remember we assumed zero hiring costs for the time being]. In that case, profit maximisation would guide the firm to expand employment beyond L_I. Actually, in a wage system in which insiders continue to receive insiders' wage and newly appointed workers, who can be periodically thrown out *before* attaining insiders' status, are paid reservation wage, it is easy to see that profit maximisation would allow employment creation up to E, and there are no obstacles to full employment. Thus, we have a two-tier wage system in which incumbents continue to receive insiders' wage (above reservation wage of outsiders – on account of firing costs) while entrants receive reservation wage – there is no obstacle to full employment *even in presence of firing costs (rent-related LTCs)*. Therefore, the

Theoretical structure of labour market flexibility 163

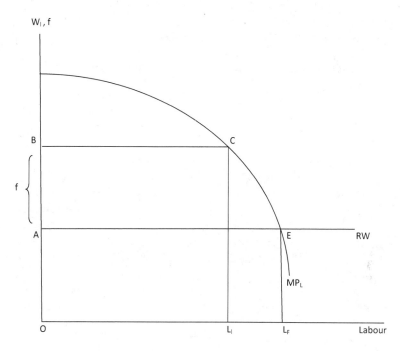

Figure 4.2 Scrutinizing the existence of unemployment in a two-tier wage system

I-O framework is *incapable* of explaining the existence of involuntary unemployment in terms of LTCs – since in spite of LTCs a two-tier wage system is capable of producing full employment.

This lacuna in I-O framework is also recognised by the authors. They briefly touch upon this point but without properly illustrating its implication. The authors argue:

> If unemployment is to be reduced, then the firms and the outsiders must find a way to 'bribe' the insiders to reduce the labour turnover costs or *to exploit these costs less in their own favor*. These . . . might take the form of. . . *two-tier wage schemes (which ensure that insider wages do not fall when the workforce is expanded)*. Such wage contracts are indeed important in some occupations and industries.
> (emphasis added) (ibid.: 63–64)

Nevertheless, they immediately dismiss the applicability of such a system arguing:

> However, it is also readily understandable, in the context of the insider-outsider theory, why such arrangements are not ubiquitous: . . . permanent two-tier wage schemes may be time inconsistent (since they may induce firms to fire the current insiders once the new entrants have been trained).
>
> (ibid.: 64)

Note that this is an inconsistent explanation in light of the firing costs. It is precisely due to the rent-related LTCs propounded by I-O theory that insiders are not freely replaceable by outsiders – therefore, insiders cannot be freely replaced by newly trained entrants as well. Thus, if firms had no incentive to replace insiders by outsiders, similarly, they will have no incentive to replace insiders by entrants. Hence, arguments of time inconsistency undermine the very foundation of I-O theory.[32]

One can argue a little further that even if insiders find the two-tier wage system time inconsistent, they nevertheless may lack the proper *tool* to stop firms from adopting such a policy if it suits the latter's purpose. In absence of such a tool – in the literature and in the hands of insiders – it is unclear how insiders can oppose such a move. Hence, even if a two-tier wage system is inconsistent for insiders, they may still simply lack the proper device to deal with it.

Further, the authors assume exogenously given output prices at the firm level (ibid.: ch.3; Lindbeck and Snower 1987), which essentially means that the product market in which the firm participates closely resembles a perfectly competitive market structure. Now a primary condition for the market structure to be competitive is *free entry and exit of firms*. In such a situation as well, the explanation of involuntary unemployment employing the I-O framework cannot stand scrutiny. The reason for this is easy to understand – hitherto, unemployed workers can simply come together and start new firms (since there is free entry and exit). Further, since the new firms have *no* insiders' pool carried over from the past, new firms can offer outsiders wages *no more* than the reservation wage (W_E). However, since existing firms offer higher wages to insiders – even when new firms enter the market – *existing firms would be simply out-competed by the new ones*. Under these conditions, the existence of involuntary unemployment is once again summarily rejected.[33]

One can argue a little further. Suppose for a moment we assume that there are only hiring- or production-related turnover costs. Figure 4.1 shows the insider wage then is: ON (i.e. we are at point K on the MPL curve). The authors argue that in this situation the economy moves to full employment at E. This is because, as the authors argued, outsiders are willing to work for a wage that is sufficiently lower than the insiders' wage to compensate the firm for all production-related turnover (or hiring) costs.[34] *The question arises: how much less should the wage of outsiders be to sufficiently compensate the firm for all production-related turnover costs?*

Now, if outsiders ask for reservation wage (RW), then the firm would have *no* incentive to replace insiders by outsiders at the margin – since the effective cost of both would be the same; consequently, the economy would be stuck below full employment at K (on the MPL curve). *Under such circumstances, the hiring cost alone would be sufficient to generate unemployment.* But this is what the authors discard. Thus, if the authors have to sustain their claim, then it must be true that the outsiders *pay for their hiring costs*, which means that outsiders accept working for *less than reservation wage by the amount of the hiring cost*. Only in this case insiders would be readily replaced by outsiders, and hiring cost alone would be unable to generate unemployment. However, if outsiders are ready to work for less than reservation wage, then this *violates* the standard definition of reservation wage.

Thus, I-O theory lands up in a theoretical contradiction in which either hiring costs alone are enough to generate unemployment – thus making LMF inconsequential,[35] or reservation wage loses its meaning (since outsiders must accept working below reservation wage and paying for their hiring costs). Therefore, the conclusions drawn from the I-O framework stand on shaky foundations. Next, we shall see Solow's argument in the insider-outsider framework – specifically, whether his model can explain involuntary unemployment due to insiders' activity.

4.2 Insider-outsider approach in an intertemporal framework: a critical assessment of Robert Solow's argument

Solow's (1985) explanation of involuntary unemployment using the Insider-Outsider (I-O) approach is set in an intertemporal framework.[36] There are three types of agents in his model, namely, employers, employed workers (or insiders) and unemployed workers (or outsiders). However, Solow offers an explanation for involuntary unemployment based on the behaviour of *only* employers and employed workers (forming union), leaving out the behaviour of unemployed outsiders as passive agents.[37] He follows the basic tradition of I-O theory and observes: 'When there is involuntary unemployment, however, the interests of employed and unemployed workers also diverge' (Solow 1985: 413).

Notice that Solow's objective is to provide an explanation of a *macroeconomic* phenomenon, namely, persistent involuntary unemployment in the economy. However, as we shall shortly see, his argument develops in a *microeconomic* setting (the model is built around a single firm confronting an insiders' union). This approach is typically followed by the neoclassical school to argue in terms of a representative firm and claim that the results arrived at the firm level *can be* transferred without alteration for the economy as a whole (note that the same method was followed in the earlier model as well). *Typically, the representative firm is assumed to be a microcosm of the whole economy.* The pitfall of such an approach has been mentioned earlier and need not detain us any further. However, while analysing the policy recommendation of the model later, we shall find out the drawback of this approach.

Let us now turn to the assumptions of the model which extends over two periods. It is assumed that a representative firm maximises its lifetime profit and starts with (i.e. period 1) a pool of workers (insiders). There is also a large pool of unemployed workers (outsiders). It is assumed that insiders possess *greater* skill (hence are *more* productive) than outsiders. However, after one period of employment (remember, this is an intertemporal model) outsiders turn into insiders, in every aspect. The author notes, 'Our key assumption is that inexperienced workers hired in period 1 are thereby transformed into experienced workers in period 2' (ibid.: 415–416). Insiders form a union that sets the wage (of insiders) unilaterally[38] (for both periods), and the union is concerned only with the welfare of its members [i.e. insiders][39] (and pays no attention to the unemployed outsiders). Outsiders' wage is assumed to be tied to some reservation level in *both* periods; with no bargaining power, outsiders are assumed to be price-takers in the labour market.

It is further assumed that in response to the wage quoted by the union, the firm (to maximise profits) chooses the employment level unilaterally (in both periods).[40] Therefore, it is possible that '[Although] The firm gains from having a large pool of insiders, *some of whom may be laid off in bad years*' (emphasis added) (ibid.: 411). Moreover, the author assumes that the firm has no long-run responsibility for its workers and 'is assumed not to make payments to laid-off members of its labor pool' (ibid.: 415).[41] However, along with this, Solow makes a very peculiar assumption that although insiders can be laid off, nonetheless insiders *cannot* be replaced even when the economy is inflicted with a large idle labour reserve. In the author's words: 'Lindbeck & Snower focus on the firm's decision whether to replace some or all of its incumbent workers with outsiders, *whereas we take it for granted that the firm cannot or will not do that*, and look only at the firm's decision whether to make a marginal addition to the size of its labor pool' (emphasis added) (ibid.: 414).

Now it is strange to assume (and we shall see later that this is pivotal for the result arrived at by the author) that the firm *can* layoff insiders but *cannot* replace them even when, to begin with, the economy is characterized by involuntary unemployment. This is a completely artificial distinction from the point of view of the firm (since maximisation of profit must be the motivation either to layoff or replace insiders); it is also artificial from the point of view of workers, since a worker once laid off cannot resist replacement. Therefore, it is a strange assumption which is at complete variance with reality – that firms *can fire* their workers but *cannot hire* new workers in their place. In fact, employers derive their enormous bargaining strength in an economy saddled with a vast reserve army of labour by the very threat of firing workers *and* replacing them with new ones. In reality, if employers *cannot replace* workers by drawing on the large reserve army of labour lying idle, then their manoeuvrability is greatly compromised. This is because firing workers *alone* does not fulfil their purpose – since a *substitute* is required to *compensate* the labour hours lost – following the separation of workers.

Based on these assumptions, Solow investigates whether there is any possibility of marginal addition (of workers) to the representative firm's existing (i.e. insiders) labour pool. Basically he is interested in examining whether there is a possibility of adding workers at the margin to the existing set of workers. He shows that insiders' activity – through union's wage claims – *negates* such a possibility and hence employment opportunity for outsiders.[42] In the author's words: 'If the insiders set their wage unilaterally, they will choose a path that . . . prevents employment of outsiders' (ibid.: 411). Now outsiders, *who are otherwise willing to be employed, remain unemployed* (for the representative firm *cannot* expand its labour pool due to insiders' activity) and this, according to Solow, provides 'a partial explanation of the persistence of [involuntary] unemployment in a mildly cyclical economy' (ibid.: 418).

Let us now look at the formal structure of the model along with the other assumptions. Since the model already assumes that the firm can *only* increase the size of its labour pool at the margin (and no replacement), amelioration of unemployment would require conditions when outsiders are *additionally* required in excess of the existing labour pool of the firm. Likewise, any persistence of involuntary unemployment would require that although there are unemployed outsiders willing to work, the representative firm's profit-maximizing labour demand is such that the outsiders are *not* demanded. Thus, in this model, involuntary unemployment is explained in terms of the representative firm's labour demand in response to insider union's wage claims, leaving out the unemployed outsiders as passive agents.

As already mentioned, the model is set up in an intertemporal framework spanning over two periods. However, the author is only concerned about whether *outsiders are hired in the first period itself* and is indifferent to such opportunities emerging in the second period. This is so for, '[Although] [t]he story extends over two periods, [. . .] we are mainly concerned with what happens in the first. This is because the second period, being the "last" period, has special characteristics that are of no real significance' (ibid.: 414). Therefore, involuntary unemployment is said to persist, *if no outsiders are hired, in the first period itself, in addition to the existing labour pool of the firm*, as 'the second period is unimportant, because the second period is – artificially – the last period, and so we forget about it' (ibid.: 415).

In order to understand the working of the model, it is necessary to take note of a few notations. For any variable mentioned below, the first subscript denotes the nature of workers: 1 for insiders and 2 for outsiders. The second subscript denotes time: the first period is denoted by 1 and the second period by 2. Hence, employment and wage claims of insiders' union in period 1 are expressed by e_{11} and w_{11}, respectively; that of outsiders employment as e_{21} (wage of outsiders in period 1 is denoted by w_2; where w_2 is the reservation wage of outsiders). Likewise, employment (and wage) of insiders in period 2 is expressed by e_{12} (w_{12}) and that of outsiders by e_{22} (wage of outsiders in period 2 is denoted by w_2). Notice that outsiders, due to lack of bargaining power, are assumed to receive only reservation wage w_2 in *both* periods. There is also a reservation wage of insiders w_0, where it is assumed that $w_0 > w_2$. The firm is assumed to start with an initial pool of m number of experienced workers (i.e. insiders). Finally, parameter s_1 describes the state of the firm's product market in the first period, and s_2 describes the state of the firm's product market in the second period.[43] We now turn to the basic building block of the model.

As mentioned earlier, unemployed outsiders are assumed to be less skilled than the employed insiders: 'They [outsiders] are therefore less productive than experienced workers [insiders]' (ibid.: 415). This idea is captured in notations as: the firm's revenue in the first period is represented by $s_1 f(e_{11}) + s_1 \varphi f(e_{21})$, where φ is a constant between $0 < \varphi < 1$. Similarly, the firm's revenue in the second period is: $s_2 f(e_{12}) + s_2 \varphi f(e_{22})$. This formulation captures the productivity differential between insiders and outsiders.

Next, look at the firm's objective function with labour as the only (variable) factor of production. The firm maximizes the present discounted value of its lifetime profit, where R is a discount factor based on pure time preference:

$$\left[s_1 f(e_{11}) - w_{11} e_{11} + s_1 \varphi f(e_{21}) - w_2 e_{21} \right]$$
$$+ R \left[s_2 f(e_{12}) - w_{12} e_{12} + s_2 \varphi f(e_{22}) - w_2 e_{22} \right]$$

Now the difficulty with such a form is that s_2 is *unknown* to the firm sitting in period 1. Therefore, Solow needs to assume: 'For now we treat s_1 and s_2 as *known*; but eventually we will want to think of s_2 as a random variable of known distribution' (emphasis added) (ibid.: 414). However, if s_2 is *known* in an intertemporal setting, then the appeal of the model is severely reduced – since it amounts to assuming perfect foresight. As perfect foresight is too strong an assumption and at complete variance with reality, the result of the model is immediately open to question. Even if s_2 is assumed to be a random variable with *known* distribution – since it is *state* of the economy in period 2 (actually product price), *as perceived by the firm sitting in period 1* – entering into the precise calculation of the firm's profit maximization, it must be true that such expectations, on average, are realized. Put differently, even if there is some error in predicting s_2 – from what emerges ultimately – *the expected value of that error must be zero*. But this amounts to assuming rational expectations – the foundation of which is highly questionable.[44] For the rest of the discussion on the model, only the version which treats s_2 as *known* is considered, since virtually negligible treatment is available with s_2 treated as random.

Let us find out how the firm decides labour demand (of insiders and outsiders). Assuming diminishing marginal productivity, the firm's choice of insiders in period 1 (e_{11}) is determined by the following condition (remember union unilaterally quotes w_{11} and the firm must *know* this to choose e_{11}):

$$s_1 f'(e_{11}) = w_{11} \qquad (1)$$

Now taking period 1 alone, it would be in the firm's interest to hire some outsiders if:

$$s_1 \varphi f'(0) > w_2$$

and the best number to hire is determined by the marginal outsider where equality is achieved. However, Solow assumes that the above inequality is *not* satisfied for the outsiders. Hence, firms are not interested in hiring any outsiders if only the first period's profits were considered. Note that this is a crucial assumption, since allowing otherwise would entail a marginal addition to the size of the firm's existing labour pool; a straightforward employment opportunity for the outsiders in period 1 itself and consequently a fall in the unemployment level. Therefore, for any explanation of persistent unemployment – as Solow promises to develop – one must, by assumption, rule out the possibility of the above inequality being held true. Yet assuming the above severely restricts the scope of the model as a special case, and the author acknowledges it:

> This condition is excessively strong. It can be read as limiting the model to periods in which s_1 is not too large. It corresponds to what employers often say, especially in not very good years, though that does not guarantee its truth.
>
> (ibid.: 416)

Despite the above restrictive assumption, the firm is said to have another motive to hire outsiders in the first period.[45] This additional motive is best captured by quoting the author in full:

But the firm has yet another motive to hire inexperienced workers in the first period: to train experienced workers for period 2. This motive becomes effective *if the firm anticipates that its second-period employment of experienced workers might profitably exceed m* [initial pool of insiders in period 1]. When this factor is taken into account the firm would be impelled to hire unemployed workers in period 1, even though first-period results by themselves would not justify it...

(emphasis added) (ibid.: 416)

This is precisely the intertemporal connection in the firm's employment decision. And this, according to the author, is the basic focus of the model: 'The central question addressed in this paper is the effect of this intertemporal connection on the firm's employment decision and the union's wage-setting decision' (ibid.: 415–416).

The additional motivation for the firm to hire some outsiders in period 1, just discussed above, actually comes into play when the following condition holds true:

$$(s_1 \varphi f'(0) - w_2) + R\{s_2 f'(m) - w_{12}\} > 0 \qquad (2)$$

Remember, the term in the first bracket is always negative by assumption. However, considering lifetime profits, the whole expression can still be positive (opening up conditions for additional motivation for the firm to hire some outsiders in period 1) only if the term in second bracket is positive and outweighs the negative profits incurred by employing outsiders in period one. Now the second bracketed term being positive signifies that even if *all* the initial insiders are employed in period 2 (remember the firm started with *m* insiders), it is still profitable at the margin to employ *another* insider. However, since the firm has already exhausted its pool of insiders, it must hire some outsiders in period 1 and train them for one period, to meet this extra demand for insiders (above *m*) in period 2. Now the exact number of outsiders to be hired for training in period one (e_{21}) is given by the following profit-maximizing condition:

$$(s_1 \varphi f'(e_{21}) - w_2) + R\{s_2 f'(m + e_{21}) - w_{12}\} = 0 \qquad (3)$$

e_{21} is *determined* by Eq. (3) and the number of insiders demanded in period 2 is given by $(m + e_{21})$. However, notice that even in equilibrium the term in the second bracket must be positive since the first bracketed expression, by assumption, is always negative.

Now it is important to note that in order to decide on the number of outsiders to be hired for training in period 1 (e_{21}), *the firm must know w_{12} in period 1 itself.* Although Solow never mentions this, this must nonetheless be true. This is plain to understand: since the union is assumed to set wage *unilaterally*, w_{12} is a parameter to the firm entering into the latter's objective function (maximised when Eq. (3) is satisfied). Since parameters of the objective function must be *known* to the agent undertaking optimization exercise – hence even to recognise that situations like Eq. (2) would emerge[46] – the firm must know w_{12}. This is similar to the case in which the firm decides on the number of insiders to be hired in period 1 by the condition: $s_1 f'(e_{11}) = w_{11}$, where the firm must *know* w_{11} in order to choose e_{11} optimally. Further, since the firm has to decide on the optimal number of outsiders (e_{21}) to be hired for training in period 1, w_{12} must be known to it in period 1 itself. For if w_{12} is *unknown* to the firm in period 1, it simply has *no* basis to predict situations like Eq. (2); therefore, additional motivation for the firm to hire some outsiders in period 1 *never* materializes. From the above discussion it must be clear that the firm must know w_{12} in period 1 itself in order to optimally choose e_{21}. *This, therefore, means that the union quotes second-period insiders' wage w_{12} in period 1 only* (along with w_{11}).

Next, we consider the union's behaviour. In particular, we consider the lifetime objective function of the union stated by the author:

$$\frac{e_{11}(w_{11} - w_0)}{m} + R\left[\frac{e_{12}(w_{12} - w_0)}{(m + e_{21})}\right] \quad (4)$$

R is the discount rate for the union, assumed to be the same as the firm.[47] The important thing about the above formulation is that the union gains utility by increasing insiders' wage above their reservation wage w_0. However, there is a trade-off, for the union suffers a direct loss of utility from the unemployment of its members. Since Solow is interested in investigating how insiders' activity may damage the employment prospect of the outsiders in period 1, *even if period 2 turns bright*, he only concentrates on period 2 (as it is already assumed that outsiders can *never* be employed considering period 1 only):

$$\left[\frac{e_{12}(w_{12} - w_0)}{(m + e_{21})}\right]$$

Next, we shall demonstrate the *implication* of the union quoting insiders' wage for the second period (w_{12}) in period 1 itself. Remember, Solow assumes the union to be only concerned with the welfare of its members (i.e. insiders) and *not* about the unemployed outsiders. If the union quotes insiders' wage for the second period (w_{12}) in period 1 itself, notice that *the number of union members in period 1 is only the initial set of insiders (m)*. Hence, the union would only be concerned with the *initial* set of insiders, m. Thus, the true objective function of the union in the second period is:

$$\left[\frac{e_{12}(w_{12} - w_0)}{m}\right]$$

Note the difference between the second period objective function of the union stated by Solow and proposed by us. The only difference is in the denominator. Solow's formulation would have been correct if some outsiders were hired in period 1 who would then turn into insiders in period 2 and *wage setting of the union for the second period was conducted in period 2*. Then the union would take into consideration only the welfare of *new* members (over and above the initial set of insiders 'm'). However, we showed that for consistency in the firm's behaviour (i.e. to even decide on the number of outsiders to be hired for training in period one), the firm must have knowledge about the second period (w_{12}) insiders' wage in period 1 itself, *which therefore means the union must quote insiders' wage for the second period (w_{12}) in period 1 only, when the number of union members is only the initial set of insiders (m)*. Since the union is only concerned with the welfare of its members, it must be concerned with the initial number of insiders (m) only. Therefore, the correct objective function for the union in period 2 is the one in which the denominator consists of only the *initial* insiders.

Now the union's strategy would be to set w_{12} such that it first ensures full employment of its members and then raises the insiders' wage as high as possible (above insiders' wage reservation wage w_0)

subject to full employment. Although Solow discusses a case where the objective function of the union is maximised at a wage such that some union members are *not* employed, this is unlikely to happen in reality, for union members would object to such a strategy (since *a priori anybody* could be retrenched), fearing loss of employment. The author himself acknowledges this case to be *less likely* to occur (see ibid.: 420). Therefore, we shall only concentrate below on the case where the union's strategy is to maximise insiders' wage claims subject to full employment of its members.

Let us now see *how* any opportunity of outsiders' employment, in addition to the existing labour pool of the firm, is choked off in the first period *due to* insiders' activity. Typically, the author argues: 'If the insiders set their wage unilaterally, they will choose a [wage] path that . . . prevents employment of outsiders even if the future employment prospects are good' (ibid.: 411). This, therefore, explains the existence of involuntary unemployment in the insider-outsider framework. The basic intuition of the model is best captured by quoting the author in full:

> Suppose market conditions in period one are not so good (i.e., s_1 not so large) that outsiders can be profitably employed on that basis. The possibility exists that they might be hired anyway if period 2 is expected to be prosperous enough (i.e., s_2 large enough) so that the firm will need an enlarged pool of skilled workers then. *This possibility will be frustrated if the insiders choose to convert the improving market prospects into a sufficiently high wage for period 2 that the firm's demand for labour can be satisfied out of its existing pool of trained workers* [i.e. insiders]. If that is the general outcome, then we have a partial explanation of the persistence of unemployment in a mildly cyclical economy.
>
> (emphasis added) (ibid.: 418)[48]

Note that Solow explicitly states the *condition* for persistence of involuntary unemployment as follows: 'if the insiders *choose to convert* the improving market prospects into a sufficiently high wage for period 2'. Now if insiders *can* 'choose to convert' better market conditions into higher wage demands, then it must be true that insiders (actually their union) *have* knowledge about the improving market conditions. *In other words, the insiders' union must know* s_2. Further, since w_{12} is quoted in period 1 only, hence, s_2 must be known to the union in period 1 itself.

The proposition that the insiders' union must have knowledge about s_2 also follows from the comparative-static analysis of the model. Remember that the union sets insiders' wage unilaterally. Let us now visit the comparative-static result obtained by the author: 'The comparative-static analysis of variations in s_2 is simple . . . with higher values of s_2. . . . It is no surprise that the skilled [insider] wage w_{12} is higher in better states' (ibid.: 420). Since the union sets insiders' wage unilaterally, unless s_2 is known to it, there is no basis for the union to claim wages higher than the insiders' reservation level wage (w_0). *Hence, the union must have knowledge about s_2 – this is an implicit assumption Solow is making without clearly stating it.* [This argument also directly follows from the objective function of the union, discussed by Solow (1985: 420) where s_2 enters as a parameter in the objective function of the union. Hence, s_2 must be known to the union.]

From all this, it is easy to see *how* outsiders' employment opportunities in the first period, in addition to the existing labour pool of the firm, is spoilt *due to* insiders' activity. Solow derives the result elaborately that the union's wage claim for period 2 would be $w_{12} = s_2 f'(m)$,[49] and employment opportunity of the outsiders in period 1 would be non-existent. The reason being, Eq. (2) turning negative with w_{12} set at $s_2 f'(m)$ – consequently, it would be unprofitable for the firm to employ even a single outsider. However, this result directly follows from the assumption of the model that *insiders can be fired but cannot be replaced* coupled with the fact that *the union knows s_2* and *claims insiders' wage w_{12} in period 1 itself*. The first of these conditions is clearly stated by the author, while the last two conditions come out from the description of the model.

The result that the union's wage claim for period 2 would always be $w_{12} = s_2 f'(m)$ – such that outsiders cannot be profitably employed – can easily be seen from Eq. (2) stated above. For convenience, we write Eq. (2) once more:

$$(s_1 \varphi f'(0) - w_2) + R\{s_2 f'(m) - w_{12}\} > 0 \qquad (2)$$

Note that the additional motivation mentioned above for the firm to hire some outsiders in period 1 occurs only when Eq. (2) holds.[50] It is clear that if conditions like Eq. (2) arise at all, then it must at least be true for insiders' reservation wage w_0 (i.e. when $w_{12} = w_0$), when *all* the initial insiders (m) must be profitably employed in the firm. Also note that the union quotes its wage w_{12} in period 1 (when there are only an *initial* number of insiders in the union [i.e. m)], and it is assumed that the union only cares for insiders. It is also noted above that the union *knows* s_2 in period 1 itself. Solow further assumes that the union can *compute* labour demands *given* various wage rates [see in (ibid.: 420) that $g(.)$ is the inverse function of marginal product of insiders $f'(.)$ – which enters into the objective function of the union] – hence the union must have information about the marginal product curve of insiders [i.e. $f'(.)$]. Now since the union can *compute* $f'(m)$ and *knows* s_2, it *can* enumerate $s_2 f'(m)$. Also remember that the union's strategy is to maximise insiders' wage claim subject to full employment of its members. It is crucial at this juncture to keep in mind that *insiders can be fired but not replaced*. Therefore, the union need not fear replacement threats, but it has to be careful that its wage claims are *not* greater than the marginal contribution of the *last* insider available in period 1 (otherwise the firm would retrench some insiders). Evidently, from the union's objective function,[51] the maximum insiders' wage consistent with full employment of union members must be $w_{12} = s_2 f'(m)$. Hence, the union's wage claim for period 2 must be $w_{12} = s_2 f'(m)$. It is clear that if $w_{12} = s_2 f'(m)$, then Eq. (2) is negative, for $(s_1 \varphi f'(0) < w_2)$ by assumption, and therefore outsiders' employment opportunities in the first period are spoilt *due to* insiders' activity. Now since outsiders remain unemployed in the first period in spite of their willingness to join the workforce, according to the author, this situation characterizes involuntary unemployment in the economy. However, there are problems with the model to which we now turn.

Checking the consistency of the argument: a critique of the Solow argument

One can imagine at least three circumstances under which the result predicted by the model does not hold (insiders' activity *cannot* spoil outsiders' employment opportunity in the first period). Therefore, Solow's explanation of persistent involuntary unemployment using the I-O framework remains open to question. We further show that the policy recommendation of the model is unlikely to solve the problem of persistent involuntary unemployment in the real world. In what follows, we shall take up these cases seriatim.

Case A

It is already pointed out that Solow makes an unduly restrictive assumption that workers can be fired but cannot be replaced. This assumption is at complete variance with reality and therefore should be done away with. Let us consider the more realistic condition in which existing insiders *can* be replaced by newly trained workers carried over from the first period. This circumstance seems all the more plausible since Solow maintains that 'the firm assumes no long-run responsibility for its workers' (ibid.: 418) and there is no firing cost in the model.

Now if the firm *can* replace its insider workers, the union loses all its bargaining power and hence wage-setting status. This is easy to see. Suppose, in response to period 2 turning bright, the union proposes to set the wage of its members above the reservation wage of insiders (w_0). By the basic tenet of the model, the union has to reveal this motive in period 1 only. Remember, outsiders hired in period 1 turn into insiders in every respect after one period of training. Since the firm gets to know the union's wage claim for period 2 sitting in period 1 itself, the firm would simply fire its *current/initial* insiders (i.e. union members) in period 2 and replace them with *newly* trained insiders (hired in period 1 for training with the condition that in the next period trained workers would work at their reservation wage w_0) to fulfil its requirement of insiders in period 2.[52] Knowing this possibility, the union can only claim the reservation wage for its members. In other words, initial insiders' (m) wage gets tethered to the reservation wage of insiders (w_0) once the firm can replace its insiders.

That being the case, whenever period 2 turns bright, the firm is faced with the following profit maximisation problem [note Eq. (2) stated above modifies to Eq. (2*)]. Note that the wage of initial insiders in period 2 is tethered to w_0; w_2 is the reservation wage of outsiders:

$$(s_1 \varphi f'(0) - w_2) + R\{s_2 f'(m) - w_0\} > 0 \tag{2*}$$

And the *number of outsiders hired in period 1*, e_{21}, is determined by the following condition [note Eq. (3) stated above modifies to Eq. (3*)]:

$$(s_1 \varphi f'(e_{21}) - w_2) + R\{s_2 f'(m + e_{21}) - w_0\} = 0 \tag{3*}$$

Since some outsiders get employment in period 1 only, involuntary unemployment in the economy falls. Thus, if one of the assumptions of the model is changed, its central result does not hold. Therefore, it can be safely concluded that the main finding of the model is already assumed; moreover, the assumption itself is clearly unrealistic.

Case B

By now it must be clear that the union's wage-bargaining power and its deciding upon a wage unilaterally, which fully negates employment opportunity for outsiders in period 1 – even if the state of the economy revives in period 2 considerably – are derived from the specific assumption that incumbent workers cannot be replaced and in the long run it is only possible to add to the size of the existing labour pool of the firm at the margin. Hence, competition in the labour market for replacing the existing insiders is ruled out by assumption. Let us revisit (2) once more:

$$(s_1 \varphi f'(0) - w_2) + R\{s_2 f'(m) - w_{12}\} > 0 \qquad (2)$$

If the above condition is true, then the following must also be true:

$$(s_1 \varphi f'(0) - w_2) + R\{s_2 f'(0) - w_{12}\} > 0 \qquad (2^\dagger)$$

This is because of the diminishing marginal productivity condition. The equation ($2^\dagger$) simply represents the lifetime profitability conditions faced by a *new* firm entering the market in period 1 with *no* incumbent worker (i.e. $m = 0$) in its labour pool. Since s_2 is assumed to be known in this model, the new firm has information about ($2^\dagger$) sitting in period 1. In such a situation, although it is the case that the existing firm cannot offer employment to the outsiders due to insider activity, the new firm, with no insiders to begin with, can nonetheless offer an overlapping wage contract of the following kind. It offers employment to the outsiders (at outsiders' reservation wage w_2) in period 1 with a *written* wage contract (such that it cannot be violated) for the second period. The contract specifies that in period 2, when these inexperienced outsiders will turn into experienced insiders, they will settle for reservation wage of the insiders, w_0. Outsiders who are otherwise unemployed have no reason to decline such offers (for $w_0 > w_2$). If that is the case, the number of outsiders getting employed in period 1 would be determined by the following condition:

$$(s_1 \varphi f'(e_{21}) - w_2) + R\{s_2 f'(e_{12}) - w_0\} = 0 \qquad \text{where, } e_{21} = e_{12}$$

Therefore, with new firms entering the market, it is possible to find conditions for outsiders' employment in period 1 itself. Hence, with new firms entering the market, involuntary unemployment in the economy falls. In such cases insiders' activity cannot spoil the employment opportunity of outsiders in period 1.

In fact, new firms armed with overlapping wage contracts – with the ability to offer reservation to insiders in period 2 can *out-compete* the existing firm by selling commodities at a lower price in period 2. In fear of losing their employment (in case the existing firm goes out of business) and joining the ranks of outsiders, union members would refrain from unilateral wage setting as described by the author, clearing the way for *outsiders' employment opportunity even in the existing firm in period 1 (once period 2 turns bright)*. Therefore, the moment some kind of outside competition is introduced in the model, its main conclusion does not hold.

Case C

The central message of the model is worth repeating here, namely, the insiders by claiming a high enough wage for period 2 (in response to period 2 turning bright) can spoil the employment prospect of outsiders in period 1. Now for this result to hold true, it was shown that Solow must assume that the union knows *exactly* the state of the economy in period 2 (s_2), in period 1 itself. Suppose this is *not* true and the union does not have perfect foresight. Instead, the union can only *imperfectly guess* the state of the economy emerging in period 2. For simplicity we assume that $s_2^e = \lambda s_2$, where $0 < \lambda < 1$ – which means that the union can only guess the actual price in period 2 *imperfectly*. In other words, this assumption is akin to the assumption that workers can be cheated.

If workers *can* be cheated, then the union would quote its wage according to the *expected* price emerging in period 2 (i.e. s_2^e). Since the union's objective is to maximise insiders' wage claims subject to full employment of its initial members (m), it would thus claim $w_{12} = s_2^e f'(m)$ as second period's wage. Now whenever the following condition [Eq. (2#)] holds true [note that Eq. (2) changes to Eq. (2#) with wage claim of the union at $w_{12} = s_2^e f'(m)$]:

$$(s_1 \varphi f'(0) - w_2) + R\{s_2 f'(m) - s_2^e f'(m)\} > 0 \qquad (2^\#)$$

this would open up conditions for outsiders' employment in period 1. The precise number of outsiders to be recruited (e_{21}) in period 1 is decided by the following condition Eq. (3#):

$$(s_1 \varphi f'(e_{21}) - w_2) + R\{s_2 f'(m + e_{12}) - s_2^e f'(m)\} = 0 \qquad (3^\#)$$

Since outsiders get employment in period 1 itself, involuntary unemployment in the economy falls. This shows that once the restrictive assumption of perfect foresight is relaxed, the main result of the model could not be sustained.

Case D

The policy recommendation of the model described by the author in order to get rid of involuntary unemployment is: 'Because outsiders are initially unskilled, it would take a discrete *reduction in the wage* below the level giving full employment of insiders to induce firm to hire outsiders' (emphasis added) (ibid.: 421).

It is clear from the foregoing observation that in this model everything operates only through the wage channel (hence purely on grounds of precise profit maximization) without any reference to the aggregate demand (AD) situation in the economy. The policy recommendation – that discrete wage reduction of insiders in period 2 (w_{12}) can create favourable employment opportunity for outsiders – does not hold if AD is considered explicitly. This is because, to begin with, the primary condition for employment of outsiders in period 1 is that the state of the economy in period 2 (s_2) should turn bright.[53] Remember, s_2 is price of the product in period 2. Now suppose discrete wage reduction of the insiders in period 2 (w_{12}) is implemented. Evidently, the share of wages in output obtained by employing the *initial* set of insiders (i.e. *m*) would *fall* and this would lead to a *reduction* of AD in period 2. This contraction of AD in period 2 must have a *negative feedback* effect for the 'state of the economy in period 2' (i.e. s_2). Thus, once AD is considered, the policy recommendation of the model challenges the basic foundation under which the model, as perceived by the author, works. Thus, we end up in a contradiction for reasons stated below.

It is clear that in a post wage cut situation, due to lack of AD, there would be an excess supply in the commodity market in period 2. This would cause a dampening effect on employment prospects of the outsiders through the following route, in contrast to the story developed by the author. An AD shortage in period 2 would turn the state of expectations about the economy (s_2) gloomy, rather than turning it bright, since a portion of the firm's output would go unsold. Clearly, this fall in price (s_2), in a straightforward fashion, would have a dampening effect on employment prospects of the outsiders [see Eq. (2)]. Moreover, even if prices in period 2 (s_2) do not fall and profit maximization justifies recruiting outsiders (i.e. inequality condition in Eq. 2 holds) – firms nonetheless will not recruit outsiders, owing to the perception of shortage of AD emerging in period 2. Thus, once AD is brought into the picture, Solow's policy recommendation – namely, discrete wage reduction of insiders in period 2 – which he believes can favourably create employment opportunity for outsiders, no longer holds. But detailed discussions of these issues are postponed until Chapter 6, where we take account of AD considerations in detail.

Conclusion

Since there is a lack of understanding in the literature about the theoretical foundation underlying LMF, we first reviewed the empirical studies which prescribe labour market reforms. From the interpretation of empirical studies it was clear that the authors arguing for LMF were basing their arguments on direct (wage) costs and indirect (adjustment) costs. They explained unemployment in terms of rigid real wages and explained real wage rigidity in terms of LTCs. Such explanation is provided by the Insider-Outsider theory of employment and unemployment – where involuntary unemployment is explained in terms of the bargaining power of insiders – derived from LTCs. Next, a detailed survey of the I-O theory was carried out. But I-O theory could not explain the existence of involuntary unemployment, if firms do not have to bear hiring cost, under following circumstances: (a) there is a two-tier wage system, and (b) when new firms enter the market. Moreover, it was shown that hiring costs alone are sufficient to generate involuntary unemployment (in which case LMF loses all its effectiveness – as hiring costs cannot be removed by LMF) or, if we assume in the authors' line (that hiring costs do not generate unemployment), then the standard definition of reservation wage is violated.

We also discussed a paper by Solow in the I-O framework with skill differentials, in which the author showed, in an intertemporal setting, that insiders' activity – by claiming higher wages in the first period – can nullify employment opportunity of the outsiders, even when the second period is believed to be good/bright. However, we showed that the existence of involuntary unemployment could not be explained if: (a) firms *can* replace existing insiders by newly trained workers; (b) either existing firms write *overlapping* wage contracts with their employees or new firms are allowed to enter the market; (c) the union does not have perfect foresight; or (d) aggregate demand (AD) is brought into the picture. In fact, the policy recommendation of Solow's model will turn out to be counterproductive in the real world (where AD has an autonomous role to play in determining the economy's output). Therefore, Solow's policy recommendation would fail to create employment opportunity for the outsiders once AD is introduced in the picture.

However, both the papers carried out their arguments without any reference to aggregate/effective demand and solely on the basis of precise profit maximization exercise. Each of them explained unemployment in terms of real wage rigidity. Thus, policy implications of both papers were to cut real wages (in order to reach the market clearing level) to restore full employment. Whether such policy persuasions would yield the desired result *unambiguously* will be the subject matter of Chapter 6, where we consider effective demand explicitly. Meanwhile, in the next chapter we look at the market clearing models which argue in favour of LMF. Interestingly, in such a framework, markets are, once again, assumed to clear through full wage flexibility.

Notes

1 It should be mentioned at the outset that the theories discussed below rule out aggregate demand deficiency that afflicts any money-using economy.
2 Actually, Fallon and Lucas (1991) is an earlier version of Fallon and Lucas (1993).
3 These adjustment costs in authors' words are:

On the hiring side certain components of these costs are apparent – the costs of attracting a pool of applicants, the costs of screening the applicants either before appointment or during an initial trial phase, and the costs of training. On the firing side costs may also be incurred. For example, if any worker possessing firm-specific skills quits, this typically imposes a net loss on the firm. Moreover, even without legislated requirements, firms may voluntarily choose to enter a contract with their employees that promises *severance* pay.

(emphasis added) (Fallon and Lucas 1991: 400–401)

By adjustment costs, the authors mean costs associated with labour *entering* or *exiting* a firm, [i.e. labour turnover costs (LTCs)]. Note that JSR may be instrumental only in raising firing costs but not hiring costs (since stipulation of training costs or, initial trial phase cannot be laid down by law).

4 LTCs operate only through the wage route in raising labour cost.
5 It may be thought that there is an element of double counting here, since it is argued that JSR increases LTCs and results in higher wage claims of the currently employed, raising labour cost. However, there is no double-counting since the argument is: removal of currently employed workers involves an expense of LTCs (hiring and firing costs) for firms. Knowing this fact, currently employed workers immediately ask for higher wages even without facing the prospect of retrenchment (their wage-bargaining power determined by the magnitude of LTC). This increases the cost of labour currently employed (in form of higher wages), since they understand that the firm would be indifferent between keeping and retrenching them. In plain terms, the currently employed workers ask for higher wages once they understand that firms would not mind paying them higher wages – for otherwise, in case they are retrenched, firms would anyway have to bear the hiring and firing costs. Thus, LTCs and rising real wages do not increase the cost of labour in additive manner; rather LTCs are instrumental in bestowing the bargaining power in the hands of current workers (as the firm has to anyway sacrifice LTCs for separating current workers) who utilize it to raise their wages.
6 Now the expropriation effect is not identified by the authors as an additional factor contributing to adoption of higher capital intensive techniques causing employment stagnation. Rather, an employment slowdown is explained through lower capital stock formation (as investment is discouraged by lowering returns on investments, due to rent-seeking activity of workers – derived from higher bargaining power following introduction of JSR) – reducing the number of workers required to work on it.
7 That is unemployed at the time of introduction of labour regulations.
8 Currently employed are known as Insiders and those unemployed are known as Outsiders. The adjustment costs typically make labour

adjustment costly and hence sluggish. In India, it is claimed, such tendencies are present: 'Inertia in employment is consistent with firing restrictions as also with insider activity, for both of which there is evidence in Indian manufacturing' (Bhalotra 1998: 25).
9 Wages of existing workers remain rigid (above market-clearing levels) since underbidding is not possible if wage costs and adjustment or turnover costs are equal at the margin.
10 Major contributions of the authors in this field have been compiled in a book titled, *The Insider-Outsider Theory of Employment and Unemployment*, Assar Lindbeck and Dennis J. Snower, 1988, MIT Press Cambridge, Massachusetts and London, England. All references made in the section are from this book unless otherwise stated.
11 Actually, outsiders comprise a larger set, according to the authors, '[T] here are two broad types of outsiders: unemployed workers and those employed in the "informal sector". For simplicity of exposition, this book deals almost exclusively with outsiders of the first type' (ibid.: 2).
12 Notice that the explanation of involuntary unemployment has something to do with rigid wages (more on this below).
13 Some 'rent-related' turnover costs may be endogenous in the sense that they are the outcome of incumbent workers' rent-creating activities. For instance, insiders may be able to influence outsiders' potential productivity and willingness to work. This is the Cooperation-Harassment version of I-O theory. This version states that insiders may refuse to cooperate with new entrants in a firm and thus reduce entrants' marginal product sufficiently to discourage firms from hiring new workers. Alternatively, the insiders may threaten to have unfriendly personal relations with newcomers, they may harass them and thereby raise the potential entrants' disutility of work sufficiently to discourage these workers from entering the firm. For a detailed discussion on the Cooperation-Harassment version of I-O theory, see Chapter 5 titled, 'Cooperation-Harassment and Involuntary Unemployment', of Lindbeck and Snower (1988).
14 Rigid wages mean these are inflexible downwards. That it is a sufficient condition for the existence of involuntary unemployment is amply clear from below:

> these [unemployed] workers must have an incentive to gain employment by offering to work less than the prevailing wages. In order for involuntary unemployment to be persistent, there must be some other agents who are both motivated and able to prevent such underbidding
>
> (ibid.: 61).

In the I-O theory, these agents who prevent underbidding are the incumbent workers or insiders (see below).
15 The authors' notion regarding the instrumentality of real wages in generating unemployment came out most clearly while they were discussing the effectiveness of demand management policies in reducing unemployment. It is best to quote them in detail:

> [There] are at least two routes whereby demand management can raise employment and production: (a) it can raise the price level before the insiders have a chance to adjust their nominal wages, thereby reducing the real product wage and inducing firms to hire more workers, or (b) it can give firms the incentive to expand employment at any given real wage. Route (a) involves a movement along a downward-sloping labour demand curve, whereas route (b) involves either an outward shift of that curve or a movement along a horizontal segment of the labor demand curve.
>
> (ibid.: 266)

16 Provided it is assumed, for argument's sake, that there are zero hiring costs.
17 Note that the question of replacement arises only in the case of successful underbidding by the outsiders.
18 The authors note:

> Under this setup, *the level at which the insider wage will actually be set depends on the size of the firm's incumbent workforce.* To illustrate why, let us assume that the firm's production technology is characterised by diminishing returns to labor. Thus, the larger is firm's incumbent workforce, the lower the marginal revenue product of this workforce will be, and the lower the entrants' marginal revenue product will be as well. When the firm's incumbent workforce is sufficiently large, the entrants' marginal revenue product (net of the marginal hiring costs) falls beneath their reservation wage, and consequently entrants are not profitable to the firm. Since entrants are then completely excluded from finding jobs in the firm, the insiders can disregard the relative profitability constraint and rather set their wage in accordance with the absolute profitability constraint. In short, the insider wage is set equal to the marginal revenue product of the incumbent workforce plus the marginal firing costs. On the other hand, when the firm's incumbent workforce is sufficiently small, so that entrants' marginal revenue product (net of marginal hiring costs) exceeds their reservation wage then some entrants will be hired. The insiders are now in competition with the entrants, and thus they set their wage in accordance with the relative profitability constraint. In this case, the insider wage is a mark up over the entrant wage with the size of the mark up determined by the sum of the marginal hiring and firing costs.
>
> (emphasis added) (ibid.: 6)

19 The reservation wages of the outsiders are typically derived from labour-leisure choice. The various combinations of reservation wages, and labourers' willingness to supply labour at those wages, generates the labour supply schedule of the economy. Note that for attaining full employment, the labour demand schedule must intersect the labour supply schedule of the economy. Therefore, full employment wage must be one, from the set of supply prices of labour.

20 The logic is the same as before. Since hiring costs have already been expended on entrants (and not on outsiders), entrants understand that the firm would be indifferent between the following two situations: (a) pay entrants wages higher than the reservation wage of outsiders to the extent of hiring cost; or (b) firing entrants and hiring outsiders (on whom hiring cost has to be expended now) in their place. This is because, from the point of view of a firm adopting either of the routes, there is no difference in terms of cost.

21 At a wage that is below the insider wage, if all turnover costs were only production-related (of course taking care of the insider-outsider productivity differences), then clearly only production-related LTCs provides no market power to the insiders such that it can generate involuntary unemployment. But note the statement that outsiders are willing to work for wages below the insider wage if LTCs were only production-related is simply an assumption.

22 That demonstrates the inability of outsiders to underbid the insiders. This shows the equivalence between unsuccessful underbidding and no replacement condition.

23 The policy suggestion (discussed later in detail) essentially entails removing the rent-related turnover costs; presently incurred due to the current provisions in law. Note that production-related turnover costs are technologically given and hence cannot be dispensed with. Precisely due to this tacit reasoning, it has been simply assumed that outsiders may be willing to work for less than the insider wage minus production related turnover costs but not for the production- and rent-related turnover costs.

24 For simplicity of exposition we abstract from the complication that insiders and outsiders have different MPL curves.

25 On the other hand, if the initial pool of insiders was more than L_I, then insiders could increase their wage only by the amount of the marginal product of the last insider plus the firing cost. The rest of the analysis that follows would be exactly the same irrespective of the size of the initial insiders' pool.

26 Remember that firing costs cause involuntary unemployment and not hiring costs. Naturally, I-O theory puts greater weight on 'power-reducing policies' vis-à-vis 'enfranchising policies' (see below). However, we would show that hiring costs alone are capable of generating involuntary unemployment if the definition of reservation wages is adhered to.

27 In Chapter 6 we will show that this is tantamount to assuming Say's law of market.

28 The authors clearly state: '[A]s a rule, hiring and training costs tend to be predominantly production-related, whereas firing costs are frequently rent-related' (ibid.: 63).

29 In this context, the enthusiasm around the Modi government's flagship 'Skill India' programme should not be lost sight of.

30 In the authors' words: 'Two-tier wage systems [are such], whereby *incumbent workers receive at least their previous remuneration level while new recruits receive permanently less. . .*' (emphasis added) (ibid.: 263).

31 Outsiders, otherwise unemployed, have no reason to oppose this.
32 This is because firing costs still protect – invoking authors' reason – insiders position vis-à-vis newly trained entrants. At the margin – due to firing costs for removing insiders – the representative firm would be indifferent between insiders and newly trained entrants, considering their equivalence in effective labour cost.
33 This particular shortcoming is recognised by authors but tactically bypassed by the simple assertion: 'The Insider-Outsider theories *are not aimed at question [as] why are the involuntarily unemployed workers unwilling or unable to employ themselves by starting new firms?*' (emphasis added) (ibid.: 51). However, they probably recognise that such a possibility is fatal to their explanation of involuntary unemployment and therefore in the policy recommendation part, they accept that with new firms entering the market, employment can go up (see the discussion on enfranchising policies).
34 Remember that we already abstracted from the productivity differentials between insiders and outsiders for simplicity of exposition.
35 This is precisely the reason why I-O theory assumes that hiring costs do not form an obstacle towards attaining full employment – since no matter what form of reforms are introduced in name of LMF, hiring costs like advertisement, screening and training costs can never be completely eliminated. Further, note that the argument that outsiders are willing to work below insiders' wage only by amount of hiring cost and not by the sum of hiring and firing cost is simply an assertion which has nowhere been proved.
36 The model which follows is from Robert M. Solow's paper, 'Insiders and Outsiders in Wage Determination', *Scandinavian Journal of Economics*, 1985, 87(2): 411–428.
37 The rationale for doing so in the author's words is:

> One of the hardest nuts to crack, it seems to me, is to explain why unemployed workers do not compete for existing jobs by offering to work at jobs for which they are qualified at a wage lower than that currently being paid to incumbents.
>
> (ibid.: 412)

Note that for the author, the existence of involuntary unemployment is purely due to the non-existence of wage competition (i.e. wage rigidity) among workers.

38 However, there is no justification provided about from where the union derives this wage-setting status (unlike in the previous model where the wage-setting status of the insiders was derived from LTCs). Nonetheless, we shall see later the crucial implication of such wage-setting status of the insiders' union on the employment opportunities of the outsiders and in what ways it creates a condition for persistent involuntary unemployment.
39 Outsiders after one period of employment turn into insiders and also get union membership.
40 In the author's words: '[W]e assume that the union is able simply to quote wages w_{11} and w_{12} for experienced labor in the two periods,

while the firm is able to choose levels of employment unilaterally' (ibid.: 415).
41 Therefore, unlike in the earlier model, there is no firing cost in this model.
42 Remember that due to the restrictive assumption of the model, employment opportunity for outsiders can only be created by expanding the existing labour pool, since there cannot be any replacement of insiders.
43 Actually, s_1 and s_2 can simply be thought of as the product price in period 1 and period 2, respectively. As the author notes: 'If it [firm] employs e_{11} of them [insiders] in period 1 it will generate an output whose market *value* is $s_1 f(e_{11})$' (ibid.: 414) (emphasis added).
44 See Patnaik (2008), Chapter 6 for critique of Rational Expectations assumption.
45 Solow is not interested in the employment opportunity of the outsiders arising in period 2, since by construction it is the last period. According to the author, only if some outsiders are hired in period 1 can involuntary unemployment fall. Hence, the author is interested in investigating the employment opportunities that may arise for the outsiders only in period 1.
46 Such that the requirement of insiders in period 2 would be in excess of what is currently available to the firm.
47 Remember that w_0 is the reservation wage of insiders and assumed to be greater than the reservation wage of outsiders w_2.
48 Solow gives an explanation for why insiders would set a high wage for period 2, which eliminates outsiders' employment opportunity, as follows:

> [W]hat may induce the incumbents to set a wage that has the effect of excluding outsiders from current employment is precisely the realization that enlarging the pool of insiders now will lead in the future to a higher unemployment rate among members, and/or to the setting of lower wages in future in order to avoid that unemployment.
> (ibid.: 417)

49 Now if the union is only concerned with maximizing the welfare of its members, then it would adopt the following wage-setting strategy in both the periods: first, full employment of its members is ensured and then insiders' wages are raised as high as possible (above the reservation wage of insiders w_0) subject to full employment; then $w_{11} = s_1 f'(m)$ and $w_{12} = s_2 f'(m)$. Evidently, $w_{11} \neq w_{12}$ since the state of the economy $s_1 \neq s_2$; in fact, it is assumed, in particular, that generally s_1 is of low value (what employers regard as 'not very good years' ibid.: 416) and that the second period turns bright [i.e. s_2 is very high] (see ibid.: 420).
50 Since by assumption: $s_1 \varphi f'(0) < w_2$ (i.e. the first period by itself does not justify outsiders' employment in period 1).
51 That is: $\left[\dfrac{e_{12}(w_{12} - w_0)}{m} \right]$

52 In order to decide on the number of outsiders to be trained in period 1, in case all the current union members have to be replaced in period 2 (for claiming greater than insiders' reservation wage w_0) – the firm has to solve the following problem:

$$(s_1 \varphi f\,'(0) - w_2) + R\{s_2 f\,'(0) - w_0\} > 0$$

The exact number of outsiders to be trained in period 1 is determined when the above inequality turns into equality at the margin.

53 Such that the representative firm perceives that its initial insiders' pool (i.e. 'm') would fall short of the requirement of insiders in period 2 (on grounds of profit maximisation).

Chapter 5

Some market clearing models on labour market flexibility

In Chapter 4 we discussed the non-market clearing theoretical framework underlining Labour Market Flexibility (LMF). It was shown that economists recommending such policy prescriptions were relying on the Insider-Outsider theory of Employment and Unemployment. Their essential argument was to get rid of the labour laws protecting incumbent workers (insiders) in the form of severance pay and other benefits at the time of retrenchment or closure of firms. This reform, they argued, would take away the bargaining power of current employees and produce a frictionless labour market, where 'thoroughgoing competition' to use Solow's term, among workers (insiders and outsiders) would finally establish full employment equilibrium. Hence, such strands of the argument recognise the *existence of involuntary unemployment*, in absence of labour reform, and explain it through downward real wage rigidity arising out of insiders' market power, supported by firing costs. This discourages employers from freely replacing insiders by outsiders, of course normalizing for productivity differentials, which prevents thoroughgoing competition in the labour market resulting in a suboptimal outcome. Therefore, they may be termed as non-market clearing arguments for LMF. And we have criticized the validity of these arguments.

However, there is another strand of theoretical argument which *does not* accommodate the existence of involuntary unemployment and confines its analysis only to full employment equilibrium outcomes.[1] Needless to say these strands assume away involuntary unemployment with complete reliance on full wage flexibility. This chapter critically discusses two such theories formulated by Professor Kaushik Basu (2007)[2] and Professors Kaushik Basu *et al.* (2009).[3] One observation should be made at the outset – if systems are assumed to operate *always* at full employment through continuous market clearing by wage adjustments, then clearly workers' welfare is primarily assessed through comparison of wages under various equilibrium (full employment) outcomes. We now turn to the specific papers.

5.1 A game theoretic approach to labour market flexibility with skill differentials

Basu (2007) uses a game theoretic approach to argue in favour of LMF. Basu (2007: 132) notes right at the beginning: 'A policy that seems obviously good for some groups of people may turn out . . . to be detrimental to their welfare . . . labour market is one area where well-meaning but erroneous policies abound'.[4] Later he clearly states the objective: 'The aim of this chapter is to construct plausible theoretical models, using India as the backdrop of stylized facts, to show that . . . India's myriad labour laws, meant to protect labourers, may have actually hurt them' (ibid.: 132). The author cites cases where disputes arise between the employer and worker. He notes that there are difficulties in laying off workers by employers, under the circumstances when a worker is not putting in enough effort (basically shirking) or/and when the worker does not possess the adequate skill for the specified job in hand.[5] The paper assumes fixed effort; therefore, the essential argument is carried out in the skill mismatch terrain.[6] The author in particular claims:

> It will be shown that in a labour market model, which *prima facie* captures the broad realities of the Indian economy, an employer's inability to dismiss workers who turn out not to possess the required skill could, in equilibrium, hurt all workers, including the unskilled.
>
> (ibid.: 133)

The basic intuition of the model is as follows:

> If worker dismissal is disallowed or very costly, firms which need specialized skills and talents may operate on a smaller scale or, worse, close down. This would of course hurt the skilled workers and, by turning them out to the unskilled labour market, could also lower wages in the latter, thereby hurting all workers.
>
> (ibid.: 133)

Therefore, workers' welfare is assessed in terms of equilibrium wages under two situations, layoffs and no-layoffs: '[I] t will be shown that enabling retrenchment and layoffs may result in larger employment and higher wages in the equilibrium' (ibid.: 134). The author therefore prescribes specific policy recommendation from the model:

> [F]irms and workers to have greater freedom to sign contracts concerning layoffs, retrenchment and closure . . . to add a clause which gives workers *the right to waive the right not to be dismissed* as conferred on them currently by the Act [IDA].
>
> (emphasis added) (ibid.: 135)

So it suggests that the unfreedom[7] to sign contracts at will on the part of employers and workers is at the root of the problem and recommends enabling amendment to IDA. Let us now consider the basic assumptions of the model.

As the model promises to capture the broad realities of Indian labour market, and the author claims that 'the modelling here is based on realistic assumptions' (ibid.: 133), it considers a set of firms which are large or dominant firms with the following characteristics: where layoff and dismissal laws apply, firms are capable of affecting the market wage [i.e. price setters (oligopsonists) in the labour market] and only require skilled labour. These firms, it may be concluded from the set of assumptions, resemble the organised sector. Another set of firms are considered which are small or fringe firms; essentially they do not come under the purview of IDA by virtue of being too small. These firms are wage takers and have no special use for skilled labour. These firms closely bear the features of the unorganised sector.

It is interesting to note how skill is defined in the paper. The author defines skill as: 'The skills needed for dealing with people, for remembering little tasks to be performed, and for punctuality often fall in this category' (ibid.: 136). Further, he claims that:

> People better endowed with these skills may not necessarily find it easier to acquire education, so even in equilibrium such skills may not be strongly correlated with the degrees and diplomas held by a worker, thus making standard job-market signaling models *irrelevant for our purpose.*
>
> (ibid.: 136) (emphasis added)

Since standard job-market signalling models become *irrelevant*, skill is *solely* defined in the specified way mentioned above. The author then assumes that workers possess only two levels of skills: either they are skilled or unskilled labour.

It is further assumed that the aggregate supply curve of labour is given by,

$$s = s(w), \qquad s'(w) > 0 \qquad (1) \; [\text{'w' is wage}]$$

Moreover, it is assumed that t proportion of the labour force is skilled, and this remains true for all levels of wages. In the author's words:

> By assuming that both skilled and unskilled workers are otherwise homogeneous or that *their labour-leisure choices are identical*, we know that if a wage of w is fixed, the supply of skilled labour is *ts(w)* and the supply of unskilled labour is *(1-t)s(w)*.
> (ibid.: 136) (emphasis added)

However, there is a problem in assuming the labour-leisure choices being *identical* across skilled and unskilled workers, *when skill is defined in the above manner*. In other words, the way skill is defined and the distinction drawn between skilled and unskilled worker is based on 'obedience' or in general what distinguishes a 'shirking-lazy' worker from a 'hard working-attentive' worker. Clearly, then, assuming that they have identical work-leisure choices is untenable. Therefore, further assuming that they can be represented by the *same* aggregate labour supply curve with t proportion being skilled and the rest unskilled, for every wage rate, is also untenable. In fact, the disobedient worker's labour supply curve should be situated *bodily to the left* of the obedient worker's labour supply curve, for all wages starting from the origin. This is easy to understand once we consider the amount of leisure chosen, for a given wage, as the indicator to distinguish between lazy and hardworking workers. Typically, for *any* wage, a lazy worker would choose *more* leisure (or *less* work) than a hardworking worker – with the result of the labour supply curve of the lazy worker lying *bodily to the left* of the hardworking worker. There is a further problem of horizontally adding skilled and unskilled workers on the horizontal axis; this is similar to the problem of adding two *different* commodities. This is because skilled labour is essentially *different* from unskilled labour and therefore *cannot* be placed on the same axis.

Let us now find out how skilled and unskilled workers are required by the dominant and fringe firms. It is assumed that from each skilled worker the dominant firms can *always* get an output of r, with $r > 0$.[8] They have no use for unskilled labour, who produce zero output in such firms. As we shall see later, this is a one-good model; therefore, assuming that unskilled or inattentive workers produce absolutely zero output in dominant firms but produce positive output of the *same* good in fringe firms is a strange assumption. It is further assumed that a fringe firm has no special use for skilled labour. Note that this also seems to be an untenable assumption, the way skill is defined. There is no reason why skilled labour (i.e. attentive and hardworking workers) would not be equally in demand in the fringe firms also (due to their higher productivity and especially when fringe firms are producing the *same* good as dominant firms) – since fringe firms are profit maximisers as well. It is further assumed that each worker, skilled or otherwise, produces an output less than r in fringe firms.

Based on these assumptions, let us concentrate on the aggregate labour demand schedule of the fringe firms. It is given by:

$$d = d(w), \qquad d'(w) < 0 \qquad (2)['w'\text{ is wage}]$$

Hence, if w is the wage, the supply of labour in excess of what is needed by the fringe firms is given by:

$$\psi(w) = s(w) - d(w) \qquad (3)$$

This is taken as the labour supply function for *dominant* firms. The dominant firm's equilibrium labour demand is obtained through profit maximization. Note that the supply of labour *in excess of what is already demanded by the fringe firms* becomes the *effective labour supply* for the dominant firms.

In the model, two situations are compared, namely, a no-layoff (N) regime denoted by the game, $G(m, N)$ and a free layoff (L) regime with the game, $G(m, L)$. The number of dominant firms operating in the industry is denoted by 'm'. The basic argument of the model is best summarized from the following quote:

> If dominant firms are not allowed to lay off workers, they are forced to make do with a labour force in which a fraction t will

be skilled and fraction *(1-t)* unskilled (since the only way to ensure that you have all skilled workers is to employ people, check them out, layoff unskilled, employ new people in their place, check them out, and so on). This will typically result in a smaller demand for labour from the dominant firms. Hence, the supply of labour in the fringe job market will be greater. This will tend to push down wages. Hence, a law preventing layoffs can actually push down *all* wages.

(ibid.: 137) (emphasis in original)

Now let us consider the contribution of a worker (i.e. productivity) recruited by dominant firms, under two regimes. Since firms have to choose workers at random (since standard job-market signalling fails) the expected output from a worker is given by rt $[= r.t + 0.(1-t)]$. When dominant firms are *not* allowed to lay off workers, then the expected output from each employed worker is rt, whereas in case of free dismissal the expected contribution from each worker is r – since through iterated churning dominant firms now can converge to a purely skilled group of workers. On the cost side, dominant firms face production cost (wage bill) and an entry fee $K(> 0)$. *Firms enter into the market only if profits net of entry fee are positive.*

Now we are in a position to look at the working of the model. It adopts a game theoretic approach and considers two time periods. In period 1, *potential* entrants (i.e. dominant firms) decide whether to enter the industry or not. Then in period 2 the ones that enter decide how much labour to employ through a precise profit maximization exercise,[9] keeping in mind that their decision will affect the labour demand of the fringe firms.[10] Equilibrium outcomes under two situations are compared [a layoff (L) regime with a no-layoff (N) regime].

If m firms are assumed to enter the industry in the first period, the second period game is described by G *(m, N)* in case of no-layoff and G *(m, L)* when layoffs are permitted.[11] However, the author only focuses on the symmetric Nash equilibrium for both situations in the second period: 'I shall here focus on the symmetric Nash equilibrium of this *m*-player game. In the examples that I consider below such an equilibrium always exists and, in fact, is the only Nash equilibrium' (ibid.: 139). Clearly, concentrating *only* on the symmetric Nash equilibrium in an oligopolistic labour market structure reduces the model's appeal. This is because in equilibrium *all* dominant firms are assumed to employ the *same* number of workers (remember symmetric equilibrium). This in turn therefore assumes that the demand functions faced by *all* dominant firms and their cost functions are identical and also that they behave as Cournot players, quite naively ignoring their mutual interdependence. This model, therefore, cannot be used for deriving *general* policy conclusions since by the set-up it restricts its application.

Before proceeding further we should keep in mind that in the situation when layoffs are allowed [i.e. $G(m, L)$ game], dominant firms arrive at a pool of workers which are *only* skilled. The contribution from each worker is expected to be r, and they would be always interested with the skilled section [i.e. *ts(w)*] of the workforce. One caveat is in order: *if the wage that dominant firms offer drops too low, then some skilled workers may prefer to go to the fringe sector.*

Now if the Industrial Disputes Act is repealed, we would switch from $G(m, N)$ to $G(m, L)$. Although the author states: 'While all kinds of welfare changes are possible, I *focus here on the relatively counter-intuitive one* and demonstrate that laborers – all laborers – can be better off under G_L [free layoff regime]' (ibid.: 141) (emphasis added). The idea here is to check whether the *method* employed by the author to arrive at the counter-intuitive result allows one to draw a *general* policy prescription. *Is the result general or a very special case? Most importantly, can one suggest freedom of signing of contracts from the model?*

Let us consider the nature of the proof. The author confines attention to class of linear models. The aggregate supply curve of labour and aggregate demand curve for labour for the fringe sector firms are assumed as:

$$s(w) = bw \qquad (4)$$

$$d(w) = A - Bw \qquad (5)$$

Let us consider employment, profits and wages for the $G(m, N)$ game below. This is obtained by maximizing the following profit equation:

$$\Pi^N_i(n_1,...,n_m) = \left[rt - \frac{\sum n_j}{b+B} - \frac{A}{b+B} \right] n_i$$

The labour employed, profits and wages earned under symmetric Nash equilibrium are given by:

$$n^N = \frac{rt(b+B) - A}{m+1} \tag{6}$$

$$\Pi^N(m) = \left[\frac{rt(b+B) - A}{m+1}\right]^2 \cdot \frac{1}{b+B} \tag{7}$$

$$W^N = \frac{mrt}{m+1} + \frac{A}{(b+B)(m+1)} \tag{8}$$

Let us now consider these expressions for the $G(m, L)$ game below. Restricting to conditions when dominant firms' wage offers *do not* drop low enough to send some of the skilled workers to fringe firms, employment, profits and wages earned under symmetric Nash equilibrium are obtained by the following profit maximisation exercise:

$$\Pi^L_i(n_1,...,n_m) = \left[r - \frac{\Sigma n_j}{tb}\right] n_j$$

The labour employed, profits and wages earned under symmetric Nash equilibrium are given by:

$$n^L = \frac{rtb}{m+1} \tag{9}$$

$$\Pi^L(m) = \frac{r^2 tb}{(m+1)^2} \tag{10}$$

$$W^L = \frac{mr}{m+1} \tag{11}$$

Now we discuss the proof (i.e. *method*) employed by the author to demonstrate the counter-intuitive case where *all* workers benefit from a free layoff regime G_L. Notice that from the expressions derived above by the profit maximization exercise, in both cases, *nothing can be conclusively said.* Neither workers can be said to benefit from a free layoff regime, nor can they be said to benefit from a no-layoff regime. Hereafter, the author takes the following route.

The author states that – *if* Π^L *(m)* $> \Pi^N$ *(m)* holds, from Eq. (7) and (10) we get:

$$\frac{r^2 tb}{(m+1)^2} > \left[\frac{rt(b+B) - A}{m+1}\right]^2 \cdot \frac{1}{b+B}$$

Then we can find an entry fee $K > 0$ such that:

$$\Pi^L(1) > K > \Pi^N(1) \qquad (12)$$

[Notice in the above inequality $m = 1$, which means that if the above inequality holds, dominant firms enter *only under* layoff regimes and *not* in no-layoff regimes, since profits net of entry fee would be negative in the latter case.]

From Eq. (7) and (10) with $m = 1$ we get:

$$\frac{r^2 tb}{4} > K > \left[\frac{rt(b+B) - A}{2}\right]^2 \cdot \frac{1}{b+B} \qquad (13)$$

After this author constructs a hypothetical example where r = 2, t = ½, b = 2, B = 8, A = 8 and $K = {}^3/_4$, Eq. (13) holds true (with $m = 1$). In such an instance, the author concludes that switching from $G(m, N)$ to $G(m, L)$ is beneficial for all workers. Hence, free layoffs should be upheld under such circumstances.

This is so, for *if* the parameters take the values as assumed by the author, *then* the structure of the argument is as follows: *if* Eq. (13) holds, then there will be no dominant firms in the industry when layoffs are banned since $\Pi^N(1)-K < 0$. So if layoffs are banned, all workers (both skilled and unskilled) will be getting a wage of $w = \frac{A}{b+B}$, which just clears the labour market that consists of only fringe sector firms and equates $d(w) = s(w)$. However, if layoffs are allowed, entry of some dominant firms in the market requiring skilled labour is bound to happen, since $\Pi^L(1)-K > 0$. Dominant firms will, of course, pay their skilled workers a higher wage, $w = \frac{mr}{m+1}$. And by virtue of dominant firms employing workers, the supply of labour to the fringe sector will fall. Hence, the fringe sector wage will also rise, and workers there (irrespective of skilled or unskilled) will receive $w = \dfrac{A}{(1-t)b + B}$. Plugging in the parameter values as assumed by the author, it is easy to see that wages received by workers in a layoff regime are greater than in a no-layoff regime. Since there is full employment everywhere, workers remain better off in a layoff regime compared to a no-layoff regime. Therefore, the author argues:

> By confining attention to situations where $\Pi^L(1) > K > \Pi^N(1)$, we here get the result that there will be no entry of [dominant] firms using skilled labor if layoffs are not permitted. In that case we can assert that allowing for layoffs will cause an expansion in the sector using skilled labor thereby pulling up wages for all workers.
>
> (ibid.: 143) (emphasis added)

The question arises: can one uphold the principle of signing free contracts at will from this particular example constructed by the author?

Now based on this particular example, the author recommends a *general* policy conclusion that:

> This paper . . . argued that legislation or even *customary practice* which makes the laying off of labor illegal or (exogenously) costly may be harmful for the workers. The same may happen if employers are *a priori* given the freedom to fire workers at will. Instead, workers and employers should have the *freedom to develop their own contract* concerning the conditions for the dismissal of labor.
>
> (ibid.: 145) (emphasis added)

The author urges that under *certain* circumstances full hire and fire may not be bad, although not always good. Workers and employers should therefore be given the opportunity to freely develop and sign contracts.[12] However, it was already mentioned that developing such *free* contracts are a myth under capitalism – especially between workers and capitalists – since all such contracts are bound to be dominated by the asymmetric distribution of power between these two classes.[13] By the very threat of unemployment, workers may be disciplined (even manipulated) by employers (Kalecki 1971).[14]

In any case, such voluntary separation route *already exists* in the current setting and need not await the proposed amendment by the author to IDA. As Fallon *et al.* (1991: 400) notes:

> The one situation in which *permission is not required for separation* in either country [India and Zimbabwe] is when *both parties agree to the termination* of employment. Naturally, this opens the possibility of paying workers to quit or retire voluntarily. *Indeed this practice seems commonplace throughout the formal wage sector in both nations and clearly represents the main escape clause available.*

(emphasis added)

However, acceding to the author's proposal for suitable amendment of the IDA – that workers should be given the freedom to reserve the right for not being fired (under some situations) and also the right for being fired (under other occasions) – could turn out to be detrimental for job security. It may end up, in effect, establishing free hire and fire rules. This is because workers can be pushed to sign a layoff contract by the employer, at the will of the latter, whenever deemed necessary, and make it appear voluntary ex post.[15]

Further, from the *limited* number of cases analysed by the author, his policy recommendation *does not* follow from the model. Note that in the model, under certain situations, layoffs are shown to be beneficial to *both* employer and the employees.[16] Therefore, from the model it appears that whenever layoffs are beneficial to the employer, they are *simultaneously* beneficial to the workers. In other words, a layoff is analysed in the context of a *positive* sum game. Interestingly, with layoffs being common knowledge, *if* layoffs were *only* a positive sum game (and better than no-layoffs in some situations) – as demonstrated by the author – then workers would *not object* to being laid off (since it is beneficial for workers also, they would never file any lawsuit). Consequently, dominant firms knowing this must not hesitate from entering the market and recruiting workers. Hence, a model with layoffs being analysed *only* in the context of positive sum *cannot* justify the policy recommendation – that workers be provided the right for 'giving up the right not to be dismissed' (ibid.: 135).[17] In other words, IDA in its *current form* need not cause any hindrance to employers for dismissing workers, *if layoffs are analysed only in the context of positive sum game.* Let us elaborate on this point.

Suppose IDA remains intact, without any kind of amendment, as proposed by the author. Therefore, effectively we are in a no-layoff regime. Now suppose some situation arises where free layoffs become more beneficial for *both* workers and employers, *simultaneously*, over no-layoffs – similar to the case analysed in the model. Clearly, since free layoffs emerge as a win-win situation for everybody, employers need not find any difficulty in laying off workers, as the latter would depart *on their own* (precisely because it is in their best interest to do so). So the benefits of a free layoff regime can be fully reaped even *without* the said amendment in place, provided layoffs are *mutually* beneficial. The author probably realizes this and therefore makes some artificial distinctions, without discussing the implications of those distinctions in terms of outcomes (in the context of layoffs being considered as mutually beneficial). The author argues:

> Over here we must distinguish between 'not resisting dismissal' and 'giving up the right not to be dismissed'. A worker can of course choose not to resist dismissal; but what is interesting is that he may not (and, in case of India, he *is* not) be able to waive the right not to be dismissed.
>
> (emphasis in original) (ibid.: 135)

However, the author is completely silent on *how* such distinctions *qualitatively* matter. Since the author only discusses the case of layoff being *mutually* beneficial to *both* workers and employers, under such situations actually emerging, nobody would report/complain to concerned authorities regarding layoffs. Therefore, it ultimately makes no difference, in terms of final outcomes, whether workers 'do not resist dismissal' or they *can* 'give up the right not to be dismissed'. Consequently, any distinction between them is completely artificial.

Moreover, even in situations when free layoffs are *potentially* beneficial to all, still the principle of free contract may not produce favourable results for workers. This is because in the real world there *is* involuntary unemployment which reduces the bargaining power of the workers drastically; with free layoffs, workers are virtually left with no bargaining power at all.[18] And if it is genuinely beneficial, then law cannot stand in its way.

However, our concern is that there can be cases (and they are more prevalent in reality) where layoffs (and therefore no-layoffs also) are actually *zero sum game*, where the interest of players (firm and workers) are in *conflict* with each other. Under such situations of conflict of interests (not discussed in the paper, but considered below), with the recommended amendment of voluntary signing of contracts in place, there can be employers' decision ruling supreme without taking the interest of employees into account. It is not difficult to imagine such circumstances, and one can imagine at least three different situations under which conflict of interests between capitalists and workers can arise. In all the cases considered below, dominant firms enter the market *both* in case of the layoff and the no-layoff regimes. In what follows, we take up these cases seriatim.

Case A

Consider the following parameter values: $r = 10$, $t = 0.85$, $b = 2$, $B = 1$, $A = 6$, $m = 1$ and $K = 20$. Note that dominant firms would be present in *both* layoff and no-layoff regimes.[19] It is easy to check that the interest of employers and workers are in *conflict* with each other. This is because, with the parameter values just mentioned, a dominant firm's profit in a layoff regime is *higher* than in a no-layoff regime [i.e. $\Pi^L > \Pi^N$ from Eq. (7) and Eq. (10)]. However, in the dominant sector, employment in a no-layoff regime is *higher* than in a layoff regime [i.e. $n^N > n^L$ from Eqs. (6) and (9)]; also, the wage in the dominant sector in a no-layoff regime is *higher* than in a layoff regime [i.e. $W^N > W^L$ from Eq. (8) and Eq. (11)].[20] Also note that the employment in a fringe (i.e. unorganized segment) sector in a no-layoff regime (n^N_f) is *less* than the employment in the fringe sector in a layoff regime (n^L_f) [i.e. $n^N_f < n^L_f$, these are directly read off from the aggregate labour demand function of the fringe sector, that is, Eq. (5)]. Further, $(n^N + n^N_f) > (n^L + n^L_f) -$ [i.e. *total workers employed (dominant + fringe) in a no-layoff regime* is *greater* than in a layoff regime]. This information can be summarized in the following chart.

Comparison between different regimes

Dominant firm's profit	$\Pi^L > \Pi^N$
Dominant firm's empt.	$n^N > n^L$
Wages	$W^N > W^L > \overline{W}$
Fringe sector empt.	$n^N_f < n^L_f$
Total empt.	$(n^N + n^N_f) > (n^L + n^L_f)$

Note: All expressions are computed at equilibrium.

Evidently, the interest of capitalists and workers regarding the preference for regimes are diametrically opposite – namely, capitalists would always prefer a layoff regime over a no-layoff regime, whereas workers would always prefer exactly the opposite – under the above parametric conditions. Under such situations, bargaining power becomes crucial, since no consensus can be reached between the agents, and the idea of developing contracts freely no longer appears harmonious. Now following the author's suggestion, if employers and workers are allowed to freely develop their own contract, essentially *only* interests of agents endowed with greater bargaining power (typically employers) would be protected. Since one counterexample is enough to disprove a general proposition – thus the author's proposal for allowing agents to develop contracts freely does not follow from the model, once we consider circumstances of conflict of interests, due to entry of dominant firms in *both* regimes.

Case B

Next consider the parameter values: $r = 1$, $t = 2/5$, $b = 1$, $B = 3$, $A = 1$, $m = 1$ and $K = 0.01$. Inserting these parameter values in the equations (as in Case A) for comparison, it can be seen that dominant firms would be present in *both* layoff and no-layoff regimes. Specifically, following conditions can be checked.

Comparison between different regimes

Dominant firm's profit	$\Pi^L > \Pi^N$
Dominant firm's empt.	$n^N > n^L$
Wages	$W^L > W^N > \bar{W}$
Fringe sector empt.	$n^N_f < n^L_f$
Total empt.	$(n^N + n^N_f) < (n^L + n^L_f)$

Note: All expressions are computed at equilibrium.

Clearly capitalists would prefer a layoff regime over a no-layoff regime. However, notice that employment in dominant firms under a no-layoff regime is *greater* than in a layoff regime ($n^N > n^L$); also, employment in the fringe sector under a no-layoff regime is *less* than in a layoff regime ($n^N_f < n^L_f$). Now although the wage in dominant firms in a layoff regime is *higher* than in a no-layoff regime ($W^L > W^N$), since $n^N > n^L$, workers in the dominant (organised) sector would prefer a no-layoff regime over a layoff regime. This is because although those who stay back in the organised sector (following adoption of layoff regime) of course do better, it is impossible to know *a priori* who would stay back. Also since in the fringe sector, the wage under a no-layoff regime is *greater* than in a layoff regime,[21] that is, $W^N > \bar{W}$ and $n^N_f < n^L_f$, so adopting a layoff regime over a no-layoff regime would mean expansion of the low-wage fringe (unorganised) sector. Evidently, under these circumstances, workers would prefer a no-layoff regime over a layoff regime. Hence the interest of employers and workers are again in *conflict* with each other.

Case C

Finally consider the parameter values: $r = 10$, $t = 3/4$, $b = 1$, $B = 1$, $A = 10$, $m = 1$, $K = 2$ and $T = 2$ (T denotes transaction cost of job switching). The distinctive feature with this set of parameter values is that dominant firms' wage offer in a layoff regime falls so low that some skilled workers go to the fringe sector[22] (the condition for this is $\bar{W} > W^L$). Following the same method as before, it can be seen that dominant firms would be present in *both* layoff and no-layoff regimes. Inserting the parameter values mentioned above, the following conditions emerge.

Comparison between different regimes

Dominant firm's profit	$\Pi^L > \Pi^N$
Dominant firm's empt.	$n^N < n^L$
Wages	$\bar{W} > W^N > (W^L - T)$
Fringe sector empt.	$n^N_f > n^L_f$
Total empt.	$(n^N + n^N_f) < (n^L + n^L_f)$

Note: All expressions are computed at equilibrium.

Now the author elsewhere admits: '[I]f we assume that workers mind the transaction cost of switching jobs, the same wage w is more attractive to the worker when it comes with a no-retrenchment clause [as against retrenchment clause]' (Basu *et al.* 2007: 10).

This, in effect, means workers in a layoff regime are interested in their wages *net* of transaction cost for job switching. Thus, for the aforesaid parameter values, workers with higher wages in a no-layoff regime (W^N) are better off than in a layoff regime receiving ($W^L - T$). However, firms would certainly prefer a layoff regime over a no-layoff regime – due to higher profits. Once again, the interests of employers and workers are in *conflict* with each other.

The discussion above clearly suggests that the argument for voluntary signing of a contract is snapped. If we uphold the freedom of signing contracts and amend IDA accordingly, based on the specific example constructed by the author, then it would undermine the interest of workers in cases (not discussed by the author but considered by us) *where the interest of workers and capitalists are in conflict with each other*. Thus, the right currently vested in workers – not to be dismissed – must be restored. This is in some sense a desired objective in itself, as Solow (1990: 80) puts it: 'The question is whether we can... *provide the job security and wage continuity* that people seem to want...' (emphasis added). Next, we turn to the discussion of the second paper.

5.2 Labour market flexibility under uncertainty: a critical assessment[23]

This paper by Professors Kaushik Basu *et al.* (2007) considers uncertainty explicitly. It theoretically investigates the effect of labour retrenchment laws on wages and employment, taking uncertainty into consideration. Basu *et al.* (2007: 3) write: 'We show that... there is no unique effect on wages: an anti-retrenchment law can cause wages to rise or fall, and aggregate employment to rise or fall, depending on parametric conditions prevailing in the market'. Therefore, they conclude that labour laws should be suitably amended to allow the market forces to operate in a way that allows the concerned parties to sign voluntary contracts instead of predetermined exogenous regulations. They question the current provisions to labour:

> these [anti-retrenchment] laws virtually prohibit the dismissal of laborers, disregarding any contract that a worker and his or her employer may have signed at the time of employment. At times, the legislation includes some form of pre-determined severance compensation. This tendency to legislate conditions

for compensation *which override voluntary contracts*, has been witnessed in many countries, with varying degrees of stringency.

(ibid.: 1) (emphasis in original)

The authors show that such simple-minded overarching protection *may at times* be detrimental to labour welfare. Thus, they construct a counter-intuitive case, the basic argument being:

> One problem with the conventional wisdom is that it fails to capture the fact that anti-retrenchment laws raise the effective cost of employing labor and, as a result, firms may hire fewer workers. Additionally, it is conceivable that, given the presence of such laws, some firms may not enter into production in the first place. Hence, the economists' view of this is often the opposite of the lay opinion: By burdening firms with the risk that they may not be able to fire their workers or that they will have to pay very large compensations in order to do so, the anti-retrenchment laws cause a decline in the demand for labor and thereby cause a lowering of wages and so ultimately hurt workers.
>
> (ibid.: 3)

However, the authors carefully draw policy conclusions from their model, emphasizing that free hire and fire is good only under certain circumstances, *not always*. So no-retrenchment can also be better under other situations. Hence, they emphasize signing of voluntary contracts.[24] In the authors' words:

> What this paper tries to show is that flexible labor laws can be in the interest of all laborers – that is, easier firing rules can increase employment and wages of all workers. The word 'can' is however important, because this need not always be so. There are contexts where the adoption of more flexible laws can hurt workers. This theoretical finding shifts our main task to determining *under what conditions* workers are better off with less protection.
>
> (ibid.: 22) (emphasis in original)

The purpose of the present review is to check the robustness of those conditions.

The authors consider two alternative legal regimes: one in which employers are free to retrench workers at will (referred to as a 'free retrenchment (F) regime') and the other in which retrenchment is not allowed at all (referred to as a 'no-retrenchment (N) regime'). The stated aim of the paper is 'to study the impact of alternative legal regimes on wages and employment' (ibid.: 6). In particular, the authors compare the effect of a switch from regime F to regime N on equilibrium wage and employment outcomes. This is done with a specific purpose in mind – checking the rationality of anti-retrenchment laws in place. In the authors' words:

> Since anti-retrenchment laws are enacted with the aim of enhancing the welfare of labor it is worth checking formally whether this actually happens. . . . The formal model below illustrates how, given *certain parametric configurations, a switch from regime F to regime N can actually lower the wage and aggregate employment. In other words, if such parametric configurations occur, the anti-retrenchment legislation would, paradoxically, work to the laborers' detriment*. It is shown that there are also parametric configurations where the non-paradoxical result occurs, that is, workers' wages rise.
>
> (ibid.: 6) (emphasis added)

Let us see whether the paradoxical result can stand logical scrutiny.

Let us concentrate on the set-up of the model. The authors assume n identical firms, each possessing the following production function:

$$x = \varphi f(L); \; f'(L) > 0, \; f''(L) < 0 \qquad (1)$$

L is the amount of labour used by the firm, x is the firm's output and φ is a stochastic variable taking the values of 1 and 0 with probability p and $(1-p)$, respectively. *It is further assumed that this stochastic shock is independent across firms and across time.*[25] Further, appealing to the law of large numbers, it is assumed that in each period a randomly selected pn firms have $\varphi = 1$ and *(1-p) × n* firms have $\varphi = 0$.[26] It is important to notice that output is dependent on only *one* input, namely, labour. Hence, other inputs like capital stock are tacitly assumed to be constant, which implies that the model restricts itself in describing only short-run phenomena. Therefore, policy conclusions are applicable essentially to the short run.

It is time to state the economic interpretation of φ. It is best to see the suggestion of the authors by quoting them in full:

> If for a certain firm $\varphi = 1$, we shall describe that as a *good year* for the firm. A *bad year* is one in which $\varphi = 0$. There are different ways of interpreting φ. It could represent input and technology shocks that firms receive. In a bad year $\varphi = 0$ and the firm is unable to produce. Alternatively, . . . we could think of φ as denoting the price of the product. The firms are scattered in different geographical locations. In each location demand for the product can be high or low. When demand is high, the price of the product is one and demand is low, it is zero.
>
> (ibid.: 7) (emphasis in original)

However, there are problems with φ interpreted as technology shock. Since we are discussing firms' behaviour producing *industrial output* in the *secondary sector*,[27] technology shock is difficult to conceive of[28] and also a very rare phenomena.[29] Thus, the application of the model, on such counts, becomes limited. The second interpretation of φ is 'price of the product'; when demand for the product is low, $\varphi = 0$, and it is $\varphi = 1$ when demand picks up. Problems with such an interpretation are clear. If Eq.(1) is stated to be a production function, then there is no rationale for including φ as a price variable. This invalidity follows from the definition of the production function itself.[30] However, there is no harm if Eq.(1) is interpreted as a revenue function. Another unrealistic assumption made by the authors is that $\varphi = 0$ in a bad year. This is too strong an assumption and is at variance with reality. This is because if we interpret φ as 'price of the product', then low demand in a bad year might cause a drop in price only by certain percent – surely in any real economy, prices cannot fall to absolutely nil. However, the authors assume this exactly, and as we shall see later, this assumption remains pivotal for the results subsequently derived; hence, the basic building block of the model is open to question.

At this juncture, it may be interesting to assess the consistency of the assumption the authors make and the *general* conclusions they derive: 'To keep the algebra simple we model this stochastic shock [φ] as being *independent* across firms and across time, there by *ruling out industry wide fluctuations and intertemporally correlated shocks*' (ibid.: 7) (emphasis added). In their footnote 3 the authors provide a justification for such an assumption:

> In a model of the manufacturing sector, such as ours, it is not unreasonable to think of fluctuations in the demand for the product of particular firms caused by *shifts in demand from one segment of the industry to another*. Our model may be thought of as a *stylized* description of this.
>
> (ibid.: 32) (emphasis added)[31]

It is important here to notice the *premise* of the model and to interpret policy conclusions accordingly. The problem addressed here is *firm-specific* and in the nature of a too-many-shirts-but-too-few-shoes kind of problem and not one of aggregate level-economy-wide technology shock[32] or demand shock. In the model, the solution to such firm-specific problems, at times, has been recommended as free layoffs. Note that the aggregate level demand constraint which is a central feature of any money-using economy is out of the scope of this analysis.[33] However, in a demand-constrained economy, the problem of demand is not firm-specific but is an economy-wide phenomenon. Therefore, any *general* policy recommendation without considering aggregate demand can only be of secondary importance.

Now we turn to the model. For our present purpose, we think the latter interpretation of φ as a price variable, with the qualification of Eq.(1) being revenue function, is more appropriate for modelling *industrial firms* than thinking in terms of technology shocks which are hardly firm-specific. *It is also assumed by the authors that in each period each firm gets to see φ before making its hiring decision*. With these observations, we now examine the working of the model.

Let us first see a firm's behaviour under an F-regime. Each firm is free to hire and fire workers suitably. In a good year, a firm's demand for labour is obtained by solving the following problem:

$$\underset{L}{Max.} f(L) - wL$$

The first-order condition is given by:

$$f'(L) = w \qquad (2)$$

Since, $f''(L) < 0$, function $f'(L)$ can be inverted and written as $g(w)$. Hence, in a good year, with market wage w, a firm's labour demand is

$$L = g(w) \qquad (3)$$

In a bad year since $\varphi = 0$, a firm's labour demand is obviously 0. Hence, in an F-regime, aggregate labour demand is given by $png(w)$.[34] The aggregate supply function of labour is given by

$$s = s(w); \quad s'(w) \geq 0$$

Assuming full wage flexibility, the labour market equilibrium in an F-regime is one in which aggregate labour demand equals aggregate labour supply. Clearly, w^F is the equilibrium wage in an F-regime if and only if

$$png(w^F) = s(w^F) \qquad (4)$$

Let us now turn to the equilibrium configuration in an N-regime. The authors claim that to work out labour demand in an N-regime, each employer must decide, *as if*, they hire labour *before* φ is revealed. The rationale for this can be best explained by quoting the authors in full:

> (A)part from the first period, the employer will (in an N-regime) be effectively stuck with a certain amount of labor in all periods without knowing each period's realization of φ. So unless the future is too heavily discounted, the fact that φ is known in one period, namely, the first period is of negligible importance.
>
> (ibid.: 8)

Adopting this method, the expected profit function of a risk-neutral[35] firm, not knowing the value of φ in advance in an N-regime, is written as:

$$\underset{L}{Max}.[pf(L) - wL]$$

The first-order condition yields:

$$f'(L) = \frac{w}{p} \qquad (5)$$

Thus, firm's labour demand is given by:

$$L = g(\frac{w}{p}) \qquad (6)$$

Where $g(.)$ is the inverse of $f'(L)$.

Because each firm is identical *ex ante*, the aggregate demand for labour is $ng(\frac{w}{p})$.[36] So an equivalent condition for market clearing as (4) in an N-regime, assuming full wage flexibility,[37] is written as:

$$ng(\frac{w^N}{p}) = s(w^N) \qquad (7)$$

where w^N is the market clearing wage.

Now to compare between the equilibrium outcomes of two regimes, the authors have taken the specific functional form of $f(L)$ as:

$$f(L) = \left(\frac{A}{B}\right)L - \frac{L^2}{2B} \qquad (8)$$

with $A, B > 0$ and $L < A$ always, for a meaningful production function.

Eq.(8) implies that the firm has a linear labour demand function:

$$g(w) = A - Bw \qquad (9)$$

Using Eq.(9), the aggregate labour demand function in an F-regime is:

$$L^F = pn[A - Bw] \qquad (10)$$

In an N-regime, it is:

$$L^N = n[A - B\frac{w}{p}] \qquad (11)$$

To compare outcomes in these two regimes, we plot Eqs.(10) and (11) in Figure 5.1. Note that the two labour demand curves necessarily cross at E.

The steeper demand curve is for an F-regime, and the flatter one for an N-regime. Now whether to choose the N-regime or F-regime depends on the position of the supply curve. Suppose initial

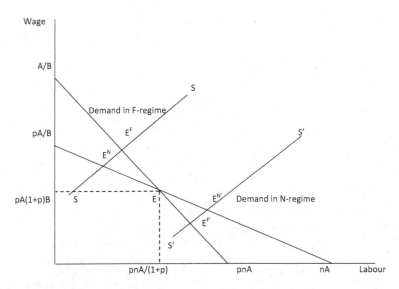

Figure 5.1 Freedom to develop voluntary contracts based on initial conditions

conditions are such that the supply curve lies to the left of E; then a move from an F to an N-regime is to the detriment of workers – as E^N lies to the south-west of E^F. The result is a fall in both equilibrium employment and wages. For the position of the supply curve to the right of E, exactly the opposite case holds. Because $E^{N'}$ lies to the north-east of $E^{F'}$, moving from an F to an N-regime is beneficial for workers. Thus, the authors argue that no prior antiretrenchment law is necessary, as initial conditions are unknown and agents should be free to sign contracts.[38] Note that as in the earlier model, this analysis does not take into consideration the specific context in which contracts are written. In a capitalist economy, production relations are dominated by capitalists and workers have to depend on capitalists for getting hired. This is because capitalists own the means of production and workers only possess labour power to earn subsistence. Such a social arrangement of ownership of means of production typically enhances the bargaining position of the capitalists vis-à-vis workers. Such a bargaining position is still strengthened by the availability of vast unused labour reserves that characterizes any capitalist economy.[39] This is because workers can always be replaced costlessly – drawing on the labour reserves – and this acts as a great disciplining device in the hands of capitalists, since workers once thrown out of employment have no other means to earn subsistence. However, workers cannot choose between capitalists, as they are few in number, and besides there is always intense competition among workers for the limited number of jobs on offer. *Such domination in production relations evidently spills over to domination of setting the terms of the contract.* Thus, any theory which is based on free signing of contracts at will misses this basic asymmetry of distribution of power between capitalists and workers.[40] To be sure, the authors get around such questions by assuming full employment – which, however, does not reflect the economic reality of any capitalist economy. Nonetheless, we check the robustness of the result.

Checking the consistency of the argument

One can imagine at least three cases when the above claim by the authors cannot be sustained. On account of the nature of problem pointed out, we consider them in three separate cases.

Case A

Note that Eqs.(10) and (11) depend on the nature of Eq.(8). Under certain functional forms of Eq.(8), it may so happen that the labour demand curve for F lies bodily to the *left* of the labour demand curve for N. Then, of course, moving from an N- to an F-regime would always be detrimental to workers, as both wages and employment fall. Of course, one may argue that if labour demand for an F-regime lies to the *right* of an N-regime, then it would be beneficial for workers. This simply points out that free contracting is not *always* necessary but is conditional upon the specific functional form of $f(L)$.[41] Also, the position of the supply curve *may* not matter (when labour demand curves do not intersect). This is clear from the following exercise.

We check whether the result derived in favour of voluntary signing of contracts is specific to the particular functional form of production technology assumed by the authors. We compare equilibrium outcomes of the F- and N-regimes with a different functional form of $f(L)$ defined:

$$f(L) = A - \frac{B}{L} \text{ for } L \gg \frac{B}{A}$$
$$= 0 \text{ } otherwise.$$

with $A, B > 0$ and as production function is only economically meaningfully defined for positive outputs over the range $L \gg \frac{B}{A}$, we shall throughout restrict our attention to such cases. Next, we derive labour demand functions for the F- and N-regimes.

F-regime

The relevant profit function in an F-regime for reasons stated earlier is,

$$\pi^F(L) = f(L) - wL$$

or, $\pi^F(L) = \left(A - \frac{B}{L}\right) - wL$

The first-order condition yields the labour demand for a *single* firm under an F-regime as, $g^F = \left(\frac{B}{w}\right)^{\frac{1}{2}}$ with, $0 < w < \frac{A^2}{B}$. Therefore, *aggregate* labour demand under an F-regime is, $L^F = np\left(\frac{B}{w}\right)^{\frac{1}{2}}$.

N-regime

The relevant profit function for the firm in an N-regime is,

$$\pi^N(L) = p.f(L) - wL$$

or, $\pi^N(L) = p\left(A - \frac{B}{L}\right) - wL$

The labour demand function for a *single* firm under an N-regime is: $g^N = \left(\frac{pB}{w}\right)^{\frac{1}{2}}$ with the restriction, $0 < w < \frac{pA^2}{B}$. Therefore, *aggregate* labour demand under an N-regime is: $L^N = n\left(\frac{pB}{w}\right)^{\frac{1}{2}}$.

We collect the values of L^F, L^N and consider the following ratio: $\left(\frac{L^F}{L^N}\right)$. On calculation,

$$\frac{L^F}{L^N} = p^{\frac{1}{2}} \rightarrow \frac{L^F}{L^N} < 1 \text{ is easy to see for: } 0 < p < 1 \text{ and this is true for}$$

any wage.

Hence, the labour demand curve for an F-regime lies bodily *below* the labour demand curve for an N-regime *throughout*. Therefore, for *any* labour supply function, equilibrium wage *and* employment outcomes in an N-regime are unambiguously favourable for workers than in an F-regime.

In particular, as earlier, if the labour supply function is, $L^S = sw$, then equilibrium wage under F-regime is, $W^F = \left(\dfrac{npB^{\frac{1}{2}}}{s}\right)^{\left(\frac{2}{3}\right)}$. However, the equilibrium wage outcome under an N-regime is, $W^N = \left(\dfrac{n(pB)^{\frac{1}{2}}}{s}\right)^{\left(\frac{2}{3}\right)}$. Comparison of W^F and W^N reveals,

$$\dfrac{W^F}{W^N} = p^{\left(\frac{1}{3}\right)} \rightarrow \dfrac{W^F}{W^N} < 1 \text{ is easy to see for: } 0 < p < 1$$

Result: Therefore, we arrive at the following results: (a) equilibrium labour demand in the F-regime is less than in the N-regime for *all* wages, and (b) equilibrium wages in the F-regime are less favourable than in the N-regime for *all* labour supply functions. Hence, workers are unambiguously better off in the N-regime in comparison to the F-regime, and the necessity for voluntary signing of contracts is snapped in this case when we merely change the functional form of how inputs are related to output. Thus, Basu *et al.* (2007) are suggesting their general policy conclusions based on a *specific* production function. *If their production function is suitably changed, their policy conclusions – allowing voluntary signing of contracts – cannot be sustained; hence, any general policy conclusions based on their model are unwarranted.*

Case B

Next we take a clue from the authors' statement, '[I]f we assume that workers mind the transaction cost of switching jobs, *the same wage w is more attractive to the worker when it comes with a no-retrenchment clause*' (ibid.: 10) (emphasis added), and take the same functional form of $f(L)$ as Eq.(8),[42] but consider a perfectly inelastic[43] labour supply curve, then Figure 5.1 modifies into Figure 5.2.

Result: Note that to the left of E we cannot unambiguously choose the F- over the N-regime. This is because equilibrium employment

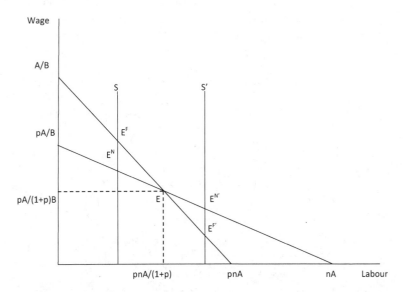

Figure 5.2 Examining the case to develop voluntary contracts based on initial conditions

levels are the same in both the F- and the N-regimes, and as the authors state, with the transaction cost of switching jobs, the same wage is more attractive to workers in the N-regime. Extending that, one may argue that a slightly *lower* wage in the N-regime may not be welfare reducing for workers. However, note that workers unambiguously choose the N- over the F-regime to the right of E. But, to the left of E we *may not* choose the F- over the N-regime depending on the distance between E^N and E^F.[44] Nonetheless, parametric conditions still matter in determining the precise distance between E^N and E^F.

Case C

Note that φ is defined as the product price [φ oscillating between 0 (bad year) and 1 (good year)]. It is argued in the paper that: '[w]hen demand is high, price of the product is one and when demand is low, it is zero' (ibid.: 7). As pointed out before, if a bad year does not signify absolutely zero price ($\varphi = 0$), but some percentage fall in price below unity, then the variation in results between the F- and the N-regimes are small. Consequently, the transaction cost of job switching is more likely to erase any gains by moving from the N- to the F-regime. More specifically, *lower* is the percentage fall in price below unity in a bad year – *closer* is the expected revenue receipts for a firm facing bad year, to its actual revenue receipts in a good year. Consequently, any distinction between the labour demand curves of the F- and the N-regimes increasingly vanishes (in the limit they actually collapse into a single labour demand curve and become indistinguishable).

This result can be arrived at from a different route as well. Since φ is defined to be the price of product, by timely government intervention in demand management (like export subsidies to tap world market),[45] the value of φ can tend to 1. This, therefore, becomes a policy variable and no longer behaves stochastically. In other words, φ took value *1* with probability *p* and *0* with probability *(1-p)*. Demand management/intervention policy can ensure that *p* tends to *1* (i.e. 'good year' materializes by design).[46] Let us look at the consequence of this on Eq. (4) and Eq. (7). Both collapse to the same equation, namely, $ng(w) = s(w)$. Hence, the aggregate labour demand curve for both the N- and the F-regimes becomes the same. It is shown in Figure 5.3.[47]

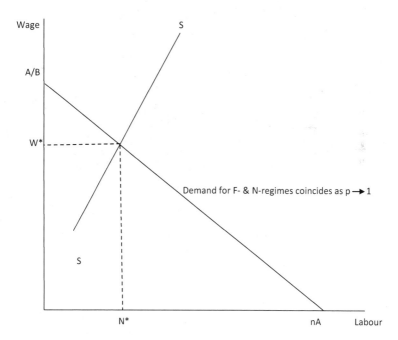

Figure 5.3 Examining the case to develop voluntary contracts with commodity market intervention

Result: We get a powerful result here that the current legislative provisions to labour – closer to the N-regime – need not be repealed. Any variation of result between the F-regime and the N-regime, in particular where the F-regime produces a better outcome, can also in principle be achieved in the N-regime *through a commodity market intervention without amending the labour laws or in a world in which price fluctuations are not extremely volatile.* This is because w* and N* are now the same for both regimes. This result is especially interesting since it *does not* depend on the specific functional form (hence is free from parametric specifications) like Eq. (8). *On a second look Eq. (4) and Eq. (7) – aggregate labour demand curves in both regimes collapse to a single labour demand curve; further, the result is also immune to the different functional forms of the supply curve. Hence, in the simple model with a fixed number of firms, the requirement for free contracting is snapped.*

5.3. Model with workers' motivation to acquire firm-specific knowledge

Let us now study the model by introducing workers' motivation *and* capacity to acquire firm-specific knowledge[48] – with the same production technology as assumed by the authors.

Stylized facts

In the literature, it is normally acknowledged that if a free/full hire and fire regime prevails in the economy, then workers will have little motivation to acquire firm-specific knowledge. This is simply because the workers are unsure as to whether they would be allowed to continue with the current firm or have to look for other opportunities outside the firm.[49] In that situation, the production function is to be suitably modified into the following:

$$x = \phi\theta f(L); \ f'(L) > 0, \ f''(L) < 0 \qquad (1')$$

where θ represents firm-specific knowledge. Other terms have the same interpretations as earlier.

Assumptions

Now assume that θ can take any value between *0* and *1* (i.e. $\theta \in [0,1]$). Also assume that $\theta = 1$ means that workers have acquired firm-specific knowledge perfectly and that $\theta = 0$ denotes that workers have no firm-specific knowledge. Intermediate values of θ signify imperfect acquisition of knowledge – with the degree of imperfection falling as θ attains a higher value.

Clearly, in an N-regime $\theta = 1$, since no hire and fire condition provides *full* motivation to the worker in terms of job security to acquire firm-specific knowledge. This is plain, since the worker knows that s/he would not have to migrate to other firms involuntarily during her/his lifetime; this assurance allows the worker to concentrate on the job at hand. Further, by offering lifetime employment, firms secure workers' loyalty towards the organization [as in case of Japan in the past century; see Morishima (1982) for details]. This contributes to improving workers' motivation to learn and perform well – *positively* affecting his/her productivity. It is interesting to see what value θ assumes in an F-regime. Note that in an F-regime firms hire workers in good years only (i.e. $\varphi = 1$), which comes with a probability p. Therefore, for higher expected values of p,[50] the greater the possibility that the worker would be retained in the *current* firm; consequently, the motivation for the workers to acquire firm-specific knowledge is larger.[51] Hence, θ would also assume a high value. Thus, we have $\theta = \theta(p); \theta' > 0$. Moreover, note that workers would be, at best, as responsive (both their motivation and ability in acquiring firm-specific knowledge) to the probability of a good year emerging (observing past trends) or less responsive[52] (i.e. $\frac{d\theta}{dp} \leq 1$). Finally, $\theta(0) = 0$. Then the association between θ and p can be expressed by the following relationship: $\theta \leq p$.

The model

With such considerations, let us revisit the results with a specific functional form of the production function, $f(L) = \left(\frac{A}{B}\right)L - \frac{L^2}{2B}$, as considered by the authors.

N-regime

Since $\theta = 1$ for an N-regime, the expected profit function remains exactly the same as before. Consequently, an individual firm's demand curve remains the same; likewise, the market demand function for labour also remains unchanged, namely, $L^N = n[A - B\frac{w}{p}]$.

F-regime

Now we consider the profit function for firms in an F-regime. It may be remembered that firms in an F-regime demand labour only in case a good year materializes (i.e. $\varphi = 1$).

$$\pi^F(L) = \theta f(L) - wL$$

With the specific functional form it becomes,

$$\pi^F(L) = \theta\left[\frac{A}{B}L - \frac{L^2}{2B}\right] - wL$$

An individual firm's demand function for labour becomes $[A - \frac{wB}{\theta}]$ and the aggregate market demand curve for labour becomes $L^F = np[A - \frac{w}{\theta}B]$. Since $\theta \le p$, the aggregate labour demand curve for the N-regime lies to the right of the F-regime *throughout*. This is shown in Figure 5.4. It is of course drawn on the basis of the strict inequality assumption (i.e. $\theta < p$).

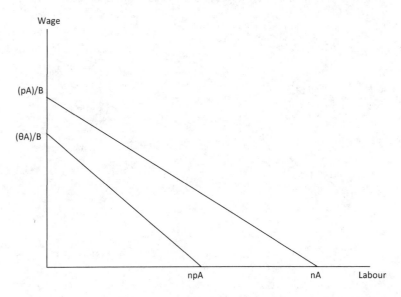

Figure 5.4 Examining the case to develop voluntary contracts with firm-specific knowledge

Result: So, for *all* labour supply curves, workers in the F-regime would be *unambiguously worse off* than in the N-regime. For example, if the labour supply curve takes the specific form of $L^S = sw$, then the market clearing wage in the F-regime is $W^F = \dfrac{npA}{\left[s + nB\left(\dfrac{p}{\theta}\right)\right]}$ and in the N-regime it is $W^N = \dfrac{npA}{[sp + Bn]}$. Looking at the denominator, one can easily see $W^N > W^F$, since $0 < p < 1$ and $\theta \leq p$. Therefore, $L^N > L^F$ is also true (labour supply function is positively sloped). Thus, with firm-specific knowledge, the N-regime is always better than the F-regime for workers in this simple model with the specific functional form of $f(L)$ as Eq. (8).

Generalizing the model

Actually, one can argue a little further. It is not necessary to restrict ourselves to the specific functional form of Eq. (8) proposed by the authors. The result derived above is a more *generalized* one when we consider firm-specific knowledge. One can derive the result by not considering any particular form of production function but considering a general production function with certain properties. Let firms under an F-regime maximise: $\pi^F(L) = \theta.f(L) - wL$ and under an N-regime maximise: $\pi^N(L) = pf(L) - wL$, for determining labour demands.

Under an F-regime, first-order conditions yield $f'(L) = \dfrac{w}{\theta}$. Thus, the labour demand at the *firm* level is $L = f'^{-1}(\dfrac{w}{\theta})$. Let the inverse function be denoted by 'g'. Hence, $L = g(\dfrac{w}{\theta})$, with , $g'(.) < 0$. Aggregate labour demand function under an F-regime is therefore written as $L^F = npg(\dfrac{w}{\theta})$.

Under an N-regime, first-order conditions yield $f'(L) = \dfrac{w}{p}$. Thus, the labour demand at the *firm* level is $L = f'^{-1}(\dfrac{w}{p})$. Let the inverse function be denoted by '*h*'. Hence, $L = h(\dfrac{w}{p})$; with, $h'(.) < 0$. Therefore, aggregate labour demand function under an N-regime is $L^N = nh(\dfrac{w}{p})$.

Now comparing the expressions for $L^F = npg(\frac{w}{\theta})$ and $L^N = nh(\frac{w}{p})$, it is easy to see that for any arbitrary wage $\bar{w}$, $L^F < L^N$, unambiguously.

Result: Thus, for *any* labour supply function and *any* production function (continuously differentiable with diminishing marginal productivity), workers are unambiguously better off in an N-regime in comparison to an F-regime when we consider firm-specific knowledge.

An example

As a specific example, let us try out the Cobb-Douglas production technology widely used in the neoclassical tradition. Therefore, the production function is $f(L) = AK^{1-\alpha} L^\alpha$; $0 < \alpha < 1$. As assumed by the authors earlier, we also concentrate only on the short run, taking technological parameter and capital stock to be constant. Hence, the production function is represented as $f(L) = H L^\alpha$; where $H = A K^{1-\alpha}$. We consider an F-regime and an N-regime seriatim.

F-regime

The relevant profit function for a firm is,

$\pi^F(L) = \theta.f(L) - wL$

or, $\pi^F(L) = \theta.HL^\alpha - wL$

The first-order condition yields the labour demand for a *single* firm under an F-regime as $\left(\frac{\theta H \alpha}{w}\right)^{\frac{1}{(1-\alpha)}}$. Therefore, the *aggregate* labour demand under an F-regime is given by $L^F = np\left(\frac{\theta H \alpha}{w}\right)^{\frac{1}{(1-\alpha)}}$.

Now, as earlier, if the labour supply function is $L^S = sw$, then the equilibrium wage under an F-regime is $W^F = \left(\frac{np}{s}\right)^{\left(\frac{1-\alpha}{2-\alpha}\right)}.(\theta H \alpha)^{\frac{1}{(2-\alpha)}}$.

N-regime

The relevant profit function for a firm is,

$\pi^N(L) = pf(L) - wL$

or, $\pi^N(L) = pHL^\alpha - wL$

The labour demand function for a *single* firm under an N-regime is $\left(\frac{pH\alpha}{w}\right)^{\frac{1}{(1-\alpha)}}$. Therefore, the *aggregate* labour demand under an N-regime is $L^N = n\left(\frac{pH\alpha}{w}\right)^{\frac{1}{(1-\alpha)}}$. With labour supply function $L^S = sw$, the equilibrium wage under an N-regime is

$$W^N = \left(\frac{n}{s}\right)^{\left(\frac{1-\alpha}{2-\alpha}\right)} \cdot (pH\alpha)^{\frac{1}{(2-\alpha)}}.$$

We can collect the values of L^F, L^N, W^F and W^N for comparison. In particular, consider the following ratios: (L^F/L^N) and (W^F/W^N). On calculation,

$$\frac{L^F}{L^N} = p \cdot \left(\frac{\theta}{p}\right)^{\frac{1}{(1-\alpha)}}; \frac{L^F}{L^N} < 1 \text{ is easy to see for } 0 < p < 1, 0 < \alpha < 1$$

and $\theta \leq p$.

$$\frac{W^F}{W^N} = p^{\left(\frac{1-\alpha}{2-\alpha}\right)} \cdot \left(\frac{\theta}{p}\right)^{\frac{1}{2-\alpha}}; \frac{W^F}{W^N} < 1 \text{ is easy to see for } 0 < p < 1, 0 <$$

$\alpha < 1$ and $\theta \leq p$.

Result: Therefore, we arrive at the following result: (a) equilibrium labour demand in an F-regime is less than in an N-regime, (b) equilibrium wages in an F-regime are less than in an N-regime and (c) equilibrium employment in an F-regime is less than in an N-regime for $L^S = sw$. Hence, workers are unambiguously better off in an N-regime in comparison to an F-regime when Cobb-Douglas technology is considered.

Argument in the context of endogenously determined industry size

Next, we turn to the case where the authors extend their argument in the context when industry size is determined endogenously. In particular, the authors assume perfect competition with free entry; with a very large number of firms and in equilibrium, the industry size gets determined endogenously by the zero expected profit condition.[53] In order to compare the equilibrium outcomes in F- and N-regimes, the following function is defined,

$$g(w) \equiv \frac{\arg}{(L)} \max[f(L) - wL].$$

The F-regime is considered first, with free entry of firms. If the wage is w, in the F-regime each firm earns a profit of,

$$f(g(w)) - wg(w).$$

So long as, $[f(g(w)) - wg(w)] \gtrless 0$, we do not have equilibrium, for there is entry or exit of firms at the margin. Thus, in an F-regime, an equilibrium wage is w'', where this is defined implicitly by,

$$[f(g(w'')) - w''g(w'')] = 0$$

Now we consider the N-regime. A firm in the N-regime facing wage w expects to earn

$$pf(L) - wL.$$

As in the earlier case, define,

$$l(w) \equiv \frac{\arg}{(L)} \max[pf(L) - wL]$$

As before, if the wage is w in an N-regime, each firm expects to earn a profit of:

$$pf(l(w)) - wl(w)$$

Therefore, with the same justification as above we find in an N-regime, w' is equilibrium wage if:

$$[pf(l(w')) - w'l(w')] = 0$$

Now since $w'' = max[f(L)/L]$ and $w' = max[pf(L)/L]$ also p < 1, it follows that $w'' > w'$. Finally, the value of L that maximizes $f(L)/L$ also maximizes $pf(L)/L$, so $g(w'') = l(w')$.

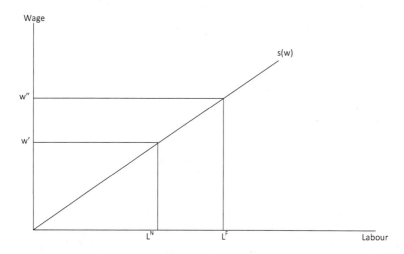

Figure 5.5 Superiority of F-regime over N-regime when industry size is endogenously determined

The aggregate supply curve is taken as upward rising and w'' and w' are shown as in Figure 5.5. The aggregate employment in the F-regime is depicted as L^F and for the N-regime by L^N.

Now we can see that $L^F > L^N$. Since $g(w'') = l(w')$, it follows that:

$$\frac{L^F}{g(w'')} > \frac{L^N}{l(w')}.$$

Therefore, it is concluded that the industry size is *larger* under the F-regime, and so too are wages and employment. Hence, it is concluded, 'in a country in which, for reasons of law, institutions or technology, there is free entry into industries, *a no-retrenchment regime is unequivocally worse for the workers*' (ibid.: 14) (emphasis added). As is seen from the quote, it is a very strong claim, since workers are said to be unequivocally worse off in the N-regime. The purpose of the following exercise is to scrutinize the claim.

Checking the consistency of the argument

Note that in cases where industry size is endogenized, $w'' > w'$ and $g(w'') = l(w')$ holds. Now suppose the labour supply curve is taken to be perfectly inelastic, as shown in Figure 5.6, which implies, $L^N = L^F$.

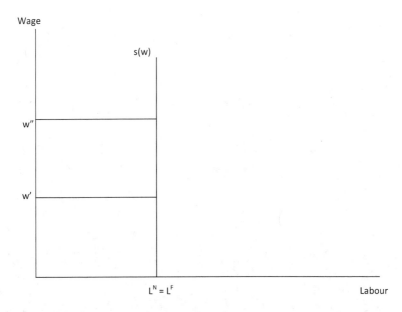

Figure 5.6 Examining the superiority of F-regime over N-regime when industry size is endogenously determined

It also implies $\dfrac{L^F}{g(w'')} = \dfrac{L^N}{l(w')}$. Therefore, we see that the claim for the number of firms in the case of the F-regime being higher than that of the N-regime and aggregate employment in the F-regime being higher than that of the N-regime merely depends upon the specification of the aggregate labour supply function being upward sloping. However, with a perfectly inelastic labour supply curve,[54] no such claim can be sustained. But still the wage in the F-regime *(w'')* is greater than the wage in the N-regime *(w')*. However, we still cannot claim that the workers in the F-regime are unequivocally better off than in the N-regime. This is because of the earlier reason – that the transaction cost of job switching makes the *same* wage more lucrative for workers when it comes in an N-regime. Hence, a slightly *lower* wage in the N-regime *may* not be welfare reducing for the workers as well. Of course, it ultimately depends on the parameter values.

Result: Therefore, in the case of endogenously determined industry size, there is no unequivocal result as claimed by the authors. It *entirely* depends on the specification of the labour supply curve and parameter values.

Relationship between severance pay and equilibrium wage

Now we shall discuss the generalized version of the model, where firms are not bound to follow two polar opposite cases, namely, no-layoff at all, or freely allowed to retrench workers. Rather, the requirement for retrenchment is that firms have to pay a severance pay *s* to the worker at the time of separation. The authors show that the relationship between equilibrium wage and severance pay is not straightforward.[55] It is V-shaped. In particular, they show that as *s* rises, starting from zero, equilibrium wages fall; however, beyond a certain point, further rises in *s* cause the equilibrium wage to rise. It follows that the w(s) curve looks V-shaped, as in Figure 5.7:[56]

In other words, the authors emphasize their earlier conclusion (with fixed firms) that no *a priori* conclusion from laws protecting labour should be drawn, as there may be situations when a rise in severance pay (a means of protecting labour) may cause wages to

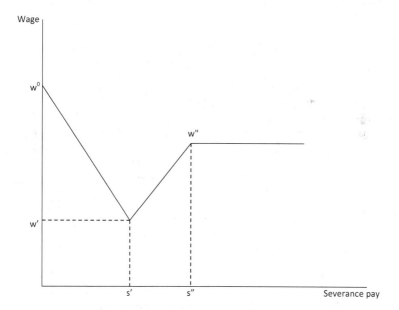

Figure 5.7 Relationship between severance pay and equilibrium wage

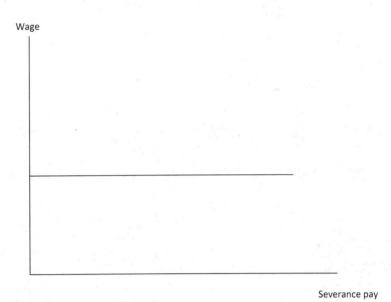

Figure 5.8 Relationship between severance pay and equilibrium wage with demand management

go down. Thus, they argue that severance pay should not be statutorily fixed but should be decided by the workers in their best interest. Let us check the robustness of this result.

For example, with a demand management policy, as discussed earlier, where p→1 it can be shown that there is *no relationship* between severance pay (s) and equilibrium wage (w) (Figure 5.8):

Thus, the V-shape of severance pay and equilibrium wage is snapped if we carry out a suitable demand management policy. Hence, the requirement for free contracting based on initial conditions is only valid under special assumptions. Therefore, any general policy conclusion, like amending the IDA 1947 to allow agents in developing voluntary contracts, based on such models is uncalled for.

Conclusion

This chapter discussed the market clearing arguments in favour of LMF. These theories assume continuous market clearing through instantaneous wage adjustment. Since they assume away any possibility of involuntary unemployment completely, their argument in favour of LMF primarily banks on wage effects. In this chapter, we discussed two such theories, and both claimed that wages are likely to be higher in regimes allowing layoffs as compared to no-layoffs, *under certain conditions*. The actual outcome, of course, depended upon initial conditions. Hence, each of the papers argued for suitable amendment to IDA: for upholding voluntary contract signing between workers and employers, since initial conditions vary and are unknown. However, it was pointed out that even if initial conditions are unknown and a regime not currently in place may be beneficial to all, negotiations may yet fail. This is simply because workers are not in a position to evaluate specific conditions concretely and it may be prohibitively costly for firms to disseminate information to each worker.

Moreover, such voluntary signing of contract is a myth under capitalism, where production relations are inherently tilted in favour of capitalists by virtue of their possessing the means of production. *Such domination in production relations evidently spills over to domination of setting the terms of the contract; moreover, such domination also ensures that the outcome of any negotiation process is represented as voluntarily agreed upon.* So any contract would be dominated by the capitalist class, and any amendment of the above kind would essentially mean no protection of employment for workers at all. To be sure, all such contracts can be represented as outcomes of voluntarily signed contracts; for example, if the employers at the time of appointment coerce workers to sign on some future-dated separation contract and attach it as an *essential* component to get employment in the first place, then all separations would *de facto* look like they had been voluntarily agreed upon. Hence, any amendment of the above kind would in effect mean full freedom to hire and fire.

However, it was also shown that the policy recommendations do not follow from the papers. Basu (2007) argued in a symmetric Nash equilibrium set-up that under certain conditions, layoffs resulted in higher wages as compared to no-layoff regimes. In order to substantiate his claim, the author resorted to a hypothetical numerical example. Now, based on a *very special* case, the author recommended a *general* policy prescription. However, it was shown that if dominant firms enter *both* in layoff and no-layoff regimes, situations of *conflict of interest* may arise between capitalists and workers. Thus, recommending voluntary signing of contracts by only analysing positive sum games is premature. If *conflict of interest* is taken into consideration (which is more relevant in reality), then the requirement for voluntary signing of contracts is snapped.

In the second paper, Basu *et al.* (2007), three different situations were discussed to argue in favour of voluntary signing of contracts. Each of them was discussed in detail, and it was shown that none of the conclusions were sustainable with minute changes in assumptions. In fact, in the simple model with a fixed number of firms, the results derived by the authors were sensitive to the specific functional form of the production technology, specification of the labour supply curve and description of a bad year when it is assumed that the product price falls to zero. Moreover, if we explicitly consider firm-specific knowledge along with uncertainty, even with the same production technology as assumed by the authors, a *no-layoff regime is always better than the regime allowing free layoff of workers*. It was also shown that *irrespective* of production technology, if we consider firm-specific knowledge, *workers would be better off in no-layoff regimes compared to free layoff regimes*.

Therefore, depriving workers from employment security by allowing hire and fire and getting rid of firing costs, as argued in the I-O framework (discussed in Chapter 4), or amending IDA suitably for developing contracts voluntarily, could not stand logical scrutiny. Thus, it is clear that the theoretical foundations underlying LMF stand on rather shaky grounds. Models discussed in this chapter assumed away the existence of any involuntary unemployment altogether by assuming instantaneous wage flexibility. In the non-market clearing models, the existence of involuntary unemployment was explained through wage rigidity due to insiders' bargaining power arising out of firing costs. It may be pointed out that neither the non-market clearing framework (insider-outsider models) nor the market clearing ones considered the aggregate demand constraint explicitly. This, however, provides a *sui generis* explanation of involuntary unemployment and was propounded by Keynes (1936). In the next chapter (Chapter 6), we investigate if LMF can get rid of involuntary unemployment through wage flexibility (as argued by the insider-outsider framework) when the effective demand constraint is binding and considered explicitly.

Notes

1 We discuss this continuous market clearing view at length since arguments for LMF are often based on these explanations (purely microeconomic in

nature; see below) and not because it captures some macroeconomic reality. As Solow (1985: 411) aptly puts it:

I take the proposal that the real-world labor market is actually in market clearing equilibrium with respect to some (mis)perceived demand and supply conditions to be a clever jeu d'esprit and not a serious description of modern capitalist economies in prolonged recession.

2 'Labour Laws and Labour Welfare in the Context of the Indian Experience', Collected Papers in Theoretical Economics, Volume III, Kaushik Basu, Oxford University Press, Oxford (2007).
3 'Labor Retrenchment Laws and Their Effect on Wages and Employment: A Theoretical Investigation', Kaushik Basu, Gary S. Fields and Shub Debgupta, in New and Enduring Themes in Development Economics, Bhaskar Dutta, Tridip Ray and E. Somanathan (eds.), World Scientific Publishers: Singapore, (2009). Also available as IZA Discussion Paper No. 2742, April, 2007. All references are based on the Discussion Paper.
4 This view has gained some support in policy circles. The Task Force on Employment (Planning Commission 2001b: 151) notes: '[I]n [the] market economy the impact of labour legislation on labour market conditions may turn out to be quite different from what was intended'.
5 Note that the hiring cost incurred for screening workers, discussed in Chapter 4, should in principle take care of the skill-mismatch problem in general. It is precisely for this reason, to have consistency in argument, skill has been defined in a very peculiar manner in this paper (discussed later) and it has been further assumed that standard job-market signalling models become irrelevant for the present set-up. Therefore, we are only left with the following: 'The *only way* for an employer to know exactly how much skill . . . a worker possesses is to employ the worker' (Basu 2007: 136) (emphasis added). Even then, the common practice followed by firms to circumscribe the skill-mismatch problem is to keep new hires on probation to 'test-out' their requisite skill for the job. Only after full satisfaction are workers offered permanent contracts. From Chapter 2 we know that restrictions on layoffs and retrenchments apply only to permanent workers. Therefore, building blocks of the model, namely, drawing attention to difficulties faced by employers in replacing employees on discovery of skill-mismatch is of little practical relevance.
6 This is also why the definition of skill and its assessment becomes pivotal.
7 Interestingly, this idea of entering into free contract, in other words, allowing market forces to play freely, has been accepted for quite some time. For example, in 1819, when the Cotton Factories Regulation Act was tabled in the British Parliament for banning child labour in this hazardous industry (although with limited scope of application for only children under nine years), it resulted in a huge controversy. 'Opponents saw it as undermining the sanctity of freedom of contract and thus destroying the very foundation of free market. . . . Their argument

said: the children want (and need) work, and the factory owners want to employ them; what is the problem' (Chang 2010: 2). However, in a class-divided society there cannot be any 'free and unbiased contracts at will', at least between workers and capitalists; these contracts are bound to be dominated by power relations.

8 Therefore, output per (skilled) worker in the dominant firm is assumed to be the same (i.e. 'r' – irrespective of free layoff and no-layoff regimes). This, however, tacitly assumes away any incentive problem on the part of the workers. In other words, it abstracts from the fact that an adverse working environment (like greater job uncertainty) can perversely affect workers' incentive to concentrate on the job at hand and hence can reduce productivity. Such persuasions are available in literature, like Standing (1991). In such cases, output per (skilled) worker in dominant firms would normally be higher in a no-layoff regime (say, r_1) than in a free layoff regime (say, r_2) – (i.e. $r_1 > r_2$). This modification, however, is not pursued here anymore; instead, we proceed along the lines of the author. Such a distinction, however, is made and remains pivotal in the discussion of the second paper (see the section on firm-specific knowledge).

9 Any possibility of aggregate demand constraint is assumed away.

10 This provides the dominant firms their wage-setting status.

11 A subgame perfect method is adopted to solve for the Nash equilibria of the game. Therefore, first the Nash equilibria in the second period game is analysed for both situations (layoff and no-layoff regime) and then the equilibrium outcomes of the full (two period) game is analysed.

12 This view has gained some support in the official policy circle; for example SNCL report notes: 'We have no doubt that *bilateralism is an essential ingredient of industrial relations*, and that both parties [workers and employers] should rely on it as far as possible' (emphasis added) (SNCL Report 2002: 16).

13 Of course any such possibility is summarily rejected by the author. Elsewhere (Basu 2011: 135) argues:

> One widely used justification for disallowing free contracts is when this occurs between parties of asymmetrical power. . . . This widely used assertion is invalid, however. If contracts between the rich and poor are not treated as valid by virtue of power asymmetry, the rich will refuse to sign contracts with the poor (knowing that the courts are likely to overturn the agreements). The poor will therefore tend to get excluded from the market. They will not be able to get loans easily or sign so many other kinds of contracts that one needs in order to get ahead in life. Hence, the asymmetry of power cannot in itself be construed as a reason for disregarding the PFC [Principle of Free Contract].

> Interestingly, if PFC is logically extended to other spheres of life, we reach bizarre results. For instance, supporters of PFC must not logically object to the flesh trade since it is apparently voluntarily agreed to and therefore must be legalized. This may be considered an extreme case, but it starkly brings out the vacuity of the argument.

14 Of course, such possibilities are foreign to the author, as his model assumes continuous market clearing. Nonetheless, such possibilities are a common phenomenon. For example, recently the Supreme Court of India has asked the Central Government to consider and interfere in the plight of the nurses working in private hospitals who are victims of the illegal practice of bond, including the retaining of their original certificates to prevent them from leaving institutions and compelling them to work for years. It was reported that about one lakh nurses were facing the problem. (The Hindu 10 December 2011). Although this is still common knowledge in the profession, fresh applicants comply with the practice voluntarily, since it is attached as a precondition for offering employment. This clearly reflects how the asymmetric distribution of power may project an illegal activity as benign and cause people to voluntarily agree to it.

15 This is widely recognised, for example SNCL Report (2002: 248) notes:

> We learn that about 8 lakh workers have been ushered out of jobs through VRS [Voluntary Retirement Schemes] and retirement schemes. Here, we must also refer to the large number of complaints that we have received on VR Schemes. We have been told that in many cases, it is a travesty to describe these schemes as voluntary. We are not asserting that all 'voluntary' retirement schemes have suffered from elements of duress. . . . But we have also been told of elements of indirect compulsion, pressure tactics, innovative forms of mental harassment, compelling employees to resign by seeking to terminate them, and in some cases, physical torture and threats of violence against themselves or dependents.

16 When layoffs are shown to be better than no-layoffs, note that it is simultaneously beneficial for both workers and firms. A dominant firm's profit increases switching from a no-layoff to a layoff regime [i.e. Eq. (12) holds], and given dominant firms' entry into the market, wages in layoff regimes become higher than in the no-layoff regimes (in no-layoff regimes no dominant firms can enter by virtue of Eq. (12), and consequently wages remain depressed).

17 In a money- and power-ridden society, this would effectively end up in draining all the bargaining power from the hands of workers.

18 The author abstracts from such phenomenon and argues that if there is a surplus to be reaped at the level of society, it would be reaped by allowing participants to develop their contracts freely. However, the argument for 'principle of free contract' is reminiscent of Ronald Coase's (1960) argument – that through bargaining (in which concerned parties can write their own contracts), the entire social surplus gets exhausted. Well-known criticisms levelled against Coase's argument also apply here, namely, that it does not consider transaction costs for negotiation, interlinked markets and distributional outcomes.

19 Until now we considered only corner solutions; these are extreme cases of either dominant firms being present in only layoff regimes or operating only in no-layoff regimes, but not together.

20 If wage, in the fringe sector, under a layoff regime, is denoted by $\overline{W}$ and calculated as, $\overline{W} = \dfrac{A}{b(1-t)+B}$, then it can easily be checked that for the set of parameter values mentioned above, $W^N > W^L > \overline{W}$. In a no-layoff regime, workers in the fringe sector receive the same wage as the dominant sector workers (see Basu 2007: 142 for details).

21 Remember under a no-layoff regime, fringe sector workers and dominant sector workers receive the same wage.

22 Basu (2007: 139) describes this as follows: '[I]f the wage that the dominant firms pay drops too low then some of the skilled labourers may prefer to go to the fringe sector'. Basically, in such a situation, dominant firms and the fringe sector compete for workers.

23 The discussion below liberally draws upon Roychowdhury (2014a).

24 This idea gives shape to the demand of the industry lobby. FICCI-AIOE (2005: 276) recommended: 'Voluntary Arbitration must be promoted to Discourage Litigation: Section 10A, has failed in its objective. Arbitration should be promoted as an alternative dispute resolution machinery to discourage litigation'.

25 By this assumption, industry-wide fluctuations and intertemporally correlated shocks are ruled out.

26 The integer problem is ignored by assuming that pn is an integer.

27 This is because anti-retrenchment legislation is only applicable to industries covered by Industrial Disputes Act, 1947. This is accepted by the authors; also see p. 32, footnote 3.

28 No concrete, real-life example of technology shock is provided. Though we have imagined some of them (see below).

29 However, this interpretation is perfectly fine if the sector in question was agriculture. Then, $\varphi = 0$ could stand for bad weather, while $\varphi = 1$ could take account of the good weather. But labour laws in India do not apply to the farm sector.

30 The production function is defined as the pure technological relationship between inputs and the resulting output. A textbook definition says: it is the maximum level of output produced by given units of input or conversely, minimum units of inputs needed for a given level of output. Thus, there is no place for prices in a production function.

31 However, note that shift in demand from one segment of industry to another is primarily due to changes in taste and preferences, normally induced by changes in income (and its distribution). Thus, such changes are typically structural rather than stochastic. Even export demand depends upon structural factors at the level of world economy and in any case exports form a minute proportion of overall demand in any industry in countries like India.

32 This assumption of firm-specificity further reduces the appeal of φ being interpreted as technology shock. Since technology shocks like shortage of raw materials, import duty on machineries etc. would affect all the firms in the industry equally and will not be firm-specific at random.

33 For detailed discussion on this, see 'Introduction' and ch.13 of Patnaik (2008).

34 This is because there are n identical firms and only pn of these have $\varphi = 1$. The rest have no labour demand under an F-regime.
35 Risk neutrality means perception of the firms towards taking risk. A risk-averse (lover) firm prefers (rejects) the certainty equivalent of expected value of profits over (for) uncertain expected profit. A risk-neutral firm only cares about the expected value of profits, irrespective of its riskiness. See Varian (2006: 224–225) for details.
36 Notice that the aggregate labour demand curve in both the F-regime and the N-regime is obtained by blowing up the demand curve of a single firm by the number of firms. Thus, the outcomes at the macro-level are obtained by simple aggregation of micro-level variables. However, this method of aggregation, which is patent to neoclassical economics, is wrong, for the macroeconomic phenomena cannot be derived from simple aggregation of microeconomic truths. A classic example to illustrate the point is Keynes' 'paradox of thrift', which holds that if the savings propensity of all individuals double, the total savings of the economy does not double – as the simple aggregation procedure would suggest. In fact, aggregate savings does not change at all (given autonomous investment, only output adjusts to a lower equilibrium value).
37 The assumption that in an F-regime there is full wage flexibility is understandable, although this is also questionable (see Chapter 6). But in the N-regime, such a Walrasian assumption is clearly untenable. Since the social circumstances under which hire and fire is prohibited, probably due to presence of unions, would also preclude the possibility of full wage flexibility by, say, claiming minimum wages and we may not get w^N, at all.
38 Note that from unknown initial conditions, if we jump to the conclusion of free signing of contracts, such reasoning implicitly assumes certain strange conditions which are at variance with reality. Note that if workers and capitalists are to sign contracts at will, then information about the exact position of the demand and supply schedules should be available to both parties. This is a bizarre assumption to make – that such information would be available with every worker (as opposed to a union) since waiving the 'right not to be fired' cannot be conferred to anybody other than the worker himself/herself. Yet this is an impractical proposition to make, for even if it is proposed that firms would inform each worker before negotiation, such information dissemination would be prohibitively costly. Thus, if initial conditions are unknown, even though a regime not currently in place may be beneficial to all – yet negotiations may fail.
39 Although the authors, by assuming full employment, simply rule out any such possibility. However, the real world is saddled with involuntary unemployment. Thus, the authors fail to recognise a defining feature of any capitalist economy in which free bargaining only remains a chimera.
40 This view gains support even in the mainstream observations: 'Asymmetry in market power between employer and employee that can lead not only to inadequate protection of workers, unsafe working conditions, and low wages, but also to inefficient economic outcomes' World

Bank (2010: 106). Interestingly, Basu (2011: 94) elsewhere recognises the problem with signing voluntary contracts, although in a different context: '[M]any seemingly voluntary land acquisitions are actually based on subtle intimidations and threats to poor farmers'. It is puzzling how workers are assessed, by the author, to possess greater bargaining power than farmers in any transaction. In our view, farmers at least have their own land to cultivate and earn their (a portion or full, depending upon the land size) subsistence and are less vulnerable than workers, who are completely dependent on employers for their subsistence.

41 That is whether labour demand curves intersect or not.
42 Thus, the labour demand curves under an F- and an N-regime are represented by Eqs.(10) and (11), respectively.
43 This is perfectly justified, since the supply curve was written as $s = s(w)$ with $s'(w) \geq 0$. We are only taking the equality, instead of strict inequality taken by authors.
44 The distance shows the magnitude of the difference between wages in the F-regime vis-à-vis the N-regime.
45 For example, in expectation of falling short of the $360 billion export target in 2012–13, the Indian government announced a 2 percent interest subsidy scheme for exporters. The then Commerce and Industry Minister Anand Sharma justified this move on the following grounds:

> Given the global slowdown and the contraction at some of the major destinations of India's exports, we are finding it difficult to meet the [export] target. . . . With these measures [interest subsidy], we should be able to give a push to our exports in the last quarter of this financial year. The objective is to stabilise the situation and try and move from the negative [current account] territory to positive.
> (The Hindu 27 December 2012)

We are recommending similar demand augmenting policies.

46 Essentially, the idea is to reduce the uncertainty level in the economy through policy interventions. Alternative policy interventions like decoupling from the world economy to reduce the transmission of volatility from the world export market, or regulating the pace of introducing technological progress can be thought of as other means to tame uncertainty.
47 Of course, the diagram is drawn on the basis of the specific functional form in Eq.(8), and the resulting aggregate labour demand curve is $L = n.[A-Bw]$ for both regimes.
48 We have seen in Solow (1985), discussed in Chapter 4, that firm-specific skill lies at the heart of his analysis. However, in our view, skill typically depends upon educational attainment and vocational training. Instead, we try to draw attention to the differential nature of 'on site' knowledge (acquired only through first-hand experience) in each industry, which has its consequent effect on productivity. For example, such knowledge acquired in the sewing industry is entirely different from that of in the printing industry. Hence, such types of knowledge is firm-specific and results in workers' specialization, affecting productivity.

49 This is similar to the argument in the Insider-Outsider framework where Lindbeck and Snower (1988: 12) talk about 'the costs arising from the effect of job security on work effort' related to turnover cost. They imagine efforts going down as a result of high labour turnover rates. Firms with high rates of labour turnover usually offer low job security, little opportunity for advancement and little incentive for workers to build reputations (ibid.: 45). We are simply assuming that it also provides little motivation for workers to acquire firm-specific knowledge. This has been widely recognised in the popular discourse; commenting on the recent introduction of contract employment for doctors at All India Institute of Medical Sciences (AIIMS), New Delhi, a senior faculty member noted: 'Contracts appointments do not benefit the employee as it leads to career insecurity, *lack of future orientation*, exploitation, financial disadvantages and stress. *Of course, this in turn does not benefit the institute either*' (emphasis added) (The Hindu 22 May 2011). This clearly draws attention to the fact that workers' motivation increases with secured (i.e. permanent) jobs. The Japanese lifetime employment system, in the past century, typically emphasized offering lifetime job contracts to workers to earn their loyalty, motivation and elicit maximum work effort.

50 Over a range in time, normally in the upswing of the business cycle when demand is high, expectations for higher p emerging in the next period is also high.

51 It is simply assumed that, with adaptive expectations on part of workers, looking at past realized value of θ, during an upswing, workers also expect a high value of p emerging in the next period. This assumption is similar to the 'common knowledge' assumption widely prevalent in game theory.

52 If workers' response is sluggish.

53 For avoiding trivial equilibria with zero production, a small modification to the function f (L) is undertaken. It is assumed that there exists some positive number, K, such that, for all $L \leq K$, $f(L) = 0$ and for all $L > K$, $f'(L) > 0$, $f''(L) < 0$.

54 Say if the economy hits the labour supply constraint.

55 Differential effects on employment are assumed away by taking a perfectly inelastic supply curve of labour.

56 The derivation of this curve involves lengthy algebra not worth repeating here. In any case, the original paper derives the V-shaped curve meticulously and may be referred to.

Chapter 6

Effectiveness of labour market flexibility in face of effective demand constraint

Explanation of persistent unemployment *solely* by analysing the labour market – in terms of real wages – was given in Chapter 4. Chapter 5, assuming full employment, forwarded a different genre of argument for LMF. Each model discussed in the Insider-Outsider (I-O) framework attempted to show 'how insiders may exercise upward pressure on wages and thereby generate unemployment' (Lindbeck and Snower 1988: 5); specifically, insiders utilize labour turnover costs (LTCs) to 'drive their wages above the market-clearing level' (ibid.: 63). Similarly, models analysed in Chapter 5 relied upon instantaneous wage adjustments to attain full employment. This is precisely the *method* all neoclassical models ultimately bank upon, namely, downward rigidity (flexibility) of real wages to explain involuntary unemployment (full employment).[1]

Explaining involuntary unemployment this way is a long-standing tradition in the neoclassical school and dates back to at least as early as Pigou (1943: 343–344). Notwithstanding sophisticated technical innovations, this logic has remained the cornerstone of all neoclassical explanations. As Solow (1980: 9), writing after almost four decades, noted: '[Real] wage stickiness is a first-order factor in a reasonable theory of unemployment'. Solow also concedes that if workers compete between themselves to bid down wages, then full employment equilibrium would *necessarily* get established: 'Pigou says the obvious thing first, and I agree that it is the first thing to say: *if there is "thoroughgoing competition" among workers, then the only possible equilibrium position is at full employment*' (emphasis added) (ibid.: 4).[2] It is obvious that neoclassical theories patently explain involuntary unemployment by downward real wage rigidity.[3]

By now it must be clear that the I-O framework (theoretical foundation underlying LMF strategy; see Chapter 4) provides a *sui generis* explanation of wage rigidity based on insiders' market power and argues for LMF, which robs insiders of their labour market power. Therefore, LMF ultimately wants to eliminate all labour turnover costs (LTCs) in order to produce a frictionless labour market so that real wages can move freely to establish full employment. In other words, LMF envisages bringing the real economy to a close approximation of the neoclassical labour market.

However, the question arises, *even if* real-life labour markets are made to closely replicate the neoclassical labour market, does it *necessarily* guarantee a full employment equilibrium outcome? According to Keynes (2010), this is not so, for the *methodology* adopted by the Classical[4] school – of analysing the aggregate labour market *directly* for determining equilibrium employment – is fundamentally flawed. Section 6.1 demonstrates why this is so. It is further shown that for the Classical conclusions (hence, I-O theory's prediction) to hold, it requires strict adherence to Say's law.[5] *Demand has no exogenous role to play here*. However, real economies fundamentally differ from the description of the Classical school (i.e. Say's law economy) since people have wealth demand for money *independent* of transaction purposes. Thus, *all* incomes generated in the production process (i.e. purchasing power) *need not be necessarily* spent back on the goods and services produced since some portion of purchasing power may be held back/diverted as *idle* cash (wealth demand for money). Therefore, every act of supply *does not*, by itself, generate demand of equal value. Hence, Say's law should be abandoned. Thus, real wage flexibility as a means of getting rid of unemployment, as prescribed by the proponents of LMF (assuming Say's law), has no relevance for any modern money-using economy.

Section 6.2 analyses the effect of money-wage cuts on employment since votaries of LMF may draw attention to money-wage cuts as a means to counter a shortfall in effective demand. However, possibilities of boosting effective demand through money-wage cuts, it will be shown, depend upon stringent special assumptions without much relevance for any real economy. Thus, the claim that revised money-wage bargains (assisted by removal of hiring and firing costs) can reduce real wages to augment employment is *incorrect* once effective demand is considered *independently*. Hence, the wage cut route (either real or money) *cannot* raise employment, since it is incapable *per se* of tackling the problem of effective demand.

However, if supply *does not* create its own demand *automatically* and effective demand is determined *independently* by certain other forces, then it is shown that a *fall in real wages (when exogenously enforced, say, with imperfect competition and cost determined prices) leads to a fall in employment*. Thus, in a capitalist economy which is perennially demand-constrained,[6] the relationship between real wages and employment is *positive* – quite contrary to the claim of the Classical school (and more recently propounded by I-O theory). Thus, it would be concluded that the argument for undertaking LMF lacks proper theoretical justification.

6.1 Similarities between determination of employment in the I-O theory and the Classical theory: some logical infirmities

Employment determination in the Classical framework is carried out by *directly* looking at the aggregate labour market. Specifically, the equilibrium level of employment is determined by simultaneously bringing in the labour demand[7] and the labour supply[8] schedules in the real wage-employment plane at their point of intersection. It is assumed that real wage moving around *freely* brings about equality between the demand for, and supply of, labour to determine full employment equilibrium (or what is same as the natural rate of unemployment).[9] The tendency for the economy to attain full employment through *full* real wage adjustments predicted by the Classical school is clear from the following assertion:

> With perfectly free competition among workpeople and labour perfectly mobile, the nature of the relation (i.e. between the real wage-rates for which people stipulate and the demand function for labour) will be very simple. There will always be at work a strong tendency for wage-rates to be so related to demand that everybody is employed. Hence, in stable conditions everyone will actually be employed.
> (Pigou, *The Theory of Unemployment*: 252; quoted in Keynes [2010: 253])

I-O theory similarly concentrates *only* on the labour market for employment determination. The only difference now is that discussions here are entirely carried out in the context of a representative firm[10] (and *not* in terms of the aggregate labour market like the Classical school). To reach conclusions at the level of macroeconomy, the representative firm is blown up by the number of firms in the economy[11] and a single firm is assumed to be a microcosm of the whole economy.[12]

Now explanation of unemployment in the I-O framework, it may be remembered, is due to insiders' activity. Specifically, incumbent workers use hiring and firing costs in their own favour to 'drive their wages above the market clearing level' (Lindbeck and Snower 1988: 63) and thereby generate unemployment. Consequently, I-O theory prescribes the following strategy for alleviating unemployment: 'power-reducing policies . . . tend [to] raise the outsiders' chances of employment at the cost of *reducing the insiders' real wage* and job security' (emphasis added) (ibid.: 261). The exact *method*[13] of raising employment of the outsiders is to get rid of the firing costs, thereby allowing 'thoroughgoing competition' among insiders and outsiders, eventually bringing down the real wages into equality with the supply price of the outsiders – restoring full employment.

The Classical theory also explains unemployment in terms of *lack* of free movement [i.e. rigidity] of real wages.[14] Specifically, unemployment is explained,

> due to the refusal or inability of a unit of labour, *as a result of legislation* or social practices or of combination for collective bargaining or of slow response to change or *of mere human obstinacy*, to accept a reward corresponding to the value of the product attributable to its marginal productivity'.
>
> (emphasis added) (Keynes 2010: 6)

It is easy to see that the I-O theory is merely using the obstinacy aspect of the Classical theory, practiced by insiders through open or tacit agreements, grounded in restrictive legislative norms (hiring and firing costs). Clearly, unemployment is generated by the insiders' activity and sustained through prevention of underbidding by outsiders due to restraining legislative practices. Basically, failure of 'thoroughgoing competition' (to use Solow's terminology) among workers causes downward real wage rigidity that results in unemployment. From the above discussion it is clear that *both* the Classical theory and I-O theory explain unemployment in terms of rigid real wages and envisage restoring full employment through real wage flexibility.[15]

However, according to Keynes (2010: 7) if unemployment is,

> due to an open or tacit agreement amongst workers not to work for less . . . such unemployment, though apparently involuntary, is not strictly so, and ought to be included under the above category of "voluntary" unemployment due to effects of collective bargaining, etc.

Therefore, the *nature* of unemployment propounded by I-O theory is only voluntary, not involuntary in the Keynesian sense.[16] This vastly reduces the appeal of I-O theory, since policy makers are more concerned with alleviating unemployment of the latter variety.[17]

Then the question arises: are the policy recommendations of I-O theory capable of eliminating unemployment? According to Keynes (2010), this is not so. In fact, Keynes argued that the explanation of unemployment (and consequently its removal) provided by the Classical school and also forwarded by I-O theory is fundamentally flawed. Let us see why.

In what follows we shall demonstrate that *even if* real wages are made flexible downwards as prescribed by the Classical school – allowing 'thoroughgoing' competition among workers – there can still be persistent unemployment due to insufficiency of effective demand in an economy with wealth demand for money. *This is the essence of Keynes' argument.* Keynes argued that it is only under the assumption of Say's law – of all savings being automatically invested – that real wage flexibility can bring in full employment.[18] Such an argument would make it clear why LMF alone – solely based on removal of LTCs for achieving completely flexible real wages – is *incapable* of augmenting employment in any money-using economy. Given this, we now turn to Figure 6.1.

Figure 6.1 depicts the aggregate labour market.[19] The market demand curve for labour is given by the (downward sloping) aggregate marginal product curve for labour (N^D) and drawn on the basis of diminishing marginal productivity assumption.[20] The labour supply curve is upward sloping[21] (N^S) along which workers equate the utility obtained from real wages with the marginal disutility of the amount of labour supplied.

Full employment is defined at the point of labour market clearing and is represented by the wage-employment combination W^*, N^*. Suppose the economy is stuck at some real wage W_1 *above* the market clearing wage W^* (say, due to trade union activity). According

Labour market flexibility and effective demand

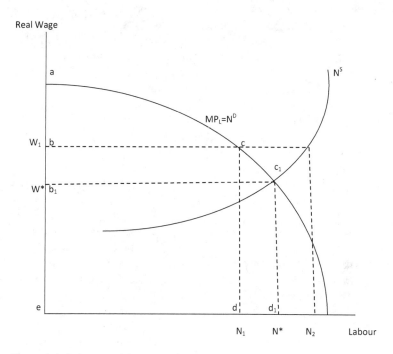

Figure 6.1 Aggregate labour market

to the Classical school, the marginal product curve of labour is the labour demand curve, and like typical demand curves, the quantity of labour demand (or employment at the short side of the market) is *determined* by the *independent variable* i.e., price of labour (real wage rate). Therefore, in the Classical framework, labour demand is determined by the equation $N^D = f\ (real\ wage)$.[22] Thus, corresponding to real wage W_1, employment is determined on the labour demand schedule at N_1, and excess labour supply or unemployment is $N_2 - N_1$.

Now the Classical school explains persistence of unemployment by downward rigidity of real wages. In other words, employment remains arrested at N_1 because trade unions run a 'closed shop'. Hence, a *necessary* and *sufficient* condition for the labour market to clear – according to the Classical theory – is to remove such labour market imperfections (by delegitimising trade union activity or complete removal of hiring and firing costs), which allows the real wage to adjust to W*. Of course, it is granted that workers – in absence of labour market imperfections – would engage in undercutting *money*-wages and bring down the real wage to the market clearing level, *curing* unemployment. Let us see what this involves.

For simplicity, let us assume that the economy is characterized by a Classical savings function (i.e. all wages are consumed and all profits are saved). Now, for historical reasons, if real wage is W_1, then employment is grounded at N_1. The magnitude of total output is given by the area under the marginal product curve to the left of N_1 by the area, *acde*. The wage bill is obtained by multiplying the wage rate with the level of employment and is denoted in the figure by *bcde*. Since national income is distributed between only two categories of income[23] – wages and profits – profits are represented by *abc*.

Now, the nature of capitalist production is commodity production (i.e. production for market). Therefore, for a certain amount of output to be *actually* produced – even in the short period equilibrium – it must be *sold* in the market or demanded. Let us see what this involves. Since national output is distributed among wages and profits, we have Y = W + P (where Y = aggregate income, W = wage bill and P = aggregate profits). The question arises: how is income allocated in a closed economy without government? Clearly, aggregate income must be allocated between consumption (C) and savings (S) – thus, Y = C + S. By virtue of the Classical savings function we have S = P. Now if Y is equilibrium output, then it must be sold in the market, and from the expenditure side, Y = C + I must hold (where I is aggregate investment expenditure).

Therefore, we arrive at the conclusion that I = P.[24] Therefore, from Figure 6.1, investment requirements associated with sustaining N_1 level of employment (to be actually generated) is *abc*.

Now suppose 'thoroughgoing competition' is introduced – maybe by scrapping hiring and firing costs – as recommended by the proponents of LMF. Assuming that workers *can* influence real wages through money-wage bargains, suppose workers successfully bid down real wage to the market clearing level W*. The question arises: does it *necessarily* imply that equilibrium employment would increase up to N* (from N_1)? From the wage-employment configuration W*, N* it is clear that the wage bill would be $b_1c_1d_1e$. This is automatically demanded, since all wages are consumed. With total income being ac_1d_1e, *potential* profit or surplus is ac_1b_1. However, from the above analysis it is clear that this potential profit needs to be *realized/absorbed* in the economy, and the only demand component available is investment purchases. Hence, aggregate investment *must* increase exactly by the amount bcc_1b_1. However, there is no obvious reason as to why this should be so, except the assumption that all surpluses (i.e. planned savings) are *automatically* used for investment purchases. This is because investment is autonomously determined and simply does not get automatically jacked up to counter any shortfall in other expenditure components. If investment is *not passively adjusting*, then accommodating expenditures equivalent to bcc_1b_1 is missing from the economy. Hence, a portion of output (bcc_1b_1) arising out of expansion of employment from N_1 to N^* goes unsold in the market, for which cost has already been incurred. This would entail a loss to the entrepreneur from expanding employment. Therefore, under the Classical assumption of profit-maximizing producers, N^* cannot be the new equilibrium position of employment (even when the supply-side conditions justify expansion of employment, essentially because the nature of capitalist production is *commodity production*), even with real wage flexibility.[25] In other words, the above discussion shows that real wages cannot be reduced *exogenously* – when real wage is determined from the marginal product of labour curve (i.e. under perfectly competitive conditions). Classical theory, nonetheless, maintains that real wage flexibility *can* cure unemployment. Hence, for logical consistency, from the discussion just carried out, we must assume that investment would passively adjust to *any* amount of planned savings automatically[26] (i.e. *any* amount of potential profits must be immediately realized).[27] But such an assumption would mean that demand has no role to play and *anything* produced would *always* be sold. In other words, this must *necessarily* assume 'supply of goods creates its own demand' (i.e. the Say's law of market).

Demand has no exogenous role to play here. It is this kind of analysis to which Keynes objected. Keynes pointed out that the economy we live in differs in fundamental ways from the description provided by the Classical school. This is because in a capitalist economy there is demand for money *per se*, independent of transaction purposes *for wealth-holding motives*. Thus, agents who earn income need not spend their *whole* income, either directly or indirectly, on *produced* goods. In other words, as Hahn (1977: 31) puts it, there can be 'resting places for savings in other than reproducible assets'. Typically, in modern money-using economies, such a 'resting place' for planned savings is money (in form of asset demand). Now suppose at any point in time the patterns of asset choice of all individuals (including banks) are such that the price of capital goods remains relatively low compared to the existing money-wages. In that circumstance, the economy's actual investment would *fall short* of full employment investment.[28] Now the price of capital goods remains relatively low precisely because people now want to hold money, as an asset, in their portfolio instead of holding claims on capital goods. This creates the shortfall in investment below its full employment level.[29] Under such circumstances, some commodities would remain unsold if full employment output is produced. Since producers suffer a loss-producing full employment output, they would simply *not* produce at full employment but something less, which could be eventually *sold*.

The moment we start recognising this fact, *autonomy* of effective demand – determining the amount of output that can be eventually *sold* – starts emerging in the picture and consequently necessitates rejection of the Say's law of market.[30] It becomes comprehensible as to why Keynes (2010: 19) objected to Marshall's analysis that 'an act of individual saving inevitably leads to a parallel act of investment', and the problem of treating investment purchases as accommodating expenditure becomes obvious.

Once it is recognised that aggregate demand (AD) has an *autonomous* role to play in determining employment, Classical (full employment) economics is reduced to a special case of Keynes's general theory.[31] Keynes (2010: 25–26) fully appreciated this point:

> The effective demand associated with full employment is a *special* case, only realised when the propensity to consume and the inducement to invest stand in a particular relationship to one another. This particular relationship, which corresponds to the assumption of the classical theory, is in a sense an optimum relationship. But it can only exist when, by *accident or design*, current investment provides an amount of demand just equal to the excess of the aggregate supply price of the output resulting from full employment over what the community will choose to spend on consumption when it is fully employed'.
>
> (emphasis added)

It follows, then, that the theories which suggest real wage flexibility (in a downward direction through competitive wage bargaining or by exogenous decree) can get rid of unemployment, assume away the *autonomous* role played by effective demand altogether and must logically bank upon Say's law to sustain their argument. Hence, the I-O theory (based on which the policies of LMF are recommended) must be logically necessarily based on Say's law, while stating that removal of hiring and firing costs would enhance employment. The logical necessity for such an assumption clearly makes the theory untenable in real-life situations.

Proponents of LMF may, however, object to the stark manner, described above, of managing the demand side – logically required for the policy recommendations of the I-O theory to hold. They may, in fact, argue that *money*-wage flexibility would be sufficient to create enough demand so as to absorb *any* planned savings in the economy. Keynes, however, assumed rigid money-wages – which is an essential requirement for the stability of the value of money and hence the stability of the capitalist system as a whole (see Patnaik 2008 for an elaboration). Hence, Keynes is inescapably interpreted as drawing attention to *money*-wage rigidity. However, this is *not* a correct appraisal of Keynes.[32] As Krugman (2006: 3) notes, writing *General Theory* was a much more difficult 'long struggle of escape' for Keynes from pre-Keynesian 'modes of thought' and submitted: 'Change one assumption in our so-called classical model, that of perfect wage flexibility, and it turns back into *The General Theory*. If that had been all Keynes had to contend with, *The General Theory* would have been an easy book to write' (Introduction to *The General Theory*).

6.2 Possibilities of stimulating effective demand through money-wage cut

Votaries of LMF may draw attention to money-wage cut and the 'roundabout repercussions' (to use Keynes's terminology) as means to tackle the demand side problem following removal of hiring and firing costs (although none of the I-O models have done so and may be accused of tacitly assuming Say's law). In what follows, we shall critically examine on the lines of Keynes and post-Keynesians – the plausibility of boosting effective demand through *indirect* routes following a money-wage cut.[33] Most important indirect routes normally discussed in the literature are repercussions on: (a) aggregate propensity to consume (APC), and (b) rate of interest.[34]

In analysing the effects of money-wage reduction on APC it may be noted that individuals' consumption depends positively upon their accumulated *real* wealth. With money-wages and prices falling – the real value of cash balances and cash-denominated assets unambiguously rise – these boost, it is argued, private consumption via the 'wealth effect'. Thus, effective demand gets stimulated through the rise in consumption demand – following the reduction in money-wages and prices.[35] This was precisely the route taken by Pigou (1943) and later Patinkin (1965) in demonstrating the self-adjusting character of a capitalist economy saddled with unemployment. It is also known as the 'Pigou-Patinkin effect' or 'real balance effect' (RBE).

However, there are obvious problems with this argument since it exclusively focuses on the asset holders' side. If, on the contrary, behaviour of the asset holders as well as those with liabilities are analysed in unison in an *inside* money world, then the positive effects on effective demand due to RBE may not be forthcoming. This is easy to understand. In an inside money economy, the financial and monetary claims of the asset holders are on a set of economic agents (liability owners) who happen to reside in the *same* economy – hence on balance, all assets and liabilities are exactly matched and *internally* held *within* the economy itself. Consequently, due to falling money-wages and prices, the rise in the real value of assets possessed by some agents (asset holders) is exactly matched by the rise in real value of liabilities held by other agents (liability owners). Hence there arises a distinct possibility that the rise in consumption by asset holders from a price fall (positive RBE) is exactly counteracted by a fall in consumption of the liability owners (negative RBE) – and on the whole, the boost to effective demand through the consumption route, as envisaged by RBE, may not materialize.[36]

Still other problems start to surface if we shift our attention from consumption spending to investment purchases. Investment decisions in a capitalist economy are typically undertaken by entrepreneurs and are partly financed through 'borrowed' capital.[37] These debts raised from the capital market are contracted in nominal (money) terms. Therefore, with continuously falling prices, *real* indebtedness of entrepreneurs would rise drastically – pushing them into insolvency. As *real* liabilities of firms go up, they eventually become bankrupt. Evidently, with a rising number of firms filing for bankruptcy, aggregate investment gets adversely affected.[38] Even if firms do not go bankrupt, fear of plunging into insolvency would make them extremely apprehensive about undertaking fresh investments, negatively affecting aggregate investment.

Additionally, deflation would put a further drag on investment by destroying business confidence. With falling money-wages and prices, entrepreneurs would be disadvantageously placed to predict future costs of production and hence profitability. With each round of price fall, the level of uncertainty in the economy would increase and *ceteris paribus*, this would put a drag on investment.[39]

Investment would also suffer since profit-maximizing entrepreneurs are discouraged by the prospect of falling business profits following deflation. This is so, for production and sale of output requires time – whereas wage contracts and other input contracts are denominated in money terms and often demanded at the beginning of the production period (more likely in face of falling prices and widespread bankruptcies, to minimize risk and uncertainty). This implies that with falling prices, products produced at yesterday's higher wages and material costs would entail/constitute a loss today, since they have to be sold at today's lower prices. This would be true irrespective of how well or how poorly business is managed, encouraging firms to scale down production and cutback investment (Wells 1979: 92). Hence, taking consumption spending and investment expenditure *together*, falling wages and prices seem to dampen effective demand rather than boosting it.[40]

Let us now turn our attention to the effects of a fall in money-wages and prices on the interest rate – remembering that investments are inversely related to interest rates. This route (of stimulating investment) is often known as the 'Keynes effect'. It operates as follows: *given* the money supply, if money-wages and consequently prices fall, the amount of money necessary for transaction purposes falls as well, resulting in a withdrawal of money from active balances that temporarily causes an excess supply in the money market. For correcting such imbalances, excess money has to be accommodated in the idle balances (speculative demand). But *given a liquidity preference schedule*, this would reduce the interest rate and boost investment, stimulating AD.

However, this line of reasoning is based on a series of underlying assumptions that need careful scrutiny. For example, this route will not be operative if, say, the market structure is characterized by oligopoly, since this would make investment interest-insensitive. Similarly, if the economy is caught in a situation like a liquidity trap, then the interest rate cannot fall any further. But even if we drop the special assumption of liquidity trap and instead note the rising *real* indebtedness of the firms due to falling prices and consequently unattractiveness of the bonds issued by them (due to apprehensions over their future solvency), then the interest rate route may not operate. This is because Keynes noted that economic recovery following the interest rate route is faced with a twofold problem: 'a moderate reduction in money-wages may prove inadequate, whilst an immoderate reduction might shatter confidence even if it were practicable' (Keynes 2010: 242).

What happens to the liquidity preference schedule with such immoderate reductions in money-wages? It leads to a loss of confidence in bond holding due to rising real debt burden of firms and their inability to respect past debt obligations, eventually plunging into insolvency. Therefore, for an asset holder deciding between money and bonds in a portfolio choice – bonds must now become *less* attractive as compared to money for any *given* interest rate. This evidently shifts the liquidity preference schedule *outwards*. Therefore, with a larger amount of money available for idle balance from each round of money-wage fall, demand for such idle balance would also rise. Hence, ultimately whether interest rates would rise or fall entirely depends upon the relative strength of these two effects. If, for instance, the liquidity preference schedule shifts outwards considerably, then interest rates would not fall at all and consequently investments need not be stimulated. In fact, if prices are expected to fall further – with the preference for holding idle cash *surpassing* the release of money from active balance – then rate of interest may well *rise* and *reduce* investment. Consequently, investments may not be encouraged from falling wages and prices.[41]

Now consider an economy in which aggregate money supply depends upon the extent of credit money created by the banking system. Is it true that the outstanding nominal stock of money would remain unchanged even if prices fall substantially (otherwise, a timid deflation would be ineffective)?[42] With debt defaults spreading due to rise in real debt burden, banks will find a large part of their assets as non-performing. Clearly, this will adversely affect their capacity and willingness to give out loans and hence create money. Further, with the asset side collapsing due to continued deflation, banks would be bound to call back outstanding loans from the market, necessarily resulting in the total supply of money stock shrinkage. Davidson (1985: 383) puts it cogently:

> An unchanged nominal quantity of money means an unchanged nominal liability total for the banking system. . . . Nominal value of the banks' portfolio of assets depends on bank borrowers

being able to meet their cash flow obligations. Consequently a coordinated fall in all prices will force private sector borrowers to default *en masse* on their obligations to the banks. The result will be a collapse of asset values on banks' balance sheets. Consequently any significant coordinated fall in wages and prices will wipe out the banks' net worth thereby inducing massive banking system bankruptcies. As banks go "belly up" on any significant scale, the outstanding nominal stock of bank money will, *ceteris paribus*, decline and *therefore the real liquidity value of the remaining money stock will not increase.*

(emphasis added)

Now if the real liquidity value of the diminished money stock does not increase, there is no reason to believe that the Keynes effect would operate.

Until now, the money supply is assumed to be exogenous; however, if the money supply becomes endogenous, falling wages and prices may push the real interest rate to higher levels, adversely affecting investments. To see this, consider the expression for real interest rate:

$$r = i - \frac{\dot{P}}{P}$$

where r and i are, respectively, real interest rate and nominal interest rate, and $\frac{\dot{P}}{P}$ is the inflation rate in the economy. Now deflation would raise the real interest rate in a straightforward fashion. Further, as the real debt burden of firms goes up, they worry about solvency. As firms' perceptions towards risk rise, they become extremely cautious about risk taking, holding up investment. Moreover, as real indebtedness of firms goes up, banks may be tempted to raise the nominal interest rate, adversely affecting investment.

Moreover, there is nothing special in the wage-flexibility path which cannot be obtained by an expansionary monetary policy. Results from both policies as well as their mode of operation would be identical. This is why Keynes came to the following conclusion:

> There is, therefore, no ground for the belief that a flexible wage policy is capable of maintaining a state of continuous

full employment; – any more than for the belief than an open market monetary policy is capable, unaided, of achieving this result.

(Keynes 2010: 242)

In fact, Keynes preferred an expansionary monetary policy path over wage-price fall for effective demand stimulation. This is because the latter route makes prices volatile with a negative bearing on entrepreneurial activities besides being difficult to implement. Keynes noted:

> The chief result of this [flexible wage] policy would be to cause a great instability in prices, so violent perhaps as to make business calculations futile in an economic society we live. To suppose that a flexible wage policy is a right and proper adjunct of a system which on the whole is one of *laissez-faire*, is the opposite of the truth.
>
> (ibid.: 244)

A critical examination of roundabout ways of tackling effective demand, following money-wage cuts revealed that, while they may be operative under stringent special conditions (theoretical possibilities in restrictive hypothetical set-up), they bear little relevance for any real economy.[43] Discussions in Sections 6.1 and 6.2 clearly indicate that employment expansion through wage flexibility (removing hiring and firing costs) as recommended by the I-O theory (in line of Classical theory) *lacks* proper theoretical justification. Wage cuts (either real or money) *cannot* raise employment, since they are incapable of tackling the effective demand problem.[44]

In fact, one can argue a little further. We found that real wages cannot be reduced *exogenously* in a Keynesian world, since this amounts to assuming the Say's law of market. Keynes instead argued real wages to be *endogenously* determined. In particular, Keynes assumed perfect competition and drew attention to *diminishing* marginal returns to labour in the short run, and espoused that a fall in real wages is an *effect* of rising employment (as opposed to its *cause* – noted by the Classical school), the latter being determined by the level of effective demand in the economy.[45] Therefore, in a perfectly competitive Keynesian world, since real wage is *determined* by the level of employment on the (diminishing) marginal product of labour curve (i.e. MPL = W/P), real wage *cannot* fall parametrically.

However, real wage *can* be parametrically reduced in a Kaleckian world of imperfect competition. In what follows, we shall investigate the effect of real wage cut on output and employment – when effective demand plays an autonomous role. In particular, it can be shown that if effective demand plays an autonomous role in determining employment, then *a fall in real wage actually leads to a fall in employment* (quite contrary to the claim of the Classical school and I-O theory). Let us make the following simplifying assumptions, which provide sufficient conditions under which real wages and output, hence employment, are *positively* related. The model, restricted to the short run assumes: (a) closed economy without government, (b) there are only two categories of economic agents – workers and capitalists with Classical savings function (i.e. marginal propensity to consume, *mpc*, for workers is unity, $C_w = 1$ and marginal propensity to save, *mps*, for entrepreneurs is unity, $S_\pi = 1$) and (c) investment is autonomously given in the short run.

It is easy to see that the marginal propensity to consume for the economy is given by $mpc^{Eco.} = \frac{W}{W+\pi}$.[46] Now with investment at $\overline{I}$, the level of AD in the economy is given by $AD_0 = \frac{\overline{I}}{1-mpc^{Eco.}} = \frac{\overline{I}}{\left[1-\frac{W}{W+\pi}\right]}$. Further, assume that: $AD_0 < Y_f$ (where Y_f is full employment output) and producers operate in an imperfectly competitive market.

Suppose producers follow the markup price setting rule $P = w_m l (1 + \mu)$, where P = price of output, w_m = money-wages, l = labour coefficient and μ = markup. Now suppose in response to unemployment, a policy of money-wage cut is undertaken that simultaneously lets oligopolists consolidate their market power, for which markup rises, so as to just offset the fall in money-wages such that prices remain unchanged (evidently real wages fall).[47] A fall in real wage leads to a *reduction* in the wage share (from the price equation, see that μ is rising) – implying a fall in the value of the multiplier. This leads to a *fall* in the economy's consumption propensity and hence AD. Since the economy's output (hence employment) is determined by *AD*, output and employment *fall further* below full employment.[48] Thus, a *reduction* in real wages leads to a *reduction* in employment, contrary to the claim of the Classical school and I-O theory.

The preceding argument leads to a further interesting observation, insofar as the organised sector workers' consumption basket includes the products produced in the unorganised sector: any rise in real wages in the organised sector, due to the greater bargaining power of workers, would have some *positive* demand spillover on the products produced by the unorganised sector, resulting in a tighter labour market condition in the unorganised sector. Thus, both organised *and* unorganised sectors benefit from rising real wages once effective demand is considered. This conclusion stands in direct contradiction to the case often made out in the orthodox circle. For example, it is widely argued that JSR creates a minuscule labour aristocracy with the relative neglect (sometimes even at the cost) of the vast majority of unorganised workers. Debroy (2005: 57) notes, 'Only a small percentage (8 to 9 percent) of the total workforce of the country is employed in the organised sector. . . . The "hire and fire" discourse is therefore about 8 percent of India's working population, those employed in the organised sector'. However, the above analysis suggests that if trade unions succeed (impossible without job security) in increasing unionized workers' real wages, then the non-unionized section also benefits once we factor in effective demand.

Conclusion

The Classical school solely banks upon the downward rigidity of real wages to explain involuntary unemployment. We established the close links between the explanations of unemployment by the Classical theory and I-O theory. Further, based on a Classical understanding, the policy of LMF was recommended (i.e. robbing off insiders' labour market power for establishing full employment). Next, we inquired: *even if* the real world is made to approximate the Classical labour market closely, is it possible to eliminate involuntary unemployment?

Following Keynes (2010) – considering effective demand autonomously – this was not so. Section 6.1 demonstrated that to sustain the policy prescription of I-O theory (i.e. real wage flexibility – removing hiring and firing costs – for attaining full employment), one must *necessarily* bank upon Say's law. The logical necessity of such an assumption makes I-O theory and the attending argument for undertaking LMF untenable in real-life situations.

Section 6.2 considered the route of effective demand expansion via money-wage cut – which, if operative, need not necessarily require Say's law to hold. We critically examined the *effectiveness* of 'roundabout repercussions' following money-wage cut, in tackling the demand side problem. A critical examination of two main *indirect* routes namely: (a) aggregate average propensity to consume (APC), and (b) rate of interest, revealed that while these may be operative under stringent special conditions (as theoretical possibilities in a restrictive hypothetical set-up), they bear absolutely no relevance for any real economy. We further demonstrated through a simple model, in an imperfectly competitive set-up, that real wages and employment, contrary to the orthodox claim, are actually *positively* related when effective demand is introduced into the picture.

Thus, in the world we live in, where effective demand has an *autonomous* role to play, there is no theoretical justification to carry out LMF to augment employment. In fact, LMF is harmful for *both* organised and unorganised sector workers in terms of employment creation. Hence, neither empirical evidence (Chapter 2) nor theoretical arguments (Chapters 3, 4 and 5) support any justification for making the labour market flexible. But, the whole discussion until now is based on a *closed* economy framework. However, there could be an argument in favour of LMF in an *open* economy context. In the next chapter (Chapter 7), we extend our analysis in an open economy context and examine the arguments in favour of introducing LMF.

Notes

1 Although real wage stickiness as an explanation of *involuntary* unemployment is a widely prevalent view in the mainstream literature, nonetheless for Keynes (2010: 7) this is not a strict definition of involuntary unemployment but instead should be termed as *voluntary* unemployment (more on this later). However, Keynes's voluntary unemployment should not be confused with the claim of a section of orthodox theorists (neoclassical) who do not recognise the existence of involuntary unemployment at all. For these theorists, *all* unemployment must ultimately be regarded as voluntary. For instance, as Lucas (1978: 334) puts it: '[U]nemployed worker at any time can always find *some* job at once and a firm can always fill a vacancy instantaneously' (emphasis in original). Thus, any unemployment must be voluntary and explained in terms of the preference of workers to choose leisure over work or to engage in a full-time job search (or training) instead of doing *any*

job at hand. This view is the market-clearing approach of the labour market. However, this view has been severely contested, even within the mainstream discourse, for being at variance with reality. As Solow (1986: S33) clarifies: 'I want to suggest that, in the case of the labour market, our preoccupation with the price-mediated market-clearing as the 'natural' equilibrium condition may be a serious error'. Hence, the continuous market-clearing approach, designating *all* unemployment as voluntary, need not be taken seriously. Moreover, from the nature of our problem at hand, the distinction between involuntary and voluntary unemployment is of no real significance and need not detain us any further.

2 Pigou's position is clearly borne out from the following:

> The classicals, if pressed, would not have denied that, should wage-earners not act competitively, but contrive, by means of combination or otherwise, to set the real rate of wages "too high," the stationary state would not be one of full employment. Their essential contention is that in *all* circumstances a full-employment stationary state is possible and, if an appropriate wage policy is adopted, will be secured.
>
> (emphasis in original)(Pigou 1943: 343–344)

He continues: '[I]f wage-earners follow a competitive wage policy, the economic system must move ultimately to a full employment stationary state; which is the essential thesis of the classicals' (ibid.: 351).

3 For this reason, the neoclassical unemployment story is solely built around theories of wage rigidity, ranging from, among others, trade unionism, efficiency wages and with special characterizations as, '[L]abor is a peculiar sort of commodity and the labor market correspondingly a peculiar sort of market' (Solow 1990: 30), from which it is concluded that the labour market is a social institution with notions of fairness for which 'there is some sort of social norm or behavioral injunction that forbids undercutting the going wage as a strategy for unemployed workers' (ibid.: 38–39).

4 Keynes (2010) used the term 'classical economists' to demarcate Marshall and his followers, the marginalists. However, according to Sweezy (1946: 297), this is misleading, for: 'It is preferable to regard John Stuart Mill as the last of the classical economists and to label the Marshallians the "neoclassical" school'. Nonetheless, in what follows, we stick to the original formulation by Keynes in General Theory (GT).

5 Close connections between the method of analysis adopted by the I-O framework and the Classical school would be established. Hence, criticisms originally formulated by Keynes against the Classical school would equally apply for the I-O theory.

6 Kornai (1979).

7 Defined as the marginal product of labour curve obtained from firm's profit maximizing behaviour.

8 Determines the supply price of labour and obtained from workers' utility maximizing behaviour (labour-leisure choice).

9   The equality of real wage and marginal product of labour on the labour demand schedule; also, the equality of utility derived from real wage and the marginal disutility of volume of employment on the labour supply schedule is subject to the condition of perfect competition prevailing in the economy [see Keynes 2010: 5]. Thus, free wage movements – even within the Classical framework – attain full employment only under perfectly competitive conditions. If this assumption is violated (as is the case for a reasonable description of any real economy), then free wage movements need not restore full employment. See Mukherji (2006) for an excellent exposition using a unified framework showing how departures from perfect competition can vary the Classical conclusions.
10 Since I-O theory 'aim (s) to provide *microeconomic* rationales for some workers' persistent failure to find jobs' (emphasis added) (Lindbeck and Snower 1988: 15).
11 Notice the methodology adopted – in the individual bargaining framework – to transfer a single firm-level argument to the whole economy (Lindbeck and Snower 1988: 70).
12 This method is fundamentally flawed and fraught with the excesses of 'methodological individualism'. For a comprehensive critique, see 'An Excursus on Methodological Individualism' (Patnaik 2008).
13 That is by applying the power-reducing policies.
14 Unemployment is additionally explained in terms of 'frictional' reasons that,

> allows for various inexactness of adjustment which stand in the way of continuous full employment: for example, unemployment due to a temporary want of balance between the relative quantities of specialised resources as a result of miscalculation or intermittent demand; or to time-lags consequent on unforeseen changes; or to the fact that the change-over from one employment to another cannot be effected without a certain delay, so that there will always exist in a non-static society a proportion of resources unemployed "between jobs".
>
> (Keynes 2010: 6)

15 The Classical school's position that real wage rigidity causes unemployment implicitly suggests that wage bargaining is in real terms. Keynes, however, rejected this view and instead argued that wage bargaining takes place in money terms; in particular, trade unions resist money-wage cut in order to protect their *relative* real wages. Keynes (2010: 13) suggested:

> in the struggle about money-wages primarily affects the *distribution* of the aggregate real wage between different labour-groups, and *not* its average amount per unit of employment. . . . The effect of combination on the part of a group of workers is to protect their *relative* real wage.
>
> (emphasis in original)

16 Keynes demarcated unemployment due to real wage rigidity as 'voluntary', since even if unemployed workers are willing (but not getting) to work at the going market wage rate (actually they are *just* indifferent

between leisure and work). However, even for a very small reduction in the real wage, workers would withdraw their labour-offerings and would prefer leisure over working. This observation, rooted in the Classical thinking, persuaded Keynes to assert that 'such unemployment, though apparently involuntary, is not strictly so'. Nonetheless, it may be argued that outsiders are not voluntarily unemployed since they may be interested to work for less than the insider's wage prevailing in the market. However, remember that unemployment is still explained by a concept of reservation wage (obtained by equating marginal disutility of work to real rewards of labour) of the outsiders below which they prefer leisure over work – 'outsiders . . . remain jobless because they are *not willing* to work for less than the insiders minus the production *and* rent-related turnover costs' (emphasis added) (Lindbeck and Snower 1988: 59) – hence outsiders' unemployment in the I-O framework also falls in the category of voluntary unemployment.

17 As Keynes pointed out, this is because 'both "frictional" and "voluntary" unemployment being consistent with "full" employment' (Keynes 2010: 14).

18 However, according to Sweezy (1963: 305), Keynes' greatest achievement in General Theory was the following: 'In particular, I still believe that his [Keynes'] greatest achievement were freeing economics from the tyranny of Say's Law and exploding the myth of capitalism as a self-adjusting system which reconciles private and public interests'.

19 Employment in the Classical framework is determined directly in the aggregate labour market. Even if the discussion is carried out in terms of aggregate labour market, the basic point of disagreement with this nature of analysis can be directly applied to the I-O framework, although the latter confines itself to the firm level.

20 However, post-Keynesians have rigorously proved that the marginal product curve is not the demand curve for labour in the real world [Weintraub (1956); Davidson (1983); McCombie (1985–86)]. Nonetheless, for simplicity of exposition, let us proceed as if the marginal product curve is the labour demand curve.

21 The argument that follows would be exactly the same even if the labour supply curve is perfectly inelastic.

22 Interestingly, Keynesians claim that the inverse function is the true relationship between real wages and employment [i.e. real wage = g (ND)], and labour demand is determined by labour productivity and the point of intersection between AD and aggregate supply curves [i.e. the point of effective demand] (see Chapter 3 of GT) (more on this below).

23 In the orthodox theory, such income categories are called 'factor incomes'. It is argued that labour and 'capital', the two basic 'factors of production' (along with land and organisation), contribute in producing final output – and receive 'factor income' in return. However, this analysis is highly misleading and ahistorical. It is misleading, since profits are justified, as if returns to capitalists' contribution to production and not by virtue of possessing private property. It is ahistorical, since returns to 'capital' is by virtue of possessing the means of production, which is specific to the organisation of production under capitalism. It does not pay sufficient attention to how capital in the first place

came to be in the possession of those possessing it. (See Bhaduri 1990: 19; Patnaik 2011b: 34.)
24 The question arises, in which way this equation is determined. Kalecki (1971: 78–79), referring to the above equation, brilliantly provides the answer (his analysis assumes that capitalists consume a part of their income):

> Does it mean that profits in a given period determine capitalists' consumption and investment, or the reverse of it? The answer to this question depends on which of these items is directly subject to the decisions of capitalists. Now, it is clear that capitalists may decide to consume and to invest more in a given period than in the preceding one, but they cannot decide to earn more. *It is, therefore, their investment and consumption decisions which determine profits, and not vice versa'*. (emphasis added)

Therefore, the equation is determined from the left- to the right-hand side (i.e. investment is independently determined).

25 This is cogently argued by Burchardt (1944: 6):'The assumption that competitive wage reductions will increase employment presupposes that entrepreneurs will always and immediately react on a temporary increase in actual profits with increased outlay'. Further,

> The crucial point in this [classical] theory is the assumption that employers react on the initial increase in profits [following wage reduction] immediately with increased outlay on capital goods or on their own consumption. If they hesitate to do so immediately, employment will not be increased'.

(ibid.: 4)

Kalecki entertained similar views. Harcourt (2006: 25), commenting on Kalecki's view on the subject, noted:

> He [Kalecki] supposes that businesspeople do not infer immediately the consequences for the expected profitability of planned investment of, say, a fall in the value of the wage unit. . . . They do nothing immediately, prices therefore fall in the same proportion as the wage unit and the "improvement" in profitability turns out to be "illusionary".

26 This logic behind an automatic increase in investment flows from, as Gerrard (1995: 448) puts it:

> The theoretical justification for Say's Law provided by the classical theory is the loanable funds theory of the rate of interest. . . . Firms allocate resources to investment with regard to the rate of interest. Household allocate their income between current consumption and saving with regard to the rate of interest. Investment and saving provide, respectively, a demand for, and a supply of, loanable funds. *The equilibrium (or 'natural') rate of interest ensures that the loanable funds market clears so that investment equals savings.*

(emphasis added)

Therefore, equality between planned savings and planned investment is always ensured through interest rate adjustments. However, this view confuses between stock and flow variables. Keynes noted that savings and investment decisions are flow variables (i.e. between two points in time when the value of the variable is *continuously* changing), and the equality between the two is established by fluctuations of another flow variable, namely, output. However, interest rate is a stock variable (i.e. between two points in time when the value of the variable remains *fixed*) determined from the portfolio choice of individuals, specifically, proportional distribution of their wealth holding between money and bonds. Therefore, equilibrium nominal interest rate is essentially derived from the equality of demand for and supply of money (just as equilibrium output is derived from the equality of savings and investment). Hence, the interest rate is essentially a monetary phenomenon determined from the money market equilibrium. Thus, under situations of planned investment *falling short* of planned savings, the interest rate has no reason to adjust downwards; moreover, if peoples' perception towards risk in bond holding increases, then interest rates would, in fact, rise, causing investment to fall further.

27 In terms of the equation I = P, this would mean that it is determined from the right- to the left-hand side, exactly in the opposite direction of what Kalecki (1971) had suggested. It is only under such assumption that it can be logically sustained that investment will exactly offset the excess amount of potential profits generated due to increased employment.

28 Peoples' choice regarding alternative forms of holding wealth determine the price of capital goods. Lower the price of capital goods for given money-wages lower would be the level of investment. For example, if one can buy an existing factory at Rs 100, no one will order a new capital good costing Rs 200 – consequently investment would be low.

29 For a fuller discussion on the subject, see Keynes (2010: ch.17), Patnaik, P. (2008: ch.13) and Davidson (1998: 827).

30 All purchasing power generated by the circular flow of income need not be used for purchasing the resulting commodities produced; part of this purchasing power (planned savings), as it were, is lost into holding assets not produced – consequently, the correspondence between the act of supply creating its own demand is also lost.

31 Keynes accused the Classical theory of being restricted to analysing only full employment equilibrium outcomes, in which 'competition between entrepreneurs would *always* lead to an expansion of employment up to the point at which the supply of output as a whole ceases to be elastic' (emphasis added) (Keynes 2010: 24). This typically means that output is constrained on the supply side and equivalent to full employment (in the Keynesian sense). Here, full employment is defined as a situation when output does not respond (i.e. inelastic) to an increase in AD. It is *not* referred to as where everybody willing to work at a given wage gets employment.

32 In fact, Keynes categorically identified the Classical method of explaining unemployment in terms of *money*-wage rigidity:'[T]he Classical Theory has been accustomed to rest the supposedly self-adjusting character of the economic system on an assumed fluidity of moneywages;

and, when there is rigidity to lay on this rigidity the blame of maladjustment' (Keynes 2010: 233). However, that his method is free from such restrictive explanations of unemployment is clearly borne out from the following:

> In this summary we shall assume that the money-wage and other factor costs are constant per unit of labour employed. But this simplification, with which we shall dispense with later, is introduced solely to facilitate the exposition. *The essential character of the argument is precisely the same whether or not money-wages, etc., are liable to change.*
>
> (emphasis added) (ibid: 24–25)

33 The discussion below has benefited from Keynes (2010: ch.19), Patnaik (2008: ch.13); Dutt (1986–87); Davidson (1985,1998); Wells (1979); Dutt *et al.* (1988).
34 Keynes also discussed boosting the marginal efficiency of capital (MEC) route to stimulate effective demand following money-wage cut. But relying on MEC is far-fetched and impractical for any real economy (see below). Beside these indirect routes, there is no way to tackle the problem of effective demand and hence augment employment permanently by administering money-wage reductions. This is demonstrated in Section 6.1 [also see Keynes (2010: 236–237)].
35 Consequently, the problem of effective demand scarcity standing in the way of employment expansion (see Section 6.1) is solved through money-wage reduction.
36 In fact, there is considerable ambiguity over whether the gainers would actually increase their consumption. Normally, gainers from a price fall are the renters. For whom 'standard of life is least flexible' (Keynes 2010: 238); therefore, induced consumption expenditure is bound to be meagre. Moreover, any additional consumption expenditure by the gainers would also depend upon how much wealth they wish to bequeath to the next generation relative to their current wealth position. Somehow, if they want to bequeath the same amount of wealth as in their own possession, then there would be no 'wealth effect' on consumption (Patnaik 2008: 155). Further, deflation – increasing the real debt burden – would reduce the consumption of debtor households. However, with sharp deflationary trends, these households are bound to default on their debts and eventually go bankrupt; then sufferers in an inside money world would be creditors. With defaults continuing, creditors would lose assets often outweighing their real asset gains. Clearly, this is going to have negative impact on their consumption spending, which may well exceed the positive RBE associated with deflation.
37 Part of it is also financed through 'own' capital. In fact, the amount of borrowed capital a firm can access in the capital market directly depends upon the amount of 'own' capital it possesses (Kalecki 1965: 91–92).
38 As Keynes (2010: 239–240) noted: '[I]f the fall of wages and prices goes far, the embarrassment of those entrepreneurs who are heavily

indebted may soon reach the point of insolvency, with severely adverse effects on investment'.

39 For detailed discussion on this, see Dutt (1986–87) and Davidson (1969).
40 Keynes also talked about effects of falling wages and prices on marginal efficiency of the capital schedule (MEC). Keynes admitted that if money-wages and prices fall very sharply, such that these are believed to have touched the minimum, then everybody would expect them to rise in future. This would have a favourable effect on investment, since MEC would be expected to rise as well. Now, all these must tacitly assume that people have some notion about the lower threshold (minimum value) of money-wages and prices, such that once these figures are reached everybody expects them to rise. However, Keynes fails to mention what determines this lower threshold for such inelastic expectations to operate. Further, in the face of falling prices since entrepreneurs' debt position worsens accompanied by worsening profit expectations, operation of the MEC route remains dubious.
41 The experience of the Japanese economy in the 1990s in this context is worth mentioning. Japan spent most of the 1990s in an economic slump, often referred to as a 'growth recession' in the literature. This was so even when the interest rate fell to zero – typically because entrepreneurs were not investing even at no cost of borrowing funds, since people preferred to hold money rather than spending on goods. This situation is cogently described by Krugman (2009: 71):

> And the 1990s were the winter of Japan's discontent. Perhaps because of is aging population, perhaps also because of a general nervousness about the future, the Japanese public didn't appear willing to spend enough to use the economy's capacity, even at a zero interest rate. Japan, says economists, fell into the dread "liquidity trap".

For a lucid discussion on the ineffectiveness of interest rate policy by the Central Bank under certain circumstances, see Galbraith (2004) and Krugman (2009: 56–76). The United States, at present, seems to have entered a similar phase like Japan after the 2008 financial crisis outbreak (see Krugman 2012: 31–34).

42 Evidently this has a crucial bearing on whether the interest rate actually falls or not following money-wage cut (to make Keynes effect operational).
43 Realizing this, Keynes (1939: 35) inferred:

> I reached the conclusion that wage changes, which are *not* in the first instance due to changes in output, have *complex reactions on output which may be in either direction according to circumstances and about which it is difficult to generalize.*

(emphasis added)

44 However, Standing (2009) points to an interesting argument forwarded by the proponents of LMF, which considers effective demand. The argument is as follows: When an economy is in the downswing of the business cycle, profits are bound to fall. Now the magnitude of the fall in profits would be more sharp in a regime of no-hire-and-fire compared

to a regime with freedom-to-fire, since some wage costs can be saved in the latter regime by retrenching workers – which cannot be done in no-hire-and-fire regime. Thus, the risk associated with employing workers in no-hire-and-fire regime is greater than in a regime with freedom-to-fire. Therefore, the returns net of risk from any particular project would be lower in a no-hire-and-fire regime compared to a regime with freedom-to-fire. This implies the marginal efficiency of capital (MEC) in a no-hire-and-fire regime would be lower than that of a freedom-to-fire regime. This would lead to lower investment (with lower output and employment) in a no-hire-and-fire regime, *ceteris paribus*, compared to a regime with freedom-to-fire. Thus, LMF should be introduced. This analysis is problematic for at least two reasons. First, in an oligopolistic market structure, if the economy is already operating in the vertical portion of the MEC schedule, then the above argument does not hold. Second, investment in a no-hire-and-fire regime can be boosted, instead of introducing LMF, by reducing the nominal interest rate through adoption of an expansionary monetary policy.

45 Keynes (2010: 15) argued:

> with a given organisation, equipment and technique, real wages and the volume of output (and hence employment) are uniquely correlated, so that, in general an increase in employment can only occur to the accompaniment of a decline in the rate of real wages.

46 Where 'W' denotes aggregate wage bill and 'π' denotes total profits of the capitalist class.
47 Alternatively, it can be assumed that prices fall, but by a lesser proportion than money-wages, resulting in real wage fall.
48 If capitalists' consumption is allowed in the model, then employment would be additionally affected by the *composition* of effective demand. This is because typically goods consumed by workers are produced using more labour-intensive methods than capitalists' consumption basket. This is emphasized by Patnaik (2011a):

> the introduction of labour market flexibility necessarily entails a weakening of the bargaining position of workers; it necessarily entails a death-blow to all forms of workers' organisations like trade unions, since anyone attempting to organise the workers will be sacked forthwith. This in turn necessarily entails a reduction in the share of wages in the net output of the economy. And since a rupee paid out as wages creates more demand than a rupee that accrues as profit (of which a larger proportion is saved), such a shift in income distribution against workers, quite apart from being regressive in itself, results in a constriction of the domestic market, with an adverse effect upon employment for this reason. Besides, . . . *since goods demanded by workers typically tend to be produced by more employment-intensive methods, the generation of employment is constricted for this additional reason too in a regime of labour market flexibility.*
>
> (emphasis added)

Chapter 7

Labour market flexibility in an open economy context

In Chapter 6 we found that if effective demand has an autonomous role to play, then there is a *positive* association between real wage and output (hence employment). Therefore, if the policy prescription of 'discrete reduction in [real] wages' (to use Solow's term) is undertaken as proposed by the proponents of LMF, it would aggravate the problem of unemployment rather than curing it. Therefore, adopting such a policy is to the detriment of the working class. What is more, this policy is likely to keep the profits of the capitalist class *as a whole at the best unchanged* (at any rate, it can never make the capitalists better off; in the limit, it can at most leave their *aggregate* economic situation unchanged). This was noted long ago by the eminent Polish economist Michal Kalecki: 'Clearly higher output and employment benefits not only workers, but businessmen as well, because their profits rise' (Kalecki 1971: 138).[1]

Thus, there seems to be little rationale left for undertaking LMF. However, the whole discussion until now has been carried out in a *closed* economy framework. The theoretical models (discussed in Chapters 4 and 5) prescribed policies of LMF based on a closed economy framework. Consequently, the criticism (other than showing their internal inconsistencies) of *not* recognising the effective demand constraint (Chapter 6) was also carried out in a closed economy context.

However, there could be an argument in favour of introducing LMF in an *open* economy context. In an open economy, it is typically assumed that the export markets would generate sufficient demand/provide enough market, and if an economy can capture the world market significantly, then it is possible to more than overcome any shortfall in domestic demand that may arise due to wage restraint following LMF – and hence effect a net expansion of employment. As noted by the UNCTAD-Trade and Development Report (2012: 104), many developed countries actively pursued such a strategy:

> [D]uring the 2000s, they [developed countries] placed greater emphasis on becoming more competitive internationally through wage restraint and reduced employment opportunities . . . This latter strategy was facilitated by . . . greater flexibility of the labour market, which strengthened the power of profit earners vis-à-vis wage earners.

This view emphasizes the role of the external market for propelling output growth. As Bhaduri (2006: 3) observes:

> *The greater economic opening in the trade of goods and services meant an increase in the relative importance of the foreign or external market compared to the domestic or internal market.* It encouraged countries to stimulate demand through export surplus, rather than through management by government's fiscal policy. As a result, each country would try to be more price competitive than its neighbours by cutting cost through wage restraint and labour market flexibility, on the one hand, and by rising labour productivity, on the other.
>
> (emphasis added)

Bhaduri (ibid.: 7) further elaborates on the cost-cutting measures as: 'wage restraint, downsizing of the labour force, change in labour laws that makes it easier to hire and fire employees, revision of pension fund laws in favour of the employer, curbing workers' right to strike'. In fact, the introductory remarks of this study noted that the Indian government – thinking along similar lines – justified its recent policy stance of 'rationalising' labour laws on grounds of attaining (and maintaining) international competitiveness, to be achieved through cost-cutting (especially, saving on labour costs by lowering wages). Recommendations of the Task Force on Employment Opportunities (2001: 171) are worth repeating here:

> India's labour laws have evolved in a manner which has greatly reduced the flexibility available to the employers to adjust the labour force in the light of changing economic circumstances. *In a globalised world, persisting with labour laws that are*

> *much more rigid than those prevailing in other countries only makes us uncompetitive not only in export markets but also in domestic markets. Some changes in the laws are therefore necessary if we want to see rapid [economic] growth.*
>
> (emphasis added)

From the foregoing discussion it is clear that the Indian government, in advocating LMF, must be emphasizing the role of the external market for driving its output and employment growth.

In what follows, we shall: (a) assess, for any economy, what are the prospects of capturing the world market by pursuing LMF?, and (b) examine the current state of cost-competitiveness in Indian manufacturing and the country's prospects of penetrating the export market further by instituting LMF. We discuss these in the next section.

7.1 Labour market flexibility as a means to capture export market

The best possible scenario for any country pursuing LMF is that it *alone* adopts such a policy while others do not follow suit (although it was noted above that many developed countries of late have actively pursued such a strategy; more on this later). This way the country in question can *then* steal a march over its competitors (through price reduction) by cutting wages and maximize export earnings, along with outcompeting imports in the domestic market. All this presumes that a country can export *as much as it likes* at the going world prices (small country assumption – this is a strong condition; weaker condition is discussed below) and *most* of its imports are price-sensitive (with the capacity of producing them domestically).[2] Now if the aforementioned condition on exports has to be fulfilled, this method of sustaining growth is self-limiting once the country's share in world exports crosses a certain threshold. However, if the country's export demand curve is *not* perfectly elastic (which is the case in reality), the extent to which such a policy would be beneficial in boosting its output growth rate (hence employment, assuming no change in labour productivity) depends upon the *responsiveness* of its export demand to price reduction. In particular, elasticity of export demand of the country in question must be considerably high, for it has to more than compensate for the loss in domestic demand due to wage compression following institution of LMF. On the other hand, if the elasticity of the export demand is *not* sufficiently high, resorting to a wage cut by introducing LMF would be counterproductive (assuming inelastic import demand), reducing output and employment growth. Let us elaborate on this point. The strategy to capture the international market through wage restraint together with rising labour productivity ends up raising the share of surplus in the output – ultimately constricting the domestic market. This is because efforts to raise the export share in the international market worsens the distribution of output in the domestic market in favour of surplus (through wage restraint and lean production). As consumption demand out of surplus is typically *less* than out of wages, efforts to increase the international market share through the above means may be *counterbalanced* by a decrease in the domestic market size due to a fall in internal absorption. To the extent domestic market shrinks *more than* export growth, owing to insufficiently high export demand elasticity, unemployment swells as output contracts with reduction in *net* effective demand. *This basic problem arises since the twin-pronged role of wage in the economy is erringly overlooked.* Bhaduri (2005: 48–49) puts it with clarity:

> The downsizing of the labour force is an example of how the micro-economic logic of corporate management differs from the macro-economic logic of managing the whole economy. . . . This confusion stems from the failure to see that major macro-economic variables like labour productivity or wage invariably have two-sided roles in the economy. *They affect both cost and demand.*
>
> (emphasis added)

But this is not all. Even if a *single* country adopts cost-cutting measures and its export demand elasticity is *considerably high*, nonetheless its actual export earnings would depend upon the *state* of world demand (absorption of the rest of the world depends upon world income). The export-led growth strategy typically assumes world demand to be fixed and invariant (which never falls). Bhaduri (2005: 40) underscores the point clearly:

> The basic logic is to apply the ideas of corporate management to the economy as a whole. The nation is a single corporation, the economy is meant to increase its international market share

by out-competing rival trading nations through cutting costs, while taking the *total* market size as *given*.

(emphasis added)

Yet treating world demand as fixed is plain wrong. The world economy may be plagued with demand shortage. There can be involuntary unemployment alongside vast amounts of capital stock lying idle at the world level due to an insufficiency of effective demand afflicting the world economy (see Patnaik, P The Hindu 05 January 2005). The Great Depression of 1929 and the collapse of economic activity at the global scale after the outbreak of the 2008 financial crisis bear testimony to this fact. Thus, if world income shrinks or stagnates at any rate, then world imports shrink or stagnate likewise – rendering the export-led growth strategy ineffective *even for a country whose export demand is responsive to price changes* (see footnote 6). This strategy will additionally fail if the trading partners of the country in question turn protectionist for whatever reasons (including saving domestic jobs in the face of falling demand).

Further problems start to surface if we abandon the hypothetical case that *only one* country – instituting LMF – adopts an export-led growth strategy. In reality, many developed (noted above) and developing countries (notably China and Malaysia) actively pursue LMF (Ghosh 2011). And yet once an export-led growth strategy is adopted by developing (or developed) nations as a bloc, the simultaneous practice of wage restraint and cost-cutting would be analogous to competitive devaluation leading to a race to the bottom. However, limitations of such beggar-thy-neighbour policy are well known from the 1929 Great Depression. Bhaduri (2005: 40–41) lucidly puts it:

> [T]he micro-logic applicable to a single corporation involves a serious macro fallacy that must not be overlooked. *It ignores the uncomfortable fact that all countries cannot be winners at the same time in the [international] zero-sum game of competitive cost-cutting for producing an export surplus, and gaining a larger share of the global market. The policy must fail in many instances, because the export surpluses of some countries must mean import surpluses for other countries. Moreover, since most developing countries tend to produce a similar range of exports, the competition among them would be more*

acute with many losers among the developing countries. The only predictable outcome of this policy would be a 'race to the bottom' among developing countries, each acting in isolation to gain a larger share of the world market. In the process they would reduce wages, lengthen working hours for the same wage, restrict workers' right, refuse pensions and social security and casualise regular employment in the name of labour market flexibility.

(emphasis added)

For a slightly different treatment of the contradictions faced by developing countries as a bloc, see Patnaik (2003: 84); Patnaik (2011: 115–117) and Krugman (2012: 28). The discussion above merely points out the various shortcomings of an export-led growth strategy based on wage compression, which is most likely to fail in the real world with many countries simultaneously pursuing it.

Nevertheless, *open* economies – operating in isolation – may be trapped in a prisoner's dilemma situation and willy-nilly engage in cost-cutting. This is the case, because failing to adopt such a policy – when others compress wages – means witnessing a fall in export share and losing out to cheaper imports in the domestic market. Therefore, it may be argued that even if it is irrational for many countries to *simultaneously* adopt a wage cut policy, nonetheless individual countries are left with very little choice. However, this is not true. This is because rather than instituting a wage cut to remain price-competitive, a country can use its exchange rate policy to achieve *exactly* the same price reduction (in foreign currency) through an appropriate real depreciation.[3] With regard to competition from cheap imports in the domestic market, it is imperative to implement some import protective measures.[4] Trying these alternative strategies may be additionally beneficial since – unlike a wage cut – these do not dampen domestic demand. Therefore, implementing a wage cut – through LMF – can only be effective in pulling up economic growth under very stringent hypothetical conditions bearing no resemblance to the real world. What is more, the same objective can be achieved through an appropriate exchange rate policy coupled, if necessary, with certain import protective/ restrictive measures.

Next, we examine the current state of cost-competitiveness in Indian manufacturing and the plausibility of capturing the export market by instituting LMF.[5] In light of India's burgeoning current account deficit (CAD) (Figure 7.1; except for past three years),[6] it may be presumed that this is a reflection of the country's exports being uncompetitive in the world market and the fact that India must urgently adopt policies to enhance competitiveness. However, it would be a wrong conclusion to draw since: 'India's export growth has almost continuously been above world export growth in the 2000s decade and in 2011' (Economic Survey 2012–13: 150) and the muted export growth between 2012 and 2015 is primarily due to the depressed world demand. Still, the large CAD is because import bills were rising at a faster pace than export earnings. Further, Figure 7.1 shows that a huge merchandise trade account deficit (export and import in goods) explains such a massive CAD, which is partially offset by invisible earnings (mainly accounting for export and import in services and remittances). Hence, the deficit in merchandise trade is the root cause of the problem, and *inter alia* some restrictions are necessary on merchandise import, apart from, if possible, raising the growth of merchandise exports.

Here, votaries of LMF may point out that the share of manufacturing exports in total merchandise exports has diminished substantially, owing to the rigid labour laws (Figure 7.2).

Let us examine, then, whether the supposedly rigid labour laws make Indian manufacturing uncompetitive in the world market. Advocates of LMF typically argue that since workers (insiders) protected by labour laws cannot be easily retrenched, they take full advantage of this to jack up wages. Let us see whether Indian manufacturing sector workers could raise their wages by taking advantage of the job security legislation. Figure 7.3 compares the mean hourly compensation of manufacturing employees across selected countries and regions in 2005. Compensation rates are converted to U.S. dollars by using the official average daily exchange rate for the referenced year (see, Sincavage *et al.* 2010 for details).

It is clear that the mean hourly employees' compensation in Indian manufacturing is among the lowest in the world. Therefore, it's difficult to sustain that Indian manufacturing exports are uncompetitive *due to higher rates of labour compensation compared to the rest of the world*. It probably also shows that there is very limited scope for any further wage compression, which LMF seeks to realize, as the floor may have almost been reached.

However, it may be argued that the low labour compensation rate is not a definite indicator of cost-competitiveness. This is because labour productivity may be so low that the *effective cost* of labour

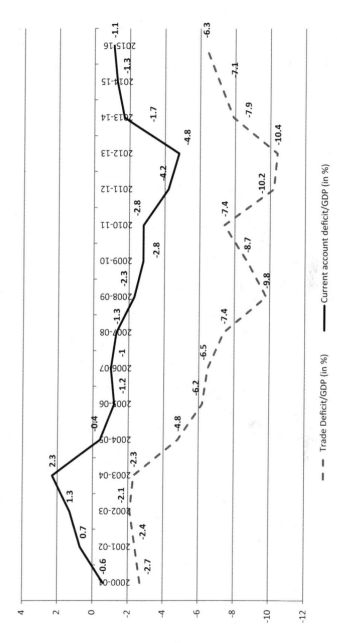

Figure 7.1 Current account deficit and trade balance as percentage of GDP
Source: Handbook of Statistics on Indian Economy, various issues

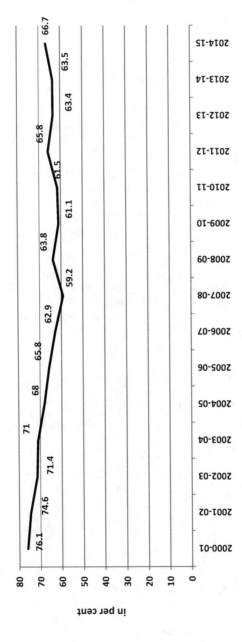

Figure 7.2 Share of manufacturing exports in total merchandise exports: India

Source: Report of the working group on Boosting India's Manufacturing Exports (2011: 18) and Economic Survey, various issues

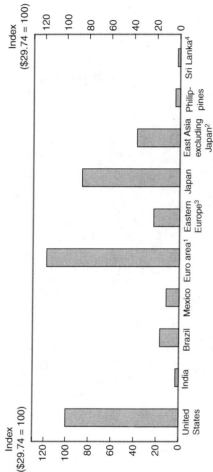

Figure 7.3 Mean total hourly compensation cost of manufacturing employees, selected countries and regions, 2005

Source: Sincavage et al. (2010: 13)

per unit of commodity may still be high – negatively affecting competitiveness. Therefore, one needs to look at the unit labour cost[7] (ULC) – recognised as the key measure of competitiveness in the international market (Ark *et al.* 2008). Figure 7.4 depicts the unit labour cost of some developing countries (taking the ULC of USA as unity)[8] and compares it with the ULC of India. Labour compensation is converted to U.S. dollars using the official exchange rate for the reference year, and labour productivities are converted at industry-specific Purchasing Power Parities (PPPs) (for details, see Ark *et al.* 2008). For the 15 years under observation, it is clear that India's ULC is way below the ULC of its competitors throughout. Therefore, it is simply wrong to argue that Indian exports are becoming uncompetitive in the world market due to high labour costs and to then blame labour laws as the reason for such high costs. *Incidentally, this also shows that the scope for penetrating the world market further, on the basis of cost-competitiveness by introducing LMF, is extremely narrow.*

Nonetheless, policymakers insist on introducing LMF to boost manufacturing growth. This argument, therefore, identifies lack of cost-competitiveness as the *primary* reason that is holding back manufacturing growth. For example, Planning Commission Deputy Chairman Montek Singh Ahluwalia (2011: 97–98), commenting on the challenges facing the manufacturing sector in the Twelfth Five-Year Plan (2012–2017), noted:

> The industrial sector was targeted to grow at an average rate 10% to 11% per year in the Eleventh Plan, but the actual achievement is unlikely to exceed 8%. . . . Industry must . . . grow faster than it has thus far . . . some consideration has to be given to the long-standing issue of the need to rationalise our labour laws to give employers more flexibility to shed labour when faced with a downturn. This is not to advocate policies of hire and fire, but only to say that more flexibility needs to be built into the labour laws than exist at present.

However, LMF would only be effective in curbing the wage rate (Chapters 4 and 6) and make us cost-competitive. But similar results can also be obtained through a depreciation of the (real) exchange rate. In other words, what is envisaged to be realized through LMF – reducing the price of our exportable in terms of foreign currency – can *equivalently* be achieved through (real)

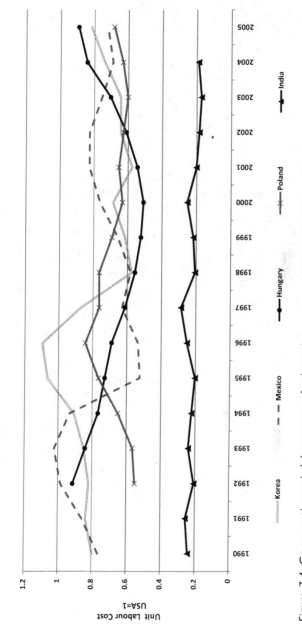

Figure 7.4 Comparative unit labour cost of selected countries, 1990–2005 (USA = 1)
Source: Data from Ark et al. (2008: 32)

exchange rate depreciation. Indeed, there is evidence of India's real exchange rate depreciating in three out of five years during the Eleventh Plan period (2007–2012) (Figure 7.5). The Real Effective Exchange Rate (REER) sharply depreciated with the outbreak of the financial crisis in 2008 and again fell in value, consecutively, for the last two years of the plan period. This must have substantially improved the cost-competitiveness of Indian products in the world (and the home) market. Yet from Ahluwalia's own comments we found that the manufacturing sector failed to achieve its growth target during the same plan period. Therefore, what LMF promises to deliver has already been brought about in the case of India by another macroeconomic variable, namely, the real exchange rate – but without producing the expected result widely underscored in the policy circle. *This casts serious doubts – at least in the Indian case – on the effectiveness of cost reduction as a means to capture export markets.*

Further, over the period April 2011 to March 2014, the rupee in real terms annually depreciated at the rate of -3.23 percent. This must have made our manufacturing products price-competitive in the export market and out-competed imports in the domestic market. Therefore, going by Ahluwalia's logic (that lack of cost-competitiveness is the main obstacle pulling back our manufacturing growth), we would expect a surge in manufacturing activity during this period.

Yet precisely during this period performance of the manufacturing sector is abysmal (Figure 7.6). If we calculate the monthly growth rate of the index of industrial production for the manufacturing sector between May 2011 and April 2014, it shows that manufacturing growth has turned *negative* in 19 out of 36 months. Additionally, positive growth is almost invariably preceded by a fall in the absolute index value (signifying negative growth), which implies that on average there was hardly any growth. Additionally, during these three years, when the currency was depreciating in real terms, India's export performance was dismal. Export growth almost halved in 2011–12 (21.8 percent) compared to 2010–11 (40.5 percent). In fact, it turned negative in 2012–13 (-1.8 percent) recovering marginally, on a low base, in 2013–14 (4.7 percent) (Economic Survey 2015–16: A101).[9]*The foregoing discussion suggests that the argument for introducing LMF in an open economy context remains unfounded for India.*

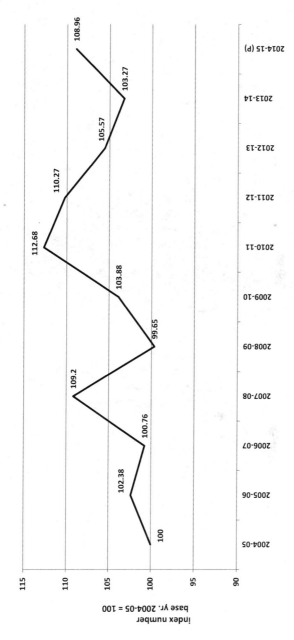

Figure 7.5 Real Effective Exchange Rate (REER) 36-currency index: India
Source: Economic Survey (2015–16: A-97) Note: (P) denotes provisional figures
Notes: Rise in index value: appreciation; fall in index value: depreciation

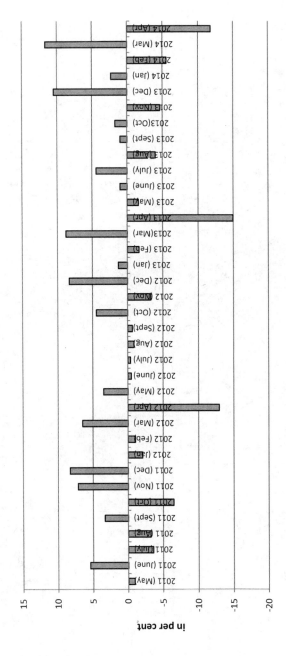

Figure 7.6 Monthly growth rate of index of industrial production: manufacturing sector
Source: Central Statistical Organization

Moreover, it must be noted that *even if* a developing country like India manages to grow in a certain period on the basis of external markets by vigorously implementing the measures described above, it must *simultaneously downplay* the importance of the internal market for sustaining this growth. In particular, it must contain domestic consumption, which is the direct fallout of restraining wages. But to implement such a policy of promoting exports and private investment at the expense of domestic consumption, the country must face stiff opposition from its people. Therefore, it is essentially undemocratic, since income inequality must rise for this strategy to work and it coerces workers to proportionally consume less. Further, the implication of this strategy for employment creation is also dismal, as labour productivity rises rapidly in a regime of export-led growth.[10] Now with respect to identifying the underlying factors responsible for the rise in labour productivity in an export-led growth regime, it may be argued that labour productivity growth itself becomes a *positive* function of the output growth rate.[11] Therefore, the more this policy succeeds on the output growth front, the more it invariably pushes labour productivity growth to even higher levels and consequently has a dampening effect on employment creation.[12] Hence, even if a developing nation grows during a certain period on the strength of external markets adopting LMF, nonetheless it fails to deplete the reserve army of labour. Ironically, the very objective LMF sets out to achieve, namely, rapid employment growth, turns out to be self-defeated by the underlying growth process. Thus, relying on external market-led growth – envisaged by Indian government through instituting LMF – is fraught with several difficulties, including being undemocratic.

Then the question arises: why is there demand for LMF at all? This is because although capitalists are concerned with profits, this concern is ensconced within a power relation whose sustenance and enhancement is vital for them – essentially because workers have to be managed (controlled) in such a manner on the factory floor that maximum effort can be elicited from them. This in turn requires organization of production in a regimented manner and crucially depends upon the authority and power that capitalists command over their workforce. Workers must listen to their 'bosses' and perfectly follow the instructions handed out in every minute detail. Therefore, capitalists always prefer to maintain a docile workforce (as organizing production becomes easy) and want to keep trade unions (TUs) at bay. This is because TUs act as a counter-force to capitalists' authority, and the latter fear that workers may 'get out of hand'.[13] And the reduced bargaining power (i.e. instructive authority) of capitalists undermines their class position in society, which thwarts production – ultimately threatening capital accumulation itself.

Now, capitalists typically maintain and consolidate their grip over workers by the constant threat of unforeseen retrenchment – a threat that acquires bite *only if* there exists a permanent pool of unemployed labour, or what Marx had called a reserve army of labour.[14] *This is the primary device capitalists use to discipline workers*. It was pointed out long ago by Kalecki that *this* is why capitalists despise full employment – as the threat of retrenchment loses its relevance and workers' bargaining power increases immensely; Kalecki (1971: 140–141) noted:

> the *maintenance* of full employment would cause social and political changes which would give a new impetus to the opposition of the business leaders. *Indeed, under a regime of permanent full employment, 'the sack' would cease to play its role as a disciplinary measure*. The social position of the boss would be undermined and the self assurance and class consciousness of the working class would grow. Strikes for wage increases and improvements in conditions of work would create political tension.
>
> (emphasis added)

Under such circumstances, the organization of production in a disciplined manner is clearly undermined. It is easy to see that the demand for LMF is to *permanently institutionalize* the threat of sack[15] – which is a prerequisite for obtaining a disciplined workforce that helps accumulation of capital. Hence, *the whole purpose of LMF seems to be to utilize it as a disciplinary device*. But then the entire argument in favour of introducing LMF, namely, to attain full employment, becomes untenable. For if full employment is actually achieved, then the threat of sack will lose its meaning and the rationale of LMF will disappear. This simply shows that the realization of full employment equilibrium by instituting LMF is internally inconsistent. For once full employment is reached, LMF would cease to act as a disciplining device – thus making it impossible to *sustain* the full employment equilibrium.

Furthermore, it was noted earlier that adopting LMF may reduce capitalists' profits (if capacity utilization falls owing to reduction in effective demand following a wage cut) – *therefore, why should they demand LMF even at the cost of profits?* Kalecki (1971: 141) made a pioneering observation in this regard:

> It is true that profits would be higher under a regime of full employment than they are on average under *laisser-faire*; . . . But *'discipline in factories'* and *'political stability'* are more appreciated by the business leaders than profits. Their class instinct tells them that lasting full employment is unsound from their point of view and unemployment is an integral part of normal capitalist system.

(emphasis added)

However, capitalists do not prioritize *between* 'maintaining discipline' on the factory floor and reaping profits. Rather, they understand that power and dominance in production relations along with maintenance of their superior class position in society is a *precondition* for garnering profits. *This is the basic premise on which profits are earned.* Any disturbance in this underlying arrangement would threaten the organization of production and the generation of profits. Capitalists, as a class, realize that any kind of workers' assertion would undermine their authority and ultimately threaten profit making. Therefore, they are acutely conscious about preserving and consolidating their power and supremacy in society. Now the ability to sack at any moment gives the capitalist class immense power, supremacy and unquestionable authority in society – which is crucial for the smooth organization of production to generate profits. Thus, capitalists would always want to introduce LMF, as it ultimately *facilitates* capital accumulation itself.

Over and above this *general* reason for demanding LMF, there is an *additional* reason to insist for free hire and fire of workers in the current juncture. In the current phase of globalisation, Foreign Direct Investment (FDI) and multinational corporations (MNCs) come to occupy an important place in the economy. MNCs always prefer to locate their production base in 'business-friendly' countries associated with low labour costs. In order to remain internationally competitive, MNCs have to continuously look out for cost-saving avenues and rapidly relocate/shift production base (i.e. moving out capital from a country and particular industry) to locations of their greatest advantage. Fulfilment of this condition primarily requires rapid adjustment in the workforce – hence the demand for LMF. However, the counterpart of this phenomenon is that the risk/burden of adjustment – on occasion of business failures – is shifted largely to the workers. Finance capital also votes for LMF, as it fears government control in the nature of labour regulations (and other forms) might spill over to other economic spheres and hurt its interest by introducing capital controls.

Finally, faced with large CADs of late, Indian policymakers are desperate to attract foreign capital – in the form of FDI and foreign institutional investments (FIIs). This came out clearly in the then Finance Minister P. Chidambaram's Budget Speech of 2013–14:

> This year, and perhaps next year too, we have to find over USD 75 billion to finance the CAD. There are only three ways before us: FDI, FII or External Commercial Borrowing. That is why I have been at pains to state over and over again that India, at the present juncture, does not have the choice between welcoming and spurning foreign investment. If I may be frank, foreign investment is an imperative. What we can do is to encourage foreign investment that is consistent with our economic objectives.

To encourage foreign investment, P. Chidambaram, in an address to the members of Parliamentary Consultative Committee of the Finance Ministry, noted that one of the ways to attract more capital inflows is to raise the FDI limits, mentioning: 'The government is looking at FDI caps to see if they are indeed serving the purpose. Otherwise the caps could be revisited' (Press Information Bureau 17 June 2013). Along with raising FDI caps – to encourage foreign capital inflow – government must adopt strategies which are typically 'liked' by international finance capital and build 'investors' confidence'. The current National Democratic Alliance government's policies are exactly along these lines. In June 2016, Prime Minister Narendra Modi, announcing a slew of reforms raising the FDI limits across various sectors, noted: 'Now most of the sectors would be under automatic approval route [rather than seeking government approval], except a small negative list', emphasizing that 'India is now the most open economy in the world for foreign direct investment' (The Economic Times 21 June 2016). Modi also instructed secretaries of different central ministries to suggest measures such that India's ranking in the 'ease of doing business' improves in 2017 (The Hindu 02 December 2016).[16] In fact, Department of Industrial Policy and Promotion (DIPP) secretary Amitabh Kant pointed out that due to the reform measures to be implemented in future, '[w]e are absolutely confident of being in top 50 [of the doing business rankings] in three years as per the target set by PM [Prime Minister]' (The Economic Times 28 October 2015). Among the key reform measures to be implemented (to gain investors' confidence) is the passage of the Insolvency and Bankruptcy Code, 2015 that will make it easier for companies to wind up (Business Line 3 May 2016). Clearly, these are policies to entice foreign investors. Therefore, to attract and keep foreign investment, government must constantly send out positive signals to foreign investors. *Viewed in this light, LMF – considered to be a crucial indicator of investor friendliness – is an important signal to attract foreign capital into India.* These, in short, are the reasons for demanding LMF: it is to advance the class interest of the capitalists (both attached to and divorced from real production) and has nothing to do with creating enabling conditions for employment generation (as claimed by LMF proponents). However, if a country does not follow such a strategy and fails to constantly send out these signals, then finance would emigrate from that economy, pushing it into a crisis. To avoid this, countries must be bold enough to institute capital controls, fixing the minimum period before which foreign investors are not allowed to call back their money and other forms of trade restrictions.

However, financing CAD through capital account inflows and/or envisaging promotion of economic growth on the strength of foreign capital is fraught with difficulties. It typically increases the vulnerability of the economy vis-à-vis external payments, as may be traced from the pattern of capital inflows into India.

Figure 7.7 shows that in most years of the new millennium, capital inflows either in the form of volatile FIIs or in debt form have dominated – especially from 2003–04[17] – over relatively stable FDI flows. Even the nature of debt inflows has been predominantly short-term (typically increasing the vulnerability of the economy); Figure 7.8 shows that the share of short-term debt to foreign exchange reserves – indicating the country's ability to respect foreign exchange claims – increased more or less continuously since 2008, touching as high as 59 percent in 2013 before settling to 57.4 percent in 2016.[18]

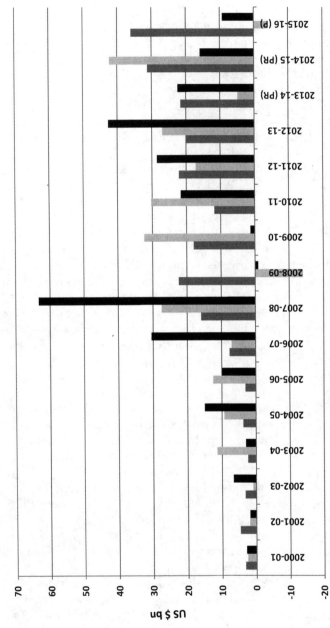

Figure 7.7 Net capital inflows to India
Notes: P: provisional; PR: partially revised
Source: Handbook of Statistics on Indian Economy, RBI

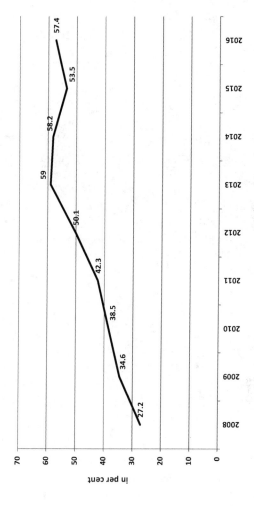

Figure 7.8 Short-term debt to forex reserves
Source: India's External Debt: A Status Report (December 2016: 58)

Thus, simply to meet external payment obligations, it is imperative for India to maintain good 'investment grade' before the international credit rating agencies – essentially through extending various concessions to capital (one key element being LMF). It appears, then, that better ways to deal with CAD are the conventional measures of curbing certain imports (luxury items) coupled with specific export-promoting measures.

Conclusion

It was pointed out at the very outset of this chapter that LMF is detrimental to the working class and is likely to keep profits of the capitalist class *as a whole* at best, unchanged. However, the whole discussion was carried out in a *closed* economy framework. Nonetheless, there could be an argument in favour of LMF in an *open* economy context. This view emphasizes the role of cost-cutting as a means to capture export markets, propelling economic growth. The Indian government wanted to introduce LMF thinking along similar lines (Chapter 1). This chapter examined the following questions: (a) for any economy, what are the prospects of capturing the world market through LMF?, and (b) the current state of cost-competitiveness in Indian manufacturing and the country's prospects of penetrating the export market further by instituting LMF?

On the first question we noted that the best possible scenario under which these cost-cutting measures are expected to deliver the desired results is only when *one country* adopts LMF policy while its competitors do not follow suit. In addition, the country must face a perfectly elastic export demand (strong condition) schedule (it has been throughout assumed in this chapter that the imports are either price-inelastic or *cannot* be produced domestically). However, if this condition is not fulfilled, then the success of such a strategy would depend upon the *responsiveness* of its *net* export demand to price reduction. In particular, the elasticity of export demand must be sufficiently high in order to more than compensate for the loss in domestic demand from wage compression due to LMF. If this is *not* satisfied, then a wage cut would be counterproductive, with the effect of reducing output and employment growth. Even if the above conditions are satisfied, still the fruitfulness of such a strategy would depend upon the *state* of world demand. For example, if world income shrinks or stagnates, then an export-led growth strategy would prove to be ineffective. Moreover, if the trading partners of a nation turn protectionist, then this strategy will fail.

Next, dropping the hypothetical case of *only one* nation pursuing LMF, we considered the more realistic case of developing (or developed) nations as a bloc adopting it. Then none of them would steal a march over its competitors, and this leads to a race to the bottom – the limitations of which are well known from the experience of Great Depression in 1929. Nevertheless, it could be argued that *open* economies, operating in isolation, may have to willy-nilly adopt such a strategy in order to remain competitive in the export and domestic markets. However, it was pointed out that whatever price reduction in exportable could be achieved through a wage cut can *exactly* be achieved through an appropriate real depreciation of the currency, and with regard to cheap competition from imports, insofar as real depreciation does not automatically curb imports, some import protective measures are imperative. Therefore, it was noted that there was nothing inevitable about cost-cutting policies, since these are achievable through an alternate set of strategies. *More importantly, it was pointed out that a wage cut policy, following the introduction of LMF, would only be effective under very stringent hypothetical conditions which bear no resemblance to the real world.*

Then we examined the current state of cost-competitiveness in Indian manufacturing and the plausibility of capturing export markets by instituting LMF. From the cross-country figures of the mean hourly compensation of employees, it came out clearly that employees' compensation in Indian manufacturing were among the lowest in the world. Thus, it is difficult to argue that our manufacturing exports are becoming uncompetitive *due to higher rates of labour compensation compared to the rest of the world*. Comparison of ULCs also showed that India's ULC is way below that of its competitors. Therefore, it was concluded that the scope for *penetrating the world market further, on the basis of cost-competitiveness, is extremely narrow.*

Nonetheless, policymakers insisted on introducing LMF and identified lack of cost-competitiveness as the *primary* reason for our slow manufacturing growth. But available evidence suggests that in spite of the real exchange rate continuously depreciating for India between April 2011 and March 2014, manufacturing growth turned *negative* in 19 out of 36 months. *Thus, there is no basis in the Indian case for arguing about the effectiveness of cost reduction (and hence the usefulness of LMF) as a means to capture export markets*. Moreover, it was noted that *even if* a developing country like India manages to grow in a certain period on the basis of external markets, it must *simultaneously downplay* the importance of the internal market. This would lead to curbing of workers' consumption and a rise in income inequality. Further, its implication on employment growth would be dismal due to its underlying thrust on labour productivity growth. Hence, *it was concluded that the very objective LMF sets out to achieve, namely, rapid employment growth, gets self-defeated*. Therefore, there lies no rationale for introducing LMF, even in an open economy context.

Then, the question was raised about why there is so much noise about introducing LMF. It was recognised at the very outset that although capitalists are concerned with profits, this concern is ensconced within a power relation whose sustenance and enhancement is vital for them. First, it was noted that capitalists would always want LMF, which amounts to *permanently* institutionalizing free hire and fire in order to acquire an obedient and disciplined workforce. Moreover, LMF gives the capitalist class unquestionable authority in advancing their class interest in society, ultimately facilitating capital accumulation. Second, in search of higher profits internationally, MNCs have to continuously lookout for cost-saving avenues – a primary condition for which is rapid relocation/shifting of production base. Fulfilment of this condition primarily requires rapid adjustment in the workforce – hence the demand for LMF. Third, to attract foreign capital in the form of FDI and FIIs (especially crucial for India to finance widening CAD until 2012–13), developing economies must provide various kinds of concessions to foreign capital. *In this context, LMF remains a crucial indicator of investor friendliness to attract foreign capital into India. In short, the demand for LMF is to advance the class interest of the capitalists (both attached to and divorced from production) and has nothing to do with creating enabling conditions for employment growth*.

Now it may be argued that failing to send out investor-friendly signals, like LMF, among others, would trigger capital outflows from an economy. But this *per se* cannot justify the institution of free hire and fire, since some measures of capital control can thwart such a contingency. Finally, financing the CAD through capital account inflows, especially in the form of volatile inflows like FIIs and short-term debt, only makes the balance of payments (BoP) situation fragile and camouflages the underlying imbalance. Hence, it was suggested, a better way of tackling the CAD seems to be the conventional measures of curbing certain imports coupled with export-promoting measures. Next, we turn to the concluding remarks of this study.

Notes

1 This may come about in the following manner. Suppose investment expenditure in any period depends upon the actual degree of capacity utilisation relative to the desired level of capacity utilisation in the previous period such that this period's investment increases (decreases) if actual degree of capacity utilisation exceeds (falls short of) the desired level of capacity utilisation in the previous period (see Patnaik 1997: 21). In such an economy with demand-determined output, implementing a real wage cut (as recommended by the proponents of LMF) would reduce the size of effective demand (see Chapter 6), and hence capacity utilisation falls. Hence, pursuing policies of high wage and employment results in a higher degree of capacity utilisation and enlarges investment (in the next period). Now since capitalists, as a class, earn what they spend, as Kalecki (1971: 79) had noted, 'It is, therefore, their [capitalists] investment and consumption decisions which determine profits, and not vice versa' – thus profits are higher in a regime of high wage and employment. However, this does not mean that individual capitalists, in isolation, would follow a high wage policy, since an individual capitalist is unsure of whether the higher cost incurred in form of higher wages to its workers would be spent back on its own product. Insofar as wages are not spent back on the firm's own product (offering higher wages), other capitalists would benefit and free-ride on the capitalist incurring a high wage cost. Knowing this, no capitalist, in isolation, would follow a high wage policy, although if all of them did so simultaneously, each one would have benefited. Hence, the capitalists remain arrested in a prisoner's dilemma. This merely shows that social rationality can be quite different (exactly opposite here) from individual rationality.
2 Yet most countries cannot adequately produce a universal input, namely, oil. For example, the share of petroleum, oil and lubricant (POL) imports in India's total import bill was as high as 31.7 percent in 2011–12 (Economic Survey 2012–13: 160). Moreover, the import of pearls, precious, semi-precious stones, gold and silver stood at 18.7 percent of India's total imports in 2011–12 (ibid.: 160) – these are not price-elastic commodities (as brought out by the surge in gold imports in the midst of massive rupee depreciation in 2013) and their imports are determined by income, taste and preference, among other things. Further, a substantial portion of these precious and semi-precious stones are used as inputs for re-exports, so if exports increase

so will the imports – without any net addition to effective demand. Thus, for India, around 50 percent of its importable is either price-inelastic (with some proportion being utilized for re-exports) or simply produced insufficiently to meet domestic demand. Given this, wage reduction would not be of much help for India in boosting domestic production (by replacing imports). In what follows, we shall throughout assume this condition to hold true. Therefore, the entire boost in domestic production due to wage reduction is assumed to come from the export end and not from import-competing industries.

3 For simplicity, if we assume all costs of production are wage costs then any percentage reduction in price brought about through cutting wages can be exactly achieved by depreciating the currency by the same percentage.

4 Real depreciation would itself make imports dearer and for price-inelastic imports some form of import control is necessary.

5 Remember that labour laws in India apply only to the (organized) manufacturing sector of the economy.

6 Improvement in the current account (and trade account) in 2013–14, 2014–15 and 2015–16 primarily occurred due to import growth turning negative, since growth in exports turned negative during this period. Economic Survey (2014–15: 15) notes:

> there has been significant deceleration in growth rates of exports which is somewhat a global phenomenon as global trade volumes have not picked up significantly since the 2011. . . [due to] sluggish global demand, which owes to a great extent to the weakness in the Eurozone.

The trend in negative export growth was much aggravated in 2015–16; Economic Survey (2016–17: 151) observes: 'In line with subdued global growth and trade, India's exports declined by 1.3 percent and 15.5 percent in 2014–15 and 2015–16 respectively'. The decline in imports mainly owed to the following two factors: (a) lower growth in oil import bill due to a sharp decline in international crude oil prices (Economic Survey 2016–17: 152), and (b) restrictions placed by the government on gold imports in 2013–14, which was only lifted on 29 November 2014 (Economic Survey 2014–15: 60).

7 Defined as, labour compensation rate upon labour productivity.

8 This simply means dividing each nation's ULC by the USA's ULC.

9 For export growth in 2014–15 and 2015–16, see footnote 6 of this chapter.

10 Labour productivity rises for three separate additive reasons. Remember that enhancing labour productivity growth is an important means to capture international market. Therefore, technological innovations, even in the developing countries take the form of a labour-saving variety. Further, since the target is to capture developed countries' markets, exportable goods produced in developing economies must be similar to those produced in developed economies. Since specific goods typically embody a particular technology and since in the developed world technological progress is primarily of a labour-saving variety, labour

productivity in developing countries increases for this additional reason. Additionally, as the share of surplus in total output increases and surplus income earners typically emulate the consumption pattern prevailing in the advanced capitalist world, this further increases labour productivity in developing countries. [For a detailed discussion, see Patnaik (2011a: 264–265)].

11 Essentially, as output growth rises, it invariably pulls up labour productivity growth; hence labour productivity growth = f (output growth) and f' > 0.

12 Remember, employment growth rate $\dot{e}/e$ is the difference between output growth rate $\dot{y}/y$ and the growth rate in labour productivity $\dot{l}/l$, that is, $\dot{e}/e = \dot{y}/y - \dot{l}/l$. Now as a consequence of adopting an export-led growth strategy, insofar as output growth itself cannot be sustained (for reasons discussed above) – whereas labour productivity rises due to the underlying growth process – its implication for employment growth remains bleak.

13 For example, other than deciding workers' wage, capitalists must also decide on overtime and ad hoc work (and their compensation rates), speeding up the work process, facilities provided at the workplace (viz. toilets, anti-sexual harassment cell, crèche, canteen, place for resting, lunch/tea/toilet-break times, emergency medical help among others), negotiating on the number (and nature) of paid and unpaid leaves, accidental and death benefits, health benefits/insurance, housing facilities, schooling for children and so on. These, in short, are demarcated as labour rights and if properly implemented tremendously increase the bargaining position of workers. This increased bargaining strength then leads to a fresh set of workers' demands and quickly spills over to increased wage claims. Hence, these labour rights are vigorously opposed by capitalists.

14 Remember that unlike in slave and feudal societies, capitalist societies do not rely on extra-economic coercion to extract labour power.

15 Humar Resource Development Minister, Prakash Javadekar's comment in the context of university and college teachers is revealing: 'The advanced countries follow the practice of hire and fire. The employees are on their toes. But we have not taken any such decision' (The Telegraph 30 July 2017).

16 India's rank in the Ease of Doing Business (DB) index, out of 189 countries, jumped from 142 in 2015 to 130 in 2016, due to the different business/investor friendly reforms adopted by the Modi government. However, India's rank in the DB index in 2015 was later revised to 134 thus, making the improvement in 2016 less dramatic. Additionally, improving the ranking is also seen as a growth-promoting strategy since the Prime Minister noted that 'ease of business is the first and foremost requirement if Make in India has to be made successful' (The Indian Express 17 October 2014).

17 This is because the then Finance Minister in the Budget Speech for 2003–04 announced:

> In order to give a further fillip to the capital markets, it is now proposed to exempt all listed equities that are acquired on or after March 1, 2003, and sold after the lapse of a year, or more, from the incidence of capital gains tax. Long term capital gains tax will, therefore, not hereafter apply to such transactions. This proposal should facilitate investment in equities.

Long-term capital gains tax before this announcement was 10 percent. This concession definitely encouraged FII inflows in India.

18 Short-term debt is defined as: Short-term debt by original maturity and long-term debt maturing within 12 months.

Chapter 8

Concluding remarks
Labour market flexibility and the proposal for *laissez-faire* capitalism

From the discussions carried out in earlier chapters, it came out quite clearly that the case for LMF is *not* logically sustainable. This is true *both* in a closed and open economy setting. In a *closed* economy setting, we showed that the underlying theoretical structure advocating LMF is *not* internally consistent. This is so for, among other things, the assumptions made in these models were at complete variance with reality, in addition to violating standard definitions in economic theory (viz. reservation wages). Further, the results thrown up by these models were liable to change with minute changes in assumptions, and *general* policy conclusions were drawn on *very special* cases. Leaving aside all these shortcomings, these models never recognised the effective demand constraint, which characterizes any modern money-using economy. Actually, the whole of the theoretical foundation on which LMF argument stood, implicitly assumed Say's law of market. The logical necessity for such an assumption to hold clearly makes the case for LMF untenable in real-life situations.

Discussions in an *open* economy setting revealed that the implication of LMF on employment growth is dismal due to its underlying thrust on rapid labour productivity growth. Thus, the very objective LMF sets out to achieve, namely, rapid employment growth, gets self-defeated. Further, it was demonstrated that the prescribed policy of free hire and fire can only work in an open economy under very stringent special conditions without much relevance for any real economy. Thus, it was concluded that the entire theoretical foundation underlying LMF stood on rather shaky grounds. Similarly, critical examination of the empirical studies arguing in favour of LMF revealed that either there were problems with the methodology employed by these studies, or the results obtained were not robust.

Therefore, the demand for LMF is so persistent, not because of its compelling logic but because the capitalist system, as known until now, requires an obedient and malleable workforce that can be governed/regulated easily. This is a *primary* condition for profit making under capitalism. Since the pursuit of profit gets precedence over everything else under capitalism, this primary condition has to be satisfied *always*. And the central condition for obtaining a docile labour force is the perpetual existence of a large pool of unemployed workers. It is the threat of replacement at any time that disciplines workers. This also shows that a reserve army of labour is an integral part and logical necessity for the smooth functioning of the system. Now the authority of capital over labour is challenged by trade unions (TUs). Thus, all forms of workers' organizations are bitterly contested and sought to be broken by various means (expansion in the reserve army of labour would itself instil fear among workers and weaken unions). *In this context, it is easy to see that job security legislation offers protection of employment by decree even in midst of a large pool of unemployed workers and thus paves the way for workers' assertion through trade union activity.* Therefore, the real reason to press for dismantling job security legislation is because it stands in the way of obtaining an obedient workforce. And neo-liberal economic policy, as part of attaining something akin to *laissez-faire* capitalism,[1] wants to institute LMF.

Laissez-faire capitalism and the quest for a humane economic order

If we design our economic system along these lines, it would be inimical to a just and humane economic order. This is because there are certain economic and social implications of arranging such an economic system [which is perennially characterized by a vast pool of unemployed workers that can be tapped anytime, is hostile to trade unions and where majority of the people (working class) live under the continuous fear of losing livelihood]. It is to the discussion of these issues to which we now turn.

Let us first discuss the economic consequences of such a system. It is amply clear that such an economic order would be *incompatible* with full employment or near full employment situations. This is because if workers can easily move from one job to another without much loss of time (which is what full employment guarantees), then the threat of retrenchment would lose its meaning.

Consequently, it would be impossible to obtain an obedient workforce, ultimately jeopardizing profit making itself. Therefore, such an economic order must be perpetually saddled with involuntary unemployment. This means that a large number of able-bodied people would *always* look for work but will *not* get work (of course the composition of unemployed may change over time). However, this unemployed lot cannot find employment *not* because of their laziness and unwillingness to search jobs or work but – as we just saw – it is a *social* condition without which the system ceases to exist. This phenomenon, other than being a severe wastage of economic resources (hence inefficient), takes a huge toll on the life of the unemployed, which includes loss of confidence, loss of skill, feeling of worthlessness, depression, deprivation and social exclusion to name a few. Clearly, this description of a society does not fit with a just economic order.

Also note that *laissez-faire* capitalism – without any restrictions on hire and fire – would fiercely oppose TU activity. Such a system will adopt various policies to weaken TUs. However, TUs, by increasing the bargaining power of workers,[2] help in checking extreme inequality in distribution of income. As Colin Gordon (2012) of the Economic Policy Institute points out in the case of the USA (Figure 8.1), there is a clear *inverse* relationship between the proportion of unionised workers and the share of income going

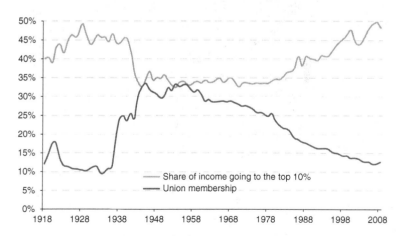

Figure 8.1 Unions and shared prosperity
Source: Gordon (2012)

to the top 10 percent of the population. From 1918, through the depression years and up to the advent of Second World War – as the share of unionised workers declined, this was associated with a more or less steady rise in the proportion of income going to the top 10 percent of the population in United States. For the next 20 years, as share of unionised workers increased, the proportion of income going to the top 10 percent of the population declined. After that, even as union membership declined, the proportion of income cornered by the top 10 percent of the population could be checked up to 1978 – probably due to the philosophy of the welfare state and its emphasis on distributive justice. But after that, the rise of neo-liberal economics under the aegis of the monetarist school and the stewardship of Ronald Reagan led to a systematic busting of unions, resulting in a secular decline in union membership associated with a sharp rise in the income share going to the top decile. Therefore, the systematic breaking of unions, which adoption of LMF *necessarily* entails, would give rise to extreme inequality in the distribution of income and wealth. This has immediate social implications to which we now turn.

Now a sharp rise in income inequality coupled with large sections of people living under constant threat of losing their livelihood, due to institution of LMF, is incompatible with a functioning democratic order. This is simple to understand. The concentration of too much economic power in too few hands typically leads to concentration of political power and state policies which are increasingly used to benefit the economic elite. Consequently, sustaining such a system increasingly requires curbing of peoples' rights effectively, with their exclusion from the decision-making process – ultimately making them voiceless spectators/passive-agents in society. Thus, an enormous social cost of promoting LMF is the stifling of democracy.

Further, TUs play a crucial role in strengthening democracy by creating class consciousness among workers. Even though workers form TUs to seek higher wages (and better working conditions), with time they tend to value the combination *itself*. They identify common secular interests, relegating other identities (viz. caste, religion, race, ethnicity etc.) and assert themselves together. As more workers (both union *and* non-union members) begin to assert themselves, decision making becomes broad-based and participatory, paving the way for a full flowering of democracy. Therefore, any system hostile towards TUs is actually antagonistic to democracy itself.

Another social ill of *laissez-faire* capitalism practicing free hire and fire is that it thwarts individual freedom. Fundamental requirements for individual freedom are people have command over their lives, realize their potentials and exercise choice to the fullest extent. However, none of these conditions can be fulfilled unless there is a certain basic security of livelihoods. But this is an unrealizable goal under capitalism, for the system cannot function without a sizeable pool of unemployed labourers. Moreover, even those employed live under continuous threat of retrenchment – which becomes more pronounced in an economy characterized by LMF. Under constant fear of replacement, realization of one's potential is impossible.

In fact, the LMF argument altogether denies acknowledging workers as human beings. It views workers merely as supplier/source of labour power (no different from other material inputs like raw materials) that creates wealth but does not recognise their capacity to think or regard them as having creativity, feelings and emotions. LMF views workers as a mere appendage to machines and believes that only by instilling fear (of retrenchment) and insecurity (of unemployment) can maximum effort be elicited from workers. Notice the obverse of this phenomenon having devastating consequences on workers' lives. Workers perennially remain in insecurity and live at the mercy and caprices of their employers. They are robbed off *all* bargaining power. Obviously, these conditions are ill suited for individual freedom.

This is the kind of society *laissez-faire* capitalism wants to design through LMF. Keynes was absolutely clear that *laissez-faire* capitalism (or its current reincarnation in form of neo-liberal capitalism) is indeed inimical to a humane economic order, noting: 'The outstanding faults of the economic society in which we live are its failure to provide for full employment and its arbitrary and inequitable distribution of wealth and incomes' (Keynes 2010: 341). However, he believed that it is *possible* to arrive at a humane and just economic order by reforming capitalism. Keynes argued:

> It is certain that the world will not much longer tolerate the unemployment which, apart from brief intervals of excitement, is associated – and, in my opinion, inevitably associated – with present-day capitalistic individualism. *But it may be possible by a right analysis of the problem to cure the disease whilst preserving efficiency and freedom.*
> (emphasis added) (ibid.: 349)

Of course, with State intervention in demand management (the basic cornerstone of Keynesian policy), often in the form of massive war-time (Second World War) expenditure and post war reconstruction in Europe, Keynes's theory was practically tested at a grand scale and proved to be a remarkable success. Adopting Keynesian demand management policies for the next 30 years, often referred to as the golden age of capitalism, advanced capitalist countries' experienced rates of output growth (coupled with near full employment condition) – unprecedented in the history of capitalism. Keynes's doctrine became the ruling orthodoxy and the Keynesian revolution swept the world. Indeed, it appeared as if Keynes's intuition that a humane system can be designed even on the basis of capitalist property relations was correct. In fact, Japanese workers were offered lifetime employment and a seniority-based wage. Haitani (1976: 98) observes: 'The distinguishing characteristics of the "Japanese employment system" are lifetime employment, wages and promotions based on workers' length of service and an elaborate system of fringe benefits'. This was to earn workers' loyalty to the firm they were employed – positively influencing their productivity and effort through job satisfaction. Morishima (1982: 116) notes: 'Employees experience considerable job satisfaction when they believe that they have made a special demonstration of their loyalty to the company; they achieve a greater degree of job satisfaction by working overtime than by their work during regular hours'. The lifetime employment system (with seniority wage) was first offered to white-collar workers and then extended to blue-collar workers (ibid.: 106). According to some estimates, workers with lifetime employment contracts constituted around one-half of Japan's total labour force in 1970 [Dore 1973; quoted in Haitani 1976: 98]. Therefore, the Japanese experiment stands in sharp contrast with the current demand for LMF.

However, Keynes's revolution did not succeed only because of the correctness of his ideas [although Keynes believed: 'if the ideas are correct . . . it would be a mistake, I predict, to dispute their potency over a period of time'(Keynes 2010: 349)]. Rather, various *independent* forces facilitated the experimentation. The foremost challenge came from the Soviet Union. Remember, all capitalist economies (except Japan) were whirling under massive unemployment (and unutilized capacity) during the 1930s' depression years. However, there was an alternative economic system which consistently produced full employment (Keynes acknowledged it: ibid.: 349) – so more and more people were getting disillusioned with the capitalist order. Hence, some temporary concessions were necessary to demonstrate the workability of the system. Further, people got disgusted with the savage inter-imperialist war – hence some concessions, in the form of welfare state became necessary, to win back their confidence. Finally, the birth of independent nations due to anti-colonial struggles meant closing of the colonial markets which traditionally provided the exogenous stimulus to drive capitalist world; this necessitated the search for other exogenous stimuli to sustain capitalist growth. State expenditure (often in form of wasteful defence expenditure) provided such a stimulus.

However, all this is presently under severe attack with the rise of international finance capital, and demand for LMF is symptomatic of this fact. But yielding to this demand will once more bring back all the social and economic ills of unbridled capitalism just mentioned above, of course in a new context.

Thus, what we need in India today is just the opposite. For instance, if raising the consumption of the masses is an end in itself (which should be the case in a functioning democracy and any just economic order), then there is a clear case for emphasizing the role of internal market-driven, employment-led growth strategy. This requires policies very different from what is advocated by the proponents of LMF. Immediately it becomes apparent that the demand-generating role of wages needs to be emphasized more than its cost side-effects. Therefore, it requires *inter alia* guaranteeing everyone minimum wages, basic income protection and regulating the pace of employment displacing technological progress for attaining full employment. Additionally, such a strategy must be based on supporting peasant agriculture and stimulating agricultural growth (employing 48.8 percent workforce). In short, it must be a broad-based development trajectory with sufficient protection of small producers (artisan and retailers). Following these strategies can result in a virtuous growth cycle sustained by the mutual expansion of the domestic market and employment, each complementing the other – ultimately leading to full employment.

Furthermore, we need to safeguard the livelihoods of existing workers by extending them employment protection. It is quite clear that indiscriminate use of contract workers would render JSR *de facto* null and void. Therefore, if workers are to be protected against arbitrary severance, then use of contract workers has to be strictly regulated. In this regard, the recently drafted labour laws in Venezuela may be a guiding principle; Articles 55–65 restricted contract workers' usage only under certain circumstances and specified transparent guidelines to convert short-term contracts into permanent ones:

> Contracts which were for a determined amount of time and have been renewed twice will be considered permanent. Further, workers can't be made to work for more than a year on a limited [time] contract. . . . A work contract then, can only be for a limited amount of time under the following conditions: when the nature of the service requires it, substituting another worker, or Venezuelans working outside the country'
>
> (http://venezuelanalysis.com/analysis/6977; accessed 23 May 2017)

The sharp contrast of this specification to the Indian contract labour law is obvious. India can adopt the guidelines discussed above to restrict the use of contract workers.[3] Next, we turn to job security of permanent workers.

Since TU activity is a precondition for a functioning democracy, therefore, we need to promote trade unionism. *Now an important prerequisite for a strong TU movement is to offer employment security to workers.* Otherwise, it would be extremely difficult to organize workers, for the organizers would be sacked immediately. *Thus, secure job tenure must extend to all non-seasonal enterprises in the organised sector (as opposed to only the manufacturing sector).* Again, Venezuelan labour laws, Articles 85–95 may be helpful: 'Stability is the right that workers have to stay in their jobs. This law guarantees work stability and . . . limits all forms of non justified firing' (ibid.). It stipulates:

> If a worker is unjustly fired, they have ten days to go to the judge of Sentencing, Mediation, and Execution so the judge can order salary payment. The employer has three days to comply, and if he or she doesn't, the judge can force compliance by confiscating property of the employer. If the employer still fails to comply, they can go to prison for six to fifteen months'.
>
> (ibid.)

Further:

> Mass firing is considered to have taken place when at least 10% of a work place with over 100 workers is fired, or 20% of a

work place with over 50 workers, and so on. In such a case the labour ministry can suspend it through a special resolution.

(ibid.)

India should adopt such principles and additionally, if permanent workers consider their firing to be unjustified, they must be given the opportunity to appeal in the court and there should be fair and speedy resolution at a trial, with full compensation to workers in the interim (until the verdict; if firing is found justified, then workers may be directed to pay back in instalments).

The preceding discussion suggests that there are essentially two broad trajectories before us to experiment – one of neo-liberal capitalism with all its features discussed above[4] and the other of proceeding towards a humane society.[5] Now if such a proceeding becomes incompatible with the capitalist property, contrary to what Keynes had thought, then it is worth considering whether these property relations themselves should be altered rather than the goal of a humane society sacrificed to preserve these property relations.

Notes

1 By *laissez-faire* capitalism, what we have in mind is no different from what Keynes had suggested to describe an economic system. In such an economic arrangement, the level of employment, output and income distribution are exclusively determined by the market forces (the forces of demand and supply) without any form of state intervention (like JSR or say, Japanese employment system). However, this definition of *laissez-faire* capitalism is perfectly compatible with the existence of oligopoly, monopoly capitalists and trade unions, and must be distinguished from the perfectly competitive or freely competitive set-up described by the Classical school.

2 Trade Unions, contrary to the account forwarded by the proponents of LMF, have an economy-wide effect in strengthening the voice and living conditions of the working class as a whole. There are many studies which identify a number of direct as well as indirect routes through which strong trade union activism would benefit non-unionized workers through 'spill over' effects (see Walters and Mishel 2003; Gordon 2012; Mishel 2012). These mechanisms could be as follows:

> There are several ways that unionizations impact on wages goes beyond the workers covered by collective bargaining agreements and extends to non-union wages and labour practices. For example, in industries, occupations, and regions in which a strong core of workplaces are unionized, nonunion employers will frequently meet union standards in the absence of a union presence. This

dynamic – the degree to which nonunion workers are paid more because their employers are trying to forestall unionisation – is sometimes called the union threat effect.

(Mishel 2012: 9)

There are many indirect ways in which trade unionism positively affects nonunion workers such as:

> A more general mechanism (without any specific "threat") through which unions affect nonunion pay and practices is the institution of norms and practices that have become more widespread throughout the economy, hereby improving pay and working conditions for the entire workforce . . . Many fringe benefits, such as pensions and health insurance, were first provided in the union sector and then became more commonplace. Union grievance procedures, which provide due process in the workplace, have been adapted to many nonunion workplaces. Union wage setting, which has gained exposure through media coverage, has frequently established standards for what workers expect from their employers. Until the mid-1980s, in fact, many sectors of the economy followed the patterns set in collective bargaining agreements.
>
> (ibid.: 9)

Thus, the positive effect of unionisation is not only restricted to its members but is instrumental in raising the average wage of the economy. Walters and Mishel (2003: 11) note in the context of the United States that 'because the nonunion sector is large, the union effect on the overall aggregate wage comes almost as much from the impact of unions on nonunion workers as on union workers'. Thus, we must not look at trade unions from the narrow angle of promoting the welfare of its members but see their widespread effect on all workers of the economy.

3 Additionally, every year enterprises using contract labour must report the number of contract workers hired. Then average number of contract workers employed in an enterprise in the past five-year period can be estimated. The contract labour law should be amended suitably such that the average numbers of contract vacancies are mandatorily turned into permanent vacancies. Moreover, since contract workers face various family obligations, they should be given some minimum employment protection and necessarily certain severance pay for separation from job with written commitment of re-employment whenever recruitment occurs. One must be clear that rising contractualization is extremely detrimental to trade union activities, and employers utilize this instrument to throttle any attempt of organizing workers.

4 Necessarily bringing in its bogie insecurity, uncertainty, poverty, unemployment and hunger with workers living under the constant threat of losing subsistence.

5 Basically targeting employment growth (exhausting reserve army of labour), enhancing gross enrolment ratio, enhancing life-expectancy at birth, reducing morbidity rate, reducing post-tax income differentials, increasing per capita food absorption and reducing poverty (by calorie norms) rather than merely concentrating on output growth.

Bibliography

Aggarwal, S. C. 2002. 'Labour Demand Function for the Indian Organized Manufacturing Industry: An Instrumental Variable Approach', *Indian Economic Review*, 37(2): 209–220.

Ahluwalia, Isher Judge. 1992. *Productivity and Growth in Indian Manufacturing*. New Delhi: Oxford University Press.

Ahluwalia, Montek Singh. 2011. 'Prospects and Policy Challenges in the Twelfth Plan', *Economic and Political Weekly*, 46(21): 88–105.

Ahsan, A. and C. Pagés. 2009. 'Are All Labour Regulations Equal? Evidence From Indian Manufacturing', *Journal of Comparative Economics*, 37(1): 62–75.

Ahsan A., C. Pages and T. Roy. 2008. 'Legislation, Enforcement and Adjudication in Indian Labor Markets', in D. Mazumdar and S. Sarkar (eds.), *Globalization, Labour Markets and Inequality in India*, pp. 247–282. Ottawa: International Development Research Centre.

Anant, T. C. A., R. Mohapatra, R. Nagaraj and S. K. Sasikumar. 2006. 'Labour Markets in India: Issues and Perspectives', in J. Felipe and R. Hasan (eds.), *Labour Markets in Asia: Issues and Perspectives*, pp. 205–300. Basinstoke: Palgrave Macmillan.

Annual Survey of Industries. 2008–09. *Factory Sector: Volume I*. New Delhi: Government of India.

Annual Survey of Industries. 2011. *Time Series Data on Annual Survey of Industries: 1998–99 to 2007–08*. New Delhi: Government of India.

Ark, Bart Van, Abdul Azeez Erumban, Vivian Chen and Utsab Kumar. 2008. 'The Cost Competitiveness of Manufacturing in China and India: An Industry and Regional Perspective', ICRIER Working Paper No. 228, New Delhi.

Bagchi, Amiya Kumar. 2002. *Capital and Labour Redefined*. New Delhi: Tulika Books.

Bardhan, Pranab. 2014. 'The Labour Reform Myth', *Indian Express*, http://indianexpress.com/article/opinion/editorials/the-labour-reform-myth/ (accessed on 22 July 2017).

Basu, Kaushik. 2007. 'Labour Laws and Labour Welfare in the Context of the Indian Experience', in *Collected Papers in Theoretical Economics, Volume III*, Kaushik Basu. Oxford: Oxford University Press.

Basu, Kaushik. 2011. *Beyond the Invisible Hand: Groundwork for a New Economics*. New Delhi: Penguin Books.

Basu, Kaushik, Gary S. Fields and Shub Debgupta. 2009. 'Labor Retrenchment Laws and Their Effect on Wages and Employment: A Theoretical Investigation', in Bhaskar Dutta, Tridip Ray and E. Somanathan (eds.), *New and Enduring Themes in Development Economics*. Singapore: World Scientific Publishers. Also available as IZA Discussion Paper No. 2742, April 2007, www.econstor.eu/bitstream/10419/34280/1/550731253.pdf (accessed on 24 July 2017; all citations from Discussion Paper).

Besley, Timothy and Robin Burgess. 2004. 'Can Labour Regulation Hinder Economic Performance? Evidence From India', *The Quarterly Journal of Economics*, 119(1): 91–134, http://econ.lse.ac.uk/staff/rburgess/wp/indreg.pdf (accessed on 12 July 2017; all citations from latter source).

Bhaduri, Amit. 1990. *Macroeconomics: The Dynamics of Commodity Production*. New Delhi: Macmillan.

Bhaduri, Amit. 2005. *Development With Dignity: A Case for Full Employment*. New Delhi: National Book Trust.

Bhaduri, Amit. 2006. *Employment and Development: Essays From an Unorthodox Perspective*. New Delhi: Oxford University Press.

Bhalotra, Sonia. 1998. 'The Puzzle of Jobless Growth in Indian Manufacturing', *Oxford Bulletin of Economics and Statistics*, 60(1): 5–32.

Bhattacharjea, A. 2006. 'Labour Market Regulation and Industrial Performance in India: A Critical Review of the Empirical Evidence', *The Indian Journal of Labour Economics*, 42(2): 211–232. Earlier version available as Working Paper No. 141, Centre for Development Economics, Delhi School of Economics. (All citations are from the Working Paper.)

Bhattacharjea, A. 2009. 'The Effects of Employment Protection Legislation on Indian Manufacturing', *Economic and Political Weekly*, 44(22): 55–62.

Breman, J. 2004. *The Making and Unmaking of an Industrial Working Class*. New Delhi: Oxford University Press.

Buchanan, D. H. 1934. *The Development of Capitalist Enterprise in India*. New York: Mc. Millan.

Burchardt, F. A. 1944. 'The Causes of Unemployment', in F. A. Burchardt (ed.), *The Economics of Full Employment*, pp. 1–38. Oxford: Basil Backwell.

Business Line. 2016. 'More Schemes Coming to Improve "Ease of Doing Business" Ranking', 3 May, www.thehindubusinessline.com/economy/policy/more-schemes-coming-to-improve-ease-of-doing-business-ranking/article8552374.ece (accessed on 29 July 2017).

Chandrasekhar, C. P. 2005. 'Who Needs a "Knowledge Economy": Information, Knowledge and Flexible Labour', *The Indian Journal of Labour Economics*, 48(4) (October–December).

Chandrasekhar, C. P. and Jayati Ghosh. 2007. 'Recent Employment Trends in India and China: An Unfortunate Convergence?' Paper presented at ICSSR-IHD-CASS Seminar on 'Labour Markets in India and China: Experiences and Emerging Perspectives', 28–30 March 2007, New Delhi, www.macroscan.net/pdfs/india_china.pdf (accessed on 27 July 2017).

Chang, Ha-Joon. 2010. *23 Things They Don't Tell You About Capitalism*. London and New York: Allen Lane.

Coase, Ronald. 1960. 'The Problem of Social Cost', *Journal of Law and Economics*, 3(October 1960): 1–44.

Contract Labour (Regulation and Abolition) Act. 1970. http://labour.bih. nic.in/Acts/contract_labour_regulation_and_abolition_act_1970.pdf (accessed on 24 July 2017).

Das, N. G. 1997. *Statistical Methods*. Calcutta: M. Das & Co. Manasi Press.

Davidson, Paul. 1969. 'A Keynesian View of the Relationship Between Accumulation, Money and the Money Wage-Rate', *The Economic Journal*, 79(314): 300–323.

Davidson, Paul. 1983. 'The Marginal Product Curve Is Not the Demand Curve for Labor and Lucas's Labor Supply Function Is Not the Supply Curve for Labor in the Real World', *Journal of Post Keynesian Economics*, 6(1): 105–117.

Davidson, Paul. 1984. 'Reviving Keynes' Revolution', *Journal of Post Keynesian Economics*, 6(4): 561–575.

Davidson, Paul. 1985. 'Liquidity and Not Increasing Returns Is the Ultimate Source of Unemployment Equilibrium', *Journal of Post Keynesian Economics*, 7(3): 373–384.

Davidson, Paul. 1998. 'Post Keynesian Analysis and the Macroeconomics of OECD Unemployment', *The Economic Journal*, 108(448): 817–831.

Debroy, Bibek. 2005. 'Issues in Labour Law Reform', in Bibek Debroy and P. D. Kaushik (eds.), *Reforming the Labour Market*. New Delhi: Academic Foundation.

Debroy, Bibek and P. D. Kaushik (eds.). 2005. *Reforming the Labour Market*. New Delhi: Academic Foundation.

Deshpande, Lalit, Alakh N. Sharma, A. Karan and S. Sarkar. 2004. *Liberalisation and Labour: Labour Market Flexibility in Indian Manufacturing*. New Delhi: Institute for Human Development.

Deshpande, Sudha, Guy Standing and Lalit Deshpande. 1998. *Labour Flexibility in a Third World Metropolis*. New Delhi: Indian Society of Labour Economics and Commonwealth Publishers.

Dore, Ronald. 1973. *British Factory, Japanese Factory*. Berkley: University of California Press.

Dougherty, S. M. 2009. 'Labour Regulation and Employment Dynamics at the State Level in India', *Review of Market Integration*, 1(3): 295–337.

Douglas, W. A. 2000. 'Labour Market Flexibility Versus Job Security – Why Versus?', www.newecon.org/labourflexibility_douglas.html (accessed on 20 May 2013).

D'Souza, Errol. 2010. 'The Employment Effects of Labour Legislation in India: A Critical Essay', *Industrial Relations Journal*, 41(2): 122–135.
Dutt, Amitava Krishna. 1986–87. 'Wage Rigidity and Unemployment: The Simple Diagrammatics of Two Views', *Journal of Post Keynesian Economics*, 9(2): 279–290.
Dutt, Amitava Krishna and Edward J. Amadeo. 1988. 'Keyne's Dichotomy and Wage-Rigidity Keynesianism: A Puzzle in Keynesian Thought', Discussion Paper No. 207 presented at History of Economics Society, Toronto, 19 June, www.researchgate.net/profile/Amitava_Dutt/publication/24123929_Keynes's_Dichotomy_and_Wage-Rigidity_Keynesianism_A_Puzzle_in_Keynesian_Thought'/links/540daac30cf2f2b29a39af0b.pdf?origin=publication_detail (accessed on 24 July 2017).
Dutta Roy, Sudipta. 2002. 'Job Security Regulations and Worker Turnover: A Study of the Indian Manufacturing Sector', *Indian Economic Review*, 37(2): 141–162.
Dutta Roy, Sudipta. 2004. 'Employment Dynamics in Indian Industry: Adjustment Lags and the Impact of Job Security Regulations', *Journal of Development Economics*, 73(1): 233–256.
Economic Survey 2005–06. New Delhi: Government of India.
Economic Survey 2012–13. New Delhi: Government of India.
Economic Survey 2014–15. New Delhi: Government of India.
Economic Survey 2015–16. New Delhi: Government of India.
Economic Survey 2016–17. New Delhi: Government of India.
The Economic Times. 2015. 'Ease of Doing Business: India Improves Ranking, Singapore Tops the List, Says World Bank', 28 October, http://economictimes.indiatimes.com/news/economy/indicators/ease-of-doing-business-india-improves-ranking-singapore-tops-the-list-says-world-bank/articleshow/49559515.cms (accessed on 29 July 2017).
The Economic Times. 2016. 'Modi Government Approves 100% FDI in Aviation and Food, Easier Norms for Defence, Pharma, Single-Brand Retail', 21 June, http://economictimes.indiatimes.com/news/economy/policy/modi-government-approves-100-fdi-in-aviation-and-food-easier-norms-for-defence-pharma-single-brand-retail/articleshow/52842211.cms (accessed on 29 July 2017).
EPW Research Foundation. 2007. *Annual Survey of Industries 1973–74 to 2003–04 (Vol. II): A Data Base on the Industrial Sector in India*. Mumbai: The Sameeksha Trust.
Fallon, Peter R. and Robert E. B. Lucas. 1991. 'The Impact of Changes in Job Security Regulations in India and Zimbabwe', *The World Bank Economic Review*, 5(3): 395–413.
Fallon, Peter R. and Robert E. B. Lucas. 1993. 'Job Security Regulations and the Dynamic Demand for Labor in India and Zimbabwe', *Journal of Development Economics*, 40(2): 241–275.
FICCI-AIOE (Federation of Indian Chambers of Commerce and Industry – All India Organisation of Employers). 2005. 'Report of Core Group on

Restructuring Labour Policy', in Bibek Debroy and P.D. Kaushik (eds.), *Reforming the Labour Market*. New Delhi: Academic Foundation.

Galbraith, J. K. 2004. *Economics of Innocent Fraud: Truth for Our Time*. Boston and New York: Houghton Mifflin Company.

Gerrard, Bill. 1995. 'Keynes, the Keynesians and the Classics: A Suggested Interpretation', *The Economic Journal*, 105(429): 445–458.

Ghose, Ajit K. 1994. 'Employment in Organised Manufacturing in India', *The Indian Journal of Labour Economics*, 37(2): 143–162.

Ghose, Ajit K. 2005. 'High Wage-Low Productivity Organised Manufacturing and the Employment Challenge in India', *The Indian Journal of Labour Economics*, 48(2): 232–242.

Ghosh, Jayati. 2004. 'Macroeconomic Reforms and a Labour Policy Framework for India', Employment Strategy Paper, ILO Working paper, www.ilo.org/wcmsp5/groups/public/---ed_emp/---emp_elm/documents/publication/wcms_114332.pdf (accessed on 24 July 2017).

Ghosh, Jayati. 2011. 'The Challenge of Ensuring Full Employment in the Twenty-First Century', *The Indian Journal of Labour Economics*, 54(1): 51–68.

Ghosh Jayati and C. P. Chandrasekhar. 2002. *The Market That Failed: A Decade of Neoliberal Economic Reforms in India*. New Delhi: Left Word.

Goldar, Biswanath. 2000. 'Employment Growth in Organised Manufacturing in India', *Economic and Political Weekly*, 35(14): 1191–1195.

Goldar, Biswanath. 2011. 'Growth in Organised Manufacturing Employment in Recent Years', *Economic and Political Weekly*, 46(7): 20–23.

Gordon, Collin. 2012. 'Union Decline and Rising Inequality in Two Charts', www.epi.org/blog/union-decline-rising-inequality-charts/ (accessed on 24 July 2017).

Guha, Atulan. 2009. 'Labour Market Flexibility: An Empirical Inquiry Into Neoliberal Propositions', *Economic and Political Weekly*, 44(19): 45–52.

Gupta, P., R. Hasan and U. Kumar. 2009. 'Big Reforms But Small Payoffs: Explaining the Weak Record of Growth and Employment in Indian Manufacturing', MPRA Paper 13496, University Library of Munich, https://mpra.ub.uni-muenchen.de/13496/1/MPRA_paper_13496.pdf (accessed on 24 July 2017).

Hahn, F. H. 1977. 'Keynesian Economics and General Equilibrium Theory', in G. C. Harcourt (ed.), *The Microfoundations of Macroeconomics*. London: Macmillan.

Hahn, F. H. and R.C.O. Matthews. 1964. 'The Theory of Economic Growth: A Survey', *The Economic Journal*, 74(296): 779–902.

Haitani, Kanji. 1976. *The Japanese Economic System: An Institutional Overview*. Northborough, MA: Lexington Books.

Harcourt, G.C. 2006. *The Structure of Post Keynesian Economics: The Core Contributions of the Pioneers*. Cambridge: Cambridge University Press.

Hasan, R., D. Mitra and K. V. Ramaswamy. 2003. 'Trade Reforms, Labor Regulations and Labor-Demand Elasticities: Empirical Evidence From India', Working Paper 9879, National Bureau of Economic Research, http://unpan1.un.org/intradoc/groups/public/documents/apcity/unpan019739.pdf (accessed on 24 July 2017).

Hazra, Arnab K. 2005. 'Labour Laws and Industrial Relations', in Bibek Debroy and P. D. Kaushik (eds.), *Reforming the Labour Market*. New Delhi: Academic Foundation.

The Hindu. 2011a. 'The AIIMS Faculty Protest Contract Appointments', 22 May, www.thehindu.com/todays-paper/tp-national/tp-newdelhi/aiims-faculty-protest-contract-appointments/article2039472.ece (accessed on 29 July 2017).

The Hindu. 2011b. 'Supreme Court Asks Centre to Consider Plight of Nurses', 10 December, www.thehindu.com/news/national/supreme-court-asks-centre-to-consider-plight-of-nurses/article2702049.ece (accessed on 29 July 2017).

The Hindu. 2012. '2% Interest Subsidy for Exports Extended for One More Year', 27 December, www.thehindu.com/business/Economy/2-interest-subsidy-for-exports-extended-for-one-more-year/article4242010.ece (accessed on 29 July 2017).

The Hindu. 2016. 'Suggest Ways to Improve EoDB Ranking: PM', 2 December, www.thehindu.com/news/national/Suggest-ways-to-improve-EoDB-ranking-PM/article16082397.ece (accessed on 29 July 2017).

The Indian Express. 2014. 'Shramev Jayate: Modi Govt Plucks Some Key Low-Hanging Fruit for Labour Reforms', 17 October, http://indianexpress.com/article/india/india-others/live-prime-minister-narendra-modi-announces-labour-reforms/ (accessed on 29 July 2017).

The Indian Express. 2016. 'Delhi University Ad-Hoc Teachers: Four Months at a Time', 28 November, http://indianexpress.com/article/education/delhi-university-ad-hoc-teachers-education-4398822/ (accessed on 29 July 2017).

Indian Labour Year Book. 2007. Labour Bureau, Ministry of Labour, Shilma/Chandigarh: Government of India.

'India's External Debt: A Status Report'. 2016. Government of India, http://dea.gov.in/sites/default/files/ExternalDebt_Dec16_E.pdf (accessed on 1 August 2017).

Industrial Disputes Act. 1947. http://labour.gov.in/sites/default/files/THE-INDUSTRIALDISPUTES_ACT1947_0.pdf (accessed on 24 July 2017).

Kaldor, Nicholas. 1939. 'Capital Intensity and the Trade Cycle', *Economica*, 6(21): 40–66.

Kaldor, Nicholas. 1979. 'An Introduction to "A Note on General Theory"', *Journal of Post Keynesian Economics*, 1(3): 3–5.

Kalecki, Michal. 1965. 'Entrepreneurial Capital and Investment', reprinted in *Theory of Economic Dynamics: An Essay on Cyclical and Long-Run Changes in Capitalist Economy*. London: Unwin University Books.

Kalecki, Michal. 1971. *Selected Essays on the Dynamics of the Capitalist Economy*. Cambridge: Cambridge University Press.
Kannan, K.P. and G. Reveendran. 2009. 'Growth Sans Employment: A Quarter Century of Jobless Growth in India's Organised Manufacturing', *Economic and Political Weekly*, 44(10): 80–91.
Kapila, Uma. 2009. *Economic Development and Policy in India*. New Delhi: Academic Foundation.
Keynes, John Maynard. 1936. *The General Theory of Employment, Interest and Money*. London: Macmillan.
Keynes, John Maynard. 1937. 'The General Theory of Employment', *The Quarterly Journal of Economics*, 51(2): 209–223.
Keynes, John Maynard. 1939. 'Relative Movements of Real Wages and Output', *The Economic Journal*, 49(193): 34–51.
Keynes, John Maynard. 1979. *The Collected Writings of J.M. Keynes*. London: Macmillan.
Keynes, John Maynard. 2010. *The General Theory of Employment, Interest and Money*. New Delhi: Atlantic Publishers.
Khan, Amir Ullah. 2005. 'Regulating Labour Markets', in Bibek Debroy and P.D. Kaushik (eds.), *Reforming the Labour Market*. New Delhi: Academic Foundation.
Kornai, Janos. 1979. 'Resource-Constrained Versus Demand-Constrained Systems', *Econometrica*, 47(4): 801–819.
Krugman, Paul. 2006. 'Introduction to the General Theory of Employment, Interest and Money', www.pkarchive.org/economy/GeneralTheoryKeynesIntro.html (accessed on 24 July 2017).
Krugman, Paul. 2009. *The Return of Depression Economics and the Crisis of 2008*. New York and London: W. W. Norton & Company.
Krugman, Paul. 2012. *End This Depression Now!* New York and London: W. W. Norton & Company Incorporated.
Lindbeck, Assar and Dennis J. Snower. 1987. 'Efficiency Wages Versus Insiders and Outsiders', *European Economic Review*, 31(1–2): 407–416.
Lindbeck, Assar and Dennis J. Snower. 1988. *The Insider-Outsider Theory of Employment and Unemployment*. London: MIT Press.
Lucas, Robert E. B. 1988. 'India's Industrial Policy', in Robert E. B. Lucas and Gustav Papanek (eds.), *The Indian Economy: Recent Development and Future Prospects*. New Delhi: Oxford University Press.
Lucas, R. E. 1978. 'Unemployment Policy', *American Economic Review: Papers and Proceedings*, 68(2): 353–357.
Mahadevan, H. 2005. 'Labour Law in the New Millennium', in Bibek Debroy and P. D. Kaushik (eds.), *Reforming the Labour Market*. New Delhi: Academic Foundation.
McCombie, John S. L. 1985–86. 'Why Cutting Real Wages Will Not Necessarily Reduce Unemployment: Keynes and the Postulates of the Classical Economics', *Journal of Post Keynesian Economics*, 8(2): 233–248.

Mishel, Lawrence. 2012. 'Unions, Inequality, and Faltering Middle-Class Wages', www.epi.org/publication/ib342-unions-inequality-faltering-middle-class/ (accessed on 24 July 2017).

Morishima, Michio. 1982. *Why Has Japan 'Succeeded'? Western Technology and the Japanese Ethos*. New York: Cambridge University Press.

Mukherji, A. 2006. 'On Wages and Employment', *The Indian Journal of Labour Economics*, 49(1): 63–77.

Nagaraj, R. 1994. 'Employment and Wages in Manufacturing Industries: Trends, Hypothesis and Evidence', *Economic and Political Weekly*, 29(4): 177–186.

Nagaraj, R. 2000. 'Organised Manufacturing Employment', *Economic and Political Weekly*, 35(38): 3345–3348.

Nagaraj, R. 2004. 'Fall in Organised Manufacturing Employment: A Brief Note', *Economic and Political Weekly*, 39(30): 3387–3390.

Nagaraj, R. 2008. 'India's Recent Economic Growth: A Closer Look', *Economic and Political Weekly*, 43(15): 55–61.

Nayyar, Deepak. 1994. *Industrial Growth and Stagnation: The Debate in India*. Bombay: Oxford University Press; published for Sameeksha Trust.

Papola, T. S. 1994. 'Structural Adjustment, Labour Market Flexibility and Employment', *Indian Journal of Labour Economics*, 37(1): 3–16.

Patinkin, Don. 1965. *Money, Interest and Prices*. New York: Harper & Row.

Patnaik, Prabhat. 1997. *Accumulation and Stability Under Capitalism*. Oxford: Clarendon Press.

Patnaik, Prabhat. 2003. *The Retreat to Unfreedom*. New Delhi: Tulika Books.

Patnaik, Prabhat. 2005. 'Need for a Universal EGS', *The Hindu*, 5 January, www.thehindu.com/2005/01/05/stories/2005010503241000.htm (accessed on 25 July 2017).

Patnaik, Prabhat. 2008. *The Value of Money*. New Delhi: Tulika Books.

Patnaik, Prabhat. 2011a. 'Labour Market Flexibility', *People's Democracy*, 8 May, http://archives.peoplesdemocracy.in/2011/0508_pd/05082011_10.html (accessed on 24 July 2017).

Patnaik, Prabhat. 2011b. *Re-Envisioning Socialism*. New Delhi: Tulika Books.

Pigou, Arthur Cecil. 1933. *The Theory of Unemployment*. London: Macmillan.

Pigou, Arthur Cecil. 1943. 'The Classical Stationary State', *The Economic Journal*, 53(212): 343–351.

Planning Commission. 1992. *Report of the Inter-Ministerial Working Group on Industrial Restructuring (J.L. Bajaj committee)*. New Delhi: Government of India.

Planning Commission. 2001a. *Report of the Steering Committee on Social Welfare of Labour and Employment for the Tenth Five Year Plan*. New Delhi: Government of India.

Planning Commission. 2001b. *Report of the Task Force on Employment Opportunities*. New Delhi: Government of India.

Planning Commission. 2011. *Report of the Working Group on Boosting India's Manufacturing Exports*. New Delhi: Government of India.

Prasad, B. B. 1963. 'Rationalization', in V.B. Singh (ed.), *Industrial Labour in India*. Bombay: Asia Publishing House.

Press Information Bureau. 2013. Ministry of Finance, Government of India, 17 June, http://pib.nic.in/newsite/mbErel.aspx?relid=96590 (accessed on 29 July 2017).

Punekar, S.D. 1963. 'Social Security Measures', in V.B. Singh (ed.), *Industrial Labour in India*. Bombay: Asia Publishing House.

Radhakrishnaiah, P. M. 2003. *The Industrial Disputes Act, 1947*, revised and enlarged by S. A. Chary. Hyderabad: Asia Law House.

Ramaswamy, K. V. 2003. 'Liberalisation, Outsourcing and Industrial Labour Markets in India: Some Preliminary Results', in S. Uchikawa (ed.), *Labour Market and Institution in India: 1990s and Beyond*. New Delhi: Manohar Publishers.

Rani, Uma and Jemol Unni. 2004. 'Unorganised and Organised Manufacturing in India: Potential for Employment Generating Growth', *Economic and Political Weekly*, 39(41): 4568–4580.

Report of the Committee on Industrial Sickness and Corporate Restructuring. 1993. (Goswami committee). New Delhi: Union Ministry of Finance, Government of India.

Robinson, Joan. 1979. *Aspects of Development and Underdevelopment*. Cambridge: Cambridge University Press.

Roychowdhury, Anamitra. 2014a. 'The Labour Market Flexibility Debate in India: Re-examining the Case for Signing Voluntary Contracts', *International Labour Review*, 153(3): 473–487.

Roychowdhury, Anamitra. 2014b. 'Recent Changes in Labour Laws: An Exploratory Note', *Economic and Political Weekly*, 49(41): 14–17.

Roychowdhury, Anamitra. 2015. 'Will the Recent Changes in Labour Laws Usher in "Acche Din" for the Working Class?', *Mainstream*, 53(16), www.mainstreamweekly.net/article5588.html (accessed on 23 July 2017).

Second National Commission on Labour Report (SNCL Report). 2002. 'Report of the National Commission on Labour, Vol. I and II, Ministry of Labour, Government of India', www.prsindia.org/uploads/media/1237548159/NLCII-report.pdf (accessed on 19 July 2017).

Sharma, Alakh N. 2006. 'Flexibility, Employment and Labour Market Reforms in India', *Economic and Political Weekly*, 41(21): 2078–2085.

Sharma, Alakh N. and S. K. Sasikumar. 1996. 'Structural Adjustment and Labour', V.V. Giri National Labour Institute, NOIDA (mimeo).

Sincavage, Jessica R., Carl Haub and O. P. Sharma. 2010. 'Labour Costs in India's Organised Manufacturing Sector', *Monthly Labour Review Online*, 133(5), www.bls.gov/opub/mlr/2010/05/art1full.pdf (accessed on 7 July 2017).

Singh, V. B. 1967. *An Introduction to the Study of Indian Labour Problems*. Agra: Shiva Lal Agarwala and Company.

Solow, Robert M. 1980. 'On Theories of Unemployment', *American Economic Review*, 70(1): 1–11.
Solow, Robert M. 1985. 'Insiders and Outsiders in Wage Determination', *Scandinavian Journal of Economics*, 87(2): 411–428.
Solow, Robert M. 1986. 'Unemployment: Getting the Questions Right', *Economica*, 53(210) (Supplement: Unemployment): S23–S34.
Solow, Robert M. 1990. *The Labor Market as a Social Institution*. New York: Oxford University Press.
Solow, Robert M. 1997. 'What Is Labour Market Flexibility? What Is It Good for?', *Keynes Lecture to the British Academy*, 30 October, www.britac.ac.uk/pubs/proc/files/97p189.pdf (accessed on 24 July 2017).
Sood, A., P. Nath and S. Ghosh. 2014. 'Deregulating Capital and Regulating Labour: The Dynamics in the Manufacturing Sector in India', *Economic and Political Weekly*, 49(26–27): 58–68.
Standing, Guy. 1991. 'Structural Adjustment and Labour Market Policies: Towards Social Adjustment', in Standing and Tokman (eds.), *Towards Social Adjustment*. Geneva: International Labour Organization.
Standing, Guy. 2009. *Work After Globalisation: Building Occupational Citizenship*. Northampton and Cheltenham, UK: Edward Elgar.
Streefkerk, H. 2001. 'Thirty Years of Industrial Labour in South Gujarat: Trends and Significance', *Economic and Political Weekly*, 36(26): 2398–2411.
Subrahmanya Bala, M. H. 2009. 'Small Industry and Globalisation: Implications, Performance and Prospects', in K. L. Krishna and Uma Kapila (eds.), *Readings in Indian Agriculture and Industry*. New Delhi: Academic Foundation.
Sundar, K. R. Shyam. 2005. 'Labour Flexibility Debate in India: A Comprehensive Review and Some Suggestions', *Economic and Political Weekly*, 41(21): 2274–2285.
Sundar, K. R. Shyam. 2008. 'Impact of Labour Regulations on Industrial Development and Employment: A Study of Maharashtra', in T.S. Papola (ed.), *Labour Regulations in India* (Vol. 6). New Delhi: Institute for Studies in Industrial Development.
Sundar, K. R. Shyam. 2009. 'Dynamics of Labour in Neoliberal Times', *Economic and Political Weekly*, 44(50): 28–30.
Sundaram, K. and S. Tendulkar. 2002. 'The Working Poor in India: Employment – Poverty Linkages and Employment Policy Options', *Discussion Paper 4*, International Labour Organisation, Geneva, www.ilo.org/wcmsp5/groups/public/---ed_emp/documents/publication/wcms_121232.pdf (accessed on 24 July 2017).
Sweezy, Paul M. 1946. 'John Maynard Keynes', in Robert Lekachman (ed.), *Keynes' General Theory: Reports of Three Decades*, pp. 297–304. London: Macmillan.
Sweezy, Paul M. 1963. 'The First Quarter Century', in Robert Lekachman (ed.), *Keynes' General Theory: Reports of Three Decades*, pp. 305–314. London: Macmillan.

Bibliography 313

Team Lease Services. 2006. *India Labour Report 2006*. Bangalore: Team Lease Services, www.teamlease.com/sites/default/files/resources/teamlease_labourreport2006.pdf (accessed on 24 July 2017).

The Telegraph. 2017. 'Minister "Sweeper" Swipe at PhDs', 30 July, www.telegraphindia.com/1170730/jsp/frontpage/story_164647.jsp (accessed on 30 July 2017).

The Times of India. 2015. 'Maharashtra to Tweak Labour Laws for Ease of Firing', 17 October, http://timesofindia.indiatimes.com/city/mumbai/Maharashtra-to-tweak-labour-laws-for-ease-of-firing/articleshow/49434870.cms (accessed on 29 July 2017).

The Trade Unions Act. 1926. Government of India, http://14.139.60.114:8080/jspui/bitstream/123456789/15520/10/The%20trade%20Unions%20ACT%2C1926%20%2877-93%29.pdf (accessed on 19 July 2017).

United Nations Conference on Trade and Development (UNCTAD). 2011. 'Trade and Development Report', http://unctad.org/en/docs/tdr2011_en.pdf (accessed on 19 July 2017).

United Nations Conference on Trade and Development (UNCTAD). 2012. 'Trade and Development Report', http://unctad.org/en/PublicationsLibrary/tdr2012_en.pdf (accessed on 21 January 2018).

Varian, Hal R. 2006. *Intermediate Microeconomics: A Modern Approach*. Seventh Edition. New Delhi: East-West Publishers.

Varshney, A. 2001. 'Mass Politics of Elite Politics? India's Economic Reforms in Comparative Perspective', in Jeffery Sachs, Ashutosh Varshney and Nirupam Bajpai (eds.), *India in the Era of Economic Reforms*. New Delhi: Oxford University Press.

Visaria, Pravin. 2008–09. 'Demographic Aspects of Development: The Indian Experience', in Uma Kapila (ed.), *Indian Economy Since Independence 2008–09*, 19th edition. New Delhi: Academic Foundation.

Walters, Matthew and Lawrence Mishel. 2003. 'How Unions Help All Workers', www.epi.org/publication/briefingpapers_bp143/ (accessed on 24 July 2017).

Weintraub, Sidney. 1956. 'A Macroeconomic Approach to the Theory of Wages', *The American Economic Review*, 46(5): 835–856.

Wells, Paul. 1979. 'Modigliani on Flexible Wages and Prices', *Journal of Post Keynesian Economics*, 2(1): 83–93.

World Bank. 1989. *India: Poverty, Employment and Social Services*. Washington, DC. http://documents.worldbank.org/curated/en/299371468751144111/pdf/multi-page.pdf (accessed on 24 July 2017).

World Bank. 2010. *India's Employment Challenge: Creating Jobs, Helping Workers*. New Delhi: Oxford University Press.

Zagha, Roberto. 1999. 'Labour and India's Economic Reforms', in J.D. Sachs, A. Varshney and N. Bajpai (eds.), *India in the Era of Economic Reforms*. New Delhi: Oxford University Press.